THE STANDARD XX

The big question

EDITORIAL · OPINION

BY ROBERT VERKAIK
LEGAL AFFAIRS CORRESPONDENT

Is extradition a fair way to deal with international crime?

A British law abused by US legal system

Failed extradition appeal has profound implications

The case of three further NatWest bankers fighting the Enron case has shocked some people but relieved others, writes Nikki Tait

Extradition rule 'unequal and insidiou[s]

Perils of doing business with Ameri[ca]

threaten such extreme penalties for a failed not-guilty plea that the vast majority of

Yes...

No...

A PRICE TO PAY

The Inside Story
of
The NatWest Three

David Bermingham

GIBSON SQUARE

First published in 2012 by Gibson Square Books

www.gibsonsquare.com

ISBN: 978-1908096197

Printed and bound by CPI Group (UK) Ltd, Croydon, CR0 4YY

CONTENTS

DEPORTED
13th July 2006

I think I probably got about two hours sleep that night. I didn't finish our tax returns until half past one in the morning, and we had to be up at four. It's funny now, of course. The UK Government was deporting me to the far side of the world, and I was spending my last few moments at home making sure our taxes were paid. Wouldn't want to get in trouble with the authorities, now, would we?

Packing had taken about thirty seconds. Toothbrush and toothpaste. Spare underwear and socks. Book to read on the plane.

At four twenty, Caroline and Simon West arrived. Both serving Army Officers. It was Caroline on whose doorstep I had first met Emma some thirteen years previously.

We had decided that we needed someone to take us to Croydon police station at that ungodly hour of the morning–Emma couldn't drive me, as that would leave her to make the long trip home alone–and we had settled on Caroline and Simon as the ideal couple. Blessed with an unerring sense of time (Gunners are never late, or infantrymen die), and the blackest of senses of humour, they would be able to look after Emma on the way home. And we knew they would be able to deal with whatever scrum we were to be met by when we got to Croydon.

It was still dark when we pulled out of the house. There was a TV van there to record it (poor guys must have been there all night), and several cameramen, including one on a motorbike who set off in pursuit. At Croydon police station, there was a sea of press waiting. This made me chuckle because Melanie had been told by Mark Spragg that under no circumstances was she to let any press know our itinerary or flight details, under threat of us being put on a military plane in chains.

Simon pulled up at about five minutes to six. Our report time was six o'clock. We had trouble opening the car doors to get out because there were so many lenses pushed at the windows.

The entrance to the police station was up a few steps, and there was a railed area just in front of the doors. Emma and I managed to find a way through the crowd and walked up the steps together, and then I turned round for one last time. It seemed churlish not to say something after such a long and protracted battle.

"This is a sad day for Britain", I said, squeezing Emma's hand. "And it's a sad day for you guys, because I suspect most of you are British, and you got let down today by your own Government". I paused for effect. Just a beat. "Get 'em out". And then we turned and walked inside.

The local police were incredibly civil. I think they were a little taken aback by the fact that there was a helicopter hovering overhead, and the whole scene was being broadcast live on all the major TV stations. Giles arrived very shortly after me with Debs. Gary was there with Julie. We were given the chance to say goodbye to our loved ones in private.

This was a particularly awful time. Somehow, through all the difficulties over the last years, I had continued to convince myself and Emma that it was all going to be okay, and that common sense would prevail. And now here I was, in a police station, telling Emma not to cry and that we'd be back soon, and that everything would be okay, knowing full well that I had no basis for saying any of these things, but hopelessly lost for anything sensible to say that would be in the slightest bit comforting.

Those who know me well will testify to my near total lack of emotion. This could be put down to me being a cold and unfeeling person, but that would be untrue. I hurt as badly as the next person, and I have even been known to cry from time to time, although generally it's in films, strangely enough. But I've always thought that a stiff upper lip and a cheery "don't worry chaps, the finish line is just round the next corner" attitude is a good philosophy when you're scared shitless and have no idea what lies ahead.

So I contented myself with asking Emma if I could have a few cigarettes from the packet in her handbag, and kissed her goodbye. Needless to say Giles and Gary had longer and perhaps more meaningful goodbyes with Debs and Julie.

We were then put in a small room with a few chairs and a TV. It was surreal. The reporters on the TV were trying to fill in with commentary over a picture from the helicopter showing the top of the police station. Dramatic footage it was not. Outside, Simon was protecting a very emotional Emma from the press gang, and marshalling her gently back to the car for the journey home.

In the meantime, we were given tea by the police, and told that there might be a little bit of a delay. It seemed that there had been an incident at Gatwick when the US Marshals had arrived to check in for the flight, because someone apparently had hacked into the Continental Airlines booking system and cancelled our seats. So the Marshals had had to use their own credit cards to repurchase seats for the three of us. The police thought it was hilarious. Given what had happened to Gary McKinnon, though, I think the person responsible was either incredibly brave or incredibly stupid, or perhaps both.

This was the time when, right at the death, I wondered if there might be an intervention. I still harboured just the faintest of hopes that a miracle might happen. The vote the previous day in the Commons had been overwhelming. The public mood was with us. At a stroke we could have been brought back from the brink.

That old scene from the movies: "Wait. It's the governor on the line. Don't pull that lever!" Some chance.

I asked if I could go for a cigarette, and was accompanied outside into a covered area in the back of the station by a policeman who turned out to have been ex Royal Signals, so we spent about 15 minutes talking about the Army, Northern Ireland, and the mess that was Iraq. And then it was time to go. We were put into a white van with blacked out windows, and driven out the rear of the station. Overhead the helicopter followed our progress to Gatwick airport. It was a bit like a flashback to OJ Simpson's white truck all those years back.

On arrival at Gatwick we spent a short while in the airport police station, before being transported across the tarmac to the plane. At the door of the aircraft, six US Marshals were waiting for us. Two women and four big guys. The women immediately took me to one side, while the guys separated Giles and Gary. Presumably they thought that I was either the least likely to start an incident, or the easiest to tackle if something kicked off. Gary had the two biggest guys.

They searched us and took away our bags, and then led us onto the empty plane. We were now officially the property of the United States, even if we were still on British sovereign territory.

We walked all the way down to the back of the aircraft, and they put each of us into a middle seat in the centre. Gary was behind me and Giles in front. On each side of us sat a Marshal. As both of my companions were relatively petite, my journey was not going to be cramped. Giles and Gary were not so lucky. The Marshals told us that under normal circumstances we would be shackled at this point for the duration of the flight, but that they wouldn't do that unless things got ugly.

They had been informed that half of the British press corps was also booked on the flight, and they instructed us to identify any faces that we knew when the passengers started boarding. If things looked in any way unsafe, they would take us off the flight and make "other arrangements". On one level the thought of a private jet was quite tempting, having never been in one. On the other hand, spending eleven hours shackled hand and foot didn't have a lot going for it, and I figured that the in-flight service wouldn't be up to much either.

My two companions were Marie-Anne and Doralees. Marie-Anne appeared to be in charge of the whole team. She was calm and professional. Doralees seemed a bit edgy, and I reckoned that she was sure there would be trouble. I was a little concerned that she might actually start it.

About the second person onto the plane was Mark Eddo of ITV News, with whom I had spent much of the previous day in our garden. I liked him very much. He had covered the story very fairly, in my view. Sympathetic but balanced. But he seemed genuinely interested in understanding the detail, so we had talked a lot off camera.

There were several other faces, mostly print journalists, that I identified to Marie-Anne and Doralees, who made notes of where each person sat down.

The flight took off on time at 9.30am. The helicopter was still filming, and so the various TV channels interrupted whatever they were doing to show live footage of the plane taking off and soaring away. Emma told me later that Mark Eddo called her several times during the flight to let her know what was happening, which was not much really, but it was a very nice gesture nonetheless. Some of the news channels were running stories on what we were reading, and what food we had ordered. Breaking news indeed.

In fact, we only missed being the headline feature on the BBC Ten O'Clock News that night because Tony Blair's friend Lord Levy had been arrested that afternoon in connection with the Cash for Honours investigation. The *Daily Telegraph's* Matt did a cartoon two days later showing a US prison cell door with "NatWest Three" written on it, and a prison guard shouting through the bars that there was a Lord Levy on the phone, wanting to know whether we wanted to make a donation to the Labour party.

When I finally got home some three years later, Emma had persuaded Matt to sign a blown up version of the cartoon with the words "Welcome Home David". It has pride of place on the wall in the kitchen.

The flight was uneventful. There were a couple of small incidents where people came down to the back purporting to want to use the loos, but in fact either carrying concealed video cameras or wanting to talk with us. They were politely but firmly turned away by the Marshals. Marie-Anne and I read throughout much of the flight, although I managed to catch a couple of hours sleep. Doralees spent much of the time playing violent games on a Nintendo. Lots of people getting shot and killed. It was a little unnerving, frankly, given that she was presumably carrying a gun.

I chatted briefly with Marie-Anne. They had come across a couple of days previously, so they had had plenty of time to see a bit of London and do some shopping. They had not appreciated how much of an issue we were in the UK until they arrived and saw the press coverage. No-one in the US was bothered.

The only awkward moments came when we wanted to go to the loo. The protocol was that the Marshals would come with you, and the door would be kept open. After some discussion on this, Marie Anne decided that I was unlikely to do anything stupid, so decency prevailed for all.

Little did we know, but at much the same time as we were making our way across the Atlantic to Texas, Home Office Minister Baroness Scotland was on her way to Washington. She had been sent by Blair to beg the members of the Senate Foreign Relations Committee to give some consideration to ratifying the extradition treaty, on whose terms we were being deported, which they were showing exactly no inclination to do, in case it resulted in the repatriation to the UK of some of the many IRA terrorists who had been safe in America for the last twenty years.

It's a funny old world.

PART ONE: ANTECEDENTS
FROM SMALL BEGINNINGS

Gary, Giles and I came from vastly different backgrounds; other than our appearance on the same charging document, probably all that we had in common was that we were born in 1962 and had worked together for a period of a few years. Gary was the oldest, then Giles. As an August baby, I had grown up always being the youngest in my class, and this would be no different.

Gary's roots were in a poor part of Glasgow. His mother struggled when his father left home, and his single-minded determination to make the best of himself in the face of adversity culminated in University, an MBA, and his first job at NatWest bank, rising rapidly through the ranks and taking in stints in both Tokyo and New York. He had fallen in love with an American girl in Tokyo, and they married a little time later in the Highlands of Scotland. They were to have two children, a boy and a girl.

Giles, the son of a diplomat whose parents had also divorced when he was young. He had joined NatWest straight from school, as a teller in his local branch in Wiltshire, and met Gary in the mid-1980s when both were working for the bank in London. Their acquaintance was struck over a game of five-a-side football after work, and they became the firmest of friends, and Godparents to each other's children. Giles had married very young and had three daughters from his first marriage, two more from his second.

If I needed reminding of it, I was the interloper. I'd only known Gary since 1998. I had met Giles back in 1990, and we had worked together for a few years in the early 1990s before leaving NatWest to go to other banks.

My background was a study in middle class conformity; Catholic family; parents who had both worked their socks off to put three children through private school. With a gap year before going to Bristol to study law, I had joined the Army on a special commission, and they agreed to pay me through University if I came back for a minimum of five years thereafter. My University life, as a consequence, passed in a state of mostly quiet inebriation, and I left with a very uninspiring lower second class degree.

My time in the Army saw me living mostly in Germany, and took in tours of Northern Ireland and long exercises in the plains of Canada. By the end of my five extremely enjoyable years it was relatively clear that my career lay elsewhere, and I resolved to go into banking as a way of finding out how businesses worked.

I left the Army on a Friday in September 1989, and started at NatWest the following Monday. To say that banking was a culture shock would be an understatement. I had left a highly disciplined and largely tax-free playboy existence in Germany, and was now commuting from a flat in Blackheath into the City to work from eight until six, and being paid a pittance. It is a common misconception that bankers are all paid vast sums of money. My fifteen thousand pound salary at Natwest was less than I had been earning in the Army, and in the Army I was living almost for free. Within months I had to sell my car, and I could not afford to go out in the evenings.

But the job was fantastic. I was working in the Aerospace group, which ran all the banking relationships for the major airline clients and aircraft manufacturers. We did everything from providing overdraft facilities to financing aircraft. Some of it was really sexy stuff, and the people working there were phenomenally clever. I absolutely loved it. I loved the complexity of the financings, and I loved the view from our twenty-eighth floor offices, right the way across London and beyond.

After a year or so, I was invited to join a recently-formed group specialising in tax-based finance, run by Peter Phillips. A lawyer by training, he was an exceptional structured financier who had helped put together the original financing for the Eurotunnel project—at the time the largest and most complex infrastructure project in the world. I jumped at the chance.

The next three years were great fun. One of the junior managers in the group was Giles. We hit it off instantly, and became very much a team within a team. The larger group consisted of a product development arm, and a marketing team. Giles and I were part of marketing, but I was the natural interface with the product development guys. They would come up with some tax efficient form of funding, and we would then identify potential clients and sell the idea.

Giles was a natural. With a very easy manner and an affable nature, he could basically sell ice to Eskimos. He was as much at ease with board members as with garage mechanics and lorry drivers, although his habit of referring to just about everybody as "mate", while commendably egalitarian, did grate from time to time.

Giles is a man's man, sports mad, and strictly beer only. If Peter Kay had been unavailable for the John Smith's beer adverts, Giles would have been the ideal stand in. Behind him, as an assistant manager, I was the technical expert, whose job was to explain the nitty gritty, and work with the client on the fine detail when it came to documenting the deals. Between us, we had all the bases covered.

These were early days for the tax-based business, and the market place was not overcrowded with banks selling their wares. The products were pretty low-tech, but in the land of the blind the one-eyed man is king, and Giles and I executed a number of highly remunerative deals with some of the biggest companies in the land.

Our pay however bore no relationship whatsoever to our earnings for the bank, and over time this became a running sore. When in early 1993 I was rewarded with a bonus of £2,000 for having spent the previous year working 15 hour days to make the bank several million pounds in cash fees, I decided enough was enough. So did Giles. He was offered a job on the main board of a small bank which had been one of our customers. I had the opportunity to set up and run a tax-based business in the London office of the giant Dutch bank ABN Amro. Neither of us blinked.

My time with the "cloggies" had many high points and several lows, and I became very fond of the Dutch, even though they are inadvertently the rudest nation on earth, as they speak their minds without filter. Over time the market became crowded with banks who had latched onto the fact that "value added" businesses such as ours were not only profit centres in their own right, but regarded by many big companies as a *sine qua non* for doing other types of business. If you wanted to be a major player, you had to offer the whole range of product groups.

If the business side of things was tough, there was a significant improvement in my personal life. Shortly after I started at the bank, in July

1993, I met and fell in love with Emma Bowman. Smart, sassy, and with a wicked sense of humour, I was hooked from the moment I met her. Well, maybe not the exact moment, since when we met on the doorstep of a friend's house in Baron's Court I was much the worse for wear, having just come from the summer drinks party of a major law firm.

The doorstep belonged to Caroline Atkinson, an old Army friend. She was hosting a table the following weekend at an Army ball at the Guards Depot in Pirbright, and had decided to have a midweek drinks party so her ball guests could introduce themselves to each other

Tired and emotional, I spent very little time being sociable at the drinks party before falling asleep in an armchair. Ever the good guest. But I did remember the stunning blonde in the pink jacket, and the following morning I asked Caroline who she was.

"Her name's Emma Bowman", said Caroline. "But forget it. She's far too good for you".

Well, I like a challenge, and a year later we got engaged, and then married in June 1995. We set up home in Fulham, because that was where Emma lived, and when it came to buying a house she was happy to move anywhere as long as it was within a four hundred metre radius of her existing flat.

Emma was born in Bath and brought up in Devon. She had come to London aged 17, and never left. When I met her she was running all of Christian Dior's promotions in department stores around the country, working in a lovely office in Grosvenor Crescent. She gave up the job in January 1998, after our first child, Jemima, was born.

By the end of 1998, I was blown out at ABN Amro. For over a year I'd been proposing a huge, tax efficient capital raising. They'd finally agreed to go ahead, but instead of going for a world first in the Dutch Market, with their own people in charge, they went for another "me too" issue in the States, with Merrill Lynch at the helm. I was beside myself.

I needed a change. And then one day towards the end of the year, the phone rang. It was Giles.

"Mate, you've gotta come back".

It was a typically forthright Giles. Straight to the point. A year or so previously he had been lured back to NatWest by Gary, who was now head of a group called Structured Trade Finance. It was part of a recently formed division called Greenwich NatWest.

NatWest had had one of its periodic major accidents a year or two previously, this time involving its investment banking business, NatWest Markets. An options trader had been falsifying the values of his trades by altering the inputs for volatility in the models, showing profit where in fact there was loss. It cost nearly £100 million, which in those days was a significant sum. The Chief Executive of NatWest Markets, Martin Owen, resigned as a consequence.

In Owen's place, NatWest's Group Chief Executive, Derek Wanless, had appointed Konrad ("Chip") Kruger, a bond trader from a little boutique called Greenwich Capital, based in Greenwich, Connecticut, which NatWest had recently acquired in its efforts to expand its US operations. Technically Kruger was co-head, with Gary Holloway, also of Greenwich Capital, but Kruger would come to live in London and Holloway would stay in Greenwich.

Kruger's demand in return for taking on the poisoned chalice of NatWest Markets was that he run it on his terms, one of which was that the business would be renamed Greenwich NatWest ("GNW"). Kruger instantly set about selling off the equities and equity derivatives businesses to Bankers Trust. He didn't know equities, and he didn't like equities. His philosophy was that if he didn't understand a business inside and out, he wasn't going to be involved in it.

Next Kruger set about reorganising the management structure of the group. Anyone guilty of "old bank" thinking would be binned. It was brutal. One victim was the erstwhile head of Structured Trade Finance, an old school British banker who inhabited a vast office in the bank's shiny new buildings on Bishopsgate. Kruger replaced him with Mulgrew.

Kruger and Holloway came from a dog eat dog world. The survival of the fittest. Cosy banking was not for them. Cut costs to the bone. Maximise revenues.

And Kruger practised what he preached. He rarely took a taxi, preferring to travel by tube. Like many great leaders, he was an unassuming looking man. Short, owlish, with glasses, and balding. But his intellect was fearsome. He had that rare gift of being able to look through complexity in an instant and get to the nub of an issue. There was absolutely no way you could bullshit him, and woe betide you if you tried it.

His senior management team worshipped him. He was Moses. His philosophy was simple. We are a partnership. We stand and fall together. The decisions of one affect all of us. Make money for me and I will pay you very well. Lose money and you will quite likely be heading for the exit.

Giles was just gushing all of this stuff down the phone at me.

"Mate", he said, "it's different. REALLY different. You'd love it. Honestly."

The fact is that if I had been having a good time at ABN Amro, I would never have considered going back to NatWest. But I wasn't.

"Giles, I'm flattered, really I am. But NatWest has a really big tax-based products group already, and I can't see what I could possibly add there."

"Mate, this is not about tax products. I want you to form a structuring group for our business. Blank sheet of paper".

I thought about it for about two seconds.

"You serious?"

"Totally. You need to meet Mulgrew. He'll like you."

And so I came to meet Gary early one morning in the breakfast room of the Broadgate Club, the high priced gym where it was apparently cool to be seen. Gary was late, a habit that I would become accustomed to. We discussed the job over breakfast, punctuated only by him asking me why I pushed my knife into my toast after buttering it. I explained that it was to clean the butter off the knife before putting it into the marmalade.

"Figures", he said. "I asked a couple of the guys who knew you from before what you were like, and one of them said "like Giles Darby, but with class"". Giles had built Gary up in my mind to be some kind of a God. I had been nervous about our meeting, but I decided then and there that I was going to get along just fine with Gary.

The following week I met Chip Kruger and the Chief Operating Officer, Neil Coulbeck.

Kruger was mildly terrifying because he asked impossible questions like "why is Mulgrew so keen to hire you?" As I really had no tangible idea of what my new role was, let alone why Gary would go out on a limb for someone he had met only once, I had no answer to this.

Neil was a quiet man of about fifty, with greying hair, whose unenviable task it was to have an exact handle on all aspects of GNW's books and risk positions from moment to moment. He was effectively the interface between GNW and NatWest PLC. He was an old NatWest guy, but given the significant downsizing of the organisation that had taken place in recent times, I knew there was no way he could be a fool and occupy the seat that he did

And so in October 1998 I began the most extraordinary period of my working life to date. At no time before or since have I so enjoyed a working atmosphere.

GNW
Autumn 1998

Many people ask what 'Structured Finance' means. The glib answer is that it means different things to different people, and it can take in a variety of evils from tax-based finance to securitisation, to funky synthetic derivatives, to plain old boring off-balance sheet finance. For Gary's group at GNW, it was mostly about the latter, but with a few added extras for spice.

Imagine you're running a supermarket chain. You own the shops and the land they sit on. Your business is selling foodstuffs and clothes, not owning lots of real estate. You're not interested in real estate. Foodstuffs produce a good, steady income, whereas the value of property can fluctuate wildly. And you want to be able to expand your business to open up more shops, but all your cash is tied up in owning your existing shops.

Let's say you've had a good year in your core business but property is way down—on paper, the land and buildings are worth less than you paid for them. You don't really care as you're planning to stay in the shops for the next 25 years, but your auditors tell you that you are going to have to show a big hit on your earnings at the end of this year. Your investors may assume that retailing business is in trouble, and run for the exits.

What you could do now is sell the shops to a third party finance company ("Finance Co") and then lease them back for a long period of time. Now they're off your books, and Finance Co will carry the risks and rewards of owning the property. But you can continue to operate your business from the premises.

Finance Co has borrowed from a bank, and is happy because the rents that you pay exceed his cost of financing the purchase of the shops. You're happy because the rents are tax deductible and Finance Co may even have given you the right to buy back the properties in (say) 25 years' time, meaning that you have security of tenure.

The bank has a loan on its books (the money it lent Finance Co, which it may also own), and security over both the shops and the cash flows (the rents you are paying).

The bank can sell the debt by securitising the cash flow—i.e. they issue a lot of securitised bonds. That way, they have a cheaper cost of financing themselves, and they don't have the risk of the finance for the next 25 years. The bond buyers are willing to make a bit less return because their money is secured against the rental flows from the retailer, who is great at his job and considered to be a good risk for 25 years.

That's an example of a structure. Someone (like me) in the bank sits down and draws the whole thing out, calculating the risks at every point. Will the tax laws change? Will some market competitor take all of your business away? Which way will interest rates move? These risks are then balanced against the amount of money to be made (in fees and interest payments), and the bank and the client then decide whether to do the deal.

To the cynic, the retailer is avoiding a lot of property taxes, paying tax deductible rents and potentially hiding a lot of assets and debt off-balance sheet. To the pragmatist, he is freeing up capital to buy more stock so that he can get bigger and better and make more money for his shareholders. You can decide who's right and who is wrong.

The London offices of GNW were at 135 Bishopsgate, part of the larger Broadgate development adjacent to Liverpool Street station. Ultra-modern. The main entrance was a large atrium with a giant escalator, which brought you up to the reception area. Marble, wood panelling, and gold-trimmed elevators. Working there felt special.

The Structured Finance group was about 100 people strong. My desk was beside a window overlooking Bishopsgate below. There were a few individual offices—Gary and Giles each had one—but most of the seating was open plan. I sat with my team at a bank of six desks. Chip Kruger and Neil Coulbeck also had offices on the floor, but there was nothing special about them. Chip's was only marginally bigger than Gary's—Kruger didn't care for the showy side. He was only interested in his businesses making money.

Despite his seniority, and the size of the business that he ran, Kruger refused to take a seat on NatWest PLC's board. The rumour was that this was because he did not want his remuneration to be published in the bank's accounts. When RBS took over NatWest in March 2000, it was said that they were so horrified by what he had been earning that they instantly decided that he had to go, and replaced him with their own man. More fool them. It's incredibly difficult to imagine RBS building a mountain of toxic debt and derivatives with Kruger at the helm. If he didn't understand it, and it wasn't priced right, there was no way on earth you would ever get to do it. I have yet to meet a man with a more acute sense of risk and reward. Often in life, you get what you pay for.

Chip's philosophy, though, was a key issue for Gary's group within the GNW organisation. Chip was a capital markets man, not a lending banker. His world was defined by securities that were tradeable. He wanted to be able to look on a screen, see a price, and execute if he liked it. He didn't like big balance sheets. You originated and structured deals. You didn't hold them. Holding risky assets was a sure fire way to get burned.

By contrast, the Structured Finance Group had begun life as a lending centre. It made loans in weird and wonderful ways to companies or projects. Often long term loans. And one of the things that defines a bank loan is its illiquidity. You lend the money. Then you wait, maybe several years, and in the meantime you earn the interest and hope the company doesn't go belly up. This was everything in life that Chip hated, and that threatened the entire existence of Gary's group. Indeed one of the only reasons that the group survived was that Gary convinced Kruger that he could shrink the loan book and leverage the really valuable client franchise for the sake of the larger business.

So one of my first projects was to help the business management guys find ways to make our group fit better with the Kruger model. First that meant being able to identify and price the risk in the existing portfolio better, by identifying the statistical probability of default. From there, we could estimate the actual loss we would sustain in the event that a borrower did default, and come up with a hard dollar number which we then deducted from our revenues and held back as a reserve.

This exercise was valuable in many ways, besides giving us a better handle on risk. It acted as a benchmark when considering new business, since if the reserve number was bigger than the potential first year revenues, we would be booking a loss to do the deal, which would automatically preclude it. And it acted as an incentive to sell existing loans in the secondary market, even at a loss. If, for instance, we had a loan asset worth

$100 million, with a credit reserve of $1 million against it, then selling it at a price of $99.5 million would actually create a profit for us on paper, because the loss of $500,000 would be more than offset by the freeing up (as profit) of the $1 million reserve.

Over the relatively short period that I was at GNW we shrunk the loan book massively and increased our profits exponentially. We moved from making huge loans for long terms to a business model where we looked to sell all of our loan assets as quickly as possible, minimising the capital tied up and maximising the fees earned.

GNW was a pure intellectual capital business, unlike any other I have worked in. You were as good as your ideas. Many firms talk of "partnerships", but GNW was the closest I have come to the real deal. Chip was so hands-on that he knew damned well who was doing what, and he rewarded cross-selling; if Giles introduced the bonds team to one of his clients, and they got some extra business, Giles would get direct credit.

There were clashes of egos, of course. The whole place was one big bucket of testosterone, with hundreds of highly paid bankers all eager to show how clever they were, but in the relatively short time that Chip had held the reins, he had transformed the old NatWest Markets group into a world class debt capital markets business, and although Structured Finance still stuck out like a sore thumb in the business model, there was no sense by the middle of 1999 that we didn't belong. In fact, we were amongst the top two most profitable parts of Chip's little empire, and things were just flying.

I was like a pig in shit. I had a job that allowed me to pursue any and every madcap idea that I or my team could come up with. We could look inwards, at ways in which to make the group more profitable or efficient, or outwards, working with the other teams to devise new financing structures and implement them. I started with a great little team and was able to build on it.

I am a great believer in surrounding yourself with people who are smarter than you, so you can bask in their reflected glory. In the group which I inherited I already had an abundance of riches. The senior statesman on the team was Malcolm Smith. Malcolm had been a NatWest banker all his life, and there was little he did not know about how it ran.

He used to worry that his face didn't fit in the cool, new, fizzing Structured Finance group, but in reality he was my right hand man. He was the voice of experience, and knew better than anyone how to get things done.

At the other end of the spectrum was Dai Clement, our resident Welsh Nationalist. Dai was about 10 years younger than I, and had joined NatWest as a graduate trainee. He had a degree in maths, a great brain, and an opinion of himself that was second in size only to the chip on his shoulder about the English. He was also incredibly inventive and worked extremely hard—usually. He was also wise beyond his years, and not afraid to take responsibility. In his youthful arrogance I could see quite a lot of myself, if the truth be told. He had a good sense of humour and a razor sharp tongue, so life was never dull with him around. That he supported Manchester United was a constant source of fun, particularly because he fitted the typical profile of a "Manc"–an armchair expert who had rarely been inside Old Trafford.

But none of the fun would have been possible without Gary. He created the environment in which we could flourish. Sigmund Freud would have had a field day with him. His garrulous and gregarious outer persona concealed a man with more insecurities than you could shake a stick at. He was capable of great kindness and total brutality.

Gary loved to challenge the orthodoxy. His management style was to invite everyone, including the secretaries, to have their say on every aspect of the business. He instituted a weekly forum, which everybody was expected to attend where we discussed all potential deals and initiatives, and everyone was invited to throw rocks or make suggestions. In this way we became a self-policing unit. A bad debt would affect all of us, so we made sure that only good deals got through our little filter before being put to the bank's risk committee, and frequently the process helped improve deal structures and pricing.

Gary would chair these sessions, and would take every opportunity to humiliate people if he thought they weren't doing a good job. It sounds harsh, but he managed to do it in a way that did not crush people, but rather made them realise that we were all in this together, and we owed it to one another to be the best.

Gary is not the world's best banker. Far from it. But nor is he stupid, and he had what amounted to second sight when it came to the strategic side of the business. Chip Kruger loved him, almost as a second son at times, it seemed. And from that we all benefited. Gary knew how to take credit for the work of his people, and none of us minded one bit.

We worked hard and we played hard. Once a year we took part in the "Ryder Cup", where Gary captained a team of twelve Celts against Giles and his team of Englishmen. We would take three days off, fly to Spain or Ireland, and play golf. The Celts, like the Americans, were much the better golfers on paper, but the English frequently walked away with the prize. Dai, who is a very good golfer, would take losing to the English extremely badly. It was great.

There were casualties, of course, and some people left Structured Finance on bad terms. When Gary took over the business he inherited a headcount of about 250, and a huge balance sheet of alarming assets in far flung places. By the time we left in 2000, the headcount was below 100, and the balance sheet was a fraction of its original size. Some of those who left would take it very personally. When we made our first appearance before the magistrate in our extradition hearing in 2004, one such person confessed to my father-in-law (not knowing who he was talking to) that he had come specifically to see Mulgrew get what was coming to him.

It's easy to look back now and be critical of the whole lifestyle. But in all honesty I don't think we were bad people. Yes, it was a highly charged environment, and doubtless there could have been accusations of sexism and all kinds of other stuff, even though many of the brightest people in the group were women. But there was never, to my knowledge, any business ethic other than doing the best deal for the client, because you didn't need to be Einstein to work out that if you shafted a client, it would likely be the last piece of business that you would do with them, and that's not good for your bottom line.

And perhaps that's what stood us apart from all the other groups within Greenwich NatWest. We had client relationships, and were responsible for all of the banking needs of these clients. We "owned" clients in Energy, Transportation and Infrastructure, sectors which all engage in extremely complex financings of big, hard assets like oil rigs, pipelines, railways, and roads, and therefore lend themselves naturally to the specialist forms of finance which were our stock in trade. If Shell needed to build an oil platform in the seas off Nigeria, chances are we would be on their short list.

Reporting direct to Gary, Giles was responsible for running the Energy group, which was the most profitable of the sectors. Whilst there were many good clients within the portfolio, by early 1999 there was one which had broken free from the pack, and was making all the running in structured finance.

It was called Enron.

FORTUNE FAVOURS THE BRAVE
1999

Enron and GNW could have been made for each other. Enron was a rapidly expanding business with a voracious appetite for capital. They valued intellectual capital highly, and would award mandates to arrange financing to those banks which brought most innovative ideas, or were prepared to work with them in structuring their deals. Enron did not give a damn if you sold down every penny of your loan exposure. They cared only that you were there for them when they needed you.

Enron was both wonderful and terrifying at the same time. In a relatively short period, it had turned itself from a gas pipeline business into the world's largest energy trading company. It is easy now to look back and scoff at how it was all a house of cards, but that would be a huge injustice. It is important to be able to see the Enron of the turn of the millennium in the context of the world and the markets at the time, rather than through the dreadful prism of bankruptcy and allegations of massive and systemic fraud that will forever be its epitaph.

You may recall that during 1999, the world had lost its collective mind over the internet. Teenagers with some outlandish idea for an incubator business would wander into an investment bank with a goatee beard and a stupid T-shirt, and wander out as the multimillionaire chairman and chief executive of happycrap.com or whatever it was called. No-one was immune to the folly, with the possible exception of Warren Buffett who kept politely trying to point out that the emperor had no clothes. That's a difficult shout when the emperor is making everyone as rich as Croesus. Buffet was old school. He just didn't get it. The guys at Enron, they got it.

Some times in life the planets just align. The zillion to one shot of the right ingredients in the right place in the right conditions creates life, or fusion, or a tsunami. In the case of Enron, it was the presence of a man called Jeff Skilling in a town called Houston, at a time when the world was not sure which way was up any more. The Enron of 1999 and 2000 was undoubtedly the product of Skilling's vision. History currently has him painted as a man sentenced to 24 years in prison for fraud. Perhaps over time that picture will alter.

Skilling was not an Energy guy by trade, nor was he a Texan. Born in Pittsburgh, he was poached from McKinsey and Co, the management consultants, by Ken Lay, the Chief Executive of Enron, in 1990. He was promoted to the Chief Operating Officer's slot in 1997, and then Chief Executive when Lay stepped up to the Chairman's position in early 2001.

Skilling's vision for Enron was as an "asset-lite" company. He realised that with the rush to deregulation in the 1990s and the arrival of the internet, the future lay not in the ownership of hard assets, but in creating physical and financial markets which could access those assets.

In 1999, Enron launched an online trading platform called EnronOnline. The brainchild of one of their London employees, Louise Kitchen, it rapidly became to the energy markets what Cyberdine Systems was to the world of John and Sarah Connor in The Terminator. Within months, Enron wasn't just making markets, Enron WAS the market in pretty much any oil or gas based commodity that you cared to mention. Enron's competitors in energy trading were just caught blinking in the headlights as the machine gobbled up all of their business.

Skilling, like Kruger, understood the value of intellectual capital. He encouraged everyone to think of the business as a partnership, and to contribute their ideas. Louise Kitchen was not a particularly senior employee, but the online trading platform was her idea, and she was encouraged to run with it.

Despite its relatively small size, Enron became the biggest hirer of MBAs in the whole of America. And it started hiring bankers as well, realising that financing would be key to its future success.

At the same time, Enron was expanding, entering areas in which it had no prior expertise. Skilling's philosophy was that Enron would get a foothold in an "old economy" marketplace, and sprinkle the Enron magic dust over the business, instantly converting it to a much more lucrative enterprise.

Skilling's 'asset-lite' philosophy was not shared by all, and there was a power struggle between him and Rebecca Marks, the head of Enron's International business. Skilling would ultimately win, but not before Enron had spent billions of dollars building power plants in India and Brazil, buying into water businesses and other assets which were hungry for capital but did not produce cashflow.

In the late 1990s, Enron could do no wrong. The markets loved it. Its stock price doubled, and then doubled again. Fortune magazine named it "America's Most Innovative Company" for six consecutive years from 1996 to 2001–the year in which it filed for bankruptcy. It was the place to go and work.

Looking back, of course, this was exactly the time that people should have been saying "hey just hang on a minute, aren't we spreading ourselves a little thin here?" But hindsight is always perfect, and at the time any skeptics were drowned out by the adoring masses. Even Enron's peers, many of whom hated it for its success and its brashness, were still happy to replicate its financing structures for their own projects.

At GNW, we were falling over ourselves to do business with Enron, even though we had our limitations. We had no position in the equity markets, nor did we do classic investment banking, and so could not advise on acquisitions and disposals. The few banks that offered these services had the top place at the table, and arguably had the best view of the overall Enron business. They included the Wall Street giants Citibank, Chase, and Credit Suisse First Boston ('CSFB').

But for a bank that was based half a world away, we were well placed with Enron. And we had a few aces up our sleeves. One of the most valuable was Kevin Howard. Kevin was a jovial old NatWest banker who had been posted to the Houston office some many years previously to run the Energy desk there, and had taken root. He was another bloody Manchester United fan, but since he actually came from the city it was a little difficult to criticise him. During the season, you would frequently find him in his favourite English pub on a Wednesday afternoon, watching the footie on ESPN.

His lack of technical banking expertise was a standing joke, and doubtless he would have been found to be surplus to requirements many years back had it not been for one thing; he was one of the best client managers you could ever come across. There was not a single person worth knowing in the Energy sector in Houston who Kevin did not know, and he could open the doors to all. Literally; for reasons which no-one has ever been able to explain, he had pretty much a free run of all the floors in Enron's 50 story glass tower in downtown Houston, and spent much of his time wandering from office to office making small talk and finding out what was on the horizon. He knew everyone by first name, and if there was gossip doing the rounds, the chances are that he was in on it.

There is simply no substitute for boots on the ground. Kevin never pretended to understand any of the complex stuff, but he always knew a man who did, and as a consequence we were always in the frame for the really interesting financings and he would always get us in to see the right person if we needed to pitch an idea. It was priceless.

Giles also made it his mission to spend as much time in Houston as he could, and became good friends with Jeff McMahon, Enron's Treasurer. The Treasurer's job is to make sure that the company has sufficient cash from day to day to pay its bills and to finance the normal operations of the business. McMahon was a key man for us. Under normal circumstances, he would have been the key man, but as this was Enron there was nothing normal about it.

Shortly after Skilling joined Enron, he hired Andrew Fastow. A banker who specialised in asset securitisations, Fastow was the middle child of three, who grew up in New Providence, and graduated in economics and Chinese. He married his University sweetheart just a year after graduation, and both would go on to obtain MBAs from Northwestern University before getting jobs at Continental Bank, where Andy was introduced to the emerging asset securitisation market.

Fastow became Skilling's protégé, and although he had limited accounting experience he was promoted to Chief Financial Officer in 1998. Such a position entails responsibility for the strategic financing of the business—how it is funded, for example how much equity and how much debt, and over what term. Responsibility for individual fundraisings would normally lie with the Treasurer. In the classic structure, Fastow would make the plan, McMahon would execute it.

But Fastow was a deals guy, and he wanted to create his own profit centre within his group, based on financing. So he set up his own little group to run specialist financial projects, initially consisting of Michael

Kopper and Ben Glisan. Kopper was a former banker from Bank of Nova Scotia, and Glisan was an accountant who worked previously at Coopers & Lybrand. With Fastow's patronage, these guys would become absolutely pivotal in much of what would go wrong at Enron in the following two years.

With this rather unorthodox arrangement, the secret to ensuring that we were in the running for deals was to forge a relationship with both Fastow and McMahon simultaneously. This was no small task, as they could not have been more unalike, and did not get on at all. Fastow was known as a difficult man, prickly and liable to outbursts of ill temper. His wife, Lea Weingarten, was the heiress to a huge grocery chain fortune, and many put his attitude down to a need to show that he was a successful businessman in his own right. Certainly he took to his new job with aplomb, earning CFO Magazine's Excellence Award for Capital Structure Management in October 1999.

Kevin Howard of course had both bases covered. Kevin had known Fastow since he had joined Enron in 1990, and had helped him out on his first structured transaction, a financing deal nicknamed Cactus. Howard and Fastow became firm friends, and regularly played tennis together. When Fastow was promoted to CFO, that relationship would pay early dividends.

In late 1998, just as I was joining GNW, Enron was looking to acquire Wessex Water, one of the UK's regulated utility businesses. It was a step into the unknown for Enron, a completely new business line in which they had no experience. It was also a very big deal for a company of their size, and they were looking for finance of over £2 billion to complete the deal. Being a UK acquisition, and through Kevin's relationship, they had approached GNW seeking an underwriting for half of this amount.

When a bank underwrites a debt deal, it agrees (in return for a fee) to take up any of the debt that they fail to persuade other banks to lend. Given the size of the deal Gary had to present it to Chip, and to the main Board of NatWest PLC. Fortunately our infrastructure team knew Wessex Water very well, and in very short order were able to assess the true risk of such a financing. Gary's pitch was that an underwriting was actually a very low risk, for which we could charge a disproportionately large amount of money. The ultimate financing would be heavily oversubscribed, but even if it went horribly wrong and we ended up holding all of it, the risk/reward ratio was acceptable given the stability of the underlying utility business.

When the bank that Enron was looking to for the other half of the money fell away, Gary saw the opportunity to create real leverage, and proposed to Enron that GNW underwrite the entire financing, but for a huge fee.

As the time ticked away, Gary received a call from Andy Fastow. Fastow was new to the CFO job, and keen to be seen to have got a "win". He asked Gary to reduce the fee, so that all sides could appear to walk away with something. Gary made a big show of his reluctance before finally agreeing. He had taken his seat at the high table. He had earned Fastow's respect by bringing a prodigious amount of money to the table in an incredibly short amount of time, whilst still making a significant fee for the bank. As anticipated, the follow on financing was oversubscribed, and we ended up with none of it on our books. It was a triumph.

Looking back, it was eerie how good a fit our organisational structure was to the one at Enron. They were an image of GNW on the other side of the looking-glass. For Fastow read Gary. For McMahon read Giles. And for Kopper and Glisan read me and my team. Of course GNW had a host of other product specialists, people with years of real expertise in the complex world of energy financing, and Howard and Giles worked hard to ensure that all of our people were constantly being introduced to the right people at Enron, to maximise our business opportunities. We were a small group, but we punched well above our weight.

Only ten years previously, none of this could have worked, but the advent of electronic commerce, and in particular e-mail, meant that running financings from thousands of miles away was perfectly feasible.

Enron was the single most valuable client in our franchise. Not just because we earned more money from them in fees than from any other client, but because they actually developed their own financing structures. New, state of the art, cutting edge financing tools. Their own in-house teams were phenomenal.

To work with them, therefore, provided a triple reward. First, the bank got paid handsomely for arranging the finance. Second, you would learn new financing techniques as you went. And thirdly, you could then go on and market these new financings to other potential borrowers.

Much has been written about the labyrinthine financing structures that brought Enron low, implying it was a hollow facade from start to finish, but this is desperately unfair. Enron's problems did not start in earnest until the second half of 2000, and were initially related to poor investments that they had made. Their attempts to keep the ship afloat thereafter exacerbated the problem hugely, and the complex financing didn't help, but what ultimately killed Enron was a classic run on the bank.

Try putting yourself in the shoes of the CEO of some major public corporation which is sailing through stormy waters and looking to raise emergency finance to stay afloat. You are on a public conference call with analysts and financiers, and someone asks whether the company is sound. If you say no, you won't get your money, the company will have to file for bankruptcy, and the shareholders will sue you personally for bringing it down.

So instead you say yes, and hope that the financing is enough to save the company, because if it isn't then you are going to get indicted for securities fraud, and sued by the financiers for making false statements.

Some choice, eh?

In any event, back in 1999, Enron were flying high. They were yet to make many of the investments that would precipitate their downfall, and the markets were set fair for them. That they were relatively highly leveraged was not in doubt, and indeed was reflected in their credit rating of BBB, a long way from the rock solid AAA rating of some oil and gas majors, but investment grade nonetheless. From our narrow perspective, which was just the financings that we were involved in, nothing appeared horribly out of kilter. When we lent money, it was against assets, and if we knew nothing about some of those assets then we would ascribe zero value to them.

We were often amused by some of the wackier proposals that came to us via Kevin Howard, and we would frequently refuse to participate if we thought the financing made no sense or the risk/reward was insufficient. But in late May 1999 we received a garbled message from one of Kevin's team in GNW's Houston office, concerning some top secret new financing proposal. It was entitled 'Project Martin'. We couldn't have known it at the time, but for Gary, Giles and me this would be the genesis of a deal which would cost us our jobs, our reputations, our freedom, and an awful lot of money.

LJM
May 1999

The Houston team had put together some verbiage and a couple of diagrams, but none of it made much sense. To understand the deal, we had to wait until Michael Kopper and Ben Glisan arrived at our offices a few days later. After some initial glad-handing with Giles and Gary, Dai Clement and I retired to a meeting room with the two Enron executives to try to get to the bottom of Project Martin.

It was quite the craziest thing we had ever come across, but Michael and Ben pitched it with such sincerity that there was no doubt that they were serious. So the least we could do was give it our serious consideration before turning it down.

Kopper and Glisan were an odd couple, but both convincing in their own ways. Glisan was in his early thirties, tall and preppy-looking. He had a square jaw and a wide mouth, buzz cut black hair and a toothy smile. If he played football at college, he would have been the quarterback, I reckoned.

Kopper was probably the same sort of age, shorter, with jet black hair expensively cut and gelled, and manicured nails. He wore fake tan, designer glasses and a seriously expensive looking suit. He was as gay as a daffodil and wanted you to know it.

Both men knew they were smart. Their business cards said Enron, and they worked for Andy Fastow. Enough said.

So Dai and I suspended our disbelief for the hour or so that the meeting lasted, and tried as best we could to ask sensible questions about something which was so far away from anything we had previously looked at that it might as well have been the master code to Microsoft's latest operating system.

Project Martin was Glisan's brainchild. A year or so previously Enron had invested $10 million to buy about 10% of a startup technology company called Rhythms NetConnections Inc ("RhythmsNet"). In April 1999, the company floated on the stock exchange, and of course as a dotcom company its value went through the roof. Shortly after the listing, Enron's investment became worth nearly $500 million. Not a bad return.

Jeff Skilling had wanted to sell the stake in RhythmsNet, but Enron was prevented from doing so by a shareholder agreement. Skilling was concerned that the wild swings in value of this technology stock would wreak havoc with Enron's ongoing earnings statement. He needed a means to protect against the value swings, and when Enron's own risk department came up short, he handed the problem to Andy Fastow's group, whose answer was to set up an unrelated third party entity which would effectively guarantee that the value of the RhythmsNet investment remained relatively static over a prolonged period.

The mechanism by which this was to be achieved was through a series of complicated derivative products. In order to give this new special purpose vehicle sufficient weight to be able to write these contracts, it would need a few million dollars of true third party equity, and Enron would agree to gift it a whole load of their own shares, as an asset base, with the stipulation that the vehicle would be prohibited from selling those shares for four years. No cash would change hands, but there would be a real transfer of value from Enron to the vehicle, in return for the promise to underwrite the RhythmsNet share price.

It was mindbending stuff, of course, because in reality Enron was robbing Peter to pay Paul. Nothing comes for free, and Enron wasn't really transferring any risk to a third party. They were solving an accounting problem by paying for something in their own stock. But in an age when all analysts ever focused on was your earnings statement, and when this "payment" to Martin would cost not one single cent of earnings, Martin was a Godsend.

At this point, it was difficult to see what possible role GNW could play. We didn't handle equities or equity derivatives. They knew that.

In fact, CSFB was going to provide the cash equity which would ensure that Martin was regarded as an unrelated party for accounting purposes. Glisan and Kopper wanted us to make a loan to Martin, to enable it to purchase some additional assets from Enron. We would have a first priority security over all the assets and all the Enron stock. It sounded relatively low risk, which presumably meant the rewards would be unexciting as well. And then they dropped the bombshell.

Martin would be run by Andy Fastow.

"What????"

Glisan explained that the importance of the vehicle to Enron actually made it comforting to have Andy in charge. It was a strange logic indeed. If you had to come up with a dictionary definition for "conflict of interest", this was it. Fastow would be running a company which would be doing a commercial, supposedly arms-length, deal with the company of which he was the CFO.

We said we'd have to take it away and think about it.

It didn't take long to decide that we had very little interest. Trying to get the bank to take all of the potential risks associated with a structure like this would be difficult enough, particularly with the news that the CFO of the company was going to be running the vehicle, but when all you were being offered was a standard debt return, there didn't seem any point whatsoever in taking it forward.

There is some dispute as to what happened next. Gary always maintained that it was his idea, and Kevin Howard likewise claimed the credit at the time, although I wonder if he still would today. In any event, one or other of them said "why don't we do the equity instead"?

In other words, we would join with CSFB in owning part of the new entity. As a purely economic proposition, it was compelling. The potential returns could be astronomic. Whatever wasn't needed to pay Enron when the RhythmsNet contract was due would accrue to the equity.

Of course it could all go horribly wrong, and you could lose your shirt. That's the nature of equity. But if you were a believer in the Enron story, and made some relatively conservative projections of share prices, the potential profit numbers involved were prodigious.

Dai and I wrote the proposition up, in all its potential horror and glory. We highlighted all the various risks associated with it, regulatory and reputational. We made sure we covered all the bases, not least with respect to the glaring conflict of interest.

Chip was incredulous.

"Are these guys nuts"?

We damned nearly didn't do it. Despite the relatively small amount of money involved, at seven and a half million dollars (we regularly made or underwrote loans in multiples of hundreds of millions of dollars to major corporations), the approvals process was no less exacting than if the bank had been buying another business, and it was ultimately signed off by Derek Wanless himself. Before that happened, Chip insisted on a general counsel to general counsel call with Enron, to assure ourselves that Enron really did understand what they were doing. Chip asked Sheldon Goldfarb, Greenwich Capital's general counsel in Greenwich, Connecticut, to make the call. He trusted Goldfarb implicitly, and if the deal was to progress, he wanted one of Goldfarb's team to be working on it.

So Goldfarb called, and got the reassurances that he needed. Apparently Enron did know what they were doing, and did want to do the deal, and in fact the main board of Enron signed off on a presentation which set out in no small detail exactly what was going on, and they waived Enron's Ethics Code to enable Andy Fastow to take a position which was so glaringly conflicted that no-one in their right minds would ever have proposed it.

The implementation of the transaction was no picnic. The vast majority of the donkey work was left to Dai and me. Kevin Howard and Gary would step in as and when needed. Sheldon Goldfarb seconded one of his brightest young in-house attorneys, James Esposito, to work with us. Negotiating a deal by phone and e-mail can be stressful, especially when you are doing it mostly on US time. Consequently, Dai and I were regularly in the office beyond midnight.

Things were given an added degree of interest by Emma giving birth to our second child, Freddie, right in the middle of the proceedings. I was summoned home on the fourteenth of June to take Emma to hospital, and Freddie was born the following day. He was smack on time, which was unexpected because Jemima had been over a week late. We had invited about 50 people to the house for the following evening some time previously, thinking at the time that we would be able to get the party out of the way before all the chaos that goes with the arrival of a child. In the event, we decided to go ahead with the evening rather than cancel, and were blessed with good weather, so the guests were met with the sight of Emma in the garden looking radiant with a one-day old baby.

Then I was back in the office, where the deal structure of Martin was constantly changing. This meant that we repeatedly had to re-seek various internal approvals from both the risk department and the Commitments Committee, which was chaired by Neil Coulbeck. Both GNW and CSFB were going to put in seven and a half million dollars of equity, and each had to set up Cayman Islands subsidiaries to make their investments.

NatWest Bank had relatively large operations in the Caymans, including a big private banking operation for wealthy clients. This was run under the umbrella of their subsidiary Coutts, private bankers to the Queen. Coutts provided a full range of services for both companies and individuals from its offices outside Georgetown on Grand Cayman.

Coutts organised the formation of a new company, resident in the Caymans, for which Coutts would provide two directors and a company secretary, and would run its day to day affairs from their offices. NatWest would provide three directors, comprising me, Kevin Howard and one of our back office managers in the London office. The company was called Campsie Limited, which particularly pleased Gary because of its association with the Campsie Fells in Scotland.

In the initial stages of the documentation, Ben Glisan and Michael Kopper did most of the work on the "Martin" end of the deal together with Anne Yaeger, their young assistant. But when it came to matters of commercial importance, Andy Fastow himself would get involved. When the first draft of the documents arrived, the partnership had been given a proper name. Codename Martin was now LJM Cayman. LJM, we were told, were the initials of Fastow's wife, Lea, and their two sons, Jeffrey and Michael.

The choice raised a few eyebrows, but perhaps it shouldn't have, because it became clear quite quickly that Fastow was quite shameless in negotiating for himself as the General Partner of LJM. The structure of his remuneration, in fact, nearly caused the whole deal to collapse.

It was in the middle of a long and difficult conference call on the documentation. On the line were Dai and myself in London, James Esposito from Greenwich, Kevin Howard in Houston, the CSFB guys, Fastow, and LJM's attorney. Fastow had adopted an entirely uncompromising attitude, and the conversation got quite heated. When I observed that I was confused as to whether I was negotiating with the CFO of Enron or the General Partner of LJM, Fastow went completely ballistic, shouting and screaming at Kevin Howard about how he had "a relationship problem here", and Kevin had to terminate the conference call.

A minute later, Kevin called me. He sounded quite shaken. I was totally unapologetic, which was unfair because he had spent years cultivating this relationship with Enron, and he really didn't need some arrogant prick on the phone from London casting aspersions at the CFO, who happened to be a good friend of his, in front of an audience of bankers and lawyers.

Kevin, though, was blessed with a wonderful ability to pour oil on troubled waters. "Look, David", he said, "I know he's a difficult guy, and yes he's greedy. But I've known him since he arrived there, and believe me, if you cut Andy Fastow, he bleeds Enron. Never, ever, question his loyalty to that company."

I got a call shortly thereafter from James Esposito, laughing at my negotiating style, and wondering how he would relate the story of how the deal cratered to Sheldon Goldfarb.

It didn't crater, of course, and despite a few more outbursts along the way, the deal got signed on 30th June 1999. But not before Gary too had an altercation with Andy Fastow, and this time it was face to face.

Fastow had come to London for Wimbledon and had agreed to meet Gary for a drink in a bar in the West End. When Gary arrived, late as ever, he discovered Fastow in a corridor screaming down the phone at Bayo Ogunlesi, who was Gary's equivalent at CSFB. The gist of it was that CSFB were holding up the signing, and that if they didn't sign in the next twenty minutes, GNW would be taking their stake as well. This was news to Gary; there was exactly no prospect whatsoever of us taking on CSFB's position in twenty minutes, or ever for that matter.

When Fastow came off the phone, Gary tried to make light of it, saying that he thought the deal had signed, and joking that it must be Fastow's fault that it hadn't. Fastow then launched into a foul-mouthed tirade at Gary. That was a mistake, because Fastow is not a big man, and Gary stands about six feet three.

According to Gary, he then pinned Fastow up against a wall and suggested that he moderate his tone. Problem sorted, they shook hands, had a drink and the deal duly got signed.

LJM was up and running.

SHOW ME THE MONEY
August to November 1999

For all the effort that had gone into the deal, there was very little celebration once it was finally signed. The potential for profits was real, but Chip Kruger was as pragmatic as ever. "Come back and tell me when you've made some money". Which was fair enough. All we had done at this stage was put seven and a half million dollars of NatWest's shareholders' money at risk.

So we set about trying to find ways to create some earnings, and consistently came up short. We went round and round in circles.

Meanwhile, over at CSFB our counterparts, Rick Ivers and Mary Beth Mandanas, were doing the same thing, but with greater success. In August 1999 they came up with new a product called SAILS, an acronym for 'Shared Appreciation Income Linked Securities', which immediately found favour with Glisan and Kopper. The nub of the idea was that they were going to monetise some of the Enron stock in LJM and use the proceeds to enable LJM to purchase some new assets from Enron.

I suppose looking back I was quite annoyed that CSFB had already convinced the Enron/LJM team of a structure, which made us feel a bit second division, having come up with nothing.

But a month later, for reasons which were not fully explained, CSFB's structure hit some problems. Fastow was apoplectic. Blaming CSFB, he leaned on them to advance a bridge loan to LJM so he could purchase some assets prior to the Quarter end on 30th September. CSFB agreed and the loan was put together in some haste.

In the meantime, both we and CSFB continued to work on ways in which we could inject extra capital into LJM, in return for some profits for ourselves. We finally came up with an idea which we thought was considerably simpler than SAILS, and put it to Anne Yaeger and Ben Glisan, who seemed to like it.

In early November 1999, a meeting was arranged at CSFB's offices in New York at which Fastow would be present, to decide once and for all how we would proceed to a recapitalisation. There was a lot at stake. Kevin Howard would fly up from Houston, and James Esposito would travel into town from Greenwich. Dai and I would fly in from London.

Shortly before the trip, while looking over the loan documents from the rushed CSFB bridge loan, Dai and I spotted an anomaly. The way the loan had been structured, and the way in which it interacted with the LJM partnership documents, was extremely complicated. But as drafted, almost 60% of the assets that were purchased by LJM with the loan proceeds would effectively belong to Fastow personally as the General Partner. It was a stupid mistake, explained by the rush in which the loan had been put together by CSFB at the end of September. But it would be ironed out when we did the recapitalisation, I figured.

CSFB's offices were on Madison Avenue in the heart of Manhattan's midtown, some way away from Wall Street. Mary Beth greeted us and broke the news that Andy Fastow would not be coming, but that Ben Glisan would attend in his stead. I recall being glad at the prospect of a thoroughly civilised discussion.

Ben duly appeared with Anne Yaeger, and immediately handed out a sheet of paper showing the latest position with respect to the partnership's assets and capital accounts. CSFB's and GNWs accounts had diminished by approximately $14 million, and Andy Fastow's had increased by a similar amount. There were some startled looks around the table. I sat and waited. Mary Beth was first to speak.

"Ben, I think there's an error here. These capital account numbers are way off base".

Ben shifted uneasily in his seat. Before he could say anything, I interjected.

"It's to do with the way the loan documents have interacted with the partnership agreement. It was a mistake. Seemingly Andy doesn't agree".

"Is that right, Ben?" asked Mary Beth.

"Well yeah, this is the position as Andy sees it."

"Well that's theft, Ben", I said. "And you can tell Andy I said so".

It went downhill from there. When I asked Ben if he realised he was working for a crook all hell broke loose, and Kevin Howard had to intervene to break up the meeting. He must have been getting used to it by now.

James Esposito was incredulous. "He's never going to hold us to it", he observed.

"Damned right he's not," I said.

But he did.

Looking back now, I cannot decide whether I was more outraged by Fastow's behaviour, or annoyed because we had screwed up by not spotting the error in CSFB's loan documents. I would like to think it was the former, but when you have to explain to your boss and your boss's boss that some $14 million has been taken by somebody else through a simple documentation error, it's difficult to do it without looking stupid and unprofessional.

Chip suggested to Gary that we were both. He said that we had been outsmarted by a Wall Street pro, and that if we were unable to play with the big boys on the street, then we shouldn't be pretending to be in that business. Of course I saw the criticism as being a direct reflection on me. Whatever may have been the mitigating circumstances, it had happened on my watch.

Chip asked Sheldon Goldfarb whether Fastow had done anything illegal. Goldfarb conferred with James Esposito and reported back that no, he hadn't. He may have driven a coach and horses through the spirit of the partnership agreement, but he had not done anything inconsistent with the letter thereof. He had not stolen anything.

We were all for taking a stand, informing Jeff Skilling (Fastow's boss), and refusing to go forward with the recapitalisation. After all, if you couldn't trust your partner in a partnership, why would you put in a whole load more of the shareholders' money? But there was also the larger picture to take into account. If we went ahead with our financing structure we still stood to make north of $20 million. If the recapitalisation did not happen, we would not be able to report any profits on the deal for the year.

So we magnanimously put the interests of the shareholders before any principles, and booked the profits.

We did try mounting a futile campaign to "persuade" Fastow to give back some of what he had taken. We thought that if CSFB also held firm, he could be shamed into backing down. But CSFB ummed and erred and danced round their handbags for a week or so, and then finally admitted that they weren't going to fight. Enron was too big a client to antagonise.

It was the grown up way to look at it, I suppose. But I still imagined lots of senior people sniggering at how we got screwed, and it made my blood boil.

Many of the extremely angry e-mail exchanges over this period between me and CSFB and Ben Glisan or Anne Yaeger would be subjected to much analysis by securities lawyers in civil depositions years later, but none of them had any idea what had happened, and why, and certainly no-one at CSFB was 'fessing up'. Instead, in one of life's little ironies, my 'colourful' e-mails were actually used as an example of how the banks plotted to put money in Fastow's pocket.

So when finally the deal was done, at the end of November, the sense of triumph at making well over $22 million in profits for GNW was muted by the feeling that it would be remembered more for our cock-up than for the money we actually made. I felt really bitter. Fastow had walked away with a bucket full of our money, and we had been left looking like amateurs. Ben Glisan called Giles after the deal had closed, and told him that he was so upset by Fastow's behaviour that he would have nothing further to do with LJM or any of its deals. It seemed a nice touch, in the circumstances.

Still, $22 million is $22 million, and right at that time we needed all the money we could get. Because a messy five month battle for control of NatWest had begun, and our group faced an uncertain future. There were three possible outcomes; NatWest might successfully defend itself, or either of the two bidders (Bank of Scotland and the Royal Bank of Scotland) might win control.

BoS stated that they would sell the GNW businesses, and NatWest, as part of its defence strategy, likewise indicated that it was going to sell GNW, together with other "non-core" parts of the group. RBS said that they would fold the UK GNW businesses into their corporate banking arm, and sell Greenwich Capital as a standalone business in the US. And if you're going to sell a business, you need to maximise its profitability.

Many businesses are sold on what is called a "multiple of earnings". If a sector is said to trade on an average multiple of (say) 10 times earnings, it means that within that sector the average company's equity is worth 10 times its annual earnings after taxes. In that kind of scenario, $1 of earnings can translate into $10 of sales price. In hostile takeovers, companies frequently change hands for more than the sector average earnings multiple, because the aggressor pays a premium to persuade the shareholders to sell to it.

So the word soon got round GNW that we needed to maximise our earnings. This would help in NatWest's defence, as the higher the group's overall earnings, the more expensive they would become, and the likelier they were to fend off a hostile challenge. And when it came to selling GNW, boosting our own numbers would ensure the best possible price.

Normally, towards the end of a good year where you've met or exceeded your targets, you think about cooling down and delaying some business so that you get off to a good start in the new year. In late 1999, however, we were encouraged to keep our pedal to the metal. Many times I've wondered whether things might have worked out differently if NatWest had not been under attack in the autumn of 1999. Would so many people have been so willing to turn a blind eye to Fastow's behaviour?

Ironically, if we had waited until early 2000 to lock in our gains, GNW would have made over twice as much money as it did. Kevin Howard was keen to defer at least some of the profit taking until the New Year, but we cashed in our chips and took what was on the table. "Show me the money", Chip had said, way back in July after LJM first signed. We showed him the money. All $22 million of it.

DAWN OF A NEW AGE
January 2000

The battle for NatWest dragged on into the New Year. By January 2000, NatWest's plan to sell GNW was well underway. Teams from other banks were regularly touring the floors, conducting due diligence with a view to making a bid for some or all of the group.

This was of course a highly destabilising and sometimes demoralising period. A good swathe of people at GNW took their annual bonuses and walked away, preferring the certainty of a new job to the uncertainty of being bought by another bank and potentially becoming surplus to requirements.

Through force of personality, Gary kept his team together during those turbulent times. Unsurprisingly, conducting business in this environment was tricky. One of our more challenging issues was that the Group effectively pulled all our lines of credit, perhaps fearing that we would saddle the bank with some crummy debt. We found ourselves constantly having to juggle issues with the clients, maintaining the façade that all was business as usual when patently it was anything but.

And then on 20th January 2000 Enron managed to surpass even their own high standards for shocking the market. They reinvented themselves as a tech stock. At a scheduled conference for analysts, Enron unveiled the formation of Enron Broadband Services, a new division which would supposedly be able to connect with every network in the world, and would pave the way for a whole new revenue stream; bandwidth trading.

Skilling expressed his view that the markets were significantly under-rating the value of Enron's stock, comparing it with peers in the Energy markets, which traded at a multiple of maybe fifteen times earnings, when this new division should be rated alongside technology stocks, which at the time commanded multiples nearer to forty times earnings. In the space of one day, Enron's stock price jumped thirty six percent, adding over $10 billion to the company's market capitalisation.

You could only shake your head in wonder, really. Every time we thought we had a handle on Enron, they would reinvent themselves. The markets loved it. The equity analysts couldn't get enough of the story. The business writers took sycophancy to a new level. The plaudits and awards just kept rolling in.

Right at this time we sent a senior team from the bank's credit risk group to Houston, to look at how Enron managed all the many and various risks in its business. They came back singing its praises to the skies. Our own in-house debt markets analyst wrote a very detailed piece, analyzing the new e-business and the company's focus on "asset-lite", and everything passed with flying colours.

If you had done a freeze frame of the company at that particular point in time, it would have been hard to think of a "better" company in the world. It had its fingers in pretty much every pie. It was a large and profitable business, expanding into new markets at a phenomenal rate. It had embraced the new paradigm of the internet age, and had the vision to see how the new technology could be used to transform 'old economy' businesses. It had its tendrils in the corridors of power in Washington, with Ken Lay advancing the cause of deregulation in the energy markets, even before his personal friend George W Bush became President.

In our little universe, the massive jump in Enron's stock price presented an interesting new possibility.

LJM had entered into its RhythmsNet derivatives contracts with Enron through a subsidiary, LJM SwapSub. SwapSub existed as a ring-fenced entity underneath LJM Cayman, its parent. Our recapitalisation in November 1999 had involved the parent. SwapSub had remained untouched.

At the end of 1999, SwapSub had a negative net worth. The value of its liabilities (the amount payable to Enron on the RhythmsNet derivatives) exceeded that of its assets (the Enron stock). It was technically insolvent.

But in January 2000, things temporarily went the other way. The RhythmsNet share price recovered, and Enron's stock went into the stratosphere. For the first time, SwapSub had positive "mark to market" value, meaning that the paper value of its assets exceeded that of its liabilities.

At the time, we were still busily looking under all tables and chairs for things to sell at a profit, to keep the earnings up for GNW. SwapSub, therefore, was an intriguing proposition. There was potentially some real value there, but it was all but impossible to capture it, because it was constantly moving. And then there was the conundrum of what was to become of us. Since SwapSub had a shelf-life of up to 5 years, any structural solution that I came up with would certainly transcend our time as part of NatWest, whatever happened. In an e-mail to Giles, I mused that I had some ideas as to things we could do, but that it might be better if I kept them to myself until we knew what was happening with our business. There was no malice intended in this comment; it was basic common sense, frankly, given the short timescale on which we were working, but it would be used against us in years to come. In fact, this e-mail would form the cornerstone of the prosecutors' assertion that we three set out to defraud our employer.

In the event, Giles and Gary were both of the view that if there was anything we could do right now, we should do it. So I spent a couple of days kicking ideas around, and came up with a structure that in the words of Edmund Blackadder was so cunning you could have put a tail on it and called it a weasel.

Most new structures consist simply of the rearrangement of various old blocks. My idea was no different, in the sense that all of the constituent components had been used before in other deals, but I'm pretty sure that nothing like this particular combination had ever been done before. I thought it was the dog's bollocks.

Many years later, when Andy Fastow was in prison and giving evidence in a civil deposition, he was asked if anyone from NatWest or the Royal Bank of Scotland had ever brought him an idea that he hadn't seen before. This was the only one that he could remember.

To this day I am proud of that structure. Although, like many before and since, it would never get done, it was nonetheless a thing of beauty, if only to those who inhabit the rarified world of structured finance. Many times in the years ahead I would imagine explaining it to a packed court-room, jurors leaning forward, transfixed. When I endeavoured to do just that with my own defence team in Houston after my extradition, I had to give up after about half an hour, with my main attorney fast asleep, and his junior seemingly losing the will to live. Horses for courses, I suppose. Some people like rap music. I like structures.

There was something for everyone in the proposal. Enron would get a guaranteed minimum level of protection over a two year period against a fall in the value of RhythmsNet shares, worth approximately twice what that protection had been back in June 1999. The banks would get to book a minimum level of profits immediately, and have a further profit potential two years hence. Fastow would also get some immediate income, and some future potential, because the partnership agreement permitted him to make money from certain of LJMs assets in certain prescribed circumstances. The banks would effectively trade some of their future potential income for some guaranteed income today. A bird in the hand....

Fastow was the key. Nothing could be done without his agreement, because as General Partner he controlled LJM. And it wasn't difficult to figure where his motivation lay.

The starting point was that on paper this thing looked like it had some excess value at that particular point in time, although the value was moving around like mad. But there was simply no way I could think of to capture the excess value, other than collapsing the whole structure.

Instead, I approached the problem from a completely different perspective. I realised that there was a way to generate a guaranteed amount of money for SwapSub by NOT collapsing the deal, but by ensuring instead that it stayed in place for at least two years.

In one of my now infamous e-mail exchanges with Gary, I touched on this aspect, and my views on it:

"If I knew there was a realistic way to 'lock in' the $40m and give him $25m, we would also jump all over it I guess, since it would give us $15m...I will be the first to be delighted if he has found a way to lock it in and steal a large portion himself."

Over a couple of weeks in February, I worked my proposal up into three separate presentations, each within the same Powerpoint file. Part one, in fact, was an internal presentation, which was designed simply to explain the thinking behind the deal to Giles and Gary.

Here I attempted to put myself inside the mind of Andy Fastow, as General Partner. I suspected that if he could find a way to pinch more money from us, legally, he would do just exactly that. So the presentation set out all the things he could conceivably do without breaking the terms of the Partnership Agreement. For each, I set out the pros and cons. The idea was to second guess where he would be going with his thinking.

As this presentation was for internal use only, I was, shall we say, direct in my use of language. I was still incandescent with rage about our run-in with Fastow the previous November, and it didn't help much that Fastow had held back the booking of some legal expenses in LJM until the end of 1999, in a way which further eroded the expected income to the two banks–prompting even Giles to remark in a widely distributed e-mail that he was a "thieving bastard".

Commenting on one possible alternative for him, I observed "problem is that it is too obvious (to both Enron and LPs [Limited Partners]) what is happening (ie, robbery of LPs), so probably not attractive. Also no certainty of making money".

In the charging documents in June 2002, and in the press and the court hearings thereafter, this little passage would be quoted again and again. In fact in the charging documents, that quote is preceded by a passage which begins "The presentation that Bermingham, Mulgrew and Darby prepared for Fastow ....discussed various alternatives which appear to be detrimental to NatWest's interest as a limited partner in LJM Cayman".

You have to laugh, really. In the same way that the events of November 1999 would somehow be recast as the two banks conspiring to enrich Fastow, so my attempts to anticipate and prevent Fastow from further eroding the bank's position in February 2000 would be recast as a conspiracy with him to do just that. According to the Department of Justice, we would walk into the office of the CFO of Enron on 22nd February 2000, and give him a copy of a presentation where we spelled out exactly how to commit a "robbery" of NatWest Bank, explicitly using that term. It was akin to accusing Churchill of planning to invade England because he possessed a map showing where the Germans might attack.

Part two of the powerpoint file was a short form presentation for Gary to show Fastow in an initial meeting of the two big cheeses. Fastow was the big picture guy. He was hardly going to be bothered with wading through page after page of complex diagrams. That presentation was the teaser, telling Fastow what the deal could do, but not how it did it.

Part three was the full presentation that Giles and I would give to (I assumed) Michael Kopper. This would explain how the structure actually worked. If Fastow didn't bite, then we would walk away without having given him the structure, so he couldn't steal the idea and take it elsewhere.

I circulated various drafts of these presentations by e-mail to Gary and Giles in mid-February, and Gary and I engaged in some e-mail discussions over the following days. I referred to Fastow in those e-mails variously as "the AntiChrist" and "our nemesis". I also referred specifically to my expectation that he would be looking to fill his own pockets if he could.

By February the package was almost ready to go. Giles and I took a deep breath and walked it through with Chip Kruger.

Chip was not dismissive of the presentation, but certainly dubious. He thought it was pretty far-fetched, and doubted that Fastow would go with it, but for the cost of a couple of plane tickets, what the hell? Why not give it a try? If GNW made a few million dollars, everyone would benefit. We'll never know if he would have ultimately sanctioned the deal, but at that time he wasn't ruling it out.

I don't think Chip liked me very much, if the truth be known. Not long before, I had clashed quite badly with a couple of senior guys down on the trading floor, and then there was the whole debacle over Fastow screwing us the previous November. I think he saw me as a bit of a loose cannon, and tolerated me only because Gary protected me. No matter. If we could get this deal done, it would go some way to redeeming me.

As Giles would put it in one of the e-mails that didn't find its way into our indictment, he and I would do all the donkey work on the deal while Gary would be back in London being knighted by Chip.

THE BIG PITCH
February 2000

I hate long-distance air travel. Luckily, my job did not necessitate huge amounts of it, unlike Giles who was seemingly always on the go. Some of the newspapers would later run stories about how we used to travel everywhere first class or in private jets. I'm sorry to admit that I have never in my life set foot in a private jet, and I have certainly flown Business Class but never First, although some might regard that as semantics. Dai Clement once got bumped up to Concorde when returning from New York, because BA had overbooked his flight. Now that I would have liked.

On the flight to Houston, with the obligatory glass of wine in hand, Gary and I spent some time going through the presentation. Gary wasn't a "pitch" sort of guy. He was the strategist. In fact he would never normally have been on the flight at all, but for two things.

The first was that he wanted to talk to Fastow about what was going on at GNW, and the various scenarios as to where we might end up. At the time, Enron was the golden goose, and if there were several potential options for us, Gary wanted to know which one might best suit his best client.

The second thing was that I was adamant that we should not give the details of our idea to Fastow unless he had agreed that GNW would get paid for it, and this required a face-to-face preliminary meeting with Gary.

So Gary was going to have his "big cheeses" meeting with the great man, and kill two birds with one stone. If there was any unpleasant talking to be done, better that those two did it in private, I figured.

True to form, though, Gary had not done his homework, and after several attempts at the "fifty thousand feet" pitch, he made an executive decision.

"Bermo, this isn't going to work. You're going to have to give him the full boona".

I protested that this was a huge tactical error, and would leave us horribly exposed if Fastow wanted to steal the idea. Gary got quite annoyed.

"Look, you're going to have to get over this whole Fastow thing, okay? He stiffed us. He's a greedy bastard. It's in the past. We have to work with this guy. You have to work with this guy. He knows we're upset about what happened. It isn't going to happen again, okay? Anyway, it would do you good to meet him. Take some of that vitriol away, maybe."

There was some truth in what he said, of course. When you have had several confrontations with someone without ever having met the person, you tend to demonise them. I had a mental image of Fastow and it wasn't a good one, as evidenced by my e mail descriptions of him.

February is not a bad time to visit Houston from London. The air is generally cool, verging on cold, and so there is little difference between the weather in the two cities. Come Summer, the Houston climate is oppressive.

This part of Texas is Bush country. George Bush intercontinental airport (named after Houston resident George H Bush, rather than his son "W") stands some way north of the City itself, outside Beltway 8, Houston's equivalent of the M25. As you make the approach in the airplane, you get an idea of the urban sprawl. It is nowhere near the size of London, but the fourth biggest City in America is sizeable, nonetheless. Like many US cities, almost all of it is low-rise, often single story buildings of wood construction. This serves to accentuate the gleaming high-rise towers of the downtown business district, which sparkle in the sunlight from many miles away.

We got a cab at the airport and headed straight for the hotel. This would guarantee that we saw little of Houston other than the concrete freeway and the mile upon mile of auto dealerships, fast food joints and cheap business premises alongside the adjacent feeder roads. There was just time to check in before heading over to the Enron building, which sat about a mile away.

Houston is a relatively young city, having grown up as a trading port in the immediate aftermath of the great Galveston hurricane of 1900, which decimated what had been America's biggest cotton port, killing over 6,000 people in the storm surge. Galveston would never recover its commercial status, and when a ship canal was dredged all the way up to Houston, some sixty miles inland, all of the shipping business moved with it. And then they struck oil, and Houston never looked back.

The downtown area of the city, consequently, is a strange mix of brick buildings from the early twentieth century, and massive modern skyscrapers. Enron's building, of course, was of the latter variety, a beautiful almost oval structure of blue-green glass that set it apart from most of the more angular buildings around it. It was fifty stories tall, but already they had outgrown it and plans were afoot for a second tower, immediately beside the first.

We were met on arrival by Anne Yaeger. She was in her late twenties I estimated, and unusually lacking in Texan brashness. Anne took us to a meeting room, where we were soon joined by Andy Fastow and a lady who was introduced by Fastow as Kathy Lynn. Michael Kopper, evidently, would not be joining us. He was away.

Fastow was shorter than I had expected, at about my height. His hair was silver grey and he looked older than his forty-odd years. In fact he was only a year older than Gary, Giles and I, but he wore an air of gravitas that seemed to put him in an older generation.

"He thinks I'm an arsehole", I thought, as I shook his hand, trying to convince myself that perhaps Ben Glisan hadn't passed on my thoughts on his behaviour the previous November.

Kathy, Andy explained, would be working full time as Michael Kopper's right hand on LJM. I guessed she was filling Ben Glisan's shoes, but I chose not to mention it. That would have been a bad start.

Andy told us that LJM was about to set up separate offices, and that certain Enron employees would be leaving to go to work there. Anne and Kathy would be amongst them, as would Michael Kopper. In the interim, Enron had signed an agreement allowing these personnel to operate from its offices, and there was apparently a cost-sharing agreement in respect of their wages. It was all a bit messy, he acknowledged, but would be sorted out as soon as LJM was a separate entity in a separate location.

He touched on LJM2, but not in any great detail, because we had declined to be involved. Unlike LJM Cayman, which was a discrete, two limited partner vehicle, LJM2 was a huge equity vehicle which had already raised a large amount of external capital, and was about to embark upon a second fundraising. Fastow had asked us back in the autumn whether

GNW would put equity into it. We had said no.

"CSFB have agreed to put in $10 million", he told us, somewhat smugly. Gary didn't blink.

Gary explained what was happening with GNW. He was as honest as he could be, given the constraints of commercial confidentiality. Andy seemed pretty unfazed by where we might end up, although he observed that the prospect of us being a new group under (say) an insurance company would be thrilling, because it was a potential investor market that Enron was very keen to explore.

And then Gary handed the floor to me, and we spent the next hour or so going through the presentation. The whole nine yards. Initially, it seemed as if Fastow was struggling with some of the derivative stuff, which was a bit funky. Had Kopper or Glisan been there, we'd have had no problems, I thought. We made progress nonetheless.

But there came a point when a light just seemed to go on, and I realised that he'd "got it". There are some hideous meetings where you struggle like mad and never see the magic moment where the client's face lights up at the idea. You just want to pack up quietly and slink away into the night, defeated.

When I was finished, he sat back in his chair and smiled. "It's ingenioussss", he said. A slight speech impediment meant that he whistled when he pronounced the letter "s" at the end of a word. It hadn't been so noticeable on the conference calls, but face-to-face it was unmistakeable.

I was flushed with pride. Gary had been right; this process had been cathartic for me. Fastow would see me in a new light from hereon in, I thought. Perhaps he might even respect me. Perhaps.

"We need to go away and think about this, but it's a great idea", he said, standing.

The meeting over, we all shook hands and then Giles and I departed. Gary was invited to take a spin in Fastow's new toy, some species of Porsche convertible that he was keen to show off. Boys' toys. Fastow couldn't have known that Gary is about as far from a petrol head as you could possibly imagine, still driving around in the same crummy old Saab a decade later.

Giles and I met up with Kevin Howard at GNW's offices on the 60th floor of the Chase Tower, Houston's tallest building.

Kevin of course was dying to know what we had been talking about, and we were adamant that he wasn't going to know. According to the FBI, Giles told Kevin not to worry because "they were going to get rich". Giles disputes ever saying this, but Gary and I still laugh about it today, because it sounds like exactly the kind of thing Giles would have said to Kevin.

The FBI would contend that this indicated that Gary, Giles and I were going to get rich by robbing NatWest. That bears a little analysis. We kept Kevin Howard out of the meeting where we discussed the heist, presumably because we wanted it to be a secret. But we then told Kevin that the three of us were going to get rich, and presumably by implication that he was not going to get rich...

The truth, of course, is much more mundane. Just as takeovers produce stress, they also produce significant opportunity. There was no doubt that our group was a valuable franchise. There were bits of GNW that no potential purchaser seemed to want, but everybody wanted us, including latterly RBS itself. Consequently, this would potentially give Gary a strong hand in negotiating terms, either with a new owner, or with RBS. Opportunities to renegotiate the remuneration of your whole group don't come along very often, and Gary was determined to make the most of it.

The evidence that he did so was there for all to see in the documentary record. Likewise Giles. That they failed was hardly their fault. By a glorious irony, Kevin Howard would ultimately parlay the situation to significantly enhance his own personal terms with new owners RBS, after Gary, Giles and I had left. Kevin did get rich!

It is impossible to overstate the importance of the Houston trip and the meeting with Fastow in our little story. During the extradition hearings, and in numerous arguments in the press and parliament thereafter, the "fact" that the three of us had travelled to Houston to discuss "the fraud" with our co-conspirators (it was always implied that Kopper was also there) was perhaps the central plank of the argument as to why we should be sent to Texas to stand trial, when all common sense screamed the opposite. The trip gave legitimacy to the US Government's claim of jurisdiction over the case, and was accepted without question by the courts at all levels. 'They came to our town. They planned their dirty deeds here. The fraud was conceived here.'

In the way that lies have of becoming fact if often enough repeated, so it became 'fact' that my presentation, like the e-mails that all pertained to it, was a key part of the "scheme to defraud", and at no stage were we ever allowed to contest this in any legal proceedings. The various judgments against us were all predicated on the lie being the truth. When we finally agreed to enter a guilty plea in November 2007, the prosecutors were happy instantly to concede the point, knowing it not to be true. The lie had served its purpose in getting us transported to Texas.

Later that evening, the four of us met up for dinner with Fastow in Morton's steakhouse in the Galleria district, a few miles to the West of downtown. Over the meal, and several bottles of very good red wine, Fastow was extremely keen to tell us all about his view of the world, and the place of LJM within it.

He was buzzing with excitement, because he had completed his initial equity raising for LJM2 at year end, and was now looking to close a second raising by the end of March or early April.

For Fastow, the original LJM Cayman deal was almost a footnote already. Whereas he had raised fifteen million dollars of equity in that deal, his target for LJM2 was nearly twenty times that. In the event, he would end up raising almost four hundred million dollars, and the list of investors would be a "Who's Who?" of the institutional investor market and many private individuals—banks, pension funds, investment trusts, wealthy Houston luminaries and even individual bankers. Over 100 employees of Merrill Lynch, who arranged the equity placing for LJM2, would put their own money into the deal alongside the bank.

As he pointed out over dinner that night, his remuneration structure was similar to the classic private equity model. A two percent per annum management fee on all assets, and a carried interest of twenty percent in any asset appreciation. The so-called "two/twenty" model. You didn't need to be a rocket scientist to work out that the management fees alone on this fund would be not far short of ten million dollars a year. Heads the manager wins, tails the investors lose.

But what about his day job? How could he possibly be doing both? He just brushed off that question with an air of "I can't believe you even asked me that". But he made no secret of the fact that he could foresee a time when LJM would become his main focus, at which point he might just walk away from Enron, having built the bridge to his golden kingdom. In fact, he was already starting to think about the possibility of LJM3.

These were strange times, indeed.

A PLACE IN THE SUN
March 2000

I travelled back to London the next day still full of the joys of Spring. Fastow had seemed genuinely interested in our idea, and I quickly set about following it up with the LJM guys.

Dai Clement had just returned from a couple of weeks' holiday. He had been away while I was developing the presentation. I had left him a brief e-mail explaining that Gary, Giles and I were on our way to Houston, that Chip was in the loop, and could he just act dumb please. I would explain everything when I got back.

It was yet another of those famous e-mails that got splashed all over the papers by the US Government. As with all the others, their spin on it doesn't really survive the slightest scrutiny. I mean, why would I ask Dai to act dumb if I was never going to tell him what we were up to? If someone told you to act dumb, wouldn't you be wanting to know why? And as anyone who knows Dai will attest, he is no shrinking violet.

I walked Dai through the presentation on my return, explaining the sensitivity surrounding it. I was genuinely excited about the prospect of getting the deal done. It was ambitious, but there was very little involved that we hadn't done already in other deals. The equity swaps would be done with AIG Financial Products. AIG was probably the largest insurance company in the world, and one of only a very small number carrying the prestigious 'triple A' credit rating which implied that the likelihood of its bankruptcy was close to zero. The irony now is not lost on me.

To compound my good humour, I was about to get on a plane again and travel to the Cayman Islands. But this time I would be taking some holiday. I had persuaded Gary, the turbulent times notwithstanding, to let me attend the annual Board meeting of Campsie, which would be held at Coutts' offices on Grand Cayman. This was unashamedly a jolly, but having never been on one before, and with the prospect of a takeover happening within the month, I thought that if anyone was going to make the trip, it might as well be me. So I took a week's holiday, and booked flights for myself and Emma.

Kevin Howard, as a fellow director of Campsie, would fly in from Houston, which was a relatively short hop across the Gulf of Mexico.

It was inevitable that we would get thrown a curve ball, I suppose. That was always the way with Enron. The night before I was due to get on the plane, Fastow (or it might have been Kopper) announced that they didn't want to go with my structure, and instead Fastow wanted to buy GNW's position in SwapSub. It was a big let-down, but I didn't really have the time to be annoyed. We had to react to the proposal before I left. The one upside was that a sale today would create instant earnings for GNW with the minimum of difficulty, whereas executing the structure in our proposal would have been complex and time-consuming.

Knowing that neither Gary nor Giles had the faintest idea about option pricing, and therefore how to do any form of a valuation on SwapSub, Dai and I sat down and did the calculations. I then put these into an e-mail for Gary and Giles, copying Dai, indicating that in my absence Dai should be able to run up to date pricings. My message was simple. Get as much as you can. I'm on vacation. Bye!

The Cayman Islands are lovely, if somewhat precariously positioned. A couple of hundred miles South of Cuba, and directly to the West of Haiti and the Dominican Republic, the group of three islands is home to some 45,000 people. Sitting alone amongst a vast expanse of open, warm water, they are particularly exposed to hurricanes, and in September 2004 were very badly damaged by winds of up to 150mph at the centre of hurricane Ivan.

The largest and most populous of the islands is Grand Cayman. Its major industries are tourism and finance—it is home to one of the world's biggest offshore financial centres. It is routinely associated with tax evasion, which always makes me smile given that it remains a British protectorate, and many of the UK Government's own buildings in London are owned by companies resident in offshore tax havens including the Cayman Islands.

We touched down in Georgetown, the island's capital, in the early evening after an 11 hour flight. The weather was hot and sunny. We got into a rickety old taxi and made the 10 minute drive to our condo, which was on the beautiful Seven Mile Beach that runs north from Georgetown up the west coast of the island.

The accommodation was a colonial style wooden building adjacent to the beach, in a small complex with its own swimming pool. Beyond the pool the white sand of the beach ran down to the azure blue sea, under a clear sky, in which the sun was getting ready to set. Paradise. The picture was missing only the cocktails.

We had two full days before the Campsie Board meeting, and there was a whole lot of swimming and sunbathing to be done. This was the first time Emma and I had been away on our own since Freddie had been born, and I was determined that it was going to be a seriously relaxing time. I was not expecting to be contacted. I did not have a mobile phone or a laptop, so the whole of London could have been consumed by the plague and I would have been none the wiser.

On the day of the meeting, I got a cab to Coutts's offices, where I met Kevin and the team from Coutts. Andrew Galloway ran the entire operation there. What a dream posting. I would imagine there were about 30 or so people working for him, mostly engaged in running offshore companies. I had been incredibly impressed by the level of understanding that Andrew in particular had shown in the LJM transactions.

Many people assume that these kinds of operations are just a "rubber stamp" for businesses that are really run elsewhere. That was clearly not the case with the Coutts guys. They were extremely sharp, and took their duties as directors very seriously.

The Board meeting took little more than an hour. We discussed the transactions that had taken place, including the refinancing in November, the investment policy of the company, and a report on Enron which had just been written by Miriam Hehir, GNW's London-based debt analyst.

That evening, Emma and I had dinner with Kevin Howard. It turned out that Kevin had not even come on a commercial flight from Houston. Fastow had changed his mind about the trip at the last minute, and had borrowed the Enron corporate jet. He had brought Lea and his two sons with him. As befitted his station in life, he was staying in a suite in the five star Hyatt Regency hotel, and Kevin told us that we were all invited to dinner there the following night.

That dinner was extremely enjoyable. Lea was absolutely charming, and instantly hit it off with Emma. Andy was also charm personified, and it was easy to see why Kevin regarded him so highly as a friend. It was almost as if he had a split personality, and moved effortlessly from one to the other depending upon whether he was in "work" mode or not. We all do that, to an extent, but with Andy it just seemed that the two personae were almost Jekyll and Hyde, so marked was the difference.

Even Emma was seduced by Andy's effortless charm, and the evening passed in a haze of tropical warmth and good conversation over seafood and some very nice wines. Lea was excited about the prospect of an imminent trip to London to search for some art on behalf of an Enron Foundation of which she had recently been made a trustee. Emma was happy to give her advice on some of London's finest galleries for both modern art and old masters.

After dinner, Andy and Lea announced that they had hired a dive boat for the following day, and invited us all to join them. The Cayman Islands have some of the best scuba diving in the world, and Andy and Lea were both experienced divers. Since none of Kevin, Emma or I had ever been scuba diving before, we would have to make do with snorkeling, but it was an agreeable prospect nonetheless, and we readily accepted.

Emma and I had images of a floating gin palace with a huge covered deck and a crew busying themselves with preparing cocktails and a sumptuous shellfish lunch. Arriving at the quay the following morning, looking out for some glistening hundred foot schooner, we were met by the sight of Andy and Lea clambering onto a rusty old tub that cannot have been more than twenty five feet long. No bar, no kitchen, no sundeck. Just a tubby captain with very few teeth. If we could have turned round and escaped back to the condo, we would have done. But we were trapped, and so we had to make the most of it.

Kevin turned up in a bright yellow pair of swimming shorts and a T-shirt. Being Kevin, he immediately said what we were thinking. "I was expecting something a bit more executive, Andy". Fastow pointed out that since they were going to spend most of their time below the surface of the water, there wasn't a lot of point in having a beautiful boat. Fair point, I suppose, although I think Emma would have begged to differ.

So off we set. Andy and Lea had brought all their own scuba gear, and began to unpack and check it. The skipper supplied masks and flippers for the three English, and Kevin took off his T-shirt, which was not a pretty sight. It quickly became apparent that not only was there no bar on the boat; there was no food, either. Andy pulled a large tub of salted nuts from his bag, broke it open and offered them round. Kevin told us later that these had come from the Enron corporate jet.

Still, it was actually a very enjoyable day. Kevin got horribly sunburned. I joked that if he was going into the water I would have to stand watch in case the Japanese whaling fleet turned up. Emma and I spent a couple of hours snorkeling over the reefs, watching the Fastows scuba diving below. I have long had a fear of open water, not being a particularly strong swimmer, but when the water is warm, you can see all the way to the sandy bottom, and you are surrounded by beautiful and unthreatening looking fish, all fear miraculously disappears.

On our return, we said our thanks and goodbyes, as the Fastows and Kevin were leaving straight for Houston that evening. Emma and I had several days of quiet sunbathing to look forward to.

Two days later I was lying by the pool at the condo when the apartment phone rang. It was Andrew Galloway from Coutts, to say that they had received a fax from London concerning the proposal to sell Campsie's interest in SwapSub. He was convening a board meeting that afternoon to discuss it, and wanted to know if I would be available. They sent me over a copy of the proposal, which consisted of a two page memo prepared by Giles and Dai. The proposal was that GNW would sell its stake in SwapSub to a new entity being set up by Kopper, for the consideration of one million dollars.

On the face of it, a million dollars seemed a disappointingly small amount of money. The memo, indeed, pointed out that at that particular point in time, the "mark to market" value of SwapSub was in the region of twenty three million dollars, of which GNW's interest was one half.

However, as the memo went on to explain, the reality was that this figure was all but irrelevant. First, because it was already out of date by the time the note had been printed and faxed, since the valuation was moving every minute of every trading day, and was wildly volatile. Indeed, just 10 days later that twenty three million dollar figure would have moved to just three million.

Second, because there was no way (as I knew from my work in February) actually to capture the mark to market number at any given point. It was an entirely theoretical number.

Third, because we had no control over what the partnership did, and Andy Fastow as the General partner had shown in the past that he would take action that was contrary to the interests of the limited partners.

Fourth, because all of the optionality in the deal was with Enron, not the two banks. Enron could decide when to cash its chips. The banks could not.

And lastly, but perhaps most significantly, because the Enron stock carried a multi-year restriction on sale which meant that its "actual" value was significantly less than its screen (or mark to market) price. NatWest's own auditors, KPMG, would subsequently put a value on that restriction at the relevant time of approximately $40 million, meaning that the 'actual' value of the asset was substantially negative at that point in time.

The note had concluded that one million dollars today was a fair price in the circumstances, and had recommended that Campsie take it. Not least because NatWest carried the stake in SwapSub on its books at a value of zero, and so the million dollars would be going straight to profit.

At the bottom of the note, Gary had scribbled his own recommendation, pointing out that we could not extract any profit from SwapSub before 2004, as the deal currently stood.

We discussed the whole matter at the Campsie Board meeting. In agreeing the proposal in principle, the Campsie board tasked Giles with negotiating firstly that the price should be increased to take into account a dividend on the SwapSub Enron stock that was due to be received in March, and secondly that the General Partner of LJM (Fastow) should agree to make distributions from income of at least a million dollars over the next two years, which would compensate for further dividends foregone. If those two points were negotiated, then the deal could proceed.

Much of what would come in the future rested on an assertion that a million dollars was an undervalue for the SwapSub asset. For the record, I stand by the price that NatWest received. Always did. Always will.

NEW PLANS
March 2000

Later that day, the phone rang again in the condo. This was getting really tedious. It was Gary.

"Hey Bermo, I trust you're not working too hard?"

"Well I was hoping to have something like a few days holiday with my wife, but it seems I made the mistake of handing out my phone number".

"Yeah well, more fool you. Look, a couple of things I need to update you on".

Gary told me that RBS had formally been declared winners in the battle for NatWest.

"They've got people in the building now doing a review of all the business groups. Chip's really struggling to hold it together. He wants to spin us out of GNW with a few of his other groups, but RBS look like they want to fold us into their own corporate banking business."

"What, you mean take us out of GNW?"

"Yeah, that looks favourite".

"They don't get it, do they?"

"No. Not right now. I'm trying, but the body language right now isn't great".

"Tossers".

"Yeah. We'll see. Chip's idea would be fantastic though, if he can pull it off. Anyway, I spoke with Andy, and he's happy to agree to the terms on the SwapSub sale, so Giles is moving ahead with that. I told him what was going on, and he's asked me if I want to do some business on a personal basis if we end up leaving."

"He doesn't miss a trick, does he?"

More than once in the past year, Fastow had made fairly unsubtle advances towards Gary with a view to him coming to work at Enron.

"Yeah I know. He wasn't specific, but I told him that any deal would have to involve you and Giles. Do you think they want us to be the European arm of LJM?"

"Looks favourite. What's your view?"

"I'd be happy to give it a crack if RBS doesn't work out and Chip's thing isn't an option. Chip seems cool with it".

"Oh, so you spoke with him?"

"Yeah, but pretty non-specific. We need to find out what it's about, and I told Andy that right now I'm up to my neck in stuff here, so you're going to have to run with it."

I felt pretty chuffed that Gary had made me part of his "inner circle", as I saw it. He told me that Fastow had initially bridled at the suggestion that I be part of any deal, but that he had insisted on it.

In the circumstances, I was more than happy to look at other opportunities, and working for what amounted to a growing private equity business, with America's newly crowned CFO of the Year at the helm–it could have been worse, whatever my past animosities towards the guy. I look back now and marvel at how easily I was seduced by my own vanity.

"You need to call Michael Kopper", Gary said. "Fix a time to go and sit down with him. Just find out as much as you can so we can see if it's a runner".

"What, now?" I asked.

"Well it's not like you're rushed off your feet, David".

"Okay, okay, I'll call him". Michael and I didn't speak for long. I told him that we were happy in principle to look at a deal. I'm pretty sure I told him that we were happy to invest our own money, and that this could be a "meaningful number".　It would of course be predicated on us leaving GNW, which was still very much up in the air. I agreed that I would travel to New York the following week to sit down with him and discuss it face to face, and suggested that in the meantime he should consider me 'out of the loop' on anything to do with Enron and GNW.

All in all, I was feeling pretty pleased with myself. Wherever we looked, people were falling over themselves to employ us. All the potential buyers of GNW had wanted us; RBS wanted us; and now Andy Fastow was apparently giving us an opportunity to become part of LJM. And given his track record, that could mean only one thing. We were likely to make a whole lot of money. It couldn't get any better, surely?

We got back from the Cayman Islands on Thursday 9th March, and I went in to the office on the following day, looking forward to showing off my suntan.

The general mood in the office was subdued. There were all kinds of rumours flying around, and in the meantime almost no business was getting done, as the credit guys had formally pulled all the lines while the takeover took place. In my mind, I had half a foot out the door already by then, and so I was pretty relaxed. There was no scenario I could foresee that would produce a bad result for me personally. The best case at that point in time would be that Chip would succeed in his plan to spin out a select number of people to a new organisation. That was Plan A.

Plan B was that the Structured Finance group would be bought by one of the suitors or allowed to continue independently under RBS, doing the kinds of deals that we had always been doing, but probably with guaranteed contractual terms.

Plan C was that I just walked away. I had been very well paid at GNW, and didn't need to find another job in the immediate future. And now there was the potential opportunity with Fastow to consider.

All we had to do was keep the plates spinning for another week or so, while everything became clear, and then we could decide which way to go. In the meantime, let's go talk to Michael Kopper.

March in New York is a far cry from March in the Caymans. The weather was dank and misty. I found Michael, Kathy Lynn and Anne Yaeger ensconced in the smart offices of Kirkland & Ellis, attorneys to LJM, on Lexington Avenue not far from Central Park. The LJM team were in New York for a round of final discussions with investors prior to the second equity raising for LJM2. Michael told me that they were on course to raise nearly four hundred million dollars, and would be looking to add a sizeable debt facility, giving the partnership the potential for over half a billion dollars of assets to manage. I thought back to the dinner in Houston with Andy, and that glint in his eye as he talked about his compensation as the General Partner.

Michael explained the proposition. He had already set up the Cayman Islands partnership that would acquire GNW's stake in SwapSub. It was called Southampton LP, named after the district of Houston where he and Fastow lived. Southampton had two partners. The general partner was

another partnership called Southampton Place LP, and the limited partner
was a Cayman Islands company called Southampton KCo. I assumed that
the "K" stood for Kopper. Southampton Place would contribute $750,000
of equity to Southampton LP, and KCo would contribute the other
$250,000.

And we were being offered the opportunity to be KCo. Not to be part
of the European LJM, as we had assumed. But to buy into the very asset
that our employer had just agreed to sell.

It took all of five minutes to figure out that we couldn't do this. Well,
certainly not right away, attractive though it might have been. This is the
point in the story where I should just have got up and walked away. I know
that now. The chances are that I knew that then. But I didn't walk away. I
can rationalise it to myself (if I want to make myself feel better) by saying
that as a structuring guy, my job was problem solving, and this was nothing other than a problem looking for a solution. Which is true. But it still
doesn't cut it. I know that.

Far from walking away, though, I sat down and wondered how we
could do this thing.

The situation was straightforward, but complex at the same time.
NatWest had agreed to sell its interest in SwapSub. That sale was being
documented and would be concluded in less than two days. We were being
offered the opportunity to buy into what NatWest was selling, but there
was no way we could do that while still employed at GNW, because it
would have been a screaming conflict of interest. But we wouldn't know
for at least a week, I thought, whether or not we were staying with GNW
or leaving, and even then we had notice periods, so I just didn't see how
we could do it.

And then it came to me. We could take an option. If we had the ability, but not the obligation, to purchase an interest in KCo, we could wait to
see what happened with GNW. If we stayed, we would just let the option
lapse. If we left, we could exercise it after we had departed, and buy into
the investment. Simple. Just holding an option would not need to be
declared to GNW's compliance people.

Michael Kopper seemed quite happy with the idea, so I sat down and
drafted an option agreement. Michael faxed my handwritten effort to the

attorney Martha Stuart, who was doing all of the documentation on the sale in Kirkland & Ellis's Washington office, and she turned it into a legal document and faxed it back.

The strange thing is that at no stage during the entire process did I ever get the sense that there was anything amiss. I was a structuring guy. This was just another piece of structuring. Apart from which, I liked SwapSub. I liked the technical challenge of SwapSub. SwapSub had always intrigued me from a structurer's perspective. It was cool. And I was being offered an opportunity to be a part owner.

What we did, I maintain to this day, complied perfectly with the letter of GNW's personal account dealing policies. But it was also undeniably in stark contrast to the spirit. Some two years later the FSA themselves would find no fault in what we had done, even while acknowledging the potential conflict of interest.

I was in New York for two days. While there, I heard that the die was cast with RBS. They had announced their firm intention to fold our group under their project finance group, run by a gentleman called Tom Hardy. This was not a positive development. RBS's philosophy was to use their balance sheet to do big deals, and sit on them. Philosophically, they could not have been more unlike us. Their focus was on absolute income; the bigger the balance sheet, the more income you could earn. Ours was on velocity of capital; originating, structuring, and selling. This was definitely not worth sticking around for.

Meanwhile, although it had yet to be announced, Chip had been told that there was no place for him within the new organisation. He was out.

In an instant, Plans A and B had disappeared. Plan C it was. I drafted my resignation the moment I got back from New York.

More than one person who knows the story has commented that what we did was not really much different from negotiating a deal for a new job with a competitor, without telling your employer what you are doing. That's exactly what happens every single day in the City, and many people sit on those offers for weeks or months, hiding what in principle is a huge conflict of interest.

But the truth is that this was different. Yes, we were leaving. Yes, what we did complied entirely with the letter of GNW's securities dealing policy.

But the fact remains that I should have told the bank the details of exactly what had happened, and let them decide whether I should be allowed to do it.

The irony is that if I had done that, the worst that could have happened was that they said no. Since I was leaving anyway, I could in theory have just waited thirty days until my notice period had expired, and then made the investment anyway, if it had still been available. It would have been exactly the same result.

But I didn't, and it's a mistake that I'll have to live with for the rest of my life.

A SMALL FORTUNE
March 2000 to 9/11

My resignation took effect from Monday 20th March. My last day as an employee, including four weeks' notice and adjustments for holidays, would be 20th April. GNW's human resources guys were content for me to spend that month at home, which is not unusual in banking, and so I circulated an e-mail about a leaving drinks on the Friday, did the rounds of the office saying my goodbyes, and prepared to leave.

Before going, however, there was the small matter of the three amigos signing the option agreement that Kopper had faxed to Gary. Giles asked me whether I thought that the SwapSub price was fair. At his behest I sat down and did a valuation of the asset as at the previous week. This valuation showed that the mark to market value of the whole SwapSub vehicle, which had been $23 million on 7th March according to Dai Clement's calculations, had since fallen to about $3 million, before taking into account the negative consequence of the restriction on SwapSub's assets. So the price was demonstrably a good one. In fact, by most measures it could have been construed as outstanding. I put all of the supporting option calculations into an e-mail, and sent it to Giles.

That afternoon, we each signed the option agreement, and Gary faxed it back to Michael Kopper.

My departure coincided with the formal announcement that Chip Kruger would also be leaving, which would precipitate a mass exodus over the coming weeks. Gary stayed for just two days longer, and Giles another month.

I was as happy as Larry. It was the first time in my adult life that I had not been employed, and I was determined to make the most of it. The job market was buoyant, so I wasn't overly concerned on that score.

In the week after I left, the Enron share price leapt to an all time high. The good news just kept rolling in.

Conscious that I had never had the opportunity to sit down with Gary and Giles and explain properly what the option entitled us to, I set about writing a detailed letter to each of them which set out the structure of the Southampton partnerships as I understood it from the New York meetings, and what we would get for our money if we invested. We had the option to acquire up to 100% of the capital of KCo, which was $250,000, at a price which increased every day, and for a period which expired on 31st May. If by then we had not exercised the option and acquired an interest, our right to do so thereafter would lapse.

I was very pleased with it, really. It was a very simple mechanism that was designed to give each of us the flexibility to decide what we wanted to do, and would allow any or all of us to walk away, at no cost.

In the letter, dated 28th March, I explained how the economics worked, and noted how we might make a lot of money, but equally might lose our entire investment.

On April 21st, one day after I had formally left the employ of GNW, the three of us signed an exercise notice indicating that I would acquire all of the equity of KCo. A week later I paid just over $250,000 from my NatWest current account to an account in the name of ChewCo Investments, as instructed by Martha Stuart of Kirkland & Ellis. The investment was in my name because Gary and Giles were still working their notices at GNW, so as the new owner of KCo I granted them options to invest which lasted until August 31st.

A week later, Fastow called Gary. He told him that we had just made $7.3 million. After tax, this was about nine hundred thousand pounds each. Not far short of a win on the premium bonds. On an aggregate investment of just over a hundred and fifty thousand pounds.

There's little point trying to pretend that this is a trifling sum. It's a prodigious amount of money.

I may alienate readers by saying this, but compared to the money we were being offered at that time to move elsewhere, a million each was certainly not enough to make us risk our careers. To put it in some perspective, it was less than I earned through my pay packet in the calendar years 2000 and 2001, and I was a long way from being amongst the top earners in GNW. Both Gary and Giles, indeed, were paid comfortably more than I. Proof perhaps that the world really had gone mad.

Having resigned from GNW, the three of us landed soon thereafter at the capital markets division of Royal Bank of Canada. RBC had been one of the suitors keen to buy our group while we were part of GNW, and when RBS had refused to sell it, RBC decided to set up their own group from scratch. Since they were not going to have to spend a vast amount of money buying a complete group, they could afford to pay individuals that they hired extremely well. As Giles commented, it's a bit like being a footballer who is out of contract. The new team doesn't have to pay a transfer fee to another club, so they can commit more to the player's ludicrous wages.

We started work at RBC in the summer of 2000, and within 6 months Gary had built a team of nearly 50 people, a good number of whom walked away from RBS to join, including Dai Clement. Kevin Howard dabbled with RBC, but ultimately used the offer they made him to leverage a better salary deal from RBS to stay.

Our year one target was to break even, which from a standing start is no mean achievement, given the costs involved in setting up a new office. We succeeded, nonetheless.

Throughout our time there, we never made mention of our investment to any of our colleagues. There was no reason to. I had declared my investment in KCo on arrival at the bank, and the existence of the option agreements with two individuals. But no-one knew the full story of what had happened.

At no time did Andy Fastow ever make any reference to the deal, either. At one stage, Michael Kopper rang Giles and asked whether the three of us wanted to be involved in another investment. Giles said no, as we were quite happy where we were, and that was the end of it.

Meanwhile, Ben Glisan was promoted to the role of Treasurer at Enron, replacing Jeff McMahon. The rumour was that McMahon's animosity towards Fastow had spilled into the open, and he had been moved sideways by Skilling. If it was a disappointment for Giles, as the two were good friends, it was tempered by the fact that we liked and respected Ben.

If 2000 was an outstanding year for us, 2001 started well, but got progressively more difficult as it went on. The dotcom bubble had burst during 2000, and the impact on the world economy began to be felt in earnest during the following year, as a huge amount of shareholder wealth had been destroyed. And then came 9/11.

I was sitting in a conference room in RBC's London offices discussing a proposal for a huge financing of BA's aircraft fleet. There was a knock on the door and Mike Ellison put his head around it.

"Excuse me David, you need to turn on the TV. A plane has just flown into the World Trade Center".

At this point, of course, no-one knew what the hell was happening, and it was as likely that it was an accident as anything else. We turned on the TV just in time to catch the second plane ploughing into the other tower.

Shortly thereafter the news started to come in about the other hijacked aircraft, and the attack on the Pentagon. We sat transfixed in front of the television, and watched both towers come down. And then rumours started circulating about planes having been hijacked in the London skies.

I rang Emma and told her that there was little point trying to get home across town, as all tube and railway stations had been closed. I said I would be home whenever I could, but not to worry. When I finally left the building some hours later, the Evening Standard carried a full-page photograph of the plane hitting the second tower, under the headline "War on America".

By the time I got home, Emma's sister Victoria was with Emma, and in a terrible state. Her fiancé Justin worked for Barclays Capital, and had been staying in the hotel right beside the World Trade Center on a business trip. He had called her after the first strike, to say that he thought a missile had gone into the tower. He had been out walking prior to his meeting in the South Tower, and had heard the explosion above. He was fine, he said, and then his phone cut off. She had switched on the TV to see the second plane crashing, and had been unable to reach Justin since.

It would be the following day before she got the message that he was unharmed, and over a week before he managed to get back from New York, on a plane chartered by the bank to bring its employees home. All of his belongings ended up under several million tons of rubble, but he was safe.

In Washington and Whitehall, the events of 9/11 would act as the catalyst for what would become known as 'The War on Terror', involving large scale military action in both Iraq and Afghanistan, and a host of draconian new laws designed specifically to transfer more powers to the forces of Government at the expense of the liberties of the citizen.

While the wider stock markets held up relatively well in the immediate aftermath of 9/11, for Enron the situation was starting to become extremely difficult. Even at that point, though, few could have anticipated that it had but a few weeks left to live.

STORM CLOUDS GATHERING
8th November 2001

On a miserable day in a miserable last quarter of a terrible year, what had once been America's seventh largest company by market capitalisation swallowed the pill that was ultimately to poison it.

I remember reading through the Securities and Exchange Commission filing and being puzzled about the consolidation of SwapSub, which didn't seem to make any sense. But a little piece right at the end of the 20 page document hit me like a train when I read it. I have since been told by an ex-colleague that he vividly remembers me sitting in front of the Bloomberg screen, staring at it, white as a sheet, before going into Gary's office, closing the door, and picking up the phone. It was Gary that I was phoning; he was in RBC's head office in Toronto at the time.

"Gary, it's David"

"Hello Bermo, what's going on?"

"Are you near a Bloomberg terminal"

"Yes, I've got one right in front of me"

"OK, go to the Enron page and pull up the 8-K they've just posted"
I waited while he found it.

"What's this about then?"

"They've just restated their accounts for the last five years".

"Oh. That's not good, is it?"

"No. But that's not the point of the call. Scroll down to page 20, and read what it says".

The relevant section of the 8-K read as follows:

Enron now believes that Mr. Kopper also was the controlling partner of a limited partnership that ... in March 2000 purchased interests in affiliated subsidiaries of LJM1. Enron also now believes that four of the six limited partners of the purchaser were, at the time of the investment, non-executive officers or employees of Enron, and a fifth limited partner was an entity associated with Mr. Fastow. These officers and employees, and their most recent job titles with Enron, were Ben Glisan, Managing

Director and Treasurer of Enron Corp.; Kristina Mordaunt, Managing Director and General Counsel of an Enron division; Kathy Lynn, Vice President of an Enron division; and Anne Yaeger, a non-officer employee. Enron is terminating the employment of Mr. Glisan...

"Jesus", he said a short while later. "They fired Ben?"

"Do you know what this is about, Gary?"

"Er, no. Are you going to tell me?"

"It's Southampton. This whole section is about Southampton. I'm ninety nine percent sure. Read it again"

There was a pause while Gary re-read it. My chest was pounding.

"Is this saying that Ben invested in Southampton? And these other people?"

"Yes Gary, that's exactly what it's saying, or at least I think so".

"Shit"

"Yeah, shit is right. Can you remember when Ben took over from McMahon as Treasurer?"

"I think it was late April, early May 2000"

"That's what I thought too. Now do you remember when we made the money from Southampton?"

"Not really"

"First week of May 2000. This really doesn't look good. What the fuck is Ben doing here? And why has he been fired? You know we've always worked on the assumption that whatever Andy did to make that money, he would have been negotiating with McMahon? Well what if he wasn't? What if he was negotiating with Ben, and Ben is on both sides of the deal? This stinks, Gary. We have to speak to someone about it. Right now".

"I couldn't agree more. Okay, where's Giles?"

"Probably on a golf course somewhere in Texas"

"Oh yeah, that's right, he's in the States isn't he? Okay, leave that with me. I'll try to get hold of him. In the meantime, I'm going to speak to compliance here. I want you to do the same your end. Go speak with Guy. Tonight. Call me back after you've spoken with him, okay?"

WITHOUT HESITATION
8th November 2001

All major corporations have compliance functions. They ensure that the company is complying with all applicable laws, and they oversee internal policy and procedures with respect to business dealings. In banks, they are all powerful because they have to deal with the regulator, which in the UK is the Financial Services Authority ("FSA"), and are responsible for huge amounts of data and reporting. The rule of thumb with compliance is that if you're not sure about something, go talk to them. They issue detailed rules for just about everything, including what employees may and may not invest in, and what must be pre-cleared on a case-by-case basis.

When I had joined RBC back in June of 2000, I had declared my interest in Southampton, because that's what the rules required. Since then, I had become a regular visitor to the compliance offices because I was an active buyer and seller of shares, and you needed their written permission for every single trade. So I knew them all well.

This was not a visit I was looking forward to, however. As it turned out, Guy Scammell, the Head of Compliance, was not around, but his number two, Gurjit Purewal was in his office.

"Hi David. What's up?"

"Um I think I may have a problem, Gurjit"

"Okay, tell me about it"

I liked Gurjit. He was very straightforward and approachable. Guy too was a really nice chap. He always used to joke about what stock I was betting on this time when I came in for approvals, and (somewhat ironically now I guess) had once told a group of people in a meeting that I was a model citizen when it came to matters of reporting dealings.

I had printed off a copy of the 8-K, and sat down with Gurjit, and tried as best as I could to give him a potted version of these issues. I told him about how we had made the investment and how much money we had made. And I told him about my suspicions that there could have been fraud on Enron's side. I remember that I could hardly get a sentence out because my mouth was so dry and I was shaking so much.

I would guess I spent half an hour with him. He took notes throughout, and when I had finished he said that obviously this looked serious, and they would have to investigate it fully. Damned right, I thought. He then advised me to go home, and said that we would need to talk to Guy and John Burbidge in the morning. John was the Chief Operating Officer, and the de facto head of RBC's London operation.

I left compliance with mixed emotions. Happy that I had got it off my chest; terrified because I had no idea what the hell had happened, and why Ben or any of the others had come to be investors in Southampton, or why they had been fired.

I called Gary as soon as I got home. He too had met with the compliance officer in Toronto, and told him everything he knew. Being Gary, this probably didn't amount to a great deal of detail, but I had no doubt he would have captured all the main points. The Toronto guy had said much the same thing as Gurjit. Well done for coming in. This looks serious. We're going to have to have the drains up. Assume we can rely on your full co-operation.

"Look, Bermo, just relax, Okay? We've done nothing wrong. This could be an unpleasant few days, but they'll investigate it, find we've done nothing wrong, and we'll move on". By now Gary had spoken with Giles. Giles had spoken to one of the guys in our Houston office, and found out that the rumour was that Ben had just been fired for not declaring his investment. There didn't seem to be any suspicion of wrongdoing.

"All we can do is our best. Get some sleep, go in tomorrow and talk John Burbidge through the whole thing, from start to finish. You know this stuff way better than anyone else. Just tell him everything you know. Okay?"

"Okay", I said, trying to make myself feel better, and failing miserably.

I can't remember if I told Emma what had happened that night. I suspect I didn't. I tend to operate on a "need to know" basis, which is a hangover from Army days. If, as Gary said, this would all be sorted in a few days, then I could tell Emma when it was all over. Telling her now would just lead her to worry, in the way that loved ones do, and I wouldn't be able to give her much comfort because I didn't have any answers. I was worried enough for both of us, anyway.

The following morning I got to the office early, and there was already an e-mail from John Burbidge telling me to come up and see him when I got in. His office was on the third floor, glass fronted so that he had a constant view over the adjacent trading floor.

It was John who had overseen the formation of the new structured finance group the year before, so he knew us all very well. In his fifties, he had a kind, slightly ruddy face and graying hair, set atop a body which was unlikely to have graced an athletics track in the recent past. He was a very cheerful sort, and enjoyed a drink and a joke. I'd heard that he also had a decent temper on him, although I had never seen it. You knew not to mess with him though, as beneath the velvet glove lay a steel fist. You don't get to run a banking business including a large trading operation without being able to fire people.

"Morning John", I said, trying not to sound sheepish or apologetic, but also looking hard for clues to his mood in his demeanour.

"Hi David. Gurjit told me about last night. We're going to have to investigate this fully. You understand that?"

"Of course". There didn't seem to be any aggression or anger in his voice, which was a good start, I thought.

"Okay, well why don't we start by you giving me as much detail as you can, and we'll see where we go from there. I'll call Gurjit and we can do this in the conference room, as I think we're probably going to need a whiteboard, right?"

I spent the next several hours trying to give the fullest possible explanation of what had happened. This involved going all the way back to June 1999, and the formation of LJM Cayman, and right the way through to the point when Gary, Giles and I came to invest in Southampton KCo, and made $7 million.

There eventually came a point when we had talked ourselves to a standstill. I have no idea what was going through John's mind, but they cannot have been happy thoughts in the light of what was happening at Enron. Even at this point when bankruptcy was not on anyone's immediate radar, Enron and Andersen looked like being embroiled in shareholder suits. Our little revelation had the potential to involve RBC, even though our participation in Southampton had happened before we ever joined the bank. But John was not known to panic, and he seemed remarkably unemotional throughout, concentrating instead on trying to understand as much of what I was saying as possible.

By now it was Friday afternoon. John thought for a moment and then asked me to go home, write down everything that I could about the whole thing, and bring it in on Monday morning. He walked up to the whiteboard tore off all the pages on which I had scribbled my diagrams, and folded them up.

There was something cathartic about writing the paper. By the time I had finished, it occupied 7 pages of small type, and included diagrams and lots of information that I was able to add by looking at all my files. I sent a copy to Gary and one to Giles for their comments. I finished it on the evening of Sunday 11th November, Remembrance Day. Then I signed and dated it, and put it into my briefcase for the morning, along with all of the papers that I had in my files. These included all the legal documents associated with our investment in Southampton, bank statements, faxes, copies of memos, plane tickets, hotel bills, and spreadsheets. A complete audit trail. Quite enough rope to hang us from several yardarms, as it would turn out.

I gave John the paper and all the documents as soon as I arrived in the office on Monday morning. Giles was also back in the office and we had a short conversation. He was relatively relaxed about the whole thing. His view was the same as Gary's. "Look, Bermo, there's nothing to hide here. We don't know what's gone on at Enron, but we know we've done nothing wrong, so all we can do is tell the truth and we'll be fine". At that stage, everyone was still jubilant at the news that the merger between Enron and Dynegy had been announced.

I had a meeting out of the office that morning, and on my return found a message asking me to call John. He wanted me to come to the Human Resources department, where they had lots of interview rooms away from public gaze. John was there with Gurjit, and they introduced me to a guy whose name I cannot remember so let's call him Peter, who worked for Kroll Associates. Kroll were a firm of forensic accountants, and the bank had made the decision over the weekend that they needed some expert help.

I think it's fair to say that Peter and I did not hit it off. It is often remarked, particularly by Gary, that a good percentage of people who meet me for the first time professionally really don't like me. I can come across as arrogant. It's not a conscious thing, and deep down I don't think I'm a deliberately arrogant man, just awkward. Peter, though, pushed all the right buttons, deliberately or otherwise.

Our meeting lasted nearly four hours, and when we were finished they spent a further two hours with Giles. Gary would be interviewed separately in Toronto. Tactically it made perfect sense–split us up and grill us all separately, then look for discrepancies in our stories.

When we saw the notes from the meetings for the first time several years later, I was staggered at how few inconsistencies there were. Certain recollections were slightly different, but in every single major aspect, our stories were the same. The nice thing about the truth is that it usually only comes in one version.

I spent the most time under the bright lights. I had written the paper, and I understood the details of the structure and all of the various trades far better than Giles and Gary. And Peter really wanted to understand the detail. Over the course of Monday and Tuesday, I sat through three separate interviews. By the end, I didn't like Peter and I don't think he liked me. He seemed to need to prove that he was way smarter than me, and he sneered a lot.

I was hugely frustrated because all I could see was the three of us trying our level best to be as helpful as we possibly could, and getting screwed in return. There was a bigger problem, though. We simply didn't know what Fastow had done that had resulted in us making $7 million on a $250,000 investment in a matter of a few short weeks. Peter saw this as being the key to the puzzle, and was determined to work it out.

By the final meeting, he had had a "eureka" moment and determined, by looking at the stock price tables of Enron and Rhythms for early May 2000, that Fastow had just persuaded Enron to unwind a whole load of derivatives trades with SwapSub on completely the wrong valuation basis. It was a very simple thesis, and supported by the relative share prices at the time, but I just knew that it couldn't be right. There was no way that Enron would have agreed to that.

I had a long journey home that Tuesday evening, made longer because someone had decided to commit suicide on the main line just outside Twyford, which added about an hour to the normal time. I spent most of the journey seething about Peter and his ridiculous thesis, and by the time I got home I was ready to burst.

After supper I had calmed down a bit. I wrote an e-mail to John Burbidge, because I was catching a plane to Toronto the following morning and probably wouldn't get the chance to talk with him. I told him that I understood that Peter was just doing his job, and that he was eager to solve the conundrum, but his theory just could not be right.

Quite apart from anything else, it would have involved a total and utter circumvention of all normal controls at Enron. They had one of the most sophisticated derivatives pricing and risk management groups we had ever come across. There was no way that they could have mis-priced those derivatives to the extent that Peter was suggesting. And even if they had, it was inconceivable that their external auditors would have missed it too. There had to have been a different explanation.

Ironically, we would discover after our extradition that, even though Peter's theory was wide of the mark, the "inconceivable" notion that all of Enron's control functions had been bypassed was in fact correct.

John called me at home early the following morning. He wanted to give me some comfort. He reassured me that they were all batting for us, and that this was just a process through which they had to go. There was nothing sinister. He explained that the head of human resources had attended one of the meetings simply to cross check things like our joining dates, and ensure that nothing of what had happened had occurred while we were employed by RBC. It had not.

I got on the plane feeling much better about life. I was mentally exhausted, but we had given RBC everything that we had, and answered every question that they had asked. There was little more to do now than let the thing take its course.

I knew from Gary that the CEO of the investment bank, Chuck Winograd, had ordered a thorough review of all the bank's dealings with Enron since our arrival, to see whether we had done anything which could appear to have put the interests of Enron before those of the bank. On the contrary, it seemed that their review threw up exactly the opposite result. Assuming there was no wrongdoing at Enron with respect to the Southampton transaction, and that Glisan and Mourdant had indeed just been fired for failing to report their investment, this minor incident would pass and we could get on with running the business.

But by the following night, RBC had decided otherwise. Stung by a relatively recent embarrassment involving an inside trader, they were fiercely protective of their reputation. Chuck Winograd told Gary that they had concluded that our actions back in March 2000 could best be construed as "stretched ethics", and that they felt it would be better if we all resigned. They could see us getting embroiled in the SEC investigation into Enron, and they didn't want to risk any negative inference if we were subpoenaed while employees of the bank.

The following morning I got on a plane back to London. It would be my last ever working day as a banker. I arrived home relatively late on that Friday evening, and had to change straight into a dinner jacket and go to a fundraising dinner for the local pre-school. Emma had gone on ahead, and I got to the fundraiser shortly after everyone had sat down for dinner.

"I have good news, and bad news", I said.

"What's the good news?"

"You're going to be seeing a bit more of me."

She looked crestfallen. "That's the GOOD news…?"

PART TWO: THE UK FIGHT

THANK YOU FOR COMING
19th November 2001

The following Monday morning, 19th November 2001, Gary, Giles and I met with the Financial Services Authority in their offices in Canary Wharf. We had agreed with RBC that we would go to them and tell them the whole story. We were accompanied by two partners from the law firm McDermott, Will & Emery—Melanie Hunt, who Giles and Gary both knew from past business, and Graham Rowbotham, who specialised in regulatory matters.

The Financial Services Authority had just moved into their new headquarters in London's Docklands area, a few miles east of the City of London. It was a vast edifice of steel and glass, handsome and very light inside. Hugely expensive, I had no doubt. But as the taxpayer was footing the bill, they could afford to go the extra mile on fixtures and fittings. We had plenty of time to admire the architecture of the glass atrium as they kept us waiting for some 15 minutes.

The FSA was the new "super-regulator", the brainchild of Gordon Brown. It had been given draconian new powers over pretty much any area of business that you could imagine by the Financial Services and Markets Act 2000. In addition to its regulatory functions, it could now investigate and prosecute whole areas of crime in its own right. For anyone working in Financial Services, being on the wrong side of the FSA was a very bad idea, as they could take away your authorisation to work in the blink of an eye.

We finally walked into a large conference room and were introduced to Giles Edwards, Peter Fox, Ken O'Donnell, Claire Young and Tim Crump. Of these, Ken seemed to be the most senior, not least because his business card had embossed lettering. It indicated that he worked for the "Enforcement" section of FSA. This didn't augur well. I had visions of Clint Eastwood and a .44 Magnum.

We sat down at a large table, and Tim Crump, also of Enforcement, indicated that they were going to be tape recording the meeting. We had no objection (I'm not sure it would have made any difference if we had), so off we kicked.

"Good morning. My name is Tim Crump. I'm in meeting room number 12 in the FSA. The time now is ten minutes to twelve, it's Monday 19th November. I'm in a meeting room with Messrs Mulgrew, Bermingham and Darby for the purposes of a voluntary meeting which you've agreed or asked FSA to attend and you wish to disclose some information to us".

Some two and a half hours later the meeting finished. We had, as with RBC, used my paper of 11th November as the framework for the discussions. RBC had given the FSA a copy of all the papers that we had given to them, which ran to several hundred pages. We all agreed that it was likely that the SEC would be wanting to talk to us, and we confirmed that we would be happy to do that, without reservation or conditions. They thanked us profusely for coming in, and said that it was "excellent" that we had brought these matters to their attention. It was a thoroughly civilised meeting, all told.

"What now?"

"Better go to the pub"

In the absence of a job to go to, it seemed like a reasonable suggestion.

And then a big fat nothing. The Enron story played out through November, culminating in its bankruptcy on 2nd December. In the second week of January the FBI and Justice Department announced that they were putting together a Task Force to investigate possible criminality at Enron.

On February 1st, 2002, Bill Powers and his internal investigation team at Enron published their report. It was a phenomenal bit of work, given how little time they had had to prepare it, and the extremely hostile circumstances in which they had to operate. For a journalist, reading it must have been like wading through treacle at times. But for me it was a treasure trove.

The report set out in some detail what had happened back in March and April 2000. It seemed that Fastow had persuaded Enron to pay

SwapSub $30 million to collapse the RhythmsNet arrangements and take back the Enron stock. The report noted that in fact, because of the stock restriction, the stake should have been worthless. No-one at Enron could explain why the restriction had been ignored. Seemingly the company's auditors had also failed to comment on it.

The report went on to say that several Enron and LJM employees had personally invested in Southampton, including Michael Kopper, Ben Glisan, Anne Yaeger and Kathy Lynn. All had made returns on their investments in Southampton significantly greater in percentage terms than ours. It also suggested that one of the limited partners had been paid $10 million for its stake in SwapSub. This was the first indication that CSFB, too, may have sold their stake, and if the price had indeed been $10 million, then something very strange indeed had happened. If I was scared before, I was starting to get really scared now. There was no doubt whatsoever that the call from the SEC would be coming, probably sooner rather than later.

Nonetheless, in one way I felt vindicated. There could be no doubt that GNW had got a decent price for its asset. This report confirmed that in no uncertain terms. But the bigger questions were how Fastow had persuaded Enron to pay $30 million for an asset that was worthless at the time, and had he really paid CSFB $10 million, and if so, why?

On 10th February, out of the blue, the *Sunday Times* published an article entitled "UK Bank Trio Behind Enron Deals", with a strap line saying "Executives wooed with skiing and lap dancers". The piece was a combination of good investigative journalism and salacious stuff. It revealed how the three of us were rumoured to have made secret investments, and then went into long descriptions of supposedly wild lifestyles.

On 4th March, the FSA wrote to Graham Rowbotham, informing him that they had now completed their "preliminary review" of our involvement in the transaction. They had decided to pass all of the papers, including a transcript, on to the SEC in New York, and would reserve their position pending the outcome of the SEC enquiries. Graham rang Ken O'Donnell at the FSA who confirmed that they had not found that we had done anything unlawful, and that in principle we were free to seek job opportunities in the financial services industry as far as he was concerned.

In the years to come, the FSA would wriggle and wriggle and tell anyone who asked that they had never conducted an investigation into us, merely made some preliminary enquiries, and that therefore it was nothing to do with them if the Americans wanted to accuse us of robbing NatWest in London. That all of the information that we supplied to them, and which they passed on to the American authorities, would become the basis of the charges against us was neither here nor there. Thanks for nothing, guys. Lesson learned.

Meanwhile RBS were sitting up and taking notice.

Gary was called at home by Helen Cockroft in their compliance department, wanting him to come in and talk with them. Gary referred her to Graham Rowbotham, which led to several months of surprisingly uncivil correspondence between their lawyers–Travers Smith Braithwaite–and ours.

We found Travers Smith Braithwaite's position incredibly frustrating, as we had no objections whatsoever to speaking with RBS, and made this clear. Both Gary and Giles had separate conversations with Helen telling her that we would be happy to come in. All we needed was some legal protection, so that anything that we said would be confidential. It was hardly a big ask in the circumstances, we thought.

We came very close to agreement. But then in early May Travers Smith changed direction, backtracking on much of what had informally been agreed, and saying that on the advice of their US attorneys they would need to meet with each of us individually, and would not be able to offer any guarantees of confidentiality. Additionally, the meetings would be a one-way street, with no possibility of them giving us any information or copies of documents that might help us in any litigation.

Funnily enough, the meetings never took place. In the years to come, Travers Smith would accuse us of refusing to meet with RBS, which whilst technically accurate was, we believed, pretty disingenuous.

In the meantime, the newly formed Enron Task Force had wasted no time in indicting Arthur Andersen, Enron's auditor, on charges of obstruction of justice for allegedly shredding huge amounts of information in the weeks before Enron's collapse. The political and media pressure on the Task Force was immense, and grew daily during the first half of 2002.

Houston's largest company had folded almost overnight, and someone had to be responsible. Someone needed to go to jail.

We expected a call from the SEC at any time. Southampton would need to be investigated. We had no doubts.

The call never came. Instead, on June 27th, 2002, following the collapse of WorldCom, amidst further allegations of accounting fraud, a criminal complaint was filed, and warrants for our arrest were issued in Houston, Texas.

IN THE FIRING LINE
28th June 2002

The following morning I was watching the BBC breakfast news. And then all of a sudden I was the news.

"Three British bankers... Fraud... NatWest... Enron".

Pictures of the Enron building in Houston. Pictures of the NatWest logo.

"David Bermingham, Gary Mulgrew, Giles Darby".

I just sat and stared at the television in disbelief. I briefly wondered whether I was dreaming. When I realised that I wasn't, I called out to Emma.

"I have to go to London", I said.

"Why?"

"Because I've just been charged with fraud".

The next few hours were a blur. As the little Thameslink train pulled out of Goring station, I remember looking out of the window across the familiar fields towards our house. I had that sick feeling in my stomach where everything is just churning. My mouth was completely dry. I had not the faintest idea what was happening, but I was certain it wasn't good.

I dialed Emma's parents, and asked her mother to go to the house and be with Emma. Then I phoned my parents. No, I told my mother, I didn't know what it was about, but I was on my way to London to meet with the lawyers. I would try to call her later.

I got to the offices of McDermott, Will & Emery ("MWE") at about half past nine. I had been there on a number of occasions over the previous few months. They were typical City offices for a major US law firm. Spacious reception area with expensive furnishings and nice art. Nice carpets. Highly efficient reception staff. Well appointed meeting rooms. A good place to do business.

That day it felt very different. When I arrived at the reception desk, I probably had the look of a frightened rabbit, but if the receptionists knew what was happening, they betrayed no sign of it.

John Reynolds and Kate Learoyd of MWE were waiting for me. They had printed off a copy of the relevant document from the internet. The Department of Justice had separately issued a press release talking about what dreadful people we were, and how they were determined to pursue criminality wherever the perpetrators were. The press release indicated that the charges were the result of a joint effort with Britain's Serious Fraud Office and the Financial Services Authority.

John and Kate were good enough to leave me alone to read the papers. We had no copy of the charging document itself, but there was a fourteen page Affidavit containing the allegations and details of what was supposed to have occurred.

The Affidavit was a right riveting read. Bang to rights. A wonderful tale of avarice and skullduggery, revealed in all its inglorious detail by the prowess of the world's finest investigators, the FBI. Even now I have more than a grudging admiration for the job that they did in weaving it together, and presenting it as a testament to their skill and professionalism. It may have been complete fiction, but never let the truth get in the way of a good story. And this was a very good story.

It all centred on Southampton LP, which we were alleged to have set up to defraud NatWest. In short, the allegation was that the three of us knew that the SwapSub asset was very valuable. We kept that information from NatWest, and schemed with Andy Fastow and Michael Kopper to persuade NatWest to sell the asset at a knockdown price. We then bought into it ourselves and sold it on to Enron for its true value, thereby netting a huge profit.

I must have read it several times by the time John and Kate came back in, but somehow it didn't get any better with the second or third readings.

John knew all about Southampton and the underlying transaction. He had not been present when we went forward to report the transaction to the FSA in November 2001, but two other members of his firm had, and we had met him before.

"This is a bloody disgrace" I said. Actually I think my language may well have been a lot more colourful, but I am hoping for the sake of Kate that it wasn't. "It doesn't look good", ventured John, which was a significant understatement.

"Do you recognise any of this, John?" I asked. "The narrative of the story, for instance?"

"Well, it bears a strong resemblance to what you told the FSA last November", he responded.

"Yes, John, it does. That's because an awful lot of what is in here comes verbatim from the stuff we gave to the FSA. Look at it. Do you remember the paper that I wrote which we talked through with the FSA? Well here it is, in bite-sized pieces. Along with some Alice in Wonderland stuff which they have just thrown in here to say it was a fraud".

"But what about the e-mails?" he asked. "They look absolutely horrible".

This of course was difficult to deny. Words like "steal", "robbery", and "greed" just jumped off the page at you. For the most part written by me.

"John, firstly these e-mails have nothing whatsoever to do with our investment in Southampton. Second, these are not whole e-mails, but extracts from e-mails. They are taken completely out of context."

I still cringe even now when I read those e-mails. Even though the full versions were clearly unrelated to any attempt to defraud our bank, as the US Government was suggesting, what possible context could justify words like 'steal', 'robbery' and 'greed'?

Looking back, I can imagine that John's reaction was "tell it to the judge, David", though being a consummate professional, he betrayed no skepticism. But John and Kate were not criminal lawyers. They were civil litigators. In fact there was not a single criminal lawyer within the London practice of MWE. It had never occurred to us for one moment that we would ever need a criminal lawyer.

I was verging on meltdown. My heart was thumping. My hands were sweating. I needed to know why this was happening. What the hell had we done to deserve this? I was lashing out at the FSA, lashing out at the Department of Justice. Wankers. All of them. We had come forward and offered our unconditional assistance. And not one of these people could even be bothered to pick up the phone to us, let alone come and see us.

We were the good guys. How dare they?

"We've got a few issues," said John, a study in quiet pragmatism amidst the storm of my outbursts. "First, we need to get you some criminal counsel in the US. Second, you are going to need to talk to an expert here about extradition. I've spoken this morning with Alun Jones, who is one of the leading Queen's Counsel on extradition. He's going to send us his initial thoughts. I'm going to get hold of our New York office as soon as they open, and find a criminal attorney for you."

I spent a good deal of time on the phone to Giles that fateful day. Living in Wiltshire, he was too busy fighting his fires from home to get on a train to London. He had found the document online. As the majority of the "bad" e-mails were actually between Gary and me, Giles was reading them for the first time.

"Mate, what the fuck is all this stuff?"

I told him exactly what it was, and what they had done with it. "Fucking bastards", he said. He was equally worked up about being quoted by an old colleague, as having said "we're gonna get rich". But that paled into insignificance next to the e-mails.

Giles coped as well as any of us in times of stress, and better than most. He was capable of losing the plot (as were we all), but for the most part his journeys off the rails were few and short-lived. Once he understood what had happened, he flipped almost instantly into "pragmatic" mode. It was his forte.

Problem number one was that Gary was in Japan, attending the 2002 World Cup. We had to get hold of him and let him know what was happening.

We needn't have bothered, as it turned out. Gary was in his hotel room ironing a shirt when he was called by a friend and told to turn on CNN. You had to hand it to the Department of Justice. Their press machine was good.

Problem number two was arrest. John wrote to the Metropolitan police, informing them that he represented us and that if we were to be arrested then we would very much like to be able to report somewhere rather than have the police turn up at half past five in the morning with the children around. In John's view, we might be facing extradition to the States within weeks.

When New York opened, John was able to speak to one of his partners there, Michael Sommer, who was a criminal attorney. Michael agreed to come to London in about ten days time. He also broke the news that we would each need to be represented by separate firms of attorneys in the US, and said he would try to identify two others who he would bring with him when he came.

John sent copies of the charging documents and all the papers that we had given to the Financial Services Authority all those months previously to Alun and Michael.

At that point, there was not a great deal else to do, so I made my way home. I had called Emma before leaving London. There had been press all over the place, she said. She was pretty upset. I had asked John what I should say if confronted by the press, and he was firm. "No comment".

I picked up an early edition of the Evening Standard at Paddington, and read all about us. I spent most of the journey home glancing furtively around the carriage to see who else might be reading the Standard, and trying desperately not to be noticed. I'm sure that the people who try hardest not to be noticed are the ones who tend to stand out a mile.

As the train pulled into Goring station, shortly before tea-time, I was seized once again with panic. I took a close look around before stepping onto the platform to make sure there were no press there. Then I walked a circuitous route home. About 500 yards from home, I thought I saw some guys hanging around the front of the house. I made a detour down a narrow lane, and across a neighbour's field into our back garden.

Ken, the local builder, was laying a patio outside the back of the house. I can only imagine what his guys thought when they saw me, dressed in smart trousers and a city shirt, appearing from the trees carrying a briefcase. It might not have been so bad had I not ripped the shirt while climbing through the barbed wire fence, leaving a small triangular patch of cloth flapping open on the right side of my chest, which was now bleeding profusely. Trying to look nonchalant at this stage was beyond me, and no explanation for my appearance sprang to mind. I just mumbled "hi guys" as I walked past them and into the kitchen.

Emma's mother Zoe was there, as was mine. We had a cup of tea, and not a great deal was said while we waited for Emma's father to arrive; it seemed senseless to go over the same ground twice. Emma's father, Brian, is a district judge. He and Zoe are 10 or so years younger than my parents. They met and married at a very young age, in the swinging sixties, and as parents-in-law go it would be hard to beat them. But on this occasion Brian was in a foul mood. He wanted to know the whole story, so I told him, which must have taken at least half an hour. He listened intently, as lawyers do, and made no comment until I was finished.

"Well I think you were bloody stupid", he said, with some understatement. What he didn't say, but implied, was that I had brought disgrace onto the family. He didn't need to say it. I knew it full well. It was a long time since I had felt like the naughty schoolboy, and it was a particularly unpleasant feeling. At times like this, though, there is no sense in trying to justify yourself. Just take your medicine.

After they had left, we waited around for my father to arrive before having some supper. He and I walked in the garden while he smoked a cigar, and I gave him a potted version of the story. "What's the worst case?" he asked.

"Five years in an American prison". Although we had not yet seen the charging document, we had been told that it consisted of one charge of wire fraud, the statutory maximum sentence for which is five years without parole.

"Is any of it true"? he asked.

"Yes, quite a lot actually. The only bit that isn't true is the bit about us committing a crime…"

After my parents had left, I had to face Emma.

"What's going to happen?" she asked.

"I don't know, sweetheart".

"Are you going to have to go to America?"

"I don't know"

"Are the police going to come and arrest you?"

"I don't know"

That uncertainty was the worst thing. Facing something terrible but definite is much easier. With uncertainty you can't make plans. You are living life from day to day. It was something we would have to get used to over the coming years.

The next few days were horrible, not least because I woke early every morning imagining the knock on the door from the police. But there were moments of levity too. The morning after being charged, Emma was bringing tea to the builders who were on their break and sitting around in the sunshine. One of them had been reading The Sun, and had turned to a page where there was a picture of the house, presumably taken the preceding day. He looked at the picture, and then over his shoulder at the house behind him, and then back at the picture, and then at Emma. Emma feigned not to notice, but managed to see the funny side when recounting the story later on that day.

On that Saturday afternoon, Giles came to the house with his wife Deborah and the children. It was a gorgeous sunny day and we ate outside in the garden, but there wasn't much in the way of merriment. Giles, like me, likes to be in control of things, and we could not have been less in control of this situation. We wondered aloud why they were doing this, why they had never spoken to us. It didn't make sense. They had taken everything that we had given to the FSA, and then just made up a story. Why?

They say that in times of crisis you find out who your friends are. We found plenty of friends. A couple of days after being charged, we had a group of the locals for supper (it had been arranged for some time and we were determined not to cancel), and ate outside as it was a lovely evening. One of the guests confided that he too had been accused of fraud several years earlier, had been arrested and investigated for quite some time before the whole thing went away. Revealing that was an unnecessary act of kindness, but it made me feel that we, too, were going to be able to get through this.

Church on the Sunday after being charged was something I was dreading. The Catholic church of Our Lady & St John in Goring is not big. The local priest, Father Tom Williams, likes very much to be amongst the congregation, so he eschews the original altar and has instead rearranged the pews so that they face each other, with a smaller altar in the middle. It works really well because now the normal congregation is just sufficient to fill the church, and there is a very cosy feel about it. But no possibility of being there unnoticed.

Goring is a relatively small village, and everyone who wishes to can know everyone else's business. As newcomers to the village (we had been there less than a year at the time) I was terrified of the opprobrium that would doubtless be visited upon us that first Sunday, particularly by some of the older parishioners. But I was determined nonetheless that we should not be hiding. We needed to look the devil in the eye.

Inevitably in life the things that you are most dreading turn out to be nothing like as bad as you have imagined. Father Tom made a point of catching my eye as we walked in, and smiled broadly. After the service, he came up to me and took my hand in both of his. "I'm sorry for your troubles", he said. "I've been praying for you". Later that day, he came ambling down the drive and knocked on the door. We talked for about twenty minutes over a cup of tea, and he was really kind and reassuring. Since 2002, not one single parishioner has ever had anything other than kind words to say. Many told us how they regularly prayed for us. It was all extremely humbling, to be honest. I have often wondered what the experience would have been like had we still been living in London.

Some time during those early days my Uncle Dick visited. Well into his seventies, he was a doctor and had a wonderfully relaxed manner. He used to do magic tricks for us when we were children at Christmas, and there would always be something of interest in one of his pockets. He was a very kindly soul, and amongst his many good deeds he played chess by correspondence with inmates on death row in America. He once wrote to George W Bush, then the Governor of Texas, asking that a particular prisoner be granted a stay of execution so that they could complete their game. Bush replied with a personal letter in which he expressed his sympathy, but declined.

He only stayed for an hour or so that day, but his advice would stand me in very good stead for the years ahead. His wife, my aunt, had died very tragically when their two children were at a very young age, and he had taken a long time to come to terms with it. He told me that he eventually worked out that there were things in life over which you had control, and it was fair to worry about those. There were other things over which you had no control, and time spent worrying over these was just corrosive to the spirit.

When experiencing periods of great stress, he said, try to set aside a little time each day for "constructive worrying", thinking about the things over which you may have some control. But dedicate specific time to this, and otherwise put the subject back in its box and don't think about it for the rest of the day.

My Mother pointed out that his words were almost certainly inspired by the Serenity Prayer:

"Lord, give us grace to accept with serenity the things that cannot be changed, courage to change the things that should be changed, and the wisdom to distinguish the one from the other."

Meanwhile, John Reynolds had received a reply to his letter to the Extradition Squad of the Met. No guarantees were given that we would be allowed to self-report if our arrest was sought.

Michael Sommer had also been busy. He had been in touch with the prosecutor, Thomas Hanusik, on the Friday, requested a copy of the charging document, and asked what bail conditions Hanusik would be looking for if we agreed to waive our rights in extradition and come voluntarily to the US.

Hanusik had taken little time in replying, indicating that we would first need to provide sworn affidavits as to assets. Michael stalled for time, indicating that until all three clients had separate legal representation, he thought it inappropriate to have substantive discussions.

Alun Jones meanwhile had produced a four page note on the extradition issues related to the charges against us. He noted that by a quirk of fate, the English equivalent of the charges as framed would be "conspiracy to defraud", and that this was not an extraditable offence under the 1989 Extradition Act.

Consequently, any request for extradition was much more likely to suggest offences under the Theft Act, which would need a fair degree of evidence to substantiate in any extradition proceedings.

The enormity of the challenge ahead was first brought home to us the following week, when we met the legal team in its entirety. John and Kate were there, and Michael Sommer, just in from New York. Michael had brought with him Mark MacDougall from Akin, Gump, Strauss, Hauer & Feld, a Washington firm. He was still working on finding a third attorney. Gary had by now flown back from Tokyo, believing that it was highly likely that he would be arrested on arrival and perhaps put on a plane to the US, and Giles had made the trip from Wiltshire. Alun Jones would join us later in the afternoon, as he was in court that day.

Michael took the lead. Slightly short, and balding, he was neatness and precision personified. He struck me as the archetypal corporate lawyer in the Hollywood films. He wore expensive suits, shirts and shoes, and carried an expensive pen. He oozed professionalism. He would lean forward intently, and his every phrase was measured.

Mark seemed somewhat more laid back. Taller, and with a full head of graying hair, he had a kindly face and constantly wore an expression of benevolent concern. He made a point of telling us about his Scottish ancestry, which played well with Gary.

The first thing we wanted to know was what the hell was happening? What did it mean? What could we expect?

Our introduction to the US criminal justice system was an unhappy one. Michael Sommer began by explaining why it was that each of us needed to instruct separate counsel, meaning separate law firms.

"Why the hell would we incur three sets of legal fees?" we asked. "We're in this together".

"Well, circumstances have a habit of changing", Michael pointed out, without humour. All three firms would of course require substantial retainers if they were to agree to act for us. Excellent. I looked around the room and started doing the maths. Even without the "third man" from the US, we were already running up expenses at the rate of approximately two thousand pounds an hour, or roughly ten pounds a minute for each of the three clients. Plus hotel bills. Plus flights. And come to think of it, the clock had already been running while Michael and Mark were on the flight, no doubt. Christ on a bike…

We ended up scribbling Michael's name, Mark's name, and "A N Other" onto three pieces of paper, screwing them up into little balls, and putting them into a bowl. Giles drew first, and picked out Michael. I went second and drew Mark. I was very pleased because Mark seemed a very nice guy, and I thought he and I would get on well.

"Oh great", said Gary, in that way he has of suggesting that the world is against him. He would have to wait to see who providence would give him as an attorney.

Michael then went on to explain that the charging document was what is known as a criminal complaint, as distinct from the more normal indictment. This, he remarked, was quite unusual because it is an informal charge, normally reserved for situations where a prosecutor is afraid that a defendant will flee, and does not have time to take his case before a Grand Jury to get an indictment. By law, the prosecutor must go before the Grand Jury with his case within 90 days and obtain an indictment, or the charges will fall away.

Given that a Grand Jury had been sitting examining evidence to do with Enron cases for some months, and there was certainly no danger of us fleeing the jurisdiction of the prosecutor, since we weren't in it in the first place, it didn't make sense that the prosecutors had opted to go this route rather than a formal indictment. Michael thought they were sending a message—not to us, particularly, but to Kopper and Fastow, who were refusing to co-operate with the ongoing investigations into Enron's collapse.

The criminal complaint outlined the case against us, but charged only one count of wire fraud—a technical device that enabled the Federal authorities to take jurisdiction over what might otherwise be a State case, by alleging that a person had used "interstate communications" (faxes, e-mails, telephone conversations etc) in furtherance of some underlying scheme.

Wire fraud had the added benefit of allowing US prosecutors to criminalise behaviour outside of the US. A scheme by UK citizens to defraud a UK bank would not naturally concern the US authorities, but the wire fraud statutes enabled them to say that any faxes or e-mails that had passed through the US would find jurisdiction there, even if the defendant had never set foot in the US. Since almost every e-mail in the world passes through a server in the US, this is a handy tool in the armoury of a US prosecutor.

The lawyers were obviously keen to get to the bottom of what had really happened.

"Let's start right at the beginning. Tell us about how you came to be working together, what you were doing, and then let's work right through from there".

"This is going to be a long story."

"Take your time".

MORE QUESTIONS THAN ANSWERS
July 2002

I did most of the talking, with Gary and Giles filling in with anecdotes and bits and pieces as we went along. We had copies of the transcript from the meeting with FSA, and hundreds of pages of documents that we had given to RBC and the FSA.

When we finally finished, Michael Sommer was rubbing his face in his hands.

"Okay, so you wrote all of this down, and gave it to RBC and the FSA with all of these papers? Did you not think to speak to a litigation attorney?"

"Er, no."

"Why the hell not?"

"Well for one thing we didn't know one. For another, we needed to report this thing instantly. And how would it have looked if we'd turned up the next day with a bunch of lawyers? We had nothing to hide. We were more than happy to answer their questions."

Michael wore a look that was a cross between quizzical and stupefied. What he really wanted to say, clearly, was "what possessed you????", but he contented himself with asking whether we realised that this created a legal record?

"Yes, we're well aware of that. But it's the truth."

"Well can you prove everything that's in here?"

"We could if we had access to the files at RBS".

"Well you certainly made the prosecutors' lives easy, that's for sure. But you say that no-one from the SEC or Justice ever contacted you?"

"Nope. No-one. Ever."

"Nice. Look, just so you understand how this works, anything that you may already have committed to the record that turns out to be wrong will be a lie. It's not a mistake. It's a lie. That's how the prosecutors will present it to a jury. The same goes for anything you may say from hereon in. Any inconsistency, no matter how small, will be used in court to undermine your entire credibility".

As Michael Sommer was explaining how foolish we had been, Alun Jones, Queen's Counsel, arrived. He immediately struck me as a character straight out of *Rumpole of the Bailey*. A big bear of a man, and of the old school. Slightly ruddy, with an expression that alternated between a mischievous grin and that of a garage mechanic who has just been asked to take a look under the bonnet and see what's wrong. I thought he would do quite well as one of the onlookers in a Bateman cartoon. His suit was slightly scruffy, and his stomach was fighting a constant battle for freedom with the bottom of his waistcoat. He could not have been more unlike Michael. I decided instantly that I liked Alun. Not that I disliked Michael. But Alun looked like he would be fun.

He spent some time talking us through the extradition rules. John Reynolds had managed to convince us, inadvertently or otherwise, that we should have our bags packed and be ready for an imminent trip to the US. Alun assured us that this was not the case, although we could of course be arrested at any time.

Alun exuded calm confidence. He had been there, done that. He had, quite literally, written the book on extradition (imaginatively entitled "Jones on Extradition"), and had been involved in numerous cases involving the US, as well as the famous Pinochet case. He was also a very distinguished criminal barrister, so there wasn't much he didn't know about the law.

As we were still functioning under the old extradition law at that time, the US would have to bring its evidence before a UK court, and we would have the opportunity to show that the case was nonsense. A UK magistrate would determine whether we had a case to answer, and the process was not a quick one. The US would have to allege offences under the Theft Act, and so would need to show evidence that the bank had indeed been defrauded. The Home Secretary was the ultimate arbiter in the decision to extradite, and had full discretion on a case-by-case basis, whatever the courts said. There were numerous levels of appeal. We weren't going anywhere quickly, unless we waived our rights and elected to go voluntarily to the US.

So why don't we just go straight to the Serious Fraud Office, we asked, as Alun had suggested in his written advice the previous week. We were accused of robbing NatWest. It was nonsense. We had gone voluntarily to the FSA all those months ago and told them all that we knew. Why would we not just go and do likewise with the SFO?

"Gentlemen" said Michael in that very deliberate delivery of his, "with every fibre of my being I would advise you not to do that".

It was a strange turn of phrase, I thought. Michael explained that in his view we were not the people that the US Government was interested in. He pointed out that although the criminal complaint alleged that we had conspired with Andy Fastow and Michael Kopper to perpetrate the fraud on our employer, neither of them had been charged.

He was right. It was so obvious. In fact none of the other investors in Southampton had been charged either, even though they must have known just as much as we did, if not a whole lot more.

Suddenly it all began to become a little clearer. Maybe that explained the criminal complaint, we thought. It's not an indictment, so it's not a formal charge. Once you are indicted you are a Federal statistic, and that means they will need to prosecute you because in America stats are everything. A criminal complaint can just be allowed to expire.

"They don't want you guys" said Michael. "They want Kopper and Fastow. They want your help, and this is their way of messaging you. So why the hell would you ask the British prosecutors to get involved, unless you actually did this thing?"

In America, information is currency, to be sold in return for promises of immunity or leniency or whatever. Nothing should ever be volunteered. When the FBI started investigating Enron, all but a very small number of individuals exercised their right to silence under the Fifth Amendment to the US Constitution, not necessarily because they had anything to hide, or had done anything wrong, but just because that's how it works over there. Meanwhile the three of us were naively assuming that going in and telling the truth was the right thing to do. One of life's more expensive mistakes, as it would turn out.

At that time, the decision not to talk to the SFO seemed sensible. Alun Jones made the point that we would have plenty of time at an extradition hearing to show why their case was nonsense, as they would have to provide evidence to substantiate charges of theft, and we would be able to respond in kind.

When we reconvened the following morning, the first discussions concerned civil proceedings. Around the time we were charged, Rabobank, a huge Dutch Bank, had brought a civil suit against RBC with respect to a transaction that we had done with Enron back in early 2001. Rabobank had effectively guaranteed the Enron risk in the deal, and was now facing massive losses as a consequence.

In an attempt to avoid their contractual obligations, Rabobank brought a suit alleging that the three of us were thick as thieves with Enron, and had fraudulently induced Rabobank to enter into the transaction with RBC. The action had been brought in New York. Whilst not defendants in the action, we would of course be key witnesses.

"I assume there's no truth in any of this?" asked Michael.

Gary answered the question. "Well let's put it this way. If we had had even the slightest inkling that Enron was a house of cards, do you think for one moment that we would have been lending money to them? We could have made a fortune shorting them. It doesn't take a brain surgeon to work out that this is just a mechanism for Rabobank to avoid payment. They probably figure that because the sums involved are so large, any kind of settlement from RBC will leave them ahead of the game."

"You have to face the fact that they are going to subpoena you for testimony", said John Reynolds.

"And you're going to plead the Fifth Amendment", said Michael.

"Why would we do that?"

"For exactly the reasons I outlined yesterday. Because you're in enough trouble already. Anything you say in this action will be used against you in a criminal trial. And these attorneys will be out to trip you up. If you trip yourself up on one little thing, no matter how seemingly unimportant it is, you will look like a liar. And the Department of Justice will use it against you. My strong advice to you is that from now on in, you make absolutely no comment on or off the record about the facts of this case to anyone under any circumstances".

"Well pleading the Fifth isn't going to help RBC very much, is it?"

"Are RBC helping you?"

It's a brutal world, the world of litigation. Every man is for himself. We believed that the Rabobank suit was completely without merit. We knew we were in a position to help RBC. But we couldn't. In a civil suit, a negative inference can be drawn from people pleading the Fifth Amendment, which suited Rabobank just fine. It stank.

Meanwhile, we had more pressing worries.

"Alright, let's go through the Affidavit".

We spent a large part of the day dissecting each part of the famous affidavit in microscopic detail. Large portions of it were entirely uncontentious. Almost inevitably these were the bits that we ourselves had supplied to the FSA, who had passed them to the SEC, who presumably had passed copies to the Enron Task Force.

Because we had given them so much information, the tremendous detail in the Affidavit looked as if it was the product of a huge amount of investigative work. Paragraph 3 read as follows:

"During this investigation, I and other FBI agents have reviewed documents, including partnership documents, bank records, hotel records, telephone records, wire transfer records, handwritten notes, transcripts of tape recorded statements, e-mails and other materials that set forth certain of the events described herein".

What the affidavit did not say, of course, is that almost all of these had been conveniently handed over by us. Stoopid limeys.

Paragraph 4 went on

"During this investigation, I and other FBI agents have interviewed witnesses with first-hand knowledge of certain events described herein"

But it did not say that those witnesses did not include the three defendants. We were the only people in the world who could have told the FBI what the e-mails really meant.

But what the hell? Anyone reading the affidavit would be overwhelmed by how much "evidence" the FBI had, and that was the point. It gave a complete and very detailed description of exactly what had happened, and it was a very compelling read.

The scheme to defraud was described succinctly at paragraph 12.

"Between approximately November 1999 and August 2000, while still employed at NatWest's GNW division, and while negotiating on behalf of NatWest, Mulgrew, Darby and Bermingham, with the assistance of persons associated with Enron and LJM Cayman, devised and executed a scheme to defraud NatWest by causing NatWest to sell its interest in Campsie for approximately $1 million at a time when [they] knew that NatWest's interest in Campsie was worth many times that amount. At the same time, [they] obtained for themselves a portion of NatWest's interest in the same partnership for only $250,000, then liquidated that interest just weeks later for $7.3 million in personal profit."

The "persons associated with Enron and LJM Cayman" were elsewhere named as Fastow and Kopper. Here was a conspiracy between 5 named people, but only three of them were being charged, as Michael had pointed out.

"Okay", said Michael, "the crux of this is that you knew the asset was worth more, and kept that fact from NatWest. From what you said yesterday, that's not true, right?"

"Not even close. $1 million was absolutely a fair price".

"Can you prove that?"

We set out at least five different ways in which we should be able to show that it was, and speculated that NatWest themselves would agree.

"Well if that's the case then it's going to be pretty difficult for the Americans to bring an extradition case on the basis of the Theft Act, because that would suggest that there was no theft", said Alun.

"Alright", said Mark, "but there are still some issues. The first is that CSFB got paid $10 million for an identical stake to the one for which NatWest got $1 million".

Indeed. It was a horrible fact. And one that would haunt us for years.

In short, Enron paid $30 million to SwapSub to unwind the Rhythms derivatives, after NatWest and CSFB had sold their interests in SwapSub to Southampton. Of the $30 million, $1 million had previously gone to NatWest, $10 million to CSFB, and $19 million had been split between Fastow, Kopper, Glisan, Mourdant, Yaeger, Lynn, a guy called Michael Hinds (who none of us had ever heard of), and the three of us.

The bald facts looked terrible. There was no getting round it. NatWest had sold for $1 million. CSFB, in the meantime, had been paid $10 million for an identical stake. Whichever way you looked at it, nothing added up. We were scrabbling around for justifications, and had none. We had no idea.

"Can you prove that you knew nothing of what Fastow and Kopper were up to, and had no knowledge of CSFB being bought out?"

"As a matter of fact, we can".

I pulled out a copy of the letter that I had written to Gary and Giles on 28th March 2000, eight days after we had taken the option to invest in Southampton. The letter made quite clear that we didn't know CSFB had been bought out, as it made several references to them still being a partner in SwapSub. It also speculated on what Fastow might do, and noted how Enron held all the cards. It described how any benefit would be split in the event that the deal made money, and suggested that we could lose all of our money if the Enron share price fell below a certain level.

The Powers Report had revealed that Fastow had actually struck the $30 million deal with Enron on 22nd March, six days before I wrote my letter.

"Okay, this is good. Assuming this letter is admissible, I think we can pretty much show that you didn't know what these guys were up to, and thought you could lose your money. That makes this nothing other than an investment, not some scheme to defraud. But it still doesn't explain why CSFB got $10 million for their stake". We would have to wait another four years for the answer.

"The big irony here", I said, "is that we went forward to report a possible fraud on Enron. Turned out that our suspicions about Fastow negotiating with Glisan were ill founded. Now we're accused of a fraud on NatWest. And it's just possible that there was never a fraud on anyone".

"You're going to have to explain that", said Alun. "Someone seems to have got shafted here. Powers thinks it's Enron. Department of Justice thinks it's NatWest. I agree that there's an irony there, but it must be one or other of them, surely?"

"Not necessarily. The SwapSub asset moved in value every minute of every day. It could change in value by tens of millions of dollars in a single day. It's quite conceivable that both NatWest and Enron got a fair price depending upon the value of SwapSub when Fastow agreed to unwind it with Enron. I know this flies in the face of what Powers says, and I happen to think that Powers is absolutely right, but I'm just saying that just because

NatWest agrees to sell for $1 million doesn't automatically make $30 million the wrong number, and vice versa, because of the volatility in price of this asset. One of the reasons that we didn't question making $7 million in a short space of time on an investment of $250,000 is that it was actually well within the range of possible outcomes. That's what made the investment so attractive. The most you could lose was your stake, which in our case was $250,000, but you could make many times that stake if both Enron and Rhythms moved the right way at the right time. It was a hugely leveraged punt".

"I don't understand how making 30 times your money in a matter of weeks can be regarded as normal", said Alun. "And I'm not sure a jury would be too ready to believe it either".

He was right, of course. The simple answer is leverage. If you buy a house for £100,000 with a loan of £99,000, then if the house rises in value by just ten percent, you will have made a return of one thousand percent on your equity. SwapSub, by its very nature, was both highly leveraged and incredibly volatile.

The problem was trying to explain that convincingly to a jury, however simple the maths.

A fantastic working example would present itself some five years later when Northern Rock collapsed in a heap and had to be rescued by the Government. The Rock was a business with about £100 billion of assets, and before it was nationalised there were a number of suitors trying to step in and rescue it, one of whom was Richard Branson. In an audacious bid in early 2008, he proposed putting in just over £1 billion of his own money to own the whole business, and in late 2011 he succeeded, albeit buying a smaller version of the bank.

Now, in very simple terms, his bet was just a bigger version of ours in SwapSub. The worst that could happen was that he would lose his stake. But if the business rose in value by just 10%, he would make ten times his money.

I laughed a lot when I read that one of the other potential bidders for Northern Rock in 2008 was a small syndicate of private equity investors led by a certain Konrad (Chip) Kruger. It really is a small world.

We finished the day discussing how the attorneys would approach the prosecutors on their return to the States. Our position was that we were more than happy to talk to these guys and tell them what everything meant. The attorneys said that this was a very risky strategy, particularly since they didn't think it was us that they were really after. We went round and round in circles.

Mark asked whether we were prepared to enter into some sort of a deal with the prosecutors. Sure, we said, as long as it didn't involve pleading guilty to something. Mark and Michael said that the possibility of the charges being dropped was real, because it was only a criminal complaint rather than an indictment. But we would have to have something of real value to them to make this a practical possibility.

The problem for us was that beyond the Southampton deal we had no information that we thought might be remotely interesting. Or at least nothing that we hadn't already given to them, which we could now no longer use as currency. In effect, we had screwed ourselves by coming forward and offering our assistance in a jurisdiction which works almost entirely on the basis that all information is sold, not given.

In particular we had no idea what had persuaded Enron to part with $30 million for something that at the time was pretty much worthless, or why Fastow had agreed to pay CSFB $10 million for its stake in SwapSub. Details, details.

We agreed that we would all go home and think about what possible help we might be to the prosecutors, and we would all talk to our attorneys over the coming days. And with that, we all said our goodbyes and left, exhausted.

THE SMARTEST GUY IN THE ROOM
July to August 2002

Michael Sommer enlisted an attorney for Gary. He was Reid Figel, who worked for the Washington firm of Kellogg, Huber, Hanson, Todd, Evans and Figel. He was a former Department of Justice prosecutor, and had been the head of the fraud squad in Washington, DC. A real heavyweight.

Meanwhile, I spent the next few days talking to Mark MacDougall and racking my brains, as to what information I had that might have been of interest to the prosecutors. One possible approach was to put together what was known as a "proffer", whereby you write down all the things that you think will be of assistance, and in return the Government agrees not to prosecute you. I was happy with this. We could only tell them what we knew, and we didn't think we'd done anything wrong, so it couldn't hurt.

I talked Mark through all of the Enron financings that we had been involved in at NatWest, or ones that other banks had done that I knew about. Mark was encouraging me to find ways in which these could be construed as "wrong", but I came up short.

Mark tried to make it easier by explaining to me that in his experience, something like Enron or WorldCom happens every ten or so years, and when it does there is a kneejerk reaction which typically takes two forms. The first is that Congress rushes to legislate, which is exactly what had happened after Enron, when the Sarbanes Oxley legislation made it a criminal offense for any director of a public company to sign off on accounts which turned out to be misleading.

The second is that the prosecutors push the boundaries of the usage of existing laws, and start labeling certain types of previously accepted activity as criminal.

"So anyway", he said, "try not to be constrained by your thinking that none of these transactions was wrong. Explain to me how they were racy, and leave it to the prosecutors to decide if they were wrong. It seems to me that your detailed knowledge of all these structures could be very useful to them. That may give us some leverage".

I tried my level best, and put together a detailed set of notes of all the transactions, and how I thought they were accounted for, and why someone might regard certain bits of them as racy. But my heart wasn't really in it because for every transaction I described, I could list a handful of other major companies in the US that had done exactly the same or very similar things.

It struck me that George Bush's comment, made after he heard about the collapse of WorldCom, that "we're gonna put some folks in jail", combined with the Sarbanes Oxley legislation, and what was happening to us, was an extraordinary state of affairs. What they seemingly needed to show was that when something went wrong, it couldn't possibly be the system that was at fault. It had to be the fault of some individuals, and if so these guys had to be crooks. So let's find a way to make them crooks. It's human nature, I suppose. And politics.

One of the major US news broadcasters had put up a big clock in the news room showing the number of days and hours since Enron had filed for bankruptcy without any charges being brought against senior officers of the company. In a weird way I almost felt sorry for the prosecutors. Under normal circumstances you would expect them to conduct an investigation, and see whether there was any evidence of a crime. But these circumstances were anything but normal. The presumption of innocence was eviscerated by a combination of political pressure and media hysteria.

If you subscribe to the view that the ends justify the means, then the Task Force approach to our case was both logical and reasonable. They didn't care two hoots about us, but they needed us to get to Kopper and Fastow, and thereafter to Skilling and Lay. It's called "peeling the onion", as one commentator at the time observed.

If we needed evidence of this, it came in the meetings that our attorneys had with Thomas Hanusik, the prosecutor. His position was simple. Give evidence against each other, or preferably against Kopper or Fastow, and plead guilty. In return, he would recommend a light sentence.

The conversations were short.

On 7th August 2002, an article by Peter Spiegel appeared on the front of the Companies and Markets section of the *Financial Times*. It was entitled "NatWest Three emerge as key figures in unlocking secrets at the top of Enron". I believe that this was the first example of the label "NatWest Three". More than one commentator suggested that it was a moniker that we ourselves had invented to give us parallels with the great injustices of the Guilford Four and the Birmingham Six. Sorry that the truth is a little more prosaic, guys. We can take no credit for it, catchy as it undoubtedly was.

Spiegel's article was fascinating. It seemed to me as if it might almost have been dictated by the Department of Justice. Here are some extracts:

"In the overall scheme of Enron's collapse, their alleged acts were small beer.......But these first charges brought by the Justice Department's Enron Task Force may soon prove more important, not because of the men who were charged in the scheme, but because of the men who were not: Andrew Fastow, Enron's former chief financial officer, and Michael Kopper, Mr Fastow's protégé. Mr Fastow and Mr Kopper have long been at the centre of the justice Department's investigation of wrongdoing at Enron, but making a case against either man has proved difficult... [t]he fact that the three have not yet been arrested and were charged in a criminal complaint rather than a formal grand jury indictment—giving prosecutors flexibility to threaten stiffer charges—has led legal experts to believe they are being pressurised to testify against Mr Fastow in return for lenient treatment."

It's funny how "legal experts" in these articles always go unnamed, but my guess is that these particular legal experts inhabited the offices of the Enron Task Force. As messages go, it could not have been clearer. "Come in and give evidence, or it's going to get a whole lot worse".

If we had known then what we know now, we would have been over there like a rat up a drain, asking where to sign. Our thought process at the time was simple, however. "We haven't done anything wrong. We have no evidence to suggest that Michael or Andy has done anything wrong. We are more than happy to help, but we're certainly not going to plead guilty to these bullshit charges".

If we were ignorant of the way the US justice system is geared towards rewarding the guilty, we got our awakening on 21st August, when Michael Kopper entered into a plea and co-operation agreement with the Government. His agreement was accompanied by an "Information", listing all the criminal acts he had been involved in. And one of them was Southampton.

I remember reading the Information over and over. All I could think was "holy shit". There was no doubt about it. Mr Kopper was really a crook, and if what he was saying was even remotely true, then so was Fastow. This was bad.

Kopper seemed to have spent a lot of time devising schemes to line his own pockets at the expense of Enron. Southampton was just the last. He'd started in 1997 with a transaction called RADR, which netted $2.2 million for his domestic partner, Bill Dodson. Then came ChewCo, a deal which ultimately helped to kill the company when its accounting had to be restated.

ChewCo had apparently netted Kopper and Dodson about $7 million, along with a whole load of kickbacks to Andy Fastow and Fastow's wife and children. And then there was Southampton, from which he had personally pocketed $4.5 million.

It would later turn out that these deals were just the tip of the iceberg. In a spreadsheet put together by Kopper for discussion with Fastow, he had identified earnings for the two of them, to be split evenly, of over $100 million from all their various dealings.

There was a common modus operandi in all three transactions which he described. Set up a partnership. Solicit investment of equity into the partnership structures by outsiders, doubtless to satisfy the magic "3% test" under US GAAP. Then use the partnership to rob Enron. In all three deals, the outside equity came from personal acquaintances, people who had no idea that they were getting involved in a fraudulent transaction. Except for us, apparently.

It did provide an answer to one of the questions our attorneys had asked the previous month. "Just why would Fastow have offered you this investment?" It seemed pretty obvious that the outside money was needed for no other reason than to satisfy US accounting rules. And there we had been, thinking that we were something special.

Kopper maximised his sentence at 15 years by pleading guilty to just two counts, one of conspiracy to commit wire fraud carrying a maximum of 5 years, and one of money laundering conspiracy with a statutory maximum of 10 years.

Kopper had also signed a co-operation agreement, however. It was an extraordinary document. Under normal circumstances, such an agreement compels the defendant to co-operate with the Government in return for a recommendation for leniency on sentencing. In this regard, Kopper's was no different to any other such agreement. What stood out about his was that he was waiving all his rights to be represented by an attorney at any meetings with the Government. And the Government would be the sole arbiter of whether or not he had indeed "co-operated" when it came to a decision as to whether they would indeed recommend a lenient sentence, which might include him spending no time at all in prison.

Kopper was the Government's bitch, as they say in Texas. This would make him a weak witness in any trial, of course, but the betting was that no-one goes to trial, so he could lie his arse off with impunity. Kopper was important because he could give them Fastow, and Fastow would give them Causey, Skilling and Lay. Kopper was the linchpin. And the charges against us were really designed to get to Kopper. Like I said, if you believe that the end justifies the means, their use of us to get to Kopper was completely defensible.

Now none of this would have mattered for us if Kopper and Fastow had not spent the previous four years with their hands in the Enron till. But they had, it seemed, and consequently the system now moved radically against us, and in their favour, not that we knew it at the time. As a guilty man in the US justice system, you have enormous potential upside. It's the magic of plea bargaining. The entire system is designed to minimise the number of cases that go to trial. Efficient use of resources, they would call it, and certainly if every case indicted went to trial then the entire court system in the US would be overwhelmed, and the cost would be astronomic. So it's certainly expedient.

From the perspective of the prosecutors, we were worthless other than as a lever. We could give them nothing. Kopper could in all probability guarantee them a conviction on us plus a whole lot more besides. And given the choice between us testifying against Kopper, and Kopper testifying against us, it was a no-brainer. Kopper was the golden goose. They needed him to be the one telling the "truth". And they could even tell him what "truth" to tell. Having waived all rights to have an attorney present at his meetings with them, they could spend as long as they wanted with him developing the stories that they needed.

Michael Kopper pleaded guilty to a litany of crimes, of which he was the architect. He had spent four years lying and stealing money from his employer. The sums of money involved were prodigious. When Enron was teetering on the edge of bankruptcy, he destroyed all his files and put his computer in a dumpster. He then pleaded the Fifth Amendment and refused to talk to any investigators, and maintained this position until the day the criminal complaint against us was filed. Then he ran to the prosecutors, agreed to tell them everything he knew and to testify to whatever they wanted against whomever they wanted. His reward was thirty-seven months in prison (two years in practice because he got a substantial discount for attending a drugs and alcohol rehabilitation course, something that is not available for foreign defendants), he was allowed to hold on to $9 million of ill-gotten gains, and he protected his partner Mr Dodson from prosecution.

For our part, at exactly the time that Kopper was destroying evidence, we were approaching authorities, telling them everything we knew, providing them with mountains of documents, and offering unconditionally to help in any investigation.

His was some deal. To quote the title of a subsequent book on the Enron story, Kopper was the Smartest Guy in the Room.

INTO THE VORTEX
August 2002 to September 2003

The plea bargain of Michael Kopper in August 2002 wasn't really a big issue in the UK media. It was in and out of the newspapers in a day or so. In practical terms, our situation hadn't really changed a great deal, although discovering that both Kopper and Fastow had apparently been up to their necks in crime was not a positive development.

We now knew that Kopper was a crook, but we couldn't really see how it would directly impact us. If the prosecutors wanted to extradite us, they would have to show evidence of theft in a London court, and we would be able to blow their case out of the water pretty smartly. After all, without a victim, there couldn't have been a theft. And NatWest (or more accurately RBS) showed no signs whatsoever of jumping onto the bandwagon of the prosecutors' wacky theory.

I remember having several conversations with Gerard Greenway, my personal banker at NatWest, someone I had–and still have–a great deal of time for. He was at pains to assure me that there were no stops on my account, and no internal warning flags raised, as far as he was aware. Two days before I learned that the US had started extradition proceedings, Gerard and I were discussing his proposal that NatWest make me a sizeable mortgage loan.

Gary and Giles, too, continued to be banked by NatWest. In fact we worked out that collectively NatWest advanced well over a million pounds in loans and facilities to their businesses in the years after we were charged, in full knowledge of our situation. If they felt they were victims of our wrongdoing, they certainly weren't showing it.

On 12th September 2002 I was called at home by a journalist from Reuters. She wanted to know if I had any comment about the indictment that had just been handed down in the Southern District of Texas. Since this was the first I had heard of it, I truly didn't have any comment.

The indictment was presumably our punishment for not getting on a plane and agreeing to plead guilty to the criminal complaint. One count of wire fraud had now been magically transformed into seven, increasing the maximum sentence from 5 years to 35. I suppose I should have been knocked sideways by this development, but by this stage I was almost numb to the continually unfolding bad news. I tried to make light of it to Emma, who wasn't convinced.

Our attorneys told us the indictment meant that the prosecutors would likely come after us now. Once indicted, you are a Federal statistic. Criminal complaints don't count, just indictments. And prosecutors like their conviction statistics. So we steeled ourselves for the inevitable extradition request. It's just as well that we didn't hold our breath.

In October 2002, Fastow was charged with seventy-eight counts of conspiracy, wire fraud, money laundering, obstruction of justice–you name it. And a whole load of charges of presenting false accounts through his fancy structures. Twenty-eight counts of money laundering alone, each carrying a maximum sentence of 10 years. In the US, once a financial crime is proved, any single movement of money thereafter, no matter how small, is an extra count of money laundering.

Amongst the 78 counts in Fastow's indictment were the identical 7 counts of wire fraud that had appeared in our indictment, but he was also charged with conspiracy and money laundering, neither of which would have been extraditable for us, thus reinforcing our view that the charges against us had been deliberately framed to permit extradition.

But if the indictment looked fearsome, Fastow was having none of it. He pleaded not guilty to all seventy eight counts.

I find it much harder to understand Fastow's motivation than Kopper's. As Kevin Howard had told me back in November 1999, if you cut Andy Fastow, he would bleed Enron. Fastow would testify that his moral compass had gone astray, which cannot be in doubt, but if you ignore the obvious vitriol that has been poured upon him, it is possible to construct a case in which Fastow, whilst knowing himself to be greedy, didn't actually believe he was doing anything criminal. He felt that everything that he did had been for the benefit of the company, and that if he made some money along the way, then that was just his reward for doing such a great job. If the accounting turned out to be wrong, then it was pretty unfair to hang that one entirely on him.

For all the harm that would accrue to us through our association with Fastow, I don't believe he ever acted with malice towards us. He would be the star witness for the prosecution in the Lay/Skilling trial, but I have always wondered whether he really believed that either man was guilty, or if he was just really upset that he was being made to carry the can for everyone else.

I believe Kopper, by contrast, was a liar and a thief, who, when the game was up would say and do anything to save his own neck. Kopper did not appear ever to have been working for the benefit of Enron. Kopper seemed to have worked for the benefit of Michael Kopper. The Michael Koppers of this world exist to test the concept of forgiveness to destruction. I met people in Houston who will absolutely never get there.

Christmas 2002 was a difficult time with the extradition hanging over us. For the first time we had the extended family to our house, and Emma spent the entire period slaving away in the kitchen. My little issues were not touched upon, but my Mother expressed the wish in her card that the New Year would see an end to all the troubles. Some chance.

After that, 2003 seemed to come and go with no overly significant events in our case, but lots happening to others. I became fixated with following the Enron cases, which seemed to grow in number and size on a daily basis. It was horrible. Like watching a car crash in slow motion and wondering who is going to be hit next by the flying wreckage. Another criminal case here. Another civil suit there. The world's biggest junket for the attorneys. A Godalmighty mess.

My routine every morning would involve a visit to the website of the *Houston Chronicle*, which won awards for its coverage of the whole Enron story. To say that their coverage was extensive would be an understatement. The wonders of the internet meant that they could compile a vast online library of information and documents.

The front page of the *Chronicle*'s coverage always contained the Prosecution Scorecard. If ever proof were needed that in America it's a game of stats, this was it. The Scorecard was an overview of all the cases charged, their progress and outcome, divided into sections according to the legal position in each case–such as Guilty Pleas, Jury Conviction, Acquittal, Conviction Overturned, Case Dropped, In Limbo, and a miscellaneous Others Charged. The numbers in each category frequently changed, and over time the first two categories actually diminished, as some defendants (including the Arthur Andersen partner who had given evidence for the prosecution in the trial against the firm) were allowed to withdraw guilty pleas, and appeal courts overturned convictions.

Initially, the category that would fill the fastest was Plea Bargains. The prosecutors needed to get to Skilling and Lay, and Fastow wasn't talking, so they had to put pressure on others. As neither Lay nor Skilling used e-mail, documentary evidence against them was hard to find. What they really needed was co-operating witnesses who would give testimony, and Fastow was the closest man to Lay and Skilling. To get to him, they had to stand pushing the dominoes over. The first to go was an in-house attorney appropriately named Larry Lawyer who was persuaded to plead guilty to not declaring income from one of Kopper and Fastow's deals in his tax return.

They also worked hard on Ben Glisan, the ex-Treasurer who pocketed $1 million from Southampton. He would be a far more credible witness than Kopper, they thought, as he had not spent four years lying, cheating and stealing. He, likewise, was keen to cut a deal. But he wanted immunity from prosecution. They weren't offering that.

In April 2003, frustrated by their lack of progress with Fastow, and under pressure to get results, the Task Force brought a superseding indictment against him, adding another twenty counts, and adding Ben Glisan as a co-defendant. By putting him on the same indictment as Fastow, the two would be tried together and Glisan would be damned by association. He faced over 20 counts, including the seven counts of wire fraud with respect to the Southampton transaction. But despite all the additional pressure, Fastow would not budge.

So the Task Force went nuclear. In May 2003 they indicted Fastow's wife, Lea. They had warned him that they were prepared to do it, but he remained unmoved. I can only imagine what that time must have been like at the Fastow family home. I know for a fact that if a prosecutor had ever threatened to charge Emma for something that I was alleged to have done, I would have signed up to whatever cockamamie theory they were peddling without blinking.

The Task Force were quite surprised at how positively this move was seen in Houston. There was no doubt that the public and media wanted blood. Enron had been Houston's largest single employer. When Enron failed, it brought shame onto the city. It wreaked financial havoc, not just amongst those who worked for the company and lost their jobs and pensions, but for many other small businesses locally that relied upon Enron for their own livelihoods. And someone had to pay.

It is a natural human emotion to look for someone to blame when something bad happens. But in this instance the media and the politicians combined to create an atmosphere that was nothing short of a witch hunt. Our attorneys were at one during 2003 in telling us to do everything in our power to avoid coming to Houston. We would be crucified, they said. I had little doubt.

At its highest point, the market value of Enron's stock was just short of $70 billion. That's a lot of wealth destroyed when the company failed. But to be controversial for just a moment, it paled into insignificance next to the total wealth lost in dotcom stocks when the market crashed. Indeed, almost twice that amount of market capitalisation was lost by shareholders in RBS alone during the period March 2007 to November 2008, when the bank had to be bailed out by the UK Government.

To the victims, it wasn't just about the money. But to the armies of attorneys and litigators, it was about nothing else. And the prosecutors could use this to their advantage. Even the threat of an indictment to an ex-Enron employee carried with it the probability of public vilification, a civil lawsuit, and with that almost certain bankruptcy.

You would have thought that the standard approach of investigators would be to look at the available documents, evidence, and witness statements, and determine whether there had been any crimes committed. For the Enron Task Force prosecutors, however, this approach was never for one moment considered. Instead, reflecting the background of many of the Task Force's prosecutors, they adopted a tactic more usually associated with mob prosecutions. They put most of their efforts into persuading witnesses to turn against their colleagues and bosses by threatening them with prosecution and bankruptcy if they didn't.

It was classic game theory, and would likely have been successful without any extra help. But to ensure that the victory was beyond doubt, the Task Force prosecutors had the Thompson Memorandum.

Named after the Deputy Attorney General, Larry Thompson, the Thompson Memorandum, was a guide produced in January 2003 for prosecutors on whether to indict a corporation. It was the product of the successful conviction of Arthur Andersen, which had consigned the once mighty accounting firm to oblivion, leaving nearly thirty thousand accountants looking for new jobs. Even the reversal of the conviction three years later by the Supreme Court was a hollow victory, because the firm had long since ceased to exist.

Even the threat of indictment in the aftermath of the Andersen case was sufficient to get most corporations to co-operate, but there were still obstacles placed in the way of prosecutors. Companies would pay legal fees for their employees, and provide access to files and witnesses. And they would often claim legal privilege over documents, the basic right to keep communications between client and attorney private unless the client agrees to their disclosure.

The Thompson Memorandum gave prosecutors enormous leeway in deciding whether a company was being sufficiently "co-operative", and the ability to use the threat of indictment as a lever, and gave companies a strong incentive to throw their employees to the lions.

Perhaps the most striking example of this was the case of Jamie Olis, an employee of Dynegy, also based in Houston. In March 2004, he was sentenced in Houston, Texas, to 24 years and 4 months without parole in Federal prison for accounting fraud. (To put that in perspective, the median sentence at the time for murder was 13 years, for drug trafficking 4 years, and for sexual abuse 3 years.) Pressure had been brought to bear on him to testify against the 'bigger fish' in the prosecutors' sights; he refused. His two co-defendants, Gene Foster and Helen Sharkey, were sentenced to 15 months and 30 days respectively. They had been charged with exactly the same offences, but had agreed to plead guilty and co-operate against Olis, rather than take their chances at trial.

Olis had made the cardinal error of asserting his innocence at trial, believing that the truth would prevail. A man of very modest resources, he was unable to fund a proper defence when his company stopped paying his legal fees, but was so sure of his innocence that he thought this would not matter. The CEO of the company had been told in no uncertain terms by the prosecutor that if they didn't withhold his legal fees, the company itself would be indicted.

Olis described how he had been encouraged to plead, but that the price of pleading was to make up a story that simply wasn't true. He was asked if he was tempted to take the deal.

"I did think about it, but there was no way I could have done it".

"Why?"

"Because it wasn't just a matter of pleading guilty. What they wanted was for me to tell the story that I and everyone else engaged in a conspiracy, and I couldn't ruin those people's lives. I'm Catholic, and I can't do that."

No firm was too big or powerful to resist the Thompson Memorandum. Over the coming years, Merrill Lynch, KPMG and doubtless countless others would pay huge amounts of money to the US Government to avoid corporate indictments, and threw very senior employees under the bus driven by the prosecutors at the Department of Justice.

Unable himself to contemplate standing trial alongside Andy Fastow, in September 2003 Ben Glisan entered into a plea agreement on one of the twenty or so counts that he faced, and was immediately sentenced to five years in prison. The count that he pled to related to a transaction named Talon, which had been executed between LJM2 and Enron, and Glisan agreed that it was accounting fraud. Glisan had always maintained that his participation in Southampton was innocent, and that the transaction was not fraudulent in his view. His plea agreement was silent on this, although he agreed to give up the proceeds of his investment. But significantly, he did not agree to co-operate with the prosecutors, and instead went straight to prison.

Glisan would become the single most impressive Government witness in the trial of Lay and Skilling. His credentials were bolstered by his lack of a co-operation agreement, meaning that he could take the stand and say that since he had already been sentenced and was in prison, he could not possibly have any ulterior motive to give false testimony at trial. This was actually untrue, as the prosecutors were secretly arranging for him to be transferred from a closed facility to a nice comfortable open prison, but that's by the by.

But as Treasurer of the company, Glisan was the most senior person to have pleaded guilty, and he had admitted that the company had committed accounting fraud through transactions that he himself had designed. Whether he actually believed this was neither here nor there. It was a good step along the way towards an indictment of Jeff Skilling and Ken Lay, because the prosecutors were determined to prove that the whole edifice had been held together by sham accounting transactions.

While all this action was happening abroad, back in England the early months of 2003 felt like the "phony war" of 1939. We changed our London lawyers. Since McDermott Will & Emery had no criminal practice in London, we needed to find a practice that did. We selected Mark Spragg, who worked for the London firm of Jeffrey Green Russell, a medium-sized partnership in which he was the only criminal partner. I hit it off with him straight away, and we have remained firm friends ever since. He is a street fighter, and will pull no punches. Just what was needed.

His first assignment was to deal with Rabobank's lawyers. They were insisting that we provide them with all kinds of information for their civil case against RBC, and telling us that we would have to foot the bill if we refused and they took us to court. I had tested Mark with this over our interview lunch and he had passed with flying colours. "Tell them to fuck off", he said. So we did. They then deposed us, and we each had to sit in a room and plead the Fifth Amendment about 150 times to a succession of questions about LJM and Southampton.

It was a ridiculous charade, but it suited Rabobank down to the ground. Invoking your right to silence can never be held against you in a criminal trial, but an adverse inference can be drawn in civil proceedings. In any trial with RBC, this would work in Rabobank's favour.

I remember having to squeeze the armrest of my chair as hard as I possibly could on more than one occasion when forced to plead the Fifth when I was absolutely incensed by the questions and wanted to tell them what I really thought about them and their bullshit legal action.

We were so enraged about it in fact that we reached out to RBC, through their lawyers, White & Case, and offered our help. After some to-ing and fro-ing, we signed a 'common interest privilege' agreement, under which we would agree to help them and they would show us all the evidence that they had collected. As litigants in a civil suit, they had powers of discovery, meaning that they could ask for documents not just from Rabobank, but also from RBS, since a lot of Rabobank's action revolved around our time at RBS. The drill was that we would go to White & Case's offices in the City, and there we would be given several binders full of documents obtained in discovery, which pertained directly to each of us. For instance e-mails that we had sent or received or were copied on. We could look at all of this stuff and take notes, but we could not take copies of the documents. Thereafter, we would sit down with the lawyers from White & Case and take them through it all. RBC of course had no idea about what all the RBS stuff meant, and so having it explained put them at a massive advantage over Rabobank.

For the first time we got to see the full copies of e-mails from which the prosecutors had done their cut and paste, a copy of our presentation of February 22nd 2000, and a whole lot more besides. I was overjoyed. I almost fell off my chair when I discovered that one of the extracts the Government cited was actually from a chain of messages that began with an e-mail from Stuart Gibson at Coutts Caymans, followed by one from me to Gary talking about asking the Coutts guys to set up and run "NewCo" for us.

The e-mail from the Coutts guy even included a standard message explaining that Coutts and Co was the private banking arm of National Westminster Bank. As it was part of the chain from which they had taken their extract, there was no way on earth that the prosecutors did not know about this e-mail. So there it was, in black and white. Gary and me discussing getting Coutts, a subsidiary of NatWest, to set up and run the company that the prosecutors were alleging was our private vehicle to rob NatWest. We were apparently hiring our own victims to drive the getaway car!

I spent many a long hour with the White & Case attorneys. The team in London was led by Margaret Cole, head of the disputes resolution team. Margaret, like most lawyers in City firms, was clearly overworked. On more than one occasion during our sessions I would notice her struggling to stay focused, although in fairness that may have been because the subject matter was so dull, because I would have exactly the same problem some years later in Houston.

In any event, I think we gave White & Case and RBC about as comprehensive an explanation for all the e-mails and other documents as we could, and it all seemed to make sense to them. Certainly they were grateful for our help, and later told us that they had subpoenaed deposition testimony from a whole load of current and former GNW and RBS employees, none of which contradicted anything that we had said.

BORIS
September 2003

It was at about this time that we first got wind of a new extradition treaty with the US. It had been signed in March, but had not yet been ratified and was still very much flying under the radar. There was little doubt in my mind how dangerous it was for us; it would completely annihilate our ability to demonstrate that the indictment was rubbish, because there would no longer be a hearing on any evidence.

It also exposed us to a superseding indictment charging all kinds of other things like conspiracy and money laundering, just to rack up the pressure on us. Since Fastow and Glisan had both had these charges thrown at them with respect to Southampton, there was absolutely no doubt in my mind that they would be coming our way too if this Treaty became law.

Mark Spragg and I spent quite some time with James Lewis QC going through the detail of the new Treaty, and what it would mean for us if it came into law. James was from the same chambers as Alun Jones, and he too specialised in extradition. Alun was unavailable at this time, as he was in court on another case, and so Mark had suggested we talk to James.

James commented that ratification of the new Treaty might take years, as the process in the US Senate is historically slow, but he pointed out that ratification might not be necessary because the new Extradition Bill that was coming towards the end of its Parliamentary passage would allow the Home Secretary to incorporate most of the operative provisions of the Treaty into our domestic law, even before the Treaty had been ratified. But surely they wouldn't do that, would they?

We would soon get our answer. Although none of us saw it, a friend called Gary and told him about a report he had just watched on the BBC Newsnight programme, where it was abundantly clear that the Government had every intention of bringing the new Treaty into UK law in fairly short order.

Scratching my head as to what to do about this, I thought I really ought to contact my MP.

I first met Boris Johnson that autumn of 2003. He was already very much a household name. Writer, journalist, editor of the *Spectator*, and Conservative Member of Parliament for Henley & South Oxfordshire. One of the country's most instantly recognisable politicians, and by enormous good fortune, he was my representative in Parliament.

Every Friday during Parliamentary sessions, MPs hold surgeries in their constituencies, where members of the public can talk to them about pretty much any issue. I had to book a time with Boris' office a couple of weeks in advance. I also prepared a short briefing and sent it to his office. I had absolutely no confidence that he would have read it, and I had a slot of just 15 minutes, although it was the last one of the day.

I arrived about 20 minutes early, and then sat outside the building in the pretty market square at Thame, trying my best to rehearse what I was going to say, since 15 minutes was a wholly inadequate time frame to talk about the Extradition Treaty, let alone about my own situation.

At this stage, the Treaty had been signed, but not yet brought into UK law. That would be done by statutory instrument sometime at the end of the year, and I was determined to stop it.

Right on time, I was ushered in to see the great man, who was holding court in a ramshackle room, sitting behind a tatty table, with his shirt-sleeves rolled up, and trademark mop of unkempt blond hair.

"Hello", he said, standing and offering his hand, and then added unnecessarily "Boris Johnson, pleased to meet you".

What happened next caught me completely off guard.

"So come on", he said, leaning forward with his hands together on the table in front of him, and a mischievous grin on his face. "Did you do it?"

"No, Boris", I burbled, completely taken aback, "I did not. It's complete nonsense".

He looked slightly crestfallen at this. It didn't occur to me at the time that Boris had some previous experience with fraudsters, a friend and schoolmate at Eton having been imprisoned for five years in the early 1990s for faking a jewellery heist in New York City in order to claim on an insurance policy.

I suppose also that I shouldn't have been surprised at Boris's question. One of his defining traits is that he is almost guaranteed to speak his mind, which some might say makes for a dreadful politician, but there are many who would elect Boris as Prime Minister tomorrow if they could. He is that rare beast: a principled man.

We chatted in the end for nearly half-an-hour about our case and the Extradition Treaty. Boris was slightly incredulous about the whole Treaty-thingy, and certainly had trouble believing that we had signed up to something on a non-reciprocal basis, but he undertook to look into it and said that he would write to me.

Within a week I had a letter from him, informing me that he had passed the matter onto his colleague, Dominic Grieve, the shadow Attorney General, and suggested that Mr Grieve would contact me with a more detailed response.

I felt a little deflated, that I was being fobbed off, even though in fairness to Boris he had done exactly what he ought to in referring the matter to the appropriate person in the shadow cabinet.

The reply from Dominic Grieve's office confirmed my worst fears. The Conservative Party, I was told, did not intend to oppose the passage into UK law of the new US Extradition Treaty, although they had significant reservations with it, as they did not wish to be seen as anti-American.

And so it came to pass. In both the Commons' and the Lords' committees in December 2003, the Tories abstained from voting, and the guts of the Treaty were duly enacted under the terms of the Extradition Act 2003, which came into force in the UK on 1st January 2004.

The Trojan horse had been safely delivered into the citadel.

Only the Liberal Democrats had the honesty to tell it as it was. Menzies Campbell, an eminent lawyer who had studied in the US, predicted that it would not be long before some member of the Committee voting "aye" would be bleating about the unfairness of the arrangements when one of his constituents was called for extradition. It was a particularly prescient comment, since on the Committee was a certain David Lepper, MP, one of whose constituents was Gary Mulgrew.

Within a matter of weeks of the Commons Committee meeting, the US Government requested the extradition of Gary, Giles and myself.

My next meeting with Boris, at a surgery in Henley, was thus a more sombre affair. Boris was sympathetic, but we both agreed that we ought to let the imminent magistrates hearing play out, as it seemed that we at least had some defences under the new Act; including, most notably, the Human Rights protections. This would be our first proper court hearing on the extradition.

Perhaps Boris' finest moment in our cause came on the day before our extradition, during an emergency debate that had been granted by the speaker. It was a raucous and full-blooded event, with the Government roundly humiliated at the end in a vote which went against them by 246 votes to 4, but refusing nonetheless to back down. Boris gave an impassioned speech in which he referred to British citizens being 'hoovered up' by the Americans.

I don't think anyone could have asked for more from their MP in a situation such as ours. Granted, I was blessed in having someone of Boris' profile on the case, but the telling thing is that his instincts from the first moment were the right ones: 'This is not about guilt or innocence. This is about bad law. I am an MP. I am responsible for bad laws. I have a duty to put this right'.

If only more saw the world through his eyes.

I THINK WE'RE ALONE NOW
November 2003

In my fluster about the Treaty at the end of 2003, I almost missed the issuance of a report that would have a profound effect on our future. Not that I knew it at the time.

Shortly after its bankruptcy filing in December 2001, Enron had asked the Bankruptcy Court in New York to appoint what is known as an Examiner. The Examiner's job is to look at all of the transactions that a company has been engaged in, to see whether there is potential for liability to be established against some third party.

Typically, there are hundreds or even thousands of creditors of a bankrupt company, each seeking to recover whatever they can from the wreckage. Banks tend to be amongst the largest creditors. If any of the creditors can be held liable in some way for the company's downfall, then their claims may be subject to subordination—being sent to the back of the queue—or indeed the bankrupt company may actually be able to get some money from the creditor itself, thereby creating a larger pot for distribution amongst the rest.

In April 2002, the Bankruptcy Court appointed Neal Batson of the law firm Alstom & Bird as the Examiner for Enron Corp. He issued a total of 4 reports over the next 18 months, and they are extraordinarily detailed pieces of work (as they should have been, for a cost of $100 million). His first two concentrated mainly on the Special Purpose Entity ("SPE") transactions that Enron had done, and in his third report in June 2003 he started to take aim at some of the banks, law firms and accounting firms, including Barclays and Merrill, that had been involved in some of Enron's more funky financings.

Batson issued his final report in November 2003. In this, he targeted CSFB and RBS, as well as the Canadian bank Toronto Dominion.

Almost immediately, all of the entities 'named and shamed' by Batson were added as defendants to the Newby Class Action suit being brought by Enron shareholders, as well as an action by the estate of Enron itself on behalf of the creditors. Not to mention a host of other suits against banks, accountants and law firms. Delicious. Trebles all round.

There is little doubt that Batson was passing everything directly to the Task Force, and blazed a path they happily followed. The indictment of four senior Merrill Lynch bankers, over a deal that became known as the 'Nigerian Barges' case, came hot on the heels of his detailed analysis of that transaction in his third report.

The significance of Batson's final report, however, and especially the section dealing with RBS, would only become apparent to us many months later. It highlighted in particular five transactions. Two of these were Greenwich NatWest deals in which we had been involved; a transaction called Sutton Bridge Financing, and the LJM1 equity investment. Of the other three, one was done by RBS before the takeover of NatWest, and another two, named ETOL 1 and ETOL 2, after the takeover (and after we had left).

The dynamite stuff in the RBS report had nothing to do with LJM1. Batson was even kind enough to see the irony in me having been indicted, as I had initially been one of the most critical voices of the lack of clarity surrounding the proposed LJM1 deal in June 1999. In a footnote to his report, having quoted one of my more forthright e-mails on the subject, he said:

"Ironically, Bermingham ultimately was indicted and charged with wire fraud for his role in allegedly improperly profiting from LJM1 and allegedly is evading authorities."

The reference to "evading authorities" came from the original charging documents, where we were described as fugitives, a term that would persist throughout the entire extradition process. It still rankles to this day.

No, the dynamite lay in the transactions known as ETOL 1 and ETOL 2, which had been done after we had left the bank. The Sutton Bridge transaction was a similar sort of deal, but much smaller than the huge ETOL trades. They bore an uncanny resemblance to the fact pattern of the Nigerian Barges deal, except that the prosecution case in the latter relied on hearsay evidence of a verbal agreement made by Enron to repurchase the barge assets from Merrill Lynch, which according to the prosecutors constituted fraud. In the ETOL trades, such an agreement was not speculation by the prosecutors; Batson had uncovered minutes of conversations between very senior RBS people and Andy Fastow, acknowledging exactly such an agreement.

Naively, I thought that Batson's report could be good news for us. Whilst we had no idea what had gone on with ETOL, we could give RBS first-hand knowledge on LJM1 and Sutton Bridge. Given that the report was immediately followed by RBS being added as a defendant to the massive Newby civil case, I was sure that RBS would want to speak to us now. We would help them rebut the allegations in the civil suit, they would assist us in our fight. All would be well with the world.

If only.

We may not have known it as we said goodbye to 2003 and hello to 2004, but we were on our own. By the end of 2003 the music had stopped and everyone had scrambled for a seat.

Everyone, that is, except us.

INTO THE FRAY
January to April 2004

On 1st January 2004, the Extradition Act 2003 took effect in the UK. Henceforth, the US would no longer need to provide evidence to support its requests for extradition. Moreover, they would no longer be restricted to seeking extradition for a narrowly defined list of crimes. Anything that would carry a maximum sentence of at least 12 months in prison would do. And the Home Secretary lost his general discretion to decide whether someone should be extradited.

Because the 2003 Treaty had not been ratified, however, requests by the UK to the US still had to go under the old Treaty. By the actions of David Blunkett, ably assisted by Home Office Ministers Caroline Flint and Baroness Scotland, Britain had effectively given the US all the substantive advantages of the new Treaty without the need to ratify it. They could have their cake and eat it too.

On 14th January the Enron Task Force got their biggest scalp to date when Andy Fastow entered into a plea bargain. In return for the Task Force dropping the other 96 counts against him, he agreed to plead guilty to one count of conspiracy to commit wire fraud and one count of conspiracy to commit wire and securities fraud. Each had a five year maximum sentence, and he agreed as part of his plea that ten years in prison was the appropriate sentence, and that he would not be asking for any lesser amount.

He would also be co-operating with the Task Force, and everyone knew what that meant. Indictments against Lay and Skilling would now surely follow.

Fastow's plea was accompanied by a simultaneous plea agreement by Lea, his wife, to one felony count of tax fraud. Her trial had been coming up shortly, which presumably was a major consideration in their decision to plead. The original indictment against Lea had contained seven counts, and the statutory maximum sentence was 37 years. Her plea agreement was one of those rare beasts that would tie the judge to the recommended sentence if he accepted the plea. The prosecutors were recommending that Lea serve no more than 5 months in prison, a term calculated to ensure that there would never be a time when both Fastows were in prison together, as Fastow himself would not be sentenced until a much later date.

But things did not go smoothly. Judge Hittner, who oversaw Lea's case, was incensed that the prosecutors were trying to tie his hands on sentencing, and so he gave Lea fair warning that he intended to sentence her as he saw fit. The maximum sentence for the crime to which she was pleading guilty was five years, and it was a racing certainty that the pre-sentence investigation report by the probation office (on which he would base his sentence) would calculate a guidelines range way in excess of five months.

Because of the nature of her plea agreement, Lea was able to withdraw the plea if the judge refused to be tied to the sentencing recommendation. So she did. And all hell broke loose.

For the prosecutors it was potentially a disaster. While Andy Fastow was tied to his plea deal, what the prosecutors really wanted was not his plea, but his co-operation. Since 10 years was the statutory maximum he couldn't be sentenced to any more. He had agreed not to ask for less. So the only incentive for him to co-operate was the Government's agreement to look after Lea, and that had just been holed below the waterline by her judge.

Needless to say, the prosecutors came up with an answer. They agreed to drop all felony charges against Lea, and replace them with one misdemeanor charge of filing a false tax return, with a maximum sentence of 12 months. They resubmitted this new plea deal, again recommending that in practice she be sentenced just to five months in prison.

Hittner was incandescent. Since his hands were effectively tied, he sentenced her to the maximum 12 months. She would spend the vast majority of it in the high security Federal Detention Center in downtown Houston. A grim place with no external facilities. For a misdemeanor charge unrelated to drugs or violence.

I remember reading about all these shenanigans on the *Houston Chronicle* website. It was almost beyond parody. The prosecutors weren't even remotely abashed by their totally transparent tactics. Who cares how you get there? Just get there. Enron Task Force chief Leslie Caldwell and her Deputy Andrew Weissmann were apparently on a mission. They did exactly what was necessary to get to Fastow. From thereon in, they presumably thought, it would be downhill all the way.

The statement of facts accompanying his plea agreement had the obligatory descriptions of his wrongdoings. He repeated the stuff in Glisan's plea agreement about the Talon trades being accounting fraud. This "financial statement manipulation" would be the overarching theme of the attack on Skilling and Lay. He then parroted the Government version of the crime in the Southampton transaction, although this one was quite intriguing. Paragraphs 14 and 15 of the agreement read as follows:

"14. Due to a dramatic increase in the value of Enron stock, the value of Swap Sub (whose primary asset was Enron stock) had also increased dramatically. I was, however, barred from profiting from any increase in value of the Enron stock held by Swap Sub. In approximately February 2000, I and others, including three bankers employed by NatWest, participated in a scheme to extract this increased value by defrauding Enron and NatWest.

15. Enron paid $30 million for the Swap Sub buyout. That price was based on my misleading representation to Enron that the limited partners of Swap Sub had agreed to sell their interests in Swap Sub for $20 million and $10 million, respectively. In fact, NatWest had agreed to sell its interest in Swap Sub for only $1 million, not $20 million. I knew that the NatWest bankers induced NatWest to sell its interest for $1 million at a time when they knew the interest was worth significantly more."

Well, if that was indeed to be the Government case against us, then we were pretty much home and dry, I thought. Fastow was admitting that he defrauded Enron to get the $30 million. We had no knowledge of this, and could prove that through my letter of the 28th March. Nor was he suggesting that we did. He was just saying we knew the NatWest stake was worth more than $1 million. If we could show that, contrary to his assertions, this was actually a fair price, then game over.

On several occasions over the coming years, Fastow wrestled under cross-examination with how it was that NatWest had supposedly been defrauded. He was clear that he had lied to Enron to induce them to pay $30 million, but since we were ignorant of this, that could only help us. The only way, in fact, that NatWest could have been defrauded was if somehow we knew that the asset was worth more than the $1 million that it was paid.

But my letter of 28th March showed clearly that we didn't.

Reading Fastow's plea agreement on the *Houston Chronicle* website, I figured that we at least now knew the direction in which the prosecution of our case would be heading, and it was one that I personally felt quite comfortable in dealing with. As long as we could get access to witnesses and evidence from NatWest.

So we reached out to RBS once again, offering our help on the Batson issues if they would help us with ours. Once again we were rebuffed by their lawyers at Travers Smith. It seemed a little silly to us. We knew they must want our help since they would struggle to defend the civil suits without it. We had asked them to sign a common interest privilege agreement in the same way that RBC had done, which seemed quite reasonable in the circumstances. But they weren't having any of it. Of course at this stage we did not know of the existence of the Thompson Memorandum.

February 2004 was a bad month. I had been working for some eighteen months as a consultant to a film finance business in Mayfair, and we were right in the middle of a big fundraising when the Government changed the law relating to film funding, killing all but three of the twenty or so films on which we were actively working. A whole year's worth of work was effectively destroyed in an instant.

A couple of days after that little bombshell, our solicitor Mark Spragg rang.

"I've got some bad news, I'm afraid", he said.

"Oh, what's that then?" Couldn't be much worse than what's just happened at work, could it?

"I've just been rung by James Lewis. He's been passed a brief seeking your extradition, and wants to know whether he should take it. In the light of our having met with him last year to discuss the Treaty, I've said I don't think that would be appropriate. Anyway, the long and the short of it is that an extradition request has obviously been filed."

Excellent. Just take me out and shoot me.

I suppose in the back of my mind I had always harboured the tiniest of hopes that it might just all go away. After all, it had been over eighteen months, and the whole Enron investigation had moved on. Perhaps they would just let our file gather dust and eventually bin it, knowing that it was all nonsense. It was a naive thought of course; the US attorneys had told us once we were indicted that the prosecutors never just let things lapse.

So, finally, the day of reckoning was at hand. They did want us.

I broke the news to Emma and my parents. There were plenty of tears.

Our problems now were acute. The case would swing on the issues of valuation and knowledge. What was SwapSub worth when NatWest agreed to sell it, and what did we know at the time? We would also need to be able to explain what the e-mails meant. In fact they would be the boil that would probably need to be lanced first, since they were the bit of the case that would always poison people against us.

But to do that we needed witnesses and we needed evidence. And in the absence of any legal action against us in the UK (either civil or criminal), we had no access to either. We could not force RBS to give us anything or anyone unless there was a pending legal action to which we were parties.

Under the old extradition legislation, this would not have been an issue. As soon as proceedings were brought, we could have subpoenaed documents and witnesses from RBS. End of case. But under the new legislation we would have no such luxury, as there was no longer an evidential test in the proceedings.

We also knew that if we were shipped to America without having obtained any of this evidence, we might never get hold of it. Knowing it exists is not good enough. And we could almost certainly kiss goodbye to the prospect of compulsory process for witnesses.

The screw was slowly tightening.

I tried my level best to put a positive spin on developments for Emma and my mother. At least now we would be able to stand up and fight, I said. It's been too long. Let's bring it on. I'm not too sure that I convinced either of them.

But we did need to face reality. No sense sitting around with your head up your arse. Grasp the nettle. In early March I sat down and drafted a personal letter to Fred Goodwin, the Chief Executive of RBS. I explained that we were keen to help RBS, but that their lawyers were refusing to engage with us. I explained what I thought we could do for them, and asked that he intervene and help us. I appealed to him as a human being, rather than as the Chief Executive of one of Britain's largest banks.

I circulated the letter to Gary and Giles. We played around a little with the draft, and then jointly signed and sent it.

Shortly thereafter we received a short response from Travers Smith. It could briefly be translated as "sod off". And they "reserved their rights", whatever that was supposed to mean. At least they had some rights to reserve. We seemingly had none.

At the beginning of April, the firebrand muslim cleric Abu Hamza al Mazri was arrested pursuant to an extradition request from the United States. He had long been preaching hatred on the streets of London, but for whatever reason the authorities did not believe that he was breaking the law. The Americans however, charged that he had helped to fund a terrorist training camp in Oregon, and had provided money and a satellite telephone to the Yemeni terrorists who kidnapped and murdered a number of tourists in Egypt–including several British holidaymakers.

Questioned as to why British authorities had never taken any action against Hamza, the Home Secretary David Blunkett was quite clear:

"Had we evidence in this country of a crime committed here then of course the police and the Attorney General would have taken action".

The Attorney General concurred that a UK prosecution would always be preferable. Strange that. It was not a view he would take in our case. Still, there's one rule for Egyptian clerics, and another for the indigenous British population. It's called equality, New Labour style.

Just six months later, charges of incitement to murder and racial hatred were brought against Hamza by the Metropolitan Police, relating to speeches that the cleric had given on the streets of north London in 1999. A UK prosecution would take precedence over the extradition application, which would be stayed. There was much speculation that the Government really didn't want Hamza involved in an extradition at a time when the issue of Guantanamo Bay was becoming a real thorn in their side. Charging him in the UK would enable them to park that little problem for a while.

Politics, politics.

ARRESTED
23rd April 2004

In mid-April the Metropolitan Police Extradition Squad contacted Mark Spragg. A date for our initial court hearing had been set. On 23rd April, we were to be arrested and taken to appear at Bow Street magistrates' court in the West End. Mark agreed with them that we could turn up at Charing Cross police station at 10.30am and be arrested by appointment. All very civilised.

Alun Jones advised us that we would need to line up some people to stand surety for us. He was pretty confident that we would be granted bail, and confident also that we would not be required to put up cash as security, but we would need some people to stand up in court and pledge a large amount of their money if we went missing.

And so on the appointed day I got into a suit and tie for the first time in months, and set off from home to begin the fight. Little could any of us have known at that stage what lay ahead, and how far the road would stretch.

Walking up the steps to Charing Cross police station, I found Mark waiting. Giles and Gary would follow shortly thereafter. Once all three of us were present and correct, Mark went to the front desk and told the duty officer that we had come to be arrested.

We were taken round the back to a long room with a desk stretching the entire length of it, behind which stood several uniformed officers. Each of us was allocated a separate officer, who read us our rights and arrested us, and then we started on the reams of paperwork that are the product of the "targets" culture that keeps policemen from performing the job of crime prevention.

We were fingerprinted and had a DNA swab taken. That incensed me, frankly, but what can you do? My DNA remains to this day on the database, ready to be lost by the authorities and misused somewhere in the world. Even if we had gone to trial and won, the DNA would still be kept.

I completed my form filling, then sat down on a bench alongside Mark, who handed me a large grey lever-arch file. "What's this?" I asked.

"It's your extradition pack", he said matter-of-factly.

The file must have contained about five hundred pages. "Blimey", I thought. "If this is what it looks like after they've removed the necessity to produce evidence, what did it look like before???"

I opened it up and started to leaf through There was a certificate from the Home Secretary, and then an affidavit from Thomas Hanusik and another one from special Agent David Hays of the FBI. And then there were several hundred pages of affidavits and exhibits. Which could better be described as... evidence.

"What the fuck is this, Mark?"

"That, David, is commonly known as a fuck job. They know you can't respond to any of this stuff, but by putting it all in there they will ensure that it gets read by the judge, and that can only count against you. They get to have their cake and eat it".

Resisting the temptation to lob the whole thing out the nearest window, I began to skip through the "evidence" to see what there was. There were a number of different affidavits from current or ex-employees of Greenwich NatWest or Coutts, and one from Michael Kopper.

Kopper's affidavit was dated January 2004, after the new Extradition Act came into force. Most of the others had been taken at the beginning of December, after the Act had received Royal Assent. This was no accident, I thought. They knew damned well that none of this was required under the new law, but they went ahead and did it anyway, knowing that we couldn't respond.

I returned to Kopper's affidavit. I was about two paragraphs in when I started to laugh. I tugged Mark's sleeve and pointed to the section that I was looking at. Mark read it and then he too started to laugh. Gary, who was still standing at the desk being processed, turned round. I pointed to him and then motioned as if tightening a noose around my neck. He looked quizzical, and pointed at himself as if to say "what, me?" Mark and I both nodded, and continued laughing.

Over the previous eighteen months, we had speculated about what story Kopper would come up with on the stand. Of the three of us, I had been most involved in the Southampton investment. It was I who had flown to New York in March 2000 to meet with Kopper. If there were conversations in dark and smoke-filled rooms, Kopper should have been claiming that he and I had those conversations. It was the lie that best fit the facts and would be most believable.

But no. According to Kopper, the whole thing had been dreamed up by Gary and him. Gary was the criminal mastermind. Giles and I didn't get a look in. I suppose the logic behind his argument was that it would make most sense for the conspiracy to start at the top rather than the bottom. Also, I was never alone with Kopper in New York, and there were two witnesses who might testify to that.

Eventually, Gary finished his processing and walked over to where Mark and I were huddled together, sniggering like little schoolboys, as we turned the pages on this fairy tale.

"What's so funny?" he asked.

"You're fucked mate, that's what", said Mark. Mark's sense of humour is an acquired taste. Gary had not spent nearly as much time with Mark as I had, so he did not seem amused.

Gary sat down beside me and I gave him the folder. I turned to the beginning of Kopper's affidavit, and pointed. "Read this, big man."

Gary started to read. I looked towards Mark and started counting, silently mouthing the words "one, two, three"…. I had reached "five" when Gary exploded.

"What the….? You're fucking joking. The lying fucking toe-rag…. "

Giles sauntered over at this point.

"What's going on?" he asked. We told him. "Is this true mate?" he asked, without a hint of irony. Mark and I just burst out laughing again, but this time it was because I was wondering whether Giles would end up needing the extradition pack surgically removed from his backside.

Luckily, at this point, fate intervened in the shape of Detective Sergeant Gary Flood of the Extradition Squad. He was a very amiable chap who introduced himself and explained what would be happening from hereon in. Then we set off on the short trip to Bow Street magistrates court,

On arrival we drove in through a large steel gate that closed behind us, into a central courtyard area. One of Gary Flood's guys offered us coffee. We thought he would come back with some lukewarm stuff from a canteen machine somewhere, but he reappeared about five minutes later with a tray of coffees from Starbucks. We offered to pay, but Gary Flood wouldn't have it.

"Wouldn't want to break into the seven million dollars, would we boys?" he said.

We must have spent about twenty minutes standing around the car, talking about the whole thing. They had read the pack, and couldn't understand why we were being extradited.

"Have I got this right?" asked Gary Flood. "You're supposed to have stolen seven million dollars from NatWest, right? Did you work in the States or something?"

"Nope"

"And NatWest hasn't accused you of anything?"

"Nope".

"So it's just the Americans who say you did this, right?"

"Yep"

"So did you?"

"Well, did we make $7.3 million? Yes. Was it stolen from NatWest? Not in a million years".

We ran through the whole story again–how the FSA had given us a clean bill of health, how we had sat around waiting for the SEC to call and ask for our help. And how no-one had ever spoken to us, and one day we awoke to find ourselves being branded as criminals on the world media.

"The thing I just don't get, though, is that if you're supposed to have ripped off NatWest here in London, why are you being extradited?"

"Is the correct question…."

And with that someone radioed to say it was time to go in. I needed to take a leak first. DS Flood suggested that I go under an old iron fire escape in the corner of the courtyard. I briefly wondered if he was joking, before realising that he wasn't and heading off to relieve myself.

It was a little surreal. I had just been arrested and was now peeing on the wall of the court building prior to my bail hearing. It would become a private metaphor for me in the months to come, one inconsequential little guy piddling in a gale in the face of the giant Government machinery that was being inexorably lined up against us. I half expected a window to open up somewhere, and a bewigged head to appear and demand that I be arrested and thrown in the cells forthwith for urinating on a public building, which doubtless in the circumstances constituted some special contempt of court.

Bow Street is an old and dusty place which first became home to a court in 1739 and grew to become the best known magistrates court in the land. Many famous people have passed through it. On the day after we were extradited, it closed its doors for the last time prior to redevelopment as a boutique hotel. Presumably as part of the whole "look forward not back" business of Government, it had been decided that you could indeed put a price on history, and that the price of this place was too high. Doubtless they'll say the same about the Tower of London at some stage and it will be redeveloped as luxury apartments or knocked down and replaced by the new home of some Russian oligarch.

The magistrate on our case that day was District Judge Nicholas Evans, a tall man with silver hair, a thin face and a very manicured appearance. He was no stranger to extradition proceedings, and had the distinction of having been the magistrate who issued the arrest warrant for the Chilean dictator Augusto Pinochet. Ours however was a strange hearing. The Extradition Act 2003 was brand new and radically different from its predecessor, so much of the time was taken up by the barristers talking him through the framework of the new Act, and what needed to be done, by whom, and by when.

On our side we had Alun Jones and his junior, a barrister called James Hines. It was not until sometime later that my sister Claire pointed out that James had been in the year above me at St Benedict's school in Ealing in the late 1970's.

The Americans were represented by the Crown Prosecution Service, who had instructed John Hardy, a barrister from the same chambers as Alun and James. He came across as a bit like Uriah Heep, with an 'ever so humble' tone, but clearly knew his business.

There would need to be two hearings, the barristers explained to Judge Evans. The first would deal with the question of whether what we were accused of constituted an extraditable offence under the new law. If the judge determined that it did, then a further hearing would be necessary to determine whether there were any bars to our extradition. The date for the first hearing was set for 21st June.

Thereafter the rest of the hearing was taken up with him deciding whether to grant us bail. This involved hearing from our sureties. Mine was my father, who was up first to be sworn in and then cross examined as to his finances, which I thought was an unnecessarily intrusive process. After my father came Rick Hill for Giles and Joe O'Brien for Gary, both old personal friends.

Bail was set at £25,000 and we were allowed to go home. There were a few members of the press in the audience, but it wasn't exactly big news.

Battle had been formally joined.

I went home that evening with my copy of the extradition pack and began to read. The scale of our difficulties became immediately apparent. Hanusik and Hays had set out to bury us in invective. There were constant references to us as fugitives. There were many references to all the mountains of evidence they had examined. Hays described our crime as "the quintessential inside job", adding that NatWest did not even realise it had been robbed until after Enron had filed for bankruptcy.

Funnily enough there was no mention of the fact that we ourselves had come forward before Enron had even filed for bankruptcy, and way before there was any criminal investigation, and supplied the vast majority of the "evidence" that these guys were now saying they had reviewed. There was no mention also of the fact that the FSA had spent quite some time talking to RBS before concluding we had done nothing wrong. There was no mention of the fact that RBS had never given the slightest indication that it thought it had been "robbed", as they so nicely put it.

To say that the whole thing was disingenuous doesn't even begin to get there. They were just playing to the crowd, knowing that nothing that they said could be challenged. We were very bad men who had been discovered solely due to the brilliance of the Enron Task Force, and were now fugitives from justice.

In point of fact, there was very little of any substance in the extradition pack from an evidentiary point of view. It was mostly stuffing. They put in all of the papers that we had given to the FSA, without acknowledging their provenance. They put in Kopper's plea and co-operation agreement behind his affidavit, and they put in Fastow's plea agreement. Thereafter, the "witnesses" who provided affidavits gave exactly nothing of any value whatsoever, and each of their statements was followed by large chunks of mostly uninteresting guff.

The most amusing affidavit by far was that of Chip Kruger, our old boss. In a very short statement, he testified that if he had known we were planning to steal money, he would have fired us. As statements of the obvious go, it would have been difficult to better that one. Certainly he had no idea that we were planning a crime, he said. Well, he was in good company there. We had no idea we were planning a crime either.

The prize for the shortest affidavit went to Neil Coulbeck, Chip's right hand man. In one and a half pages of double spaced type, there were but three paragraphs. The first was a brief CV. The second indicated that he had not been in any way responsible for the decision to make the original LJM investment, and in the third he said that he had no recollection of being involved in any way in the sale of the SwapSub asset. He retired from RBS shortly after making his statement.

If these were supposed to be witnesses against us, the line-up was thin. I sat back thinking "is that it?" I mean, if you are going to put evidence in to the request, then make it something compelling. So I started to ask myself what was missing.

Three things, I figured.

The first was any evidence of a victim. Although there were several affidavits from current or former employees of NatWest, not one suggested that there had been a crime, nor gave material testimony against us. Special Agent Hays was clear that NatWest didn't know it had been robbed until after Enron filed for bankruptcy. The clear implication is that at some point NatWest DID realise it had been robbed. And yet there was not one person saying "yes, it was a crime. We was robbed, guv". Nor would there ever be.

The second thing missing was evidence from Fastow. They put his plea agreement into the pack, but no affidavit from him. And yet he was implied to be the head of the conspiracy. Now I'm no Sherlock Holmes, but I reckon that he never gave an affidavit because he told them that Michael Kopper's story was bullshit.

Lastly, there was no affidavit from Dai Clement. We knew, because a friend had told us, that Dai had been flown to Washington shortly before we were indicted, and had been torn a new arsehole by the FBI. Dai would not talk about it, presumably because he had been instructed not to, but it was clear that it had been a very unpleasant experience for him.

And Dai was the closest material witness to the facts. He had been my right hand man on all our dealings with LJM. He had been there when I was going toe to toe with Fastow on conference calls. He had been there when I had lost the plot in New York with Ben Glisan and called Fastow a crook. And he had been intimately involved in the sale of SwapSub while I was sunning myself on a beach in the Cayman Islands. All they really needed Dai to say was "I have no idea what the value was, I was just doing as I was told". But Dai is too proud to have said that. Given how anaemic the other witness affidavits were, the fact that there was none from Dai suggested that he was not to be bullied into falsehood. I figured that he must have told them that $1 million was a fair price and their theory was utter shite, and yet they went ahead and indicted us anyway.

THE LAW IS AN ASS
Summer 2004

Our preparations for the hearing quickly revealed how bad a piece of legislation the Extradition Act really is. Our first hearing was to determine whether what we were accused of was an extraditable crime. That question would turn on what was deemed to be our "conduct", and where this conduct was deemed to have taken place. That should be a relatively simple point, but the Act is a monument to poor drafting, and a lawyer's paradise.

Critical to the debate was the allegation that we travelled to Houston to discuss the fraud, which established the "nexus" with the US. We were unable to argue this point, because disputing evidence was prohibited under the new law. For the record, not one person involved in the Southampton transaction ever said that that meeting was part of any scheme to defraud. Only the prosecutors made that leap of imagination. And yet, this allegation became fact for the purposes of the Extradition Act, and would just keep on screwing us in much the same way as the e-mails did.

As you will have guessed, we lost that first battle in June. Judge Evans ruled that the "conduct" was what was set out in the narrative of the indictment; that even if as little as 5% of the conduct could be said to have occurred in America, then it would be covered by the Act; and that since we had travelled to Houston as part of the scheme to defraud, that would do.

The next hearing was set for 28th September, to last three days. That hearing would examine all the possible defences to extradition. In our case there were just two relevant provisions. The first was called "passage of time", and the second was human rights. Our argument on the first was effectively an abuse argument. Prosecutor Thomas Hanusik had clearly delayed the extradition request until the law changed and there was no necessity to produce evidence, and therefore it would be unjust to extradite.

The human rights argument had two limbs. The first was that we could not get a fair trial in the US in these circumstances. Everything that we needed to conduct our defence was in the UK, and would be extremely difficult to access from the US. The second argument, which was particularly strong, was that everyone has a right to a private and family life, and that this right, while qualified, should only be disturbed if it is "necessary" or "proportionate" to do so. Well, to any rational, objective person, it was neither necessary nor proportionate to extradite us to the US, since any trial could and by any sensible argument should take place in the UK.

This was the genesis of the "natural forum" argument that became the centrepiece of the campaign to change the law and keep us in the country a couple of years later. The bald fact is that there is no provision anywhere in the Extradition Act for determining which jurisdiction would be best suited to trying a case when more than one could do so. Article 7 of the European Convention on Extradition (ECE), to which the UK is a signatory, contains such a provision, and most sensible countries (in fact pretty much all countries except Britain) reserve the right either never to extradite their own nationals (in which case they will try them in their home country if requested to do so), or to decline to extradite if the conduct could be deemed to have been committed in whole or in part on their own soil.

I would be the first to admit that if we were standing trial alongside an American defendant, where the US prosecutors had got there first, then there would be some sort of a logical argument in favour of a single trial in one jurisdiction. But we weren't. There were no other defendants. Fastow and Kopper were at best witnesses for the prosecution, and maybe not even that. So if you did a ledger by jurisdiction, you had:

"Victim" (NatWest):	UK
Defendants:	UK
Witnesses for the Prosecution:	US and UK
Witnesses for the Defence:	UK
Documents for the Prosecution:	US and UK
Documents for the Defence:	UK

In fact, the extradition pack contained only one piece of evidence that had not come either from NatWest or the three of us, and that was the Kopper affidavit. Every other witness affidavit was from a current or ex-employee of RBS, NatWest or Coutts. No-one in their right mind could say that this should naturally be dealt with in the US, surely?

In the heated debates that would follow in the years to come, the Government consistently tied itself in knots over this one. They argued that prosecutors rather than judges should determine questions of forum. Given the provisions of article 7 of the ECE, and the fact that judges decide questions of forum on a multiplicity of issues on a daily basis, this was probably the most asinine argument in the world, but when hurled in the faces of whimpering Labour backbenchers by a brutish Scottish Home Secretary, this kind of specious argument can find its appeal.

They also said that the old Extradition Act had no forum provision, so why were people now bleating about it? This was true, but the old Act gave the Home Secretary a general discretion to refuse any extradition on any grounds, and so submissions on forum could be made to him directly, and his ruling could be subject to judicial review. The new Act took away all general discretion from the Home Secretary.

To defend against the extradition request, we needed to do two things.

The first was to get some expert testimony as to how the US legal system in general and the Texas system in particular worked in practice, so that we could show how difficult it would be for us to defend this case. Mark and Alun jollied off to Texas at our expense and spent a few days tracking down our expert.

The second, bizarrely, was to ask every single one of the relevant authorities in the UK to please consider prosecuting us. Mark Spragg wrote to Ken Macdonald, the Director of Public Prosecutions, Robert Wardle, the Head of the Serious Fraud Office, and Andrew Proctor, the Head of Enforcement at the FSA, pointing out David Blunkett's comments on the arrest of Abu Hamza, and inviting them to commence an investigation with a view to a prosecution if there were evidence to merit it.

While Mark and Alun were away, we decided to open up a new front. All the lawyers were agreed that not only was the legislation badly drafted, but that it lacked some very basic protections for defendants. We needed to get the law changed.

I picked up the phone to a group called the Policy Partnership. Set up by Lord Paddy Gillford, the Policy Partnership website says that they provide strategic, financial and political communications counsel. To you and me, they are a lobby group, who specialise in helping people get to the right parts of the Parliamentary process to effect change.

I explained our circumstances to Andrew Smith, one of their senior advisers. Andrew said he would get back to me. He rang back the next day and said that he didn't think they could help, but he gave me the name of someone to contact.

It was Richard Elsen, who ran a little business called Bell Yard Communications. They were what Andrew described as a crisis management company, and Richard was well hooked into the workings of the Government, having until recently headed up what was known as an "attack and rebuttal" team for Alistair Campbell. Their sole purpose in life, apparently, had been to find ways to rubbish any Tory policy announcements, and no holds were barred. This group would morph over time into the aggressive little machine run by Gordon Brown's chum Damian McBride, whose e-mail ideas on personal smears against senior Conservatives would become front page news in April 2009.

I really didn't like the sound of this at all, but in our circumstances I thought that I should put my own political persuasions in my pocket for a while. Might as well follow up the lead. Richard was happy to talk to us.

Gary was supportive. Giles was adamant that it was bad idea and he wanted nothing to do with it. In his mind, all we would do was upset the Government, and potentially make things far worse for ourselves than they already were. It's one of those scenarios in which you can never prove one way or another who's right, and so we agreed to differ.

Through all the years of our struggles, we fought about many many things, but there was an unwritten rule that the majority would prevail, and in this case Giles was in the minority. He maintained his stance that he wanted nothing to do with it, however, and for good measure refused to contribute to the cost, leaving Gary and me to pick up half of the tab each.

Gary and I met up in London and made the journey to Bell Yard's offices together. They were above a small shop on the south side of Fleet

Street, directly across from the Royal Courts of Justice. Two steep and narrow flights of stairs brought you to a heavy door with their name on it. Inside was old and decrepit. But the location could not have been better for a firm which spent a lot of its time working for clients that were in and out of the High Court.

Richard was not at all as I had pictured him. He was polite and smiling, unimposing with a warm handshake and no obvious air of malice. Not a natural candidate to have worked alongside Alistair Campbell, I thought. He introduced us to his business partner, Melanie Riley. Melanie came across as very professional, and slightly more serious than Richard, who had the laid back air of someone who wasn't too fussed about where the next job was coming from.

The office was small and open plan, with only three desks, a couple of printers and a photocopier. The walls were covered with various enlargements of press cuttings and newspaper headlines. Michael Jackson here, City workers there.

I had little or no idea what to expect that they could do for us. I wanted the law changed. They seemed to be PR guys. I wasn't sure I saw the connection. But they listened as Gary and I poured forth, and Melanie took copious notes.

"Wow", she said as we finally finished. "That's quite a story. I assume you guys are not the only ones being extradited under this new law?"

"Oh no, I suspect there are quite a few, and there will be lots more to come. We're just at the front of the queue."

"Okay. Well, there are numerous angles to this, but I think Richard and I should take some time to think about whether we can help, and if so what we can do. We will also need to agree a fee structure if we are going to work for you. Let me give you each a pack with our standard terms in it, and you can go away and look through that. And we'll get back to you in a couple of days and let you know what we think".

True to her word, she rang a couple of days later and invited us back in. Gary couldn't make it, so I went alone. Melanie had drawn up an action plan, and wanted to talk me through it.

The major problem, as Melanie saw it, was that the issue of extradition is not one that naturally interests people. It affects a very small number of people, and the natural instinct is to assume that if someone has been charged with a crime in a foreign country, then they probably have at least a case to answer.

It is in our nature to believe that there is no smoke without fire. In Britain, we still mostly believe that if someone has been charged, the likelihood is that he or she is guilty of at least some wrongdoing. Miscarriages of justice are the exception rather than the rule.

We were trying to highlight the fact that the Extradition Act was a very dangerous piece of legislation, because it essentially obliterated any protections for people accused of crimes in a foreign country. But it's a pretty dry topic, and you've got to go some to get people enthused.

Oh yes, and we were three "rich bankers", as far as the world at large would be concerned, who had by their own admission made a ton of money by investing with a guy who was now the poster child for the biggest corporate fraud in history. Not a good starting point, really.

Justice should be blind, of course. We needed to highlight the principle in order to get any traction, and in that regard we had quite a good story to tell. Whatever preconceptions people may have had of us as individuals, the fact is that we were three Brits who lived and worked in England, who had been accused by a foreign Government of committing a robbery of our own employer in London. What possible business could that be of the Americans? The only reason that this extradition was happening was that a new law allowed it. So something must be wrong with the law, surely?

The argument had a certain strength to it. There were other things going for us. The Abu Hamza affair, which was such a good contrast; the fact that the new law had been bullied through Parliament on the back of the War against Terror, and yet was now being used against bankers; and some other cases including Ian Norris, the former chief executive of Morgan Crucible, who had just been indicted with price fixing. This was the thin end of the wedge.

Melanie had identified a number of people and organisations that she believed we should be briefing, with a view to getting a powerful and educated consensus to see the dangers of the new legislation. Key to the task would be to focus on the legal principles. High on her list were some of the usual suspects like Liberty and Justice, and eminent human rights campaigners such as Dame Helena Kennedy.

She also suggested that we go to see a lobbying firm that she knew, who could target many MPs and brief them on the issues.

It was a relatively simple strategy. Neither Melanie nor Richard was particularly confident of success, because it was just such a minority issue, and it was difficult to see people caring unless it impacted them directly. We are most of us very selfish, even if we pretend otherwise. I see things completely differently now, of course. But ten years ago I would have looked at an article about three blokes being charged with fraud and wanted in America, and thought "put them on a plane. Why are we wasting taxpayers' money?"

It was with much enthusiasm but little expectation, therefore, that we embarked upon the journey to educate those who we thought mattered. We couldn't possibly have known what a storm we would kick up.

In his book *Flat Earth News*, published in 2008, the journalist Nick Davies wrote a whole section on our campaign. Melanie was very upset about his portrayal. His view, coloured by our guilty plea a few months previously, was that we had cunningly diverted people away from the mountains of incriminating evidence, and instead focused on the "poor me" aspects of principle, and that the whole thing was a triumph of spin over substance.

In one sense, he was right. We absolutely did focus on the principle, and not the facts of our case. But the implication that we did it as a diversion from our guilt is not only wrong but misses the point. Our innocence or guilt never mattered. Nor should it have. Criminal cases should be tried in the courts, not the newspapers. What matters is the law that allows British citizens to be shipped to the other side of the world and incarcerated by some foreign Government, without the necessity to produce a single shred of evidence.

From that perspective, all the credit goes to Melanie and Richard for their clarity of vision. They saw how to advance the argument. In military terms, they set out the strategy. Everything that followed was the execution of that strategy, and if it were to be measured in column inches and hours of Parliamentary time, I would say it was an outstanding success. Not a total success, of course, because the law remains unchanged, but we came agonisingly close, and the war isn't over yet.

Much as I would like to be able to trumpet our brilliance in the field of PR, however, much of the success of our little campaign was down to the Home Office and the Government themselves, to whom I am indebted for their arrogance, condescension, and the assumption that all members of the public and the Fourth Estate are stupid and incapable of making up their own minds when presented with the unalloyed facts.

Of those journalists who followed the story through from those early days in 2004, none that I know of has ever condemned the three of us after our guilty plea. They knew that our fight against the extradition laws was about principle, and that it was the right fight. It remains so to this day, as the followers of Gary McKinnon, Ian Norris and the hundreds of other citizens already extradited and the hundreds more already in the pipeline will surely attest. It was a fight about bad law, never about innocence or guilt.

If we had not fought as we did, the Extradition Act would almost certainly never have become front-page news. That we had the resources to bring the fight to the Government would of course be used against us. A collection of backbench Labour MPs masquerading as class warriors would latterly line up to denounce us as millionaire bankers, as if somehow that fact alone should justify our extradition. But if not us, then who would fight?

Someone had to speak up. I'm glad it was us, for all the vitriolic column inches it would bring. Now don't get me wrong; our motivations at the start were almost entirely selfish, but we correctly identified that we would be the thin end of the wedge, and so 'our' fight became a 'just' fight.

Our critics have often argued that it was all about developing sympathy for us. It was never about developing sympathy for us. We were about as unsympathetic a bunch of characters as it would have been possible to imagine in the circumstances. But bad law affects rich and poor alike, and generally speaking its effects tend to be felt disproportionately by the poor, since they do not have the means to fight.

For Melanie, Gary and me, those days in the summer of 2004 saw the beginning of a beautiful relationship that would last to this day. When

Gary and I informed Melanie in early 2006 that we simply couldn't afford to pay her any more, she refused point blank to walk away, and would be a champion of the cause over the following years without ever being paid a penny by anyone. Not quite the multi-million dollar PR campaign that the Government wanted everyone to believe we were running.

Melanie worked hand in hand with Liberty and a few influential individuals to keep taking the fight to the Government, and when Gary McKinnon's case began to be front page news in the spring and summer of 2009, it was Melanie who was working away feverishly behind the scenes, still unpaid.

In the early days, though, the going was slow. Educating people on such a dry matter is a tough ask. Liberty and Justice were with us in principle, having opposed many of the aspects of the Act before it became law. Others were slower to come on board.

BOW STREET
September 2004

The summer of 2004 was not an easy time. I continued to work during the week in London, but I was privately consumed with the dread of what was to come. My way of dealing with it was to immerse myself in the fight, but frequently this was to the detriment of my home life. If it was bad for me, it was so much worse for Emma, who had to bear the burden whilst pretending for the sake of the children that everything was well with the world.

It's very hard to rationalise something like this. With many crises in life, decision making is unpleasant but relatively straightforward. The problem with this situation was that it was impossible to predict the outcome, the timetable, or the consequences of the many possible outcomes. We might win the extradition fight, but then be stuck in the UK for the rest of our lives, unable to take a foreign holiday for fear of arrest, imprisonment in a foreign jail, and extradition.

We might win the extradition fight and then face a UK prosecution. Oddly enough that was the best possible scenario, since we would then be able to defend ourselves and put the issue to bed once and for all.

We might lose the extradition fight and then be locked up for years and years before agreeing to a plea deal. Or we might plead straight away but be sentenced to a long term in prison. We might or might not be allowed to transfer back to the UK to serve any sentence if convicted. We might fight all the way to trial, and win, but be bankrupted by the costs, and mentally scarred for life by the trauma of a trial, when the stakes for losing are so high.

The money worries were always there. By this stage, we were funding five different sets of lawyers on two continents. We knew that if extradited, we had no realistic chance of being able to take the matter to trial because we just couldn't afford it.

You simply cannot plan in these circumstances. You have to wake up every day, and see what the day brings. In my own little cocoon, this was not a problem. I enjoyed my day job and found the intellectual challenge of the legal fight extremely interesting. Odd as it may seem perhaps, I'm an incredibly principled person, and I am good at channeling anger in positive directions. I knew that whatever they threw at me, I would survive, and I was damned if I was just going to roll over and let this happen. So I insisted that we try to maintain as normal a life as we possibly could, for the sake primarily of the children, but also because once you start behaving like you're defeated, then defeat will surely follow.

For those around you, though, it's so much harder, and that's what eats away. It is torture. I guess that families who have loved ones who are diagnosed with some awful illness go through similar emotions. A death is dreadful, but at least has certainty. An illness with an uncertain prognosis both as to time and result leaves you living from one day to the next. For us, this would go on for over five years. I would be lying if I said it took no toll on us as a family. But in other ways it galvanised us, and the love and support of our families and friends not only sustained us, but made us stronger.

In the Army you learn that although you can train as hard as you like, it is only when the bullets start flying that true character is revealed. Thankfully, I was never tested in combat. But the trauma we went through brought out the character in Emma and our close families in a way that I could never have imagined. None was found wanting.

We had taken the conscious decision not to tell the children, partly because I genuinely believed that we would prevail, and so we would be able to explain to them after it was all over, and partly because once the genie is out of the bottle, you can never put it back. It was hard enough for Emma to cope with the stress as it was, without adding the extra complexity of young and inquisitive children asking questions that we couldn't possibly answer.

Mark Spragg and Alun Jones had found a witness on their trip to the US who would be prepared to give evidence on the practical workings of the US criminal justice system and was willing to travel to the UK to appear in person. James Hines was very enthused about our prospects of prevailing on the issue of human rights. He had done a lot of investigation into the European authorities, and thought that we had a very strong case.

It was a matter of forum, and since the Act did not specifically provide for a decision on forum, therefore the human rights laws should step in and do just that.

I was particularly pleased that Caroline Flint, the Minister for Extradition, had already highlighted the inclusion of human rights protections in the Act, when persuading the select committee the previous December of the merits of allowing the US to extradite without evidence:

"[o]ne of the very positive aspects of the Extradition Act 2003 is that it includes many safeguards, which were not clear before, to protect citizens' rights. They provide ample protection for UK citizens.

[…]

Most important, extradition cannot take place when it would be contrary to the person's rights under the European convention on human rights. An ECHR case established that our obligations in that respect extend to the person's likely treatment after extradition. Those are solid safeguards for protecting UK citizens".

Mark had also managed to secure the agreement of Liberty to intervene in our case. Whichever side won in the magistrates' court, there was bound to be an appeal to the High Court, because this was the first big test case for the new law. Liberty wished to ensure that the Human Rights arguments would be thoroughly rehearsed, so they wrote a letter to the court formally stating their intention to intervene in any High Court appeal.

It was a massive result for us, and a hugely brave decision by Shami Chakrabarti, the Director of Liberty. We were about the least likely candidates in the world to be actively supported by Liberty, but Shami to her enormous credit recognised that justice should be blind, and the issues of principle in our case would have profound implications for all who would follow. It is a decision that she has stood by through all the intervening years, in the face of some truly dreadful criticism from many bigoted senior figures both in Government and outside, including supporters of Liberty.

As the date of our hearings drew close, I became more excited. It seemed to me that we had strong arguments on just about all of the points of law. In retrospect I realise that probably everyone thinks the same when they read their lawyer's arguments, but only one side can prevail.

On the morning of 28th September, I set off early for our hearing in London with Emma. I was in two minds as to whether it was a good idea that she came, but she was insistent. We were in this together, for better or worse. As we approached the court, we could see the posse of press photographers outside. Chin up. Be polite.

Getting in to the court from the street could be a bit of a palaver. Immediately inside the entrance lobby was a large metal detector, through which you could only walk one at a time, so if you arrived in a group, the chances were that several of you would be stuck waiting outside the doors. Luckily, I wasn't trying to avoid the press.

Inside, scores of people milled around. We made our way up the dark stairway to one of the upper courts, where we found my parents, Melanie, Mark Spragg and Emma's father, Brian, amongst those waiting in the corridor outside.

Gary and Giles duly turned up, with a large crowd of family and supporters. Giles' wife Debs was there, but Laura Mulgrew was not. Laura, who is American, had filed for divorce the previous Friday evening.

Alun Jones arrived about two minutes before we were due to kick off. He was wearing his wig and gown, although neither was on straight and he was looking rather hot and bothered, presumably from running with a large bundle of documents under his arm. It was quite comical, really.

What came next wasn't nearly so comical. Mark handed each of us a copy of a letter received the previous day from Robert Wardle, the director of the Serious Fraud Office. It was his response to Mark's request that he look at investigating us here, with a view to a prosecution, and it made my blood boil. Not because he refused to investigate us, which was wearily predictable, but because of the timing of his letter, and the reasoning within it, which as far as I was concerned was a bloody disgrace.

He had copied the letter to the CPS, so our judge would be able to take account of it in his deliberations, even though Wardle himself would not be there to be cross-examined on it. Although Mark Spragg had sent two further letters asking for a response to his original request, Wardle had somehow managed to wait until the very eve of the hearing to send his reply, leaving no opportunity for us to respond. Coincidence, he might claim. To us it seemed a shitty little trick, particularly copying the CPS, so that it could be entered into the proceedings.

In the letter he set out his rationale for his refusal to investigate. The central plank was as follows:

"In particular, the other participants in the alleged conspiracy–Kopper and Fastow–are to be dealt with in the United States. In these circumstances I think it more likely to be in the interests of justice for your clients to be tried in the United States".

It made no sense. Having made a deal with the prosecutors, Kopper and Fastow were now at worst witnesses against us. Not co-defendants. And Fastow wasn't even mentioned as a potential witness in the extradition pack. It was a shocking decision.

Wardle also distanced himself from the press release of the Department of Justice on 27th June 2002, which had said that "the investigation that led to today's complaint was coordinated with Britain's Financial Services Authority, Britain's Serious Fraud Office, and the Securities and Exchange Commission". The letter implied that all that the SFO had done was to provide help to the US in obtaining evidence for the Enron investigation generally.

This letter would turn out to be one of the single most important contributing factors to our extradition. Because the UK authorities would not even investigate, let alone prosecute, we would have to be extradited to ensure that we did not "get off scot free", as Home Office Minister Hazel Blears would later describe it. It would be a betrayal that would be visited upon many others over the years, Ian Norris and Gary McKinnon among them.

As I saw it, the actions of this one man, who at a stroke could have saved us, would condemn us to make the journey to Texas, from which there would only ever be one way back, as convicted criminals. He was able to stand in the long grass, out of our reach, and snipe, knowing that we could not engage him. He was able to prejudice the case against us with a letter like this but never have to stand up and be counted in cross examination. Like Macavity the cat, he just wasn't there, but the prejudice he had created would count against us.

At the appointed hour the clerk of the court opened the doors and in we trouped. The courtroom was old and musty. I imagined the assorted drunks, pickpockets and ne'erdowells of the eighteenth century had probably faced much the same layout as we now did, absent the dirty electric light fittings and padded seats for the court staff.

The bench where the judge would sit was an impressive wooden edifice, raised so as to give him a view downwards over the court from his large chair. In front of the bench were the tables for court officials, stenographer, clerks, and the counsel for the two sides of the case. Behind them was the dock, to which we were shown, which was a raised platform surrounded by metal rails, containing a narrow bench, which was monumentally uncomfortable. But I guess that's what being a defendant is about.

Around three sides of the court were wooden benches for members of the press and the public, and before Judge Evans came in, I glanced around to see who else was there. There were many friendly faces. The journalists were relatively easy to spot, as they had pads and pens poised. In one corner, right at the back, sat Margaret Cole, the White & Case partner representing RBC in its civil action against the Dutch bank Rabobank.

Judge Evans, when he entered, suggested that the three defendants might like to take seats in the benches behind the dock, as these were more comfortable. It was a nice gesture, and the only one he would afford us in all of our dealings with him.

The hearing lasted three days. The first morning was largely taken up with opening statements and procedural stuff. In terms of the order of play, we would get to go first, and then John Hardy would have a go on behalf of the United States, and then both sides would be able to sum up.

Our plan was that I should be the primary mouthpiece for the three of us, because my knowledge of the details of our case and of the wider Enron related issues was becoming close to encyclopedic.

I was due to take the stand in the afternoon on the first day. It is impermissible for witnesses to be coached in England (a sharp contrast to the practical workings of the US system), and Alun Jones was therefore keen not to be seen conversing with me over lunch, so I took myself away to a pub round the corner from the court, and sat down with a large glass of red wine, a packet of cigarettes, and my thoughts.

I had never taken the witness stand before in any court proceeding, and to be honest I was absolutely terrified. It wasn't that I had any specific concerns. It was just first time nerves. You have no idea how it's going to pan out. What if the judge lays into me? What if they start asking questions about the merits of the case? Should I answer them, or refuse to do so on the grounds that this is not an evidential hearing? How would that look? So many things go through your mind, and I figured that I would need Dutch courage and a significant hit of nicotine to see me through the ordeal.

I was called to the stand immediately after lunch, and sworn in. I needed a glass of water because my mouth was so dry, and my heart was pounding.

Alun Jones spent an hour or so questioning me, to ensure all of the information that we wanted to convey would be put into evidence. He was a skillful inquisitor, putting me at ease, and coaxing out what he wanted without ever seeming to "lead" the witness.

We talked about the Enron investigations, the farce of the Fastows' plea deals, Kopper and Glisan's deals, the clear indication that our criminal complaint was a device to get to Kopper and Fastow, and ultimately to Jeff Skilling, Ken Lay and Rick Causey, Enron's Chief Accounting Officer.

We discussed how difficult it would be to conduct a defence of our case in Texas. All of the witnesses and evidence that we needed would be here in England, and we would have no powers of subpoena. The jury pool was irrefutably tainted by the anger in the Houston community at the loss of their largest employer. The prosecutors would use the threat of further charges to lever a guilty plea out of us.

I explained what had happened to Jamie Olis and his two co-defendants, and how attorneys at the time had commented that in these circumstances, everyone would be rushing to do the best plea deals for their clients, even if they were obviously innocent. I testified that if extradited, given the circumstances we would face, we would be "insane" not to enter into a plea agreement, our innocence of the charges notwithstanding.

I went on to talk about how it was standard practice for the US prosecutors to threaten potential defence witnesses with indictment, and thereby prevent them from testifying. I said that in these circumstances it would be highly likely that many of the people that we might wish to call as witnesses would be unwilling to make the trip to the US, and who could blame them?

By the end, all of my nerves had gone and I was talking with confidence. I figured we had made our points as well as we could possibly have done. But when Alun sat down, it would be John Hardy's turn, and this was not going to be an easy ride.

During Hardy's cross-examination, I remember being very irritated by his Uriah Heep, ever so humble style. Looking back after the event, his was a masterclass. Of course I had no idea what he was trying to get out of the cross-examination, and he was far too skilled to let me see much, so I satisfied myself with answering the questions that he asked. I was polite but firm, and the questioning was never hostile.

He concentrated on three main issues. The first was the e-mails and the copy of the February 2000 presentation that were contained in the extradition pack. I was immediately concerned that his detailed questions were going to matters of evidence, and said so. I emphasised that the e-mails were mere extracts, taken spectacularly out of context, that the February 2000 presentation was not remotely connected with any fraud, but was in fact a perfectly good business proposition, and that one million dollars was absolutely a fair price for the SwapSub asset.

Next he tried to corner me into admitting that we had made no attempts to interview witnesses, even though they were all here in the UK. I pointed out that you cannot interview a witness without the documents, because unless you have materials to refer to, and to present at trial, any interview is a waste of time.

Lastly, he asked whether I had declared my investment to the compliance department of Greenwich NatWest. "No sir", I said. And that was that.

Thereafter, Gary and Giles both got up and were cross examined very briefly. Hardy really just wanted to elicit from each that neither had declared his investment to GNW's compliance department. Neither had.

Job done.

On the way out, Margaret Cole offered her hand and her condolences on the way things had panned out for us since we had last met. She wished us well.

The whole team went to the pub afterwards. Several ex colleagues had come along to give us support, and the general consensus was that it had gone as well as it could possibly have done. I was ecstatic at having survived my little ordeal without making an arse of myself.

The following day, I made the trip to London alone. On the way, I picked up a couple of the newspapers. The coverage of the case was detailed but unbiased. They had picked up on the issues very well. I was extremely pleased, because Melanie had been working really hard to ensure that the journalists knew what was at stake here, and that this case was the test of a brand new and very dangerous law.

First up was our expert witness, Doug McNabb, who practised as a defense attorney in Houston. His job was to "tell it how it is", as to the workings of the US criminal justice system. A huge bear of a man, he was very charming and impressive.

Alun took Doug through his testimony. I thought it was brilliant. The picture that he painted of Houston was of a City torn to shreds by what had happened to Enron, and a jury pool that a recent survey had shown to be at least eighty percent tainted.

He described a system in which our chances of bail were extremely slim, because the US regarded us as fugitives, and because we were aliens, with neither homes nor family in the US. Consequently, even if granted bail by a Federal judge, we would be liable to be locked up immediately by the immigration authorities.

He described the inside of the Federal Detention Center in downtown Houston, where we would be incarcerated, and how it was all but impossible to prepare for trial from there. And he opined that getting a Texas court to issue subpoenas for documents and witnesses overseas would be to all intents and purposes impossible.

Hardy's cross-examination was brief. He pulled out a copy of the Sixth Amendment to the US Constitution, guaranteeing a defendant a fair trial, and he took Doug through it sentence by sentence, asking whether or not each was still in effect. Each was.

Next, he pulled out a copy of article 6 of the European Convention on Human Rights, which bore a fairly strong similarity to the Sixth Amendment, and which would be the test under the Extradition Act as to whether we would get a fair trial if extradited. A simple but quite brilliant tactic. Doug did his best to point out that the practice is a long way from the theory, but Hardy had made his point.

After we had finished, it was Hardy's turn to go into bat for the US Government. This was necessarily going to be a much shorter session, because he had no witnesses. Consequently he spent some time walking through the written testimony of Thomas Hanusik and Special Agent Hays from the extradition pack, and a further affidavit recently submitted by Hanusik.

Three points that he kept emphasising were the under-valuation of the asset, identity of the victim (NatWest, not Enron), and the importance of the February meeting in establishing jurisdiction. The first and last were utter nonsense, but would be taken as fact because the US prosecutors said that it were so.

On valuation, Hardy quoted from Hanusik's affidavit:

The essence of the scheme was that, by misrepresentations, omissions, and deceit, the co-schemers caused NatWest to sell its interest in a limited partnership for $1 million to an entity that the co-schemers secretly controlled. The co-schemers knew that NatWest's interest in the partnership was worth well in excess of $1 million.

When asked by Judge Evans about the actual value for the SwapSub stake, in the view of the US prosecutors, Hardy responded:

In opening the case to you in June, the Government's position was, and now remains, that, contrary to Mr Bermingham's assertion in evidence yesterday, one million was in fact too low a sale price, but that the price of thirty million could not be said to be an unreasonable market price. That was the Government's position and it remains so. In other words, the Government's case to you is that the purchase by Enron of Swap Sub for $30 million was a reasonable purchase at a reasonable price.

What? Even the American prosecutors weren't claiming that! And they were sitting on a mountain of evidence that proved the exact opposite of what he was saying. In all the years since I have yet to see a single piece of evidence that $30 million was "a reasonable purchase at a reasonable price".

On the issue of the February meeting, and the appropriate forum for trial, he said:

"We respectfully submit that if and in so far as the facts of this case fall to be considered at all…we submit that the meeting on or around the 22nd February in Houston is of cardinal importance."

He followed this up with:

"We submit that on the evidence that is before you at the moment, bearing in mind in particular the email of the 19th February prior to the meeting, the meeting itself, the presentation included in the bundle at page 382 … gives a picture of what the meeting in Houston was actually about and how important it was. That is why we respectfully submit that not only is Houston a convenient forum, but an entirely appropriate one for the trial of this matter."

You see here the critical problem with the Extradition Act. The prosecutor submits his charging documents, and (if he desires) an affidavit in support. He can make whatever allegation he wishes, completely unsupported by evidence. It can be totally false. It will necessarily be taken by the court as being true, and the lawyers for the Government requesting extradition will faithfully represent that it is so, having no reason to believe otherwise.

When we wound up on the afternoon of 30th September, Judge Evans indicated that it would be his intention to pass judgment on 15th October, at a hearing that we would be required to attend. We took our leave and repaired as ever to the pub.

FRIENDS EXTRADITED
October 2004

We all duly reconvened at Bow Street on 15th October. The verdicts had just come in on the 'Nigerian Barges' trial of the Merrill Lynch bankers in Houston. Five convictions, including the four bankers, and one acquittal of a relatively junior Enron accountant. The prosecutors were pushing for sentences of fifteen to thirty years, to set an example, they said.

The press were outside Bow Street in force, and our gang of family and friends were also with us. I'm an optimistic sort, and I was hoping for the best even though I rather expected the worst. We thought our article 8 argument was particularly strong. Extradition was neither necessary nor proportionate because a trial not only could, but to any reasonable observer should, be held in the UK.

Before Judge Evans entered, I heard his assistant ask another member of the court staff for some bail forms. Mark Spragg had also overheard the remark, and when I caught his eye he gave me a thumbs down. It was disappointing, but in practice the result would make no difference because whichever side lost was bound to appeal to the High Court, and that's where the real war would take place.

I hadn't expected the judge to read out his judgment, but he did. It was eleven pages long, but he was no more than a couple of paragraphs in when I started to get really angry.

"The Government's opening note", he said, "provides an admirably succinct overview". All rubbish, but admirable and succinct, sure enough.

"Although this case proceeds under the Extradition Act 2003, the request was prepared to meet the requirements of Schedule 1 to the Extradition Act 1989. There is therefore available affidavit evidence giving considerable factual detail of the allegations. As a matter of interest that evidence makes a case to answer."

I nearly leapt off my seat at that point. He did go on to say that whether there was in fact a case to answer was irrelevant under the new Act. But it didn't matter. The damage was done. We live in an age of spin and soundbites. Things taken out of context, just like my e-mails.

Time and again from Government Ministers, and even from Tony Blair at Prime Minister's Questions, it would be thrown back in our faces that the judge had effectively determined that we would have been extradited under the old 1989 Act anyway, when in point of fact he had decided no such thing.

Next up was his commentary on Robert Wardle's letter:

"Of course, these defendants could have been tried here but it would seem they are not going to be. Mr Wardle, on behalf of the SFO... gives the reasons... The reality is that were the SFO now to commence an investigation, then by the time they were ready to launch a prosecution, there would be defence submissions inviting the court to stay the prosecution as an abuse. Additionally and crucially, Kopper and Fastow are important witnesses for the prosecution. They are readily available to give evidence in the States but not in the UK. If this extradition request is defeated further criminal proceedings are unlikely."

It's difficult to know where to begin really. Every single statement, as far as we were concerned, was totally incorrect. Far from trying to forestall a UK prosecution, it would have been the ONLY way to clear our names and prevent extradition. Why did he think we had asked for it? It would ALWAYS be quicker to have a UK prosecution of this case than to follow through the extradition process and then have to spend up to two years waiting for a US trial while we attempted to access witnesses and documents from the UK.

And who said Fastow would be a crucial Government witness? There was no evidence to support that. And even if he were, it was simply wrong to suggest that he and Kopper could not come to the UK. Their plea agreements specifically tied them to giving evidence wherever and whenever the US Government ordered them to do so. Or they could give evidence from the US by vidcolink.

And if the extradition was defeated, all the US Government would have to do was to ask the UK authorities to prosecute it. It's called Mutual Legal Assistance. We have treaties on the subject.

I could go on and on about Nicholas Evans' judgment, but it wouldn't achieve much. He dismissed our human rights arguments without blinking, and of our expert witness he opined that "he is entitled to his view. I am not bound to accept his view". He went on to say that "It must be rather depressing for him to practice as a defence attorney in the Federal Courts when he is of the opinion that fair trials and justice are not available".

He summed up thus:

"I accept the defendants could have been prosecuted in the UK. There was, however, no obligation to prosecute them in the UK. They are not going to be prosecuted in the UK. There is a good and proper basis for prosecuting them in the US. The US wants to prosecute them in the US. The process of extradition is 'necessary in a democratic society' and proportionate".

So there. With that, he sent the case to David Blunkett, the Home Secretary, who would be limited under the new Act to deciding whether or not we could face the death penalty, and whether the extradition should be barred by reason of 'specialty'—the doctrine that someone can only be tried for the offences for which they have been extradited, and no others.

In the absence of evidence, the void is filled by prejudice. Under the old Act, you could argue your case. Now, the other side got to make whatever allegations they wanted, and these would be taken as fact, untested, and then form part of the judgment against you. It was like something out of a Kafka novel. I mean either there is evidence, or there isn't. And if there isn't, then the statements made must not form part of the decision, because they are untested. But human instinct just doesn't work that way. If the US Government says something is so, then we must take them at their word, because of course they never lie or get it wrong, do they?

At this point, it is worth touching upon the case of Lotfi Raissi, an Algerian born man who was accused in early 2002 of training the 9/11 pilots. Imagine for a moment that his hearing had taken place under the 2003 Act, in front of Judge Evans. It is a racing certainty that the outcome would have been the same as our own. In fact the judge who presided over his case testified as much to the Commons Select Committee in November 2005. The allegations against Raissi were truly awful, and if recited as fact would have painted him as one of the world's most wanted men.

But they weren't fact. They weren't even close. They were a total and utter fabrication, much like the allegations against us. And this was only discovered because under the 1989 Extradition Act, Raissi's American accusers were required to support the allegations in their charging documents with evidence, and they couldn't because it didn't exist.

It's all very well saying that it will all come out in the wash, because Raissi could have won at trial in America, but Raissi would never have got near to a trial in America. He would have languished for years, or perhaps for ever, in a SuperMax facility, along with other suspected terrorists, until such time as he was ready to confess to his 'crimes'. It's an absolutely terrifying thought.

So whatever your feelings may be about 'the NatWest Three', put those to one side. It's not about us anymore. It's about all those who are swept up in this madness as I write, and all those to come.

There are those on the Conservative benches who argued that they only supported this legislation because they thought it would just be used for terrorists. That is an appalling proposition. The more serious the crime, and therefore the potential sanction, the greater the protections we should have against injustice

So off to the pub again. Melanie meanwhile was doing her level best with the press to cast at least a neutral light on what had been a very bad day.

In the pub, Gary introduced me to Julie Fielding, a childhood friend who had been extremely supportive of Gary through the last few months. They would later become an item, but at this point they were still just good friends.

Julie was an effervescent sort with piercing eyes and a huge smile, and she was in no mood to let a little stumble on the road divert us. She had the "can-do" manner of someone who had managed to make a success of running her own business while bringing up two small children on her own.

She had been giving some thought as to what we could do, and had decided that a website was a must. Gary had a couple of friends who were capable of setting up the site, and would run it. It would act as a bulletin board, and a means of conveying our message to a growing audience. Julie even had a suggestion for the name of the site.

It would be called Friends Extradited, in homage to the social networking site Friends Reunited, the precursor to the modern Facebook and others. She had even mocked up some web pages, and I had to admit that it looked great. There was a picture of the three of us, next to the caption "Make it Not Happen", in reference to RBS's slogan at the time "Make it Happen". And how could you not like the name? It was just so catchy. I was sold.

Melanie too was extremely enthusiastic. She reckoned that a standalone site like that would be an invaluable tool when dealing with the press, because it could act as a repository for information in an electronic format, something that makes journalists' lives so much easier.

The site was up and running within a couple of weeks. An old work colleague, Vincent Kane, and his wife Jane, would do all of the hard work in receiving and sorting messages, and sending e-mails from the site.

The launch coincided with the opening shots in our battle proper against the Government. In the years ahead, we would win all the intellectual arguments, and fall at the final hurdle in actually getting the law changed in late 2006, not through any fault of our own, but through a failure of moral courage by the Conservatives when the chips were down. But by then, we would have brought the issue to the national consciousness in a way that none of us could possibly have imagined when sitting in the pub that day.

Encouraging people to write to their MPs or the Home Secretary, we produced specimen letters on the website for them to personalise as they saw fit. If they wanted to make the letters about our case, then fine. If they wanted them to be general about the lack of protections in the law, then fine. We encouraged everybody who got a reply to scan it and send it to the site.

It took a couple of weeks, and then the replies started coming back. A trickle at first, and then a flood. By convention, a Minister should reply to correspondence from an MP within two weeks, although the reply almost always comes from a designated civil servant.

So we quickly got a sense of where the Government was on the issues, and it was jaw-dropping stuff. In defence of the fact that we had put into law a Treaty that remained unratified by the US, and was non-reciprocal, the Home Office breezily suggested that reciprocity wasn't the be all and end all of treaties, and that ratification would doubtless take place sometime quite soon.

As to the right of the US to ask for extradition of British citizens without evidence, the Home Office cited France and Ireland as other countries which did not require the US to produce evidence. This simply could not be true, I thought. After all, the film director Roman Polanski had fled to France (where he had citizenship) some twenty something years previously to avoid being sentenced on US charges of underage sex, and I recalled that there had been a high profile case of French financiers whose extraditions to the US had been refused by France. Time to do some digging.

Doug McNabb's website provided links to all of the US's international extradition treaties, so I sat down and pulled up the French and Irish ones.

In a very limited sense, the Home Office was correct. Neither treaty required that the US should provide evidence in support of its requests. But this was a totally misleading picture. The French treaty contained a clause whereby France would decline to extradite its own citizens, purely on the basis of their nationality. So in effect they were saying to the US, "you can have anyone you want as long as they are not French". This "own nationals" clause is a very common one in international extradition treaties, the logic being that countries reserve unto themselves the right to try their own citizens. In the Irish treaty, they had provisions allowing Ireland to refuse to extradite if the crime could have been deemed to have been committed on Irish soil, or if the Irish authorities had declined to prosecute.

The Home Office was peddling deliberate misinformation by suggesting that our new extradition arrangements were merely following the lead of other friendly countries. I wondered whether that had ever been the subject of discussions in parliament. So I went onto the Hansard website and did a search, and up it popped.

In December 2003, in persuading parliament to accept the new arrangements, Home Office Ministers Caroline Flint (in the Commons) and Baroness Scotland (in the Lords), had used exactly these arguments. As Flint said on 15th December:

"There is another important, and more modern, precedent. Such extradition relations with the US are not unique in Europe. The bilateral extradition treaty between the US and Ireland, which dates from 1984, contains exactly the same evidential provision. Perhaps more significantly, so does the bilateral treaty between France and the US, which is less than 10 years old. Whatever unjustified suggestions there may be about relations between the UK, or even Ireland, and the US, I trust that no honourable Member would seriously suggest that France is subservient to the US, that it automatically does the US's bidding, or that the US is uninterested in the rights of French citizens. Both Ireland and France have accepted the restraints imposed by the terms of the US constitution. They see nothing wrong with treaties that impose differential evidential requirements, and we should follow their example."

The following day, Baroness Scotland had addressed the Lords in almost word for word the same manner.

Next I went looking for details on the French extradition case that I recalled from the previous year. On 9th December 2003, it was reported that a US request to extradite four senior French financiers had been turned down because it was not French policy to extradite French citizens. Commenting on the case the French Finance Minister, Francois Mer, had observed that "in the United States it seems money buys everything, even innocence or guilt". The French had difficulty understanding how to operate in such a system, he said.

So just two months before Flint and Scotland got up and spun the line that we were following the lead of our French and Irish colleagues, the French position on extradition had been made abundantly and very publicly clear. "We don't extradite our citizens".

So, what to do with this information? After all, the fact that politicians dissemble is hardly newsworthy any more, and at this point our issue was still very much small print in the business pages.

In the end, I went through all one hundred and twenty or so US bilateral extradition treaties with countries around the world. It took some days, but at the end of it I had what I believed to be a bullet-proof document, which we posted on the website. It confirmed that in the entire world, there were only three countries that did not require the US to provide evidence in support of its requests. Ireland, France, and now the UK. But both Ireland and France had far more substantial protections for their own citizens, and we had none.

In a nutshell, our position was worse than that of any other country in the world. To give you some idea of how low British citizens now rank, the US negotiated new extradition treaties at the end of 2006 with Latvia, Macedonia and Estonia, in all three cases being happy to provide evidence to those countries in support of its extradition requests.

A special relationship indeed.

Armed with all this, I resolved to get an appointment to see Boris Johnson. A letter wouldn't do. I was going to sit down with him, show him the evidence and some of the correspondence. I badgered his assistant Oliver Dommett daily until he agreed to set up a meeting in Boris's office at the Commons.

On Wednesday 10th November 2004, I arrived in the early afternoon at Portcullis House, the brand spanking new building for MPs' offices just across the road from the Palace of Westminster.

It's an old cliché that when a public company builds itself a new head office, it is time to sell the stock. That certainly applied to Enron. And in that context it is interesting to note how New Labour spent vast sums of taxpayers' money building new offices for, variously, the Scottish Parliament (original estimate £40 million, final cost over £400 million), the Welsh Assembly, the Home Office, the Treasury, and of course the MPs themselves.

I waited with Olly for about 10 minutes in Boris's office, and then in he crashed, sweating profusely from what had obviously been a brisk cycle ride from somewhere, and flushed from the cold November air. He was wearing a crumpled grey suit, the sleeves of which seemed way too short, with the cuffs of a red sweater protruding underneath.

"Sorry I'm late", he said, and we began. We talked for the best part of an hour. I told him where we were with the extradition proceedings, and took him through our whole argument. How it wasn't about us, it was about the principle. How in many senses we were the lucky ones, with the resources and the resolve to fight. But this could happen to anybody, any day.

I gave him the document that I had prepared showing the key points of every single one of the 120 extradition treaties, and explained how Ms Flint was being at best disingenuous in her comments on the French and Irish arrangements.

"Well when you put it like that", said Boris, "I think it's a bloody outrage".

I walked away that day thinking that it may well come to nothing, but at least I had been given the opportunity to sound off.

I could not have been more wrong.

The following morning, Armistice Day, I was standing as usual on the fast train from Reading to London, reading the *Telegraph*, when I turned to the comment page and found that Boris had written, as his weekly piece, an article entitled "Special Relationship or One-Way Street?"

Within a couple of paragraphs, I realised to my astonishment that the whole piece was about our meeting.

Private Eye satirises Boris mercilessly for the style in which he writes. "Cripes", "Blimey", "Gadzooks". They run comic strips in which he appears in the guise of Dennis the Menace, from the Beano.

On this occasion, Boris excelled himself. His *Telegraph* piece was outstanding. If I was a little put out at him describing me as a "bit of a yuppy" (the first and only time anyone has leveled that description at me), he nonetheless hit the nail on the head about the law.

There are many nuances to the interaction between the Treaty and the Act, and even in the ways that other countries deal with extradition, but he didn't miss a beat. I was not aware of him taking any notes during our meeting, but he didn't get a single fact or observation wrong.

He made it clear that our innocence or guilt was not the issue, but that the law was just fundamentally wrong, and needed to be changed forthwith.

I can only assume that he must have said goodbye to me and just got straight down to writing the copy, as I would imagine that his deadline would have been about 5pm that same day. It begs the question as to whether he does this every week, hoping that some topic on which he can wax lyrical will just present itself out of nowhere in particular.

My heart soared. Not in my wildest dreams had it occurred to me that he would use his *Telegraph* column for these ends. But if we had wanted a platform from which to launch an attack on the law, we could never have asked for a better one.

But he went further. He tabled what is called an Early Day Motion ("EDM"), which is a bit like a petition that sits in the Commons and attracts signatures from MPs. The EDM called for the law to be changed to incorporate provisions on natural forum (such that cases that could be tried in the UK would be), to remove the provision in the Act allowing America to request extradition without evidence, and to stop all extraditions to the US until America ratified its side of the Treaty.

EDMs are of little practical use, other than as a survey of opinion. They sit on the books for months, and signatures can be added at any time. The signatures started to come in at a steady pace, and not just from the Tories and Lib Dems. There were eventually over fifty Labour signatories too.

It would be interesting that when, unusually, the exact motions as proposed in Boris' EDM were tabled as amendments to the Extradition Act several months later, almost none of the fifty two Labour MPs who had signed the EDM would vote for the amendments. History would repeat itself four years later in the case of Gary McKinnon, the computer hacker. In that case, no fewer than 59 Labour MPs who had signed an early day motion calling for a stop to his extradition then voted with the Government to prevent the rules being changed.

In November 2004, however, I was cock-a-hoop. Some of the other newspapers began to pick up on the issue. We posted Boris's article and a link to his EDM on the Friends Extradited website, and encouraged people to write to their MPs urging them to sign it. We were beginning to get some traction, I thought.

I got the usual Christmas card from my parents, wishing for the third successive year that the new year would bring an end to this nightmare. The difference this time was that my Mother was a changed person. Being a relatively insensitive sort, and coming from a family where soppiness and cuddles weren't ever high on the agenda, I tended not to think too much about what was out of sight, and it wasn't until we started getting engaged in the political fight that I realised how much pain and anxiety my Mother had been stoically carrying over the previous two years.

She had suffered terribly when the story first broke. Parents' love for their children tends to be unconditional, but the shame that the allegations visited on the family was felt most acutely by my parents, who are both of a generation where propriety was everything. Mother had mostly suffered in silence, I suppose because she saw that as her duty. She had longed for a way to be involved, and to help, but there was none. Until now.

The moment that we took on the political process was the moment that my Mother rediscovered her self-esteem. Seeing at first hand the rank injustice in Nicholas Evans' judgment, and being possessed of a steely determination that I had never previously seen, she set about the task with a vengeance. She wrote letters to everybody that she knew, explaining what was going on, and urging them to get involved. She wrote to her MP. She wrote to the Home Secretary. She wrote to the newspapers. She even wrote to the Prime Minister, and ultimately the Queen.

The campaign gave her a purpose, and she became totally dedicated to it. In a way, she and my father were like Margaret and Denis Thatcher. My Mother was the driving force, with my father in the background, playing golf, drinking beer and providing moral support.

My Mother gave me strength, and I think she found strength herself when she realised that all of her friends, and many others, were four square behind her.

JUDICIAL REVIEW
January 2005

January 2005 began much as 2004 had ended, with a lot of paper flying around. We had made our submissions to Home Secretary David Blunkett the previous November. The Act required that he make a decision within 42 days, but fate intervened in December 2004 and Blunkett was forced out of office over allegations of fast tracking a visa application for his girlfriend's nanny. His replacement was Charles Clarke, and there was some optimism that Clarke, not having been the author of the extradition Treaty, might take a somewhat more sympathetic view of the whole thing.

The campaign to flood the Home Office with correspondence was bearing quite some fruit. Boris Johnson had got the bit firmly between his teeth and was relentlessly pursuing Caroline Flint, who managed quite quickly to box herself into a corner. By now, Flint had begun to argue in their correspondence that of course forum was an issue, and that it was right that trials should take place where the witnesses and evidence were, rather than where the crime could be deemed to have been committed. Boris quickly seized on this change of tack, and asked, not unreasonably, where in the statute it indicated who should determine which was the appropriate forum, and on what basis?

In successive letters, Flint tied herself in knots before finally refusing to engage further on the issue, saying that the interpretation of the law was a matter for the courts.

Undeterred, Boris, wrote to Home Secretary Charles Clarke, but got back another non-reply from Flint. So he wrote again, and eventually was rewarded with a non-response from Clarke.

At this point, the responses to the public also changed tack to reflect the new "forum" position, quoting from Robert Wardle's letter about how the natural forum for the trial was Texas.

If pressed on specifics, they would say that they could not discuss the details of a case which was still before the courts and still awaiting the decision of the Home Secretary. But when it suited them, they would quote selectively from Evans judgment ("there is a case to answer") or Wardle's letter.

Meanwhile, we were still struggling to get the UK authorities to look at our case. After Wardle's letter, Mark Spragg had put together a huge pack and sent it to the Attorney General, Lord Goldsmith, asking if he would pull his finger out and order an investigation. It was an incredibly detailed submission.

Some two months later, we got a one paragraph reply from some minion in Goldsmith's office indicating that the great man saw no reason to "interfere in the statutory process". So according to Judge Evans, we were going to be extradited because no-one in the UK was interested in investigating, and according to Goldsmith no-one was going to be investigating because we were being extradited.

We had also asked each of our MPs to write to Wardle, pointing out some of the problems with his letter, including the factual inaccuracies and the total lack of consideration for any of the "defence" sides of the argument in determining what would be in the "interests of justice".

On 5th January 2005, Giles received a letter from his MP, Andrew Murrison, which enclosed a copy of Wardle's response. It was a cracker. Giles faxed it to me, and I nearly fell off my chair. Previously, Wardle had made one small error. This time, he had committed to a detailed explanation of his decision, and it was a litany of factual inaccuracies and consequently wholly false conclusions.

We convened a conference call, and Gary was adamant. We should challenge this in the courts. Alun Jones was keen, Mark was less so, citing the costs associated with bringing such an action. But the costs would be paid by the other side if we won, and we were quite sure we would win. How could we not? Wardle had got the reasoning for his decision completely, totally and utterly wrong.

Wardle had made four clear factual errors, all of which we have thoroughly refuted earlier in these pages—that the losers were both Enron and NatWest, that the evidence was in America, that "Fastow and Kopper are to be tried in the United States", and that "any investigation in this country would lead to further delay". As a public official, any "decision" is open to judicial review. This, in our view, clearly constituted a "decision", and seeing now how things were starting to stack up against us, we were in the mood to fight.

This time, the battle would be fought on our terms. It was clear that for whatever reason there was a concerted action by Government officials to ensure we were extradited. They were feeding off each other. All of these people were now the enemy.

During January we worked to put together the papers for the application to the High Court.

As part of the process, we wrote again to Fred Goodwin (now "Sir" after being knighted in June 2004 on Gordon Brown's recommendation for his services to banking). We asked just one thing of Sir Fred. Please take a position on whether the $1 million sale price for the SwapSub stake in March 2000 was fair or unfair. This was something which they would already have taken a position on internally. It was something that was independently assessable. It was not a big ask.

The response from Travers Smith a fortnight later said it all really.

"Acting on the advice of its US lawyers and in view of the status of the criminal proceedings against your clients in the US, our client believes that it would be inappropriate for it to respond substantively to your clients' requests".

Of course, it would be highly inappropriate for the supposed victim to have a public position on whether it was indeed a victim, as alleged.

Before battle commenced, we sat down with Melanie, and discussed our media strategy. We decided that we would selectively and thoroughly brief certain key journalists a day or so in advance of the filing, to get some feedback and ensure that our arguments were clear and accurate.

As part of this process, at the start of February Melanie set up a meeting at her offices with Andrew Gilligan, who was working at the Evening Standard after being forced out of his job at the BBC by the criticisms of Alistair Campbell for having accused the Government of "sexing up" its dossier on the Iraq War. This of course was the story that would lead to the death of the scientist David Kelly, and the disgraceful smear campaign launched against him posthumously by the Government.

Gary didn't make the meeting with Andrew Gilligan. As time went on, the media side of things fell more and more to Melanie and me. Gary had relocated to Brighton after being thrown out of his house the previous September, and so coming into London was not something he could do at the drop of a hat, whereas I was based every day in the West End, and so always available at short notice.

We spent an hour or so going through the issues. Gilligan described the idea of people suing the Serious Fraud Office for failing to investigate them as "quite jolly", but he seemed to understand the seriousness of what we were doing, and that this was not just a publicity stunt.

Over the next couple of months I would spend a lot of time talking to journalists who Melanie identified as key figures who wrote influential opinion pages. Patience Wheatcroft at the *The Times*. Joshua Rozenberg at the *Telegraph*. Nikki Tait at the FT. My philosophy was simple. If you give me time with these people, I think I can get them to focus on what's important here, which is the principle of bad law. The rules of engagement were that I would answer questions on any subject other than the facts of our case. Those should be the province of a court of law. It didn't seem unreasonable.

None of the initial meetings was straightforward. Joshua Rozenberg, the *Telegraph*'s legal correspondent, was the most interested in the legal principles. I first met him with Gary in London. I sensed that he was hugely cynical, and probably thought we were guilty as hell, but he was at least very engaged on the legal issues at stake.

Gary thought the meeting went really badly, because we hadn't sufficiently conveyed our sense of righteous indignation. Gary's view has always been that we were being hugely wronged, and that we should get that message across. My view was that no-one was interested in a 'poor me' story. Why waste time trying to get people to feel sorry for us? Concentrate on what's important. Bad law.

Joshua Rozenberg got it. Nikki Tait and Patience Wheatcroft were far harder nuts to crack. Both were extremely cynical and evidently found it difficult initially to get beyond their natural prejudices. By this I mean that as business journalists, they had covered the Enron stuff in detail, which at this point looked like one giant crime scene with the words "greed" and "venality" plastered all over it. We were in some way involved, so the likelihood was that we were part of the problem. They were quite obviously convinced that we were engaged in a campaign to deflect attention from our guilt.

Both came around. By the time we were extradited in July 2006, they were firmly in our court, not because they were taken in by my devilish charm, but because by then they had taken the trouble to look beyond the obvious prejudices and focus on the wider principles.

One journalist that I got to know quite well was Megan Murphy of Bloomberg, a friend of Melanie's who I met over a pizza and a glass of wine in the West End one lunchtime. An American with a law degree, she had embarked on a career with an eminent firm of US attorneys, only to give it up to pursue her love of legal journalism. As Bloomberg's courts' correspondent in London, she was in and out of the High Court every day. Her nationality and the legal issues at stake in our case gave her a heightened interest in the proceedings, and she and I would talk frequently over the next eighteen months.

On 14th February we served the papers on Wardle at his offices, and the story went live. The Evening Standard carried it prominently that day. All of the newspapers that we had briefed in advance rang Wardle's office to ask for a quote, and of course he had none to give, because the whole thing had come out of the blue.

The following day, the press coverage was excellent. Melanie had done a great job ensuring that she was available to answer any last minute questions that the journalists had, and they all got the story spot on. I was over the moon. The fight back begins here, I thought.

There were two great significances to the action. The first was that if we prevailed, Wardle would be forced to remake his decision, almost certainly following the guidelines handed down by the court. We were satisfied that any sensible decision on which forum to try our case would always fall in favour of the UK.

The second was that by bringing an action in the UK, we would be able to subpoena papers from the SFO, which would open other doors and might just enable us to get papers direct from RBS itself.

The response from the SFO came on 3rd March, seeking the dismissal of the claim. A 'permission' hearing was set for 7th April, where two High Court judges would decide whether or not we should be allowed a full hearing on the matter.

It would be my first ever visit to the Royal Courts of Justice. For any watcher of the television news, the façade is instantly recognisable. A huge, ornate, Gothic building built out of stone in 1882, which houses all of the Appeal Courts for both civil and criminal cases, and several other functions besides.

Stepping inside the courts was like walking into a vast Cathedral. An immense galleried hall, stone floored and replete with statues along side walls, a testament to the skills of the old stonemasons.

The sheer size of the space, and the arched roof some sixty or so feet above meant that the chamber echoed with the sound of footsteps and voices. Only two concessions to modernity were evident. Electric lighting and airport-style walk-through metal detectors and x-ray machines.

Our hearing was to be in one of the first floor courts, in front of Lord Justice Laws and Mr Justice Ouseley. Alun had seemed a little concerned when we had first been told their names. I wondered whether he had some difficult history with either of them, but if so he wasn't saying.

Of one thing there was no doubt, though. According to both Alun and James Hines, these two were among the finest legal minds in the country. Laws LJ was a possible contender for elevation to the Law Lords, and Ouseley, much the younger, was tipped for future greatness. If they approved our application and granted the judicial review, it was a racing certainty that they would also hear the extradition appeal. This was the 'A' Team.

Walking into the courtroom, I was again struck by the size of the space. It was about fifty or sixty feet square, with a double height ceiling and ornate wooden carvings on the wood paneled walls. On three sides of the court were tiered rows of what could have been church pews.

The pews to the rear of the court were evidently for the public, and those to the left and right seemed to be earmarked for the press. The legal teams occupied the front benches of the public section, and the court officials sat in the well of the room underneath the vast, almost altar-like judges' bench at which were two large thrones.

As this was not a criminal hearing, we sat with our families and friends in the public gallery, bystanders rather than participants in our own pro-

ceedings. I cast my eye around the press benches and saw a number of
familiar faces. All of the key journalists were in the High Court, along with
many more that I did not recognise. Whichever way this hearing went, it
was going to be well reported.

As we waited for the judges to come in, I surveyed the opposition.
David Perry, QC, was instructed by the Treasury Solicitor's Office, acting
for the Director of the Serious Fraud Office. Perry looked about mid-for-
ties, and had a 'solid' air about him, I thought. Neither good nor bad looking. Neither overweight nor under. Just solid.

The hearing would involve oral argument, where both sides made their
case as to why the judicial review should or should not be granted, and
then the judges would make up their minds. It would all be over in a few
hours. If we prevailed, the judges would set a date some months in the
future for the full hearing. It would almost certainly be at the same time as
the extradition appeal.

It was obvious from the moment that they walked through the door
which judge was which, their identical robes and wigs notwithstanding.
Lord Justice Laws was a short, rather overweight man with a ruddy face
that I thought rather resembled a bulldog chewing a wasp. Had it not been
for his thick, square framed spectacles, he would have been the absolute
caricature of a Dickensian lawman, whose morning would have consisted
largely of condemning pickpockets and assorted ne'erdowells to be
hanged before retiring for an extremely long lunch.

Mr Justice Ouseley must have been five or ten years younger, I guessed,
and had an owlish, intellectual look about him. Both wore long red robes,
tied at the waist with a purple sash, and a stiff white collar. Their wigs were
short rather than the long, flowing ones which for some reason I had
expected.

All of the barristers were also bewigged. The scene in this courtroom
could not have changed much in a couple of centuries, I thought.

As the plaintiffs in the case, we went first.

We put forward three main lines of argument; Robert Wardle had mis-
directed himself in his decision not to investigate us, because he had made
substantial errors of fact in coming to his decision. Second, he had acted
unreasonably in his decision-making. And thirdly, he had a duty under the

Human Rights Act to consider the appropriate forum for our case, since any logical analysis would show that it was very much a UK matter, and that therefore he should be obliged to investigate us, since a likely consequence of his failure to do so would be our extradition.

David Perry, for the SFO, gave a solid but unspectacular set of arguments as to why none of our reasoning was correct, then the judges retired to consider their response.

The consensus in the corridor outside the court was that we had done as well as we could have done. Our wait was mercifully brief, and we all filed back in less than thirty minutes after the judges had retired.

Laws LJ did the talking. Or more accurately reading. In a scene reminiscent of Judge Nicholas Evans the previous October, he began to read from a folio of typed sheets. It was soon evident that we were going to be there some time, and that this document had been written before we had ever set foot in the court that morning. Had the oral arguments been a charade?

The first ten minutes or so were scene-setting, and I kept looking at Alun and James for any sign as to whether it was going well or badly. Eventually I managed to catch James's eye, and he gave me a half-smile and an almost imperceptible nod. He thought we had won.

Within another minute, he was proved right. On one line of argument after another, Laws LJ ruled that we had points sufficiently strong as to be arguable at a full hearing. I was almost beside myself with happiness. When Laws LJ finally looked up from his papers, I wanted to jump up and scream "yes!!!!"

Laws LJ, as anticipated, indicated that the hearing should take place alongside the extradition appeal. Since the Home Secretary still hadn't ruled on our extradition yet, it was not possible to set a date for such an appeal. Consequently, there would be a status hearing in three months' time. By then, hopefully, it would be possible to set a date for both the extradition appeal and the judicial review.

Drinks in the pub across the road were a lively affair. We now had two bites at the cherry. If we won the Judicial Review, Wardle would be forced to investigate our case in the UK, which would either result in him deciding that there was no case to answer, or that there was a case and it belonged in the UK. Either result would do us just fine. Although the former would not in itself stop our extradition, it would reveal just how totally idiotic the whole new Act was, and force someone to intervene at that point.

Even if we lost the Judicial Review, however, we might still win the extradition appeal, and the mere exercise of going through the review would inevitably have a subtle influence on the judges' decision in the extradition appeal. Because even though the issues were meant to be separate, human beings—even High Court judges—find it extremely difficult to ignore information once it is out there.

The press loved it. I would say that this was a real turning point in our journey. No longer would people be able to claim that this was a cheap publicity stunt. We were serious, and the High Court had agreed that on the face of it there seemed to be a big hole in the law.

We did a series of interviews on the national radio stations. Commentators described the situation variously as Orwellian and Kafkaesque, both of which suited me just fine.

The US Government immediately asked permission to be joined as 'interested parties' in the case, which was duly granted. It was also suggested that both the Home Secretary and Attorney General had a dog in the fight, and so should also be invited to make representations. As interested parties, each would be able to submit evidence and make oral argument. Our list of adversaries had grown from one man to three separate divisions of Her Majesty's Government, and the American Government to boot. All would be represented by counsel. It was going to be crowded in the lawyers' benches.

The US instructed Rosie Fernandez of the Crown Prosecution Service who submitted a lengthy affidavit explaining why it was so important that the case be tried in Texas rather than the UK.

It was going to be the most spectacular own goal, I thought. There wasn't a single point that she made that we weren't going to be able to turn on its head and use against her clients. This was going to be fantastic. A bloodbath. I couldn't wait.

Home Secretary Charles Clarke finally ignored all of our arguments on specialty, and in May 2005 he ordered our extradition. Only now did the law allow us to formally lodge an appeal of the extradition, which we duly did. The date for that appeal would now be set by Laws and Ouselely at the directions hearing on 7th July.

THE EUROJUST CONSPIRACY
7th July 2005

On the day of the hearing, Laws LJ and Ouseley J decided that our Judicial Review should be heard over two days in mid-November, and the extradition appeal a fortnight later. Discovery would begin immediately in the Judicial Review, meaning that the SFO would now be required to send us all of their papers on the subject. Mark Spragg, Alun Jones and I emerged into the sunlight outside the High Court, pleased with the outcome, and then stood for ten minutes waiting for a taxi to appear. None did.

Mark rang his office to find out that news was breaking of multiple bombs on the tube network. London was in chaos. All public transport had been shut down. Alun decided to walk back to his chambers, which were only half a mile or so. Mark and I opted for a pub with a television, to find out what was going on.

Days like that put one's own troubles into perspective. Fifty six people died, including four suicide bombers, and nearly seven hundred more were injured. Having passed through Edgware Road tube station not five minutes before one of the bombs exploded there, the random chance of the carnage was not lost on me. So many people headed off to work that day and never came home.

Tony Blair would waste little time in using the incident to accelerate his wholescale assault on our civil liberties, saying that the 'rules of the game have changed'.

Terrorist outrages notwithstanding, though, the summer of 2005 was one of mostly good cheer. I was thoroughly enjoying my work, and self employment meant that Emma could always rely on me being available in case of unforeseen circumstance. As a family, we had perhaps never been happier. The sword of Damocles was still hanging over us, but after three years it was now hanging around in the background rather than dominating our lives on a daily basis.

We holidayed in Cornwall, as had become our custom over the past couple of years because we feared arrest if we set foot outside the coun try, and whilst the weather wasn't exactly Mediterranean, it was still a wonderful place to be.

I was spending a lot of time with Mark, Alun and James, both professionally and socially. Mark and I would have lunch at the Chopper Lump in Hanover Square once or twice a week, and the four of us would frequently have a drink after work in Vats Wine Bar on Lambs Conduit Street, a well-known watering hole for the legal profession.

There was a feeling that things were moving inexorably in our direction.

The letter writing campaign continued to bear fruit. The Home Office eventually stopped peddling the falsehoods about Ireland and France, and switched tack to arguing about natural forum, which played directly into our hands. The issue was very straightforward. In a case which could be tried in more than one country, who should decide which would be the better venue, and according to which guidelines?

This, at its heart, was the root of our judicial review.

Luckily for us, the Home Office civil servants seemed quite keen to engage on the issue, and we started to see letters from them and from Caroline Flint which acknowledged that there would be cases which could be dealt with in more than one country, and where decisions would need to be made as to which was the most appropriate.

Perfect. They were acknowledging that there was an issue. So who should be making the decision, and on what criteria? It should be for the prosecutors, they said, not the courts.

Okay, so where are the rules dictating who will make the decisions, and what to take into account?

Answer came there none. Yes, we know there's an issue, but we plan to do nothing to fix it.

Well, not quite. We didn't know it at the time, but the Home Office and the Attorney General were engaged in some behind the scenes juggling on this rather thorny issue. From as early as 2002, the Home Office had been corresponding with the European Union on the subject of Conflicts in Jurisdiction on Criminal Matters. The EU was keen to foster international co-operation in criminal cases, and to this end they had set up a body with the mildly Orwellian name of Eurojust, based in Brussels, to which the

UK contributed both funding and personnel. Indeed, in 2005 the top job at Eurojust was held by a British citizen. Eurojust recognised the complexities associated with modern crime, where in increasing numbers of cases more than one country might have a claim to prosecute. They were keen to establish an international framework for deciding where the trial ought to be held.

In furtherance of this rather worthy aim, Eurojust had published in its 2003 Annual Report a set of guidelines as to which jurisdiction should prosecute. James Hines had found a copy of these, and they could have been written specifically with us in mind. Underpinning the guidelines was the principle of 'territoriality', that a crime should ideally be tried where the majority of the conduct took place, or where victim was situated.

The guidelines set out a large number of factors to be taken into consideration. Location of alleged perpetrators. Location of victim. Location of witnesses. Location of evidence. The needs of the defendant in preparing a defence should be given the same weight as those of the prosecutors, they said.

This document was surely our salvation. An internationally recognised set of guidelines which, if applied to our case, would ensure that any prosecution would take place in the UK. But what was the UK Government's view? Well, none at all, seemingly.

In October 2004, the Commons Select Committee on the European Union had written to Caroline Flint on two occasions, asking for the view of the Home Office on these guidelines. Flint never responded. When she was replaced as Minister for Extradition by Andy Burnham in June 2005, the Committee wrote to him, asking him to give the matter his attention He too failed to answer.

Correspondence from the Home Office dating back to 2002 made it clear that the position of Her Majesty's Government was that territoriality was the key, but by mid-2005, this stance had obviously become politically inconvenient. Although our case was taking most of the headlines on the issue, there were several other notable cases of extradition requests from the US in which the issue of forum would be live. Neither Baba Ahmad nor Gary McKinnon had set foot in the US when supposedly committing their crimes, and in both cases the Metropolitan Police had investigated and decided not to bring charges.

In August 2005, Khawar Qureshi, the barrister for the Home Office, submitted a legal note in the judicial review case, suggesting that the concept of 'forum non conveniens', or natural forum, had no place in a criminal context, and was in fact a strictly civil law concept.

But in a letter dated 31 July 2005 to the Commons Select Committee, Qureshi's own client, Andy Burnham, had been fulsome in his praise of the Eurojust Guidelines. This letter did not come to light until much later; a copy of it was forwarded to me directly by the clerk of the committee in January 2006. He informed me that it had not been received in July 2005, but sent to him just a day previously by the Home Office. Much too late to use as evidence in our judicial review proceedings. How very convenient for the Government. Tell Parliament one thing, and the courts the opposite, and misfile the evidence. It would not be the last time.

DISCOVERY
September 2005

The High Court judges had set a timetable of events for the months prior to the judicial review and extradition appeal. As part of the process, each side was ordered to make discovery of all evidence that was pertinent to the case. In the judicial review, this meant that the Serious Fraud Office had to give us all the documents that they had on their files.

Supposedly.

The package, when it arrived, consisted of several pages of files from the City of London police, including interview notes and internal memoranda, and some internal SFO file notes. There was not much of any significance, but the files referred to correspondence between the SFO and the FSA. This correspondence was missing.

So we asked the SFO to produce it.

No, they said. The FSA apparently objected to its disclosure, claiming 'public interest immunity'. Excellent. The High Court was going to decide whether or not the Director of the SFO had erred in his decision making, but would not be allowed to see the documentary evidence that surrounded that decision making.

Fate conspired to give us a gift, however, in the shape of Margaret Cole. She had been a partner at White & Case when we were helping the Royal Bank of Canada in their civil case against Rabobank. In July 2005, she took up a new position as Head of Enforcement at the FSA.

We decided to test a friendship. Mark Spragg wrote to Margaret, asking her to intervene for us with her colleagues. We fully expected her to rebuff our advances; people in high places will often actively discriminate against former friends or associates, for fear otherwise of being accused of favouritism.

Sure enough, we received a very charming response from Margaret, pointing out that in the circumstances she was conflicted, and thus unable to help. She did, however, say that she had asked one of her colleagues to look into the matter.

To our great surprise, a week or so later, we got a letter from the FSA saying that it had resolved its difficulties, and was happy for the SFO to disclose the relevant correspondence and some file notes, albeit with some redactions. The papers duly arrived a few days later. I am quite sure that she would deny it if asked, but equally sure that Margaret Cole had a word in the right ear.

The critical document was a letter from the FSA to a Tricia Howse at the SFO dated 13th June 2002. It was quite obvious why neither the FSA nor the SFO had wanted it made public. Written by Tim Crump of the FSA's Enforcement division only two weeks before we were charged, it referred to a presentation made by the FBI and Enron Task Force to the SFO at their offices on 12th June. Now Robert Wardle, the Director of the SFO, had clearly implied in his witness statement that the SFO had had no involvement in our case before the charges were filed. Tim Crump's letter unequivocally proved the opposite—there was no way to misinterpret it. The verbatim text is as follows:

"Dear Ms Howse. I refer to your recent telephone conversation with Ken O'Donnell in relation to the activities of Messrs Darby, Mulgrew and Bermingham as disclosed to you at a presentation by the FBI on 12 June 2002."

The letter consisted of a 'handover' by the FSA to the SFO of all the FSA material pertinent to our case, and contained a redacted paragraph. It referred to all the papers that had been sent by the FSA to the SEC in March 2002, and appended a four page summary of the FSA's conclusions following their enquiries into the transaction. The summary also contained redactions, as did two interview notes from the City of London police.

If my spirits had been high before, they were sky high now. The Director of the SFO had surely been caught red-handed, and to add insult to injury the authorities were censoring our discovery. Marvellous.

Melanie could hardly contain her glee. Mark immediately pointed out the inconsistency to the SFO, and asked for the missing file notes relating to the FBI presentation on 12th June. Who was there from each side, and what was said? And could we please have unredacted versions of all the documents that they had sent us?

A week or so later, we got our response. There were no file notes.

There had been no such presentation. Ms Howse was travelling in the Cameroon, and was uncontactable, and no, we couldn't have unredacted versions of the papers, as the redactions were there at the behest of the FSA.

That's how it works. As a Member of Parliament or a civil servant, you have licence to say much as you want, and to keep saying it until you are caught out publicly and red-handed, at which point you apologise unreservedly for the unintentional misunderstanding, and if possible blame some junior faceless functionary. Rarely if ever will you have to face any adverse consequences.

Faced with this obstacle, we told the SFO that we were going to ask the court to order the production of the unredacted documents. We then wrote to Rosie Fernandez of the Crown Prosecution Service, who was representing the US as interested party in the hearing, and asked for a copy of the presentation that the FBI had given to the SFO on 12th June, together with the identities of the people involved. One way or another, we figured, the truth would out.

The response from the CPS was almost instantaneous. They filed a request with the court for their client, the US Government, to be removed from the case as an interested party, saying that they could be of 'no further assistance' to the court, but asking that Rosie Fernandez's witness statement arguing why the US was the best jurisdiction for the case should remain as part of the case papers.

It was history repeating itself. Although he must have known that the new Extradition Act had no provisions for discussing evidence, Thomas Hanusik had gone ahead in late 2003 and stuffed the extradition request full of inflammatory affidavit material which we couldn't contest. And now, two years on, the US had persuaded the eager beavers at the Crown Prosecution Service to write a load of tosh about natural forum, none of which would have stood up under cross-examination, which would now lie on the file unchallenged because they were withdrawing as an interested party. And their withdrawal meant they could now ignore our request for documents, which is exactly what they did.

Why is this such a big deal? Well, it's simple really. What we are ninety nine percent sure is what happened, but which the SFO's evasions and the

US Government's refusal to engage prevented us from proving, is that on 12th June 2002 the Enron Task Force arrived in London and told the UK prosecuting authorities to get out of their way.

Subsequently, they conducted interviews with several members of Natwest/RBS in London, at least one of whom was sufficiently intimidated by them ultimately to take his own life. They trampled all over the UK authorities' jurisdiction, sharing little or no information, and then flew back to Washington to compile an Alice in Wonderland tale accusing three bankers of conspiring to rob their own bank in London. Oh yes, and despite being in London conducting interviews, they never bothered to interview the three people who were the subject of their enquiry, who had all volunteered their unconditional assistance to any investigation some six months previously, and whose very own documents, produced to the FSA and forwarded to the SEC, were now being used against them.

Imagine if you will the roles being reversed. Some members of the SFO fly into Washington. They meet with the SEC and the FBI, and tell them that they are planning to interview several senior US bankers in connection with a major fraud, and they don't expect either the SEC or the FBI to be involved. Can you imagine how that conversation might go?

Now, it's possible of course that the SFO didn't just roll over, but did the right thing and insisted on accompanying the FBI to their interviews. But if that's the case, then that would mean that Wardle was wrong when he said his department wasn't in any way involved in the investigation into our case. So take your pick.

On 6th October, we convened at the High Court for the hearing to decide whether the SFO would be required to produce the unredacted versions of the documents. About ten minutes before the hearing was due to begin, we were all milling about in the corridor outside the courtroom. All of the barristers were there, including John Hardy for the US Government, waiting to find out whether his client was to be allowed to walk away from the proceedings as they had requested. He looked extremely agitated.

I had thoroughly disliked John Hardy at the magistrates' hearing the year before, but the passage of time had given me cause to reflect on his professionalism, and I didn't think he bore any personal animus towards us. He was doing his job as an advocate to the best of his abilities, and he had to trust what his client was telling him. We knew it to be lies and fabrication, but you could hardly blame John Hardy for that.

I wondered whether the honourable man in John Hardy suspected that the SFO and the US Government were engaged in what I believed could even amount to a conspiracy to pervert the course of justice. He had seen the correspondence. There can surely have been no doubt in his mind that the Enron Task Force had come to town in June 2002, and had made a presentation to the SFO. The SFO was now denying this, his client was refusing to answer questions on the matter, and was now seeking to extricate itself from the judicial review, meaning that no further information could be compelled from them. I reckoned it would be enough to make anyone look agitated.

All of a sudden, there was a flurry of activity. Someone from the Treasury Solicitors' office approached Mark Spragg and handed him a wad of papers. They were the unredacted versions of most of the documents that we had asked for.

Mark handed the papers to me, knowing that of all of us I would be able to spot the bits of clear text that had previously been redacted in the shortest time. I went straight for the FSA letter of 13th June, and the summary of the FSA's conclusions, which was attached to that letter. My audible reaction when I got to the latter echoed around the stone corridors, and must have turned every head.

"Fucking hell!!"

I could not believe what I was reading. As the team gathered round, I pointed to the last page and a half of the FSA summary, which had been sent to the SEC in March 2002. Most of the previously redacted bits related to the FSA's interaction with RBS after we had met with them in November 2001.

The FSA, it turned out, had asked RBS to go back and do a thorough review of all transactions to do with LJM and Swap Sub, from the original set up of the deal in June 1999 through to the sale of the Swap Sub interest in March 2000.

RBS had reported back to the FSA that it had examined all of the transactions in detail, that everyone had followed all internal procedures correctly, and that in the case of the valuation of the Swap Sub asset, $1m was seemingly an objectively fair price. They had re-run all of the option valuations from the time, and had come up with a number that was pretty much the same as the valuation that I had done at Giles' request, and which was sitting on the files.

In plain English, the Swap Sub asset had been properly disposed of, following the correct procedures, at a fair price.

There was no fraud on NatWest.

In fact, even the FSA said as much. Reflecting the fact that we had failed to report our investment to GNW, about which we had been perfectly candid in our meeting, the FSA concluded that there was prima facie evidence of a major conflict of interest, but that this alone would not be something on which they would take any action. The summary finished by stating that it was possible that the $7.3 million that we had made from the investment was indeed the proceeds of a fraud, but that any such fraud would have taken place in the US, in other words against Enron. Just as we had reported to them.

It's almost comical when you think about it. The three of us had gone forward to the FSA to report out suspicions of a fraud on Enron. The FSA had conducted its enquiries and come to exactly the same conclusion. And RBS, quite independently, had formed the same view. In the interim, the Powers Report had reinforced this possibility by concluding that the Swap Sub asset, for which Enron was to pay Fastow $30 million, was indeed worthless.

There were in fact only a handful of people on the planet who believed that Natwest could possibly have been defrauded, and all of them worked for the Enron Task Force. But in the US criminal justice system, that belief was sufficient. The facts and the evidence, where inconvenient, were to be ignored, destroyed or buried, and in any event, they had no place in proceedings under the Extradition Act 2003.

The unredacted version of one of the police file notes memorialised a conversation with a member of the FSA who suggested that the Department of Justice had bigger fish to fry, and speculated that the FBI were probably aiming to use the three of us to prosecute the Enron people.

Seemingly, the UK authorities had no issue with this.

It seems crazy, but the discovery of this stunning set of facts could potentially hurt us rather than help us. We now had was strong evidence to support what we had always contended, that there was no way that Natwest had been defrauded. NatWest didn't even think it had been defrauded. That should really have been that. Pack up the tents and go home. In the Alice in Wonderland world into which we had now stumbled, however, it was not quite that simple.

Ignoring for a moment the obvious fact that we were convinced that the SFO were dissembling about the FBI presentation in June 2002, the opinion of both the FSA and RBS that there was no UK fraud would, bizarrely, support the decision of the SFO that proceedings in the UK were unreasonable. They could argue that there seemed to be no evidence of a UK crime. If the US chose to take a different view, that was up to them, wasn't it?

Here, in a perfect nutshell, was the lunacy of the Extradition Act. We could be extradited because no-one in the UK thought that a crime had been committed. No other country would extradite in these circumstances—even Ireland will refuse when it seems clear that there is no crime.

The evidence that no-one here believed there was a crime would likely result in us losing the judicial review without helping in the fight against extradition. The Act gave us no platform to discuss evidence or introduce any evidence of our own. Evidence one way or another was simply irrelevant. Allegations were all that counted.

In years to come, Government Minister after Government Minister would get to the despatch box and say how our case had been thoroughly examined in the courts, and how we were found to have had a case to answer, and how we would certainly have been extradited under the old regime anyway. All rubbish. Bad law makes for injustice.

ALICE IN WONDERLAND
14th November 2005

And so it was that we found ourselves in the High Court on 14th November 2005, setting out our arguments as to why Mr Wardle should be forced by the court to remake his decision, and to do so based on the correct facts, and using the right balancing act. All logic and common sense was with us. The law, such as it was, was wholly against.

For Gary, Giles and me, the frustrations with process and legal nicety were agony. The SFO had stood by and allowed agents of a foreign Government to tread all over their turf. Then they prevaricated and dissembled to prevent their role in the whole affair coming to light. But in law, all of this was irrelevant.

One of the originally redacted documents was a file note from the City of London Police, memorialising a conversation with Tim Crump from the FSA who had opined that he thought we were being used to get to the bigger fish. Another police file note referred to the involvement of Tricia Howse at the SFO. Ms Howse, on her eventual return from the Cameroon, would indicate that she had no recollection of this or any presentation from the FBI. Most convenient.

In subsequent correspondence with the FSA in the weeks leading up to the Judicial Review, we had established that the FBI had indeed visited them on 12th June 2002, but it was a courtesy call only and they had indicated that they were on their way to the SFO. The FBI had given no inkling that they were considering charges against us, and the first the FSA had known of the charges was when they were filed and posted on the internet. This is the standard US version of Mutual Legal Assistance. Britain bends over. The Americans shove something large up our backside.

But for all our anger at what was so clearly happening, Alun Jones was determined to play it by the book. He did not believe that Laws LJ would have any truck with wild accusations and histrionics. So he pulled all his punches.

Personally, I would have hauled Wardle and Howse into court, put them under oath and asked them in front of the judges and the world's press what in fact had happened. Perhaps there was a perfectly innocent explanation.

But we didn't. We played by the book because hey, we're British and we need to maintain a sense of decorum. Gary was sitting next to me in the courtroom, and he had a lined pad open in front of him. Every ten minutes, he would draw a line, graphing our performance. The graph started downwards, and with the odd hopeful blip continued on that trajectory throughout the day. Alun's arguments were worthy indeed, and meticulously put, but our challenge was effectively to create a legal duty where no statutory scheme existed, and that was a tough ask. The 'equity' of our arguments was really neither here nor there.

That first night, I got howling drunk and ended up venting my spleen at the total unfairness of it all. Emma's father Brian took quite a lot of the brunt of it because he is a judge, and so by extrapolation all of the inequities of the system and our situation must have been his fault.

Gary would have been proud of me. Being a very emotional person himself, he always accuses me of bottling up my emotions. He's all for public displays of angst. I'm not. I get angry with the best of them in private, but generally I can keep my other emotions to myself.

When it was over, I apologised to Brian and went to bed. Perhaps the next day would be kinder.

It wasn't.

We got to listen to David Perry QC defend the indefensible for the SFO. The nub of his argument was that there was no duty in law for him to investigate, and that if he chose not to do so, this could not possibly breach our human rights, notwithstanding that it must have been plain to him that the consequence of his refusal was that we would be extradited. It was a predictably solid performance.

Next up was Hugo Keith on behalf of Lord Goldsmith, the Attorney General, who was on a mission, seemingly, to cook our goose not just in the judicial review proceedings but in the extradition appeal as well.

Keith's performance will live with me to my dying day. He wanted to nail the issue of natural forum once and for all. It was a masterclass in double standards. He told their Lordships that the desirability of honouring our international extradition treaties should almost always trump the rights of the individual.

The concept was breathtaking in its arrogance. When selling the new Act to Parliament, Baroness Scotland, Caroline Flint and other Home Office ministers had gone to great lengths to trumpet the 'robust' protections for individuals in the new human rights bar to extradition. 'Solid safeguards for UK citizens', as the Ministers had said.

And now, in the very first public test of that very same law, the Attorney General was arguing that these 'robust' protections should in fact apply only in the 'most exceptional' circumstances.

OVERSIGHT
22nd November 2005

If my regard for politicians and their attorneys was low after the judicial review hearing, it was about to plumb new depths. Sandwiched neatly in the fortnight between the judicial review and our extradition appeal was an open hearing of the House of Commons Home Affairs Select Committee. At extremely short notice, they had decided to take evidence on the US-UK Extradition Treaty, and had called several witnesses to appear before them on 22nd November 2005, one of whom was Andy Burnham, Minister for Extradition.

I'm not sure what had prompted this little demonstration of democratic accountability. Most likely it was the number of Parliamentary Questions about the Treaty, in the light not only of our case, but the growing number of others that were following us.

There were two distinct issues, and over the years the Government would quite skillfully dance between them, confusing MPs and journalists alike. The first was that the Treaty itself was non-reciprocal, in favour of the US. The second was that notwithstanding this evident bias in their favour, the US Senate had yet to ratify the Treaty. And they had no significant incentive to do so when they could already avail themselves of most of its advantages through the Extradition Act.

Back in December 2003, Baroness Scotland had told the House of Lords that she expected the US to ratify the Treaty in the near future, and that no problems were expected. In the absence of any evidence to the contrary, I shall give her the benefit of the doubt and assume she was merely misinformed. Even the slimmest understanding as to how Treaties are ratified in the US should have given her pause for thought, and the fact that the 1972 Treaty between the two countries had taken the US until 1976 to ratify should have been a decent indicator that these things are not simply a rubber stamp over there.

There are many things to criticise about US politicians. But they are pretty damned good at protecting the interests of American citizens against those of foreign powers. All International treaties are fully scrutinised before being passed into law, a process which can be extremely lengthy and often results in substantial amendments along the way. And in the case of the US-UK treaty, as we mentioned earlier, there was particularly strong opposition from supporters of the old on-the-run IRA terrorists.

The issue of non-ratification, therefore, became a highly emotive one, and ultimately the Government used it rather skillfully to deflect attention from the far greater error that they had made, in negotiating a totally non-reciprocal arrangement in the first place. This lack of reciprocity was openly acknowledged by both Flint and Scotland in December 2003, but when we began to make some traction with it in our letter-writing campaign, they changed tack and began to argue that in fact there was no imbalance in favour of the UK. The new Treaty, they said, actually provided as close to equality as the two legal systems could manage, unlike its predecessor, which they claimed was actually biased in favour of the UK.

Having been alerted to the Select Committee meeting, therefore, I was determined not to waste the opportunity. The committee were to take evidence from Sally Ireland of the human rights group Justice, from Timothy Workman, the senior extradition magistrate at Bow Street, and from Andy Burnham, the shiny new Extradition Minister.

Mark Spragg, Melanie and I spent a couple of days putting together a short but comprehensive briefing paper, and then sent copies to every single member of the Committee and to Sally Ireland. By convention, representation in Committees tends to be roughly proportionate to the size of the parties in Parliament, so the Home Affairs Select Committee had a Labour majority, but we were nonetheless hopeful that we could make some headway.

The brief was divided into an explanatory section, and a section suggesting key questions for the Minister. We highlighted the problems with the Treaty. We explained the issues on ratification. We pointed out that the US now had no incentive to ratify. We pointed out the problems with natural forum.

On the day, I travelled to the Palace of Westminster to sit and listen. It was to be my first ever glimpse of the workings of Parliament.

I had no sooner sat down in the public section of the committee room than in walked Detective Sergeant Gary Flood of the Extradition Squad. He grinned and came over to sit next to me.

"Well" he said, "you've been causing a bit of a stir, haven't you?"

"Well you didn't just expect us to bend over and take it up the arse did you Gary?"

"No, I suppose not".

The Chairman called the meeting to order, and called District Judge Timothy Workman as the first witness.

Workman was the most senior magistrate at Bow Street, and consequently was at the cutting edge of administering Blair's new law. As he took his seat, I noticed that a number of the MPs around the table had our brief in front of them, and one or two of them were turning the pages of the document. I felt chuffed. Information is power.

Judge Workman was, well, workmanlike. He was extremely measured in his testimony. The Committee really wanted his views on how well the new system was working. Relatively well, apparently. Better than the old regime? Well, they were different. All fairly straight bat stuff. But then, out of the blue, the Conservative MP Nick Herbert asked one of our planted questions. What about the case of Lotfi Raissi, the Algerian born man accused of training the 9/11 pilots? They were asking the right man, because it was Workman who had presided over the case and dismissed it.

He was clear. Raissi had not been extradited because under the old Act, the US was required to support its requests with evidence, and had been unable to do so. Under the new law, he thought he would have been powerless to prevent Raissi's extradition on at least one of the counts.

Bingo! From the horse's mouth.

Sally Ireland, following Judge Workman, gave a very solid if dispassionate set of arguments as to why Justice had concerns over the operation of the Treaty.

Last to the table was Andy Burnham. He arrived only a minute or so before his appointed time, and so did not have the benefit of listening to the other witnesses.

I was struck by how young he looked. He was younger than me, in fact, yet he was a Minister of State. He has rather extraordinary eye-lashes that make him look as if he is permanently wearing eye-liner, and comes across as just, well, a bit pretty really. And he had that incredibly annoying 'I'm just a man of the people' air about him which had become a feature of so many Government Ministers under New Labour.

Burnham, like Flint before him, had a script and was determined to stick to it.

No, he wouldn't be giving draft copies of the Treaty to the Committee so that they could trace its development. This would be a breach of our undertakings of commerciality to our treaty partners. Of course, the interests of the Americans must take priority over those of Parliament and the British Public. I laughed to myself. I could just see the Senate Foreign Relations Committee's response to that little one if the boot had been on the other foot.

Burnham was shocked and angered by all the misleading press there had been on the subject of the Treaty. Of course it wasn't non-reciprocal. That was a scurrilous rumour. The Treaty was actually of great value to Britain. The old Treaty had produced an average time of nearly 30 months to extradite someone, whereas under the new arrangements this was down to 7 months, and that was surely good for justice.

This was true, in its most limited sense, but utterly disingenuous and misleading. Burnham was implying that if the US had to provide evidence in support of its requests, the process would be hugely delayed. This was quite simply wrong. The Act provided a timetable that was the same whether a country was required to produce evidence or not.

I had come very late to an interest in politics, but seeing it in the flesh, close up, gave me a sense of outrage that I had not previously thought possible. It was a bit like being in the High Court the previous week. You're there, but you're not there. The theatre plays out in front of you, and even though it's all about you, you are allowed no role in it. The characters stroll on and say whatever they see fit, and then go off to the bar, or home to their wives, or back to the office, and think nothing more of it. All in a day's work.

Burnham wasn't quite finished, though. He needed to add arrogance to the mountain of misleading guff. He was given the opportunity when asked about the Raissi case. It was put to him that Judge Workman had testified that he would have had little choice but to extradite under the new Act. Burnham disagreed. Workman must have been mistaken. He was only a judge after all. Burnham was a Minister of State.

Gary Flood had not stayed to the end, and Sally Ireland had left after her testimony, so I had no-one at whom to vent my spleen.

Mark Spragg wrote to the Committee members, pointing out all the inaccuracies and misleading statements in Burnham's testimony, but I knew that it would make no difference. This was never about determining whether the Treaty should be renegotiated. It was about going through the motions so that the Government could always say that Parliament had examined all the issues.

EXTRADITION APPEAL
December 2005

The following week we all reconvened at the High Court for our second bite at the cherry. The hearing was well trailed in the papers, and by now we were starting to get leading articles published. The case had migrated from the business section to the main pages, and we were making good inroads with public opinion.

I had done a number of interviews for radio, and one or two for television. Many of these interviews were hard going, but little by little we started to win the argument.

Our life was made much easier because the Home Office consistently refused to field anyone for the shows, and would inevitably provide a proforma statement saying that the extradition arrangements were fair, and not much more. It just looked terrible for them, and as my confidence grew with practice, I never missed the opportunity to stick the knife in about Government accountability.

Melanie taught me that media these days is about soundbites, and so I would always try to condense our major arguments into short, very quote-friendly pieces. One of the first of these, which resonated very well, was that the first duty of any Government is the protection of its own citizens. It happens to be a fundamental belief of mine, but it was also a good lead in to describing how no other nation on the planet had come close to giving up its own citizens' rights in the way that Blair, Blunkett and Co had. Part of me was aching for the Home Office to respond with the old chestnut of Ireland and France, so that I could pronounce them liars in a public broadcast.

Slowly but surely, almost all of the national press was falling in behind our arguments. Melanie, Mark and I made it a point of principle that there was no-one with whom we would not engage, and we worked hard at persuading the journalists and opinion formers of the merits of our case. I'm a great believer in the power of argument. You should always be prepared to tell people what you think, and why. Not to do so is cowardice, and above all an insult to people. In our case, the Home Office approach was Diktat. 'It's right because I say it is'. A few years earlier the press might have bought that, but after being sold hook, line and sinker on the Iraq War, they were starting to bite back. The days of the Government's free ride were well and truly over.

I was perplexed by the attitude of *The Times*, however. In more than one leader article, they came down in favour of our arguments, but took a side swipe at our modus operandi. I was intrigued as to how they thought we should have gone about it. Perhaps one day I'll find out. I was relaxed about people assuming we were guilty. I'm sure I'd have thought exactly the same thing if I'd been in their shoes, and there was no doubting the quality of the smear job on us. Giles and Gary used to get very upset by the whole thing, but it never got to me.

The protagonists in the High Court appeal were Alun Jones and James Hines for us, John Hardy for the US Government, and Khawar Qureshi for Home Secretary Charles Clarke. Judgment on both the Judicial Review and the appeal would be given together, probably in time for Christmas.

None of us harboured any particular confidence in the result of the Judicial Review, but it had been an invaluable exercise as it had enabled us to touch on issues which were really important to our case, but which had no place in the extremely narrow scope of the extradition hearing. Laws LJ and Ouseley J, therefore, would be making their decision on the extradition appeal with a far greater knowledge of our case than they would otherwise have had, and this should be helpful, we thought, even though the revelation that no-one thought there was a crime in the UK might count against us.

The first day, in which Alun went through all of his arguments, went reasonably well. Liberty had submitted a lengthy written intervention, drafted by their counsel Stephanie Harrison, on the human rights arguments.

I remember coming away from that session in chambers thinking 'this is going to be a historic victory'. I loved the fact that so many Government agencies had lined up against us. It would make winning all the sweeter. I loved the fact that Liberty had intervened in our case, because it was so unlikely on the face of it.

There was a problem of course. If we won in the High Court, the US would appeal to the Lords. If we won in the Lords, and became the legal precedent for all extradition cases, we might be stuck in the UK for the rest of our lives—because no-one here was going to prosecute us, and the US wouldn't drop the indictment. If we set foot in another country we were liable to be arrested and extradited, as Roman Polanski would find out in 2009.

But as problems went, that would be a luxury one, and we could deal with it on our own terms.

By the end of the first day of the hearing, Alun Jones had worked away at the judges sufficiently to elicit the question that was at the heart of our case. With the benefit of all the evidence from the judicial review, the judges knew that NatWest did not think it had been defrauded, or at least it certainly seemed that way. They had an indictment which clearly claimed that NatWest had been defrauded. And they had plea agreements from Kopper and Fastow which both seemed to indicate that it was Enron that had been defrauded, in which case all of the inflammatory e-mails, supposedly pointing to a fraud on NatWest, must surely have meant something completely different. It was a mess.

Laws expressed his confusion to John Hardy. He put it to him that if the US Government knew that NatWest did not think it had been defrauded, then this had the appearance of a 'bad case', and an abuse of the extradition process. My heart soared. And why, he asked, was the US Government so keen to pursue an allegation of a fraud on a UK bank?

Hardy found the latter question easier to answer.

"In short, my Lord, because they can."

I glanced at the press benches. Megan Murphy, my friend from Bloomberg, was staring straight at me, her face a picture of astonishment. She was undoubtedly thinking exactly what I was thinking.

John Hardy had just thrown the case, surely?

Article 8 of the European Convention on Human Rights enshrines the right of an individual to a private and family life. Carting someone to the far side of the world would undoubtedly interfere with this right. But the article 8 right is 'qualified', which means it could be legitimately breached if it were necessary and proportionate to do so.

And now John Hardy, good old right-minded John, had essentially committed legal hari-kari in the High Court. The US did not seek our extradition because it was necessary or proportionate. They sought it because they could.

Game, set and match.

On the confusing question of whether NatWest had or had not been defrauded, John Hardy asked that he might be given overnight to confer with his client, and give a response the following morning. The judges were happy to grant him the time.

I discussed the matter with Emma's father Brian that evening. He was in agreement with me. Hardy certainly appeared to have thrown the case, whether intentionally or otherwise.

Overnight, the US Department of Justice produced a letter. Our prosecutor Thomas Hanusik was away traveling, but the author of the letter had contacted him and asked about the FSA paper which seemed to indicate quite clearly that NatWest did not seem to think it had been defrauded. Hanusik apparently had 'no recollection' of such a document, which struck me as more than a little odd. But he went on to say that even if he had seen the document, it would not have made any difference to his case. It was 'unsurprising' that NatWest might not wish to admit to being a victim, since they presumably felt very foolish having been robbed!

For good measure, Hanusik drew attention to one of my e-mails from January 2000 as evidence that we knew that the Swap Sub asset (whose value changed every minute of the working day) was worth a lot of money when NatWest sold it two months later.

Alun Jones was purple with rage. I, on the other hand, could barely contain my excitement. To me, the letter was just so ridiculous that it would probably win the case for us on its own. If the judges wanted evidence of a bad case and an abuse of process, here it was in black and white on Department of Justice headed notepaper. Laws LJ and Ouseley J would see it for what it was.

Hardy, to his credit, made a good fist of trying to reconcile the irreconcilable. He said that there was no evidence to suggest that the $30 million that Enron had paid was not a fair price. This was wholly incorrect, but of course he did not know that and we were not allowed to challenge it. But he hedged his bets nicely by saying that even if $1 million was the correct price, we might still have defrauded NatWest by breaching our fiduciary duties to them in not reporting that we knew that Enron was willing to pay more. It seemed a fairly ludicrous proposition, and I was confident that the judges would see it for what it was.

All in all, we were very pleased with the way the appeal had gone. A few days later, Alun Jones sent me an article about a Green Paper that had just been published by the EU on Conflicts of Jurisdiction in Criminal Matters. It was a lengthy consultation document looking ultimately towards a mandatory EU Framework to resolve conflicts. In effect, it was suggesting enshrining the Eurojust guidelines in EU law, and putting in place a formal system for monitoring the decision making process. Our cup runneth over, I thought. We submitted it to Laws LJ and Ouseley J, as evidence of the formal concept of natural forum in criminal matters, the existence of which had been denied by Mr Qureshi in the High Court. I couldn't wait to see how the Home Office would respond on behalf of the UK Government.

STUFFED
Early 2006

I was much looking forward to Christmas in 2005. We all thought that we would have our victory by then, and could start to plan once again for our futures.

In mid-December, Mark Spragg attended a party in Buckingham Gate, next to the Palace, hosted by DS Gary Flood and his team. All the great and the good of the extradition world were invited. Barristers, solicitors, Treasury Solicitors, Crown Prosecutors and sundry Home Office staff. According to Mark, person after person came up to congratulate him on our impending victory. The question was not who were the victors, but as to the magnitude of the victory. Would it be so crushing as to prohibit the US taking the matter to the Lords?

December 2005 turned into January 2006, and then January became February, and still no judgment. What could possibly be taking them so long? Melanie was fielding calls from journalists asking what on earth was happening. We had no idea. Alun and James were perplexed. Mark, who was good at picking up rumours, could shed no light. My mood began to darken. Something was wrong. Very wrong. It still seems odd now, but when I got the call from Mark on 19th February, I was almost expecting the news.

"It's not good, I'm afraid David. We've lost"

"On everything?"

"Yes. Pretty comprehensively. I've got a copy of the draft judgment here, which I can share with you, but it cannot go any further than that. Judgment will be handed down at the High Court in two days' time. It can't be made public before that."

I felt sick. That really, really sick feeling you get in the pit of your stomach. My mouth was dry, and my head was spinning. Mark sent the draft judgment to me by e-mail, and it was nearly one hundred pages long. One hundred pages of utter awfulness.

It was almost impossible to read the document because my mind was all over the place. How the hell was I going to tell Emma? We had spent the past ten weeks thinking we had won a huge victory. No doubt about it. No doubt.

Except that we hadn't. Not even close, it seemed.

The last time I had felt like this was the morning of the 27th June 2002, when the whole thing started. Your whole world gets turned upside down. Shit. Shit. Shit. Shit.

Eventually I rang Gary. There was little point ringing Giles. It would just depress me even more. Giles had always been of the view that taking on the Government as publicly as we had done was a huge error, because it would just make them determined to fuck us. And sitting in my office that day, it was difficult to find an answer to any of the questions that didn't involve a Government stitch-up.

Gary, like me, was shellshocked, but we agreed to meet up at Alun's chambers the following day and take stock. Obviously we would be seeking leave to appeal to the Lords. He would speak to Giles.

I really struggled on the journey home that day. It occurred to me not to tell Emma at all. To give her one more day of happy and normal living before dropping the bombshell. But I've never been much good at secrets or lies, and I had long believed that the basis of a happy marriage was to have neither. There was no choice. I would have to tell her that evening.

I figured that it was possible to make light of it by saying that it was a disappointment, but that the case was always going to go to the Lords anyway, so no big deal. I didn't think I could carry off that deception, however. The weight of defeat was crushing. Emma deserved the truth. We were in this together.

My greatest frustration was that I couldn't explain what had happened. There had never been any doubts in our mind that we had won in the High Court. Not a scintilla of doubt. And yet the scale of our defeat was enormous. We didn't come close to winning on a single point. Laws LJ even had a pop at Alun for being prepared to wound but afraid to strike, a criticism perhaps of Alun pulling all his punches on the behaviour of the SFO.

Over the years, I have read and re-read this judgment countless times, not least because it would become a legal precedent for all the other cases that were to follow. I have tried to find a way in which it makes sense, in all the circumstances. Granted, I am not a lawyer, but we had a strong legal team, the intervention of another legal team, and a whole host of legal minds watching the case, all of whom thought we had won.

I have come up with three possible answers after all this time.

The first is that we were all just deluding ourselves, and that our legal arguments just didn't hold water. I don't buy this, because there was so much consensus that we had prevailed.

The second explanation is that the judges wanted to use our case as a lightning rod to demonstrate quite how bad the law really was. British judges have an unparalleled reputation for impartiality. Their job is to enforce the laws passed by Parliament, not to question Parliament's judgment in passing the laws in the first place, unless the law itself is in conflict with another. Bad laws lead to injustice. Ours was a very high profile case. By ruling against us, the judges might have been expressing an unspoken criticism of the law itself. But this seems fanciful.

The only other explanation that I can come up with is that, faced with a direct challenge to the Government, the judiciary backed down. It's a far-fetched theory, I know, but frankly there wasn't much about our case that was normal.

My deep interest in politics has been almost exclusively driven by the events of the last decade, and it's a very personal thing. If you had asked me in 2000 whether Government Ministers would openly lie in Parliament, I might have ventured that it would happen incredibly infrequently. Now, I'm the world's greatest cynic. When I see a Minister at the despatch box, I naturally assume that he or she is dissembling.

We have seen that there were almost no lows to which Blair's Government would not stoop. I am ashamed to say I fully supported the war in Iraq. I even had a blazing row with Emma's father Brian about it. My perspective was simple. If the Prime Minister stands up in Parliament and tells us that this madman is potentially only 45 minutes away from launching weapons of mass destruction at other countries, we have a duty to intervene. Brian's instincts of course were correct. I was a dummy. Blair misled Parliament.

Over the following years, Blair's people briefed against the dead scientist David Kelly, who had been Andrew Gilligan's source in what turned out to be the truthful story that the Government had 'sexed up' the dossier in support of war in Iraq; they consistently told Parliament that they had no knowledge of CIA rendition flights or secret CIA interrogation centres in Eastern Europe; they connived in the torture of detainees in foreign lands, attempted to pass laws allowing the use of information known to have been produced under torture, and introduced a raft of 'anti-terror' legislation that has seen the greatest attack on our civil liberties since Magna Carta in 1215.

So do I think that the Government law officers were capable of trying to put pressure on the judges in our case to come up with the 'right' result? Actually, yes I do. Is there any evidence to support this theory? No, not a scrap. Would they even be moved by such pressure? I sincerely hope not.

Maybe the answer is more simple. Maybe the judges, like Nicholas Evans before them, were just so convinced that we must be guilty, that they did not think we should be allowed to 'escape justice'. You couldn't blame them I suppose. Faced with all the invective and fantastical allegations from the prosecutors, if you accepted them as being fact then we must be very bad men indeed. Who knows? That result still remains a mystery to me.

Still, another day, another battle. There would be plenty more. Alun and James were pretty deflated the following day, but still hopeful that we could turn it around in front of the Law Lords. Getting there was not an automatic right, however.

By convention, the High Court would refuse leave to appeal to the Lords, but might agree to certify certain points as being of public importance. We would then petition the Lords directly, and they would agree to hear the case. Once there, everything was up for grabs again.

We had to decide how we were going to deal with the press. We couldn't let Melanie know the result in advance, as this would have been contempt of court. But we could tell her that we would agree to be interviewed after the judgment was handed down. This would enable Melanie to tell them all not to bother hassling us before we went in.

"Time to take the gloves off", I said. As I saw it, we were being royally screwed, and sitting back and letting it happen simply wasn't an option.

Giles vehemently disagreed.

"Mate, you've seen what these guys can do. Why do you want to make it worse than it already is?"

We argued long and hard about it. Gary was with me, so we carried the day. We would come out fighting.

"Mark, we need Shami Chakrabarti there. Standing beside us. Can you fix that please?"

Mark agreed that he would. In the event, he had enormous trouble, because he was unable to tell Liberty that we had lost, and Shami seemingly had more important things to do than take part in our victory celebrations. Eventually he persuaded Gareth Crossman, Liberty's policy director, that it was really important that Shami was there.

That evening, I rehearsed what I was going to say on the steps of the court. This was the single most important event in our journey so far, and we could not waste the opportunity. Stories like this are news for twenty four hours maximum, after which they sink back into media oblivion.

The journey to court the following morning was difficult. I was in pugnacious mood, but Emma was still extremely upset. As we approached the court we could see the scrum of photographers, TV cameras and assorted trucks.

"Chin up. Smile. Be Polite. They're just doing their jobs". This was the biggest press pack I had ever encountered, and the cameramen ran towards us before forming a huddle which enveloped us and moved with us like some amorphous, many-legged creature as we proceeded towards the court steps. Once inside, we found our case listed on the board, and headed up towards the courtroom.

It was a bit of a family gathering. My parents were there, as was my sister, and Emma's father Brian. And a large number of friends including former NatWest colleagues. All expecting to be cracking open the Champagne afterwards.

My sister Claire, who is a lawyer by training, gave me a big hug. She told me afterwards that she knew as soon as she saw me that we had lost, but even so she felt shocked and sick as the result was announced.

All of the usual suspects were in the press benches, and I recall the looks of astonishment as it all unfolded. Megan Murphy looked particularly taken aback. She looked over at me. I smiled ruefully back as if to say "I know, go figure."

Melanie was particularly distraught. She was like one of the family, and I felt that we were letting her down as much as our loved ones. Gary and I had recently told her that we couldn't afford to keep paying for her services, as the legal bills just kept mounting. I figured that I would have to take on the press role myself. Melanie, however, wouldn't hear of it.

"If you think I'm walking away from you guys after all we've been through, you don't know me very well". For Melanie, this was personal. She knew we were fighting for the right reasons. She believed passionately in what we were trying to do, and she would stick with it to the bitter end.

As it would turn out, Melanie would remain engaged in the fight, unpaid by anybody, for years to come. For her, getting this law changed became something of a religious crusade.

She gave me a hug. "I'm so sorry", she said.

After the judgment had been handed down, the judges agreed to certify three points of law, which was what we needed to seek permission to appeal to the House of Lords, although not before they had altered the wording of what we wanted to argue. We wandered out into the corridor. Melanie asked whether we still intended to talk to the press outside. Yes, we did. And then I saw Shami. I had never met her before, but her face was familiar from so many television appearances. She was the voice of civil liberties in Britain.

She caught my eye and came over. I thanked her profusely for coming, and asked whether she would be willing to stand alongside us and say a few words on the steps outside.

"It's why I'm here", she said.

"Well, there's no time like the present".

It was all a bit theatrical really. As we came through the huge wooden doors, we could see the press posse below us. They waited as we came down the steps, three former bankers in suits and overcoats, and the Director of Britain's leading human rights organisation. Not a picture you would easily have imagined.

I cannot recall in what order we spoke, but Gary said a few well-chosen words, Shami gave a passionate speech about how bad the law was, and I did my little bit. In the press the following day, Shami was hilariously mis-quoted by some journalists. She had talked about people being carted off to the far side of the world like sacks of carrots, but many of the papers had printed it as 'sacks of parrots'. It reminded me of Monty Python's Life of Brian, and the sermon on the mount—'Blessed are the cheesemakers'.

For my part, I was not holding back. I suggested that the Government was using its own citizens as political currency to curry favour with America, and that in matters of criminal justice we were now effectively the fifty first state of America. I reminded people that the first duty of any Government is the protection of its own citizens, and assured them that the fight would continue.

As the melee finally dispersed, I saw a friendly face amongst the TV cameras. It was Chris Atkins, one of my friends from the film business. He had brought his cameraman along, and they had videoed the whole show. He was making a feature-length documentary called Taking Liberties about how the Blair Government was eviscerating some of our oldest rights in the name of the War on Terror, and we were to be a chapter in the film, it seemed.

'Nice speech', he said.

'Thanks. Fancy joining us for a beer? I've got to do a couple of radio interviews, but hook up with Emma and I'll see you there in a bit.'

NEW FRONTS IN THE FIGHT
March 2006

Our loss in the High Court prompted a surge in media interest, greater than we could ever have predicted. The case was now attracting international attention, and many opinion pieces. A few were unflattering, but most focused on what was important, the principle of extradition on demand.

Nor did the statistics make happy reading for the Government. In the two years that the new law had been in force, the number of extradition requests from the US had jumped sharply, and only a very small percentage were terrorism related. The US Senate Foreign Relations Committee, meanwhile, still stubbornly refused even to schedule a hearing on the Treaty, let alone ratify it.

On 1st March 2006 Menzies Campbell put a question to Tony Blair at Prime Minister's Questions about the arrangements. Blair's answer was a disgrace to democracy, but quite revealing of his frustration at the situation. He lambasted the Liberal Democrats for being anti-American and soft on terror. It was a shoddy response from a shoddy Prime Minister.

Jeff Randall, the TV and Radio journalist, and Business Editor of the *Daily Telegraph*, wrote an extensive editorial comparing our treatment with that of a group of Afghanis who had hijacked an aircraft in Europe, flown it to Stansted Airport and then claimed political asylum. They had been convicted in a British court of hijacking, a verdict that was overturned on appeal, and were now living in Britain with their extended families at an aggregate cost to the British taxpayer of tens of millions of pounds. In a wonderfully jingoistic piece, Randall suggested that the three of us should be kept in the land of our birth, while these foreign criminals should be the ones being deported.

On the day that this piece was published in the *Telegraph*, Melanie took a call from Radio 5 asking if I would appear as a guest on Randall's Sunday evening programme, which was recorded live at Shepherd's Bush. I readily agreed. I had been on the Today programme and a few news slots immediately after our High Court verdict, but this one might reach a different audience.

In the event, my appearance was brief. I got to answer one question and listen to some professor of law from America rambling on down a phone line for a bit before time ran out.

As the show closed, however, Jeff announced that it was tradition for him to buy drinks for all his guests, and so we retired to the bar where the great man lit up a large cigar and held court. He talked animatedly to his other guests, before turning his attention to me.

"Now then young David, better have another beer. I don't suppose they'll have many of those where you're going". I agreed that they probably wouldn't. "Tell me all about it", he said.

He listened to me while I explained all the shortcomings in the law, and why it was so important that we get it changed. He studied me with a critical eye while blowing smoke. When I had finished, he smiled.

"A funny thing happened last week", he said. "I don't often get a call from either of the Barclay brothers, but I got one the moment we went to press with my editorial in the *Telegraph*. I must admit I wondered whether they were going to sack me. Far from it. They agreed with me that the whole thing is a bloody disgrace. They want to run a campaign. What do you think of that?"

Utterly astonished, I burbled something about not realising that the country's largest selling broadsheet did 'campaigns'. As a rule, he agreed, they didn't. Until now.

Bloody hell.

"There is a God", I thought. I spent the journey back in the BBC car chuckling to myself.

The news would coincide with the opportunity to open up another front in the fight. One of my greater frustrations over the past couple of years had been that despite the growing awareness of the issues in both Parliament and the media, the possibility of actually getting the law changed still seemed terribly remote.

The Government controls the legislative agenda, and allocates time as it sees fit to debating legislation. Blair's Government had made an art form out of emasculating the Commons as a debating chamber. The technique was relatively simple. First, they had cut the number of hours available for debate, supposedly as a sop to all of the Blair babes who had to go home and cook dinner, or some such nonsense.

Next, they flooded the chamber with a torrent of ill-conceived legislation, meaning that serious debate on the entirety of any Bill was all but impossible. This little trick had the added advantage of enabling them to smuggle highly contentious measures into law by hiding them deep in the small print of much larger bills on a totally different subject.

The upshot of all of this, given Labour's large Parliamentary Majority, was that it was all but impossible for the opposition to table legislation of its own. Early March 2006, however, brought a potential opportunity to use the Government's own tactics against them.

It was Oliver Dommett, Boris's assistant, who alerted me to it. Boris, in turn, had been tipped off by Sadiq Khan, the MP for Babar Ahmad.

It had become traditional that each new legislative year brought yet another Justice or Terrorism Bill from the Home Office. In less than 10 years, this department had spewed out more criminal legislation than in the previous fifty, creating over three thousand new criminal offences.

The 2006 version was the Police and Justice Bill, which promised a major overhaul of the police system in England and Wales, along with hundreds of sundry measures on criminal justice and evidence.

Right at the back of this vast tome, however, hidden in Schedule 12, were a number of suggested amendments to the Extradition Act 2003. These were all nitty bitty little changes, of no great substance. But Schedule 12 could be the Trojan Horse. We could table our own amendments.

This was our moment, surely.

We all met in the House of Commons. Mark and Melanie came in with me. Boris was there with Sadiq Khan, who introduced Babar Ahmad's wife Maryam.

For Sadiq Khan, this was difficult territory. He was a young, thrusting Labour MP with good prospects. He was a lawyer, and highly regarded. But he was also a Muslim and a good friend of Babar Ahmad, and he knew that the law was wrong.

The substance of the amendments was easy enough. Boris had already set that out in his Early Day Motion, which by this time carried the signatures of over 150 MP's of all parties, including over 50 from Labour. If those 50 voted for the amendments, we would win.

So it was agreed. We would seek to remove the designation of the US as a country that could request extraditions without evidence, and we would insert a new clause into the Act which would preclude extradition if the case could be tried in the UK, unless the requesting state could demonstrate that the interests of justice would be better served by a trial taking place abroad. That decision would rest with the courts, not the prosecutors.

We needed sponsors for the amendments. Boris agreed that he would persuade Dominic Grieve, the shadow attorney general, to draft the clauses. My mother had been in constant correspondence with Grieve, and he was wholly supportive.

We knew that the Liberal Democrats would support us, because they had opposed bringing the new arrangements with the US into law in December 2003, warning of what they saw as the very real dangers. The Tories had abstained, not wishing to be seen as anti-American.

The first opportunity to insert the amendments would be at the Committee stage of the Bill in the Commons in a few weeks' time. Thereafter, the Bill would pass to the Lords, where the amendments could be re-proposed if the Government had thrown them out in the Commons Committee stage. We would get more than one bite at the cherry.

We were fighting a guerrilla campaign here. The Government would be taken by surprise, but it would not take long to marshal its forces. We needed to mount an effective lobbying campaign aimed at winning in Committee, where the absolute numbers involved were quite small. We needed to find out which MPs were appointed to debate the legislation and get to them. Hopefully, we could then identify, through the Friends Extradited website, at least a handful of their constituents, and get them letter-writing. Make it personal.

I was so excited the next day that I couldn't work. I also hated leaving things to chance. So I sat down with the Extradition Act, and drafted the amendments that I wanted to see, in language that I hoped would drop seamlessly into the fabric of the Act without causing problems elsewhere.

I sent the drafts to Alun, James and Mark for their comments. Then I produced a one page brief in support of each of the two draft amendments, designed as speaking notes for whoever would be proposing them, and e-mailed the whole package to Dominic Grieve, Boris Johnson and Nick Herbert, who would be the lead Tory in the Committee. This was excellent news, because Nick Herbert had been a member of the Home Affairs Select Committee the previous November when they had taken evidence on the Treaty, so the subject matter was hardly new to him. He was also a rising star in the Tory Party, and a lawyer to boot.

That done, we needed to start quietly lobbying. After our High Court loss, one of the mothers at school had approached Emma and offered help. She worked for a PR company, and one of her colleagues was an ex-Tory MP called Adrian Flook. A former stockbroker, he had lost his seat at the 2005 election, but had maintained strong connections inside the Palace of Westminster.

I talked to Melanie, and if she was at all put out about the notion of another PR company, she didn't show it. This guy's brief was wholly the politicians. No press. And he too was working pro bono.

In the meantime the *Daily Telegraph* had begun their campaign. It was centred in the Business Pages, and was grandly entitled The *Daily Telegraph* Fair Trials for Business Campaign. I was a little alarmed that it had the potential to be seen as elitist, which might damage the wider message. But as the *Telegraph* pointed out in one of their opening editorials on the issue, the new laws put British businessmen in unique peril, since these were the people most likely to have day to day interaction with America. The extradition statistics supported them, and there was growing alarm in the City of London about the aggressive extra-territorial approach being taken by US prosecutors since the new laws had come into force.

There were a number of journalists working on the campaign, and I got to know them all quite well. Christopher Hope and Russell Hotten were the two most frequent writers, with Katherine Griffiths doing some of the more complex investigative work. They reported to Damian Reece, who in turn reported to Jeff Randall. Others contributed periodically, including from the US. It was quite a team.

CLUTCHING AT STRAWS
March 2006

After the devastation of the High Court decision, we were now fighting back on two fronts. The media, and the Police & Justice Bill.

We wrote a final letter to Sir Fred Goodwin, begging him once again to help us. If we were going to be sent to Texas, our chances of defending ourselves would be vanishingly slim, given that all the material that we needed was in the UK, and most of it was at RBS. Could he please, please, just give us access to the evidence we would need to conduct our defence, even if he didn't have the spine to come out and take a position on whether he thought his own bank had been defrauded.

No, of course he couldn't, came the answer from Travers Smith a week later. If extradited, they opined that there were doubtless good legal processes for obtaining documents and witnesses, and the bank would respond to any court order. Travers Smith should have known as well as anyone else, and better than most I reckoned, that if we set foot in Texas, we were fucked. We would have no chance whatsoever of securing document or witness production. But that was not their concern. Their only concern was protecting their client.

The *Telegraph* campaign gave us ample opportunity to keep upping the ante. Every day, more senior business leaders, politicians and notable people wrote letters or articles for the paper expressing their support for the campaign. Even though the *Telegraph* was fastidious in ensuring that the campaign was about the law rather than us, the two had become almost inseparable one from another. If you mentioned the word 'extradition' to anyone at that time, the likelihood is that the first words out of their mouths would have been "NatWest Three".

Keen to be even handed, the paper offered the Government all the space it wanted to put its case. But there wasn't much. On 14th March they ran a two column piece from Andy Burnham in defence of the arrangements, entitled "Provisions are fair and proportionate". In fairness to Andy Burnham, I don't suppose he wrote a word of it. His performance in front of the Home Affairs Select Committee the previous November had suggested that his grasp of the issues was tenuous at best, and that he was really just a mouthpiece for the Government.

Nonetheless, the piece made my blood boil. It wasn't a terrorist treaty; No no no, said Mr Burnham, even though Tony Blair had defended it on exactly those grounds less than a fortnight earlier. And the evidential arrangements were not imbalanced. Whatever pretty much every single legal commentator in the country might say. They were all wrong.

The bit that finished me off, however, was his insistence that the *Telegraph* was wrong to state that the human rights protections in the Act would always be trumped by an extradition request. No, sir, said the Minister. The human rights protections were enshrined in the Act, and were alive and kicking.

He seemed quite oblivious to the arguments made in our High Court appeal by his very own lawyers, which now formed the legal precedent, that the human rights protections should, other than in the most exceptional of cases, always be trumped by the desirability of honouring our international extradition treaties.

When I had stopped throwing things around the room, I picked up the phone to Russell Hotten, who was co-ordinating the campaign at the *Telegraph*, and asked if I could be given the right to reply. Russell gave me a word limit, advised me to be as measured as I could, and set me on my way.

The *Telegraph* published my piece almost without amendment. Gary and Giles were apoplectic. Melanie didn't know which way to turn. Alun Jones hated it. Mark Spragg thought it was bloody marvelous.

It all depends on your point of view, really. If, like me, you took the view that the Labour Government wasn't remotely susceptible to rational argument, but only to newspaper headlines, then my approach was entirely justified. I accused Burnham of talking total drivel, and in journalistic terms "offered him outside"—I suggested that he nominate a TV or radio station of his choosing, with a moderator of his choosing, and then he and I could have a proper debate on the law.

Of course he was never going to respond. Nor did he.

I found justification for my fairly blunt approach just a few days later, when the Conservatives formally tabled the proposed amendments to the Extradition Act at the Committee stage of the Police & Justice Bill. I went along to watch the proceedings in the Palace of Westminster.

For the Tories, Nick Herbert was reason personified, and he was ably supported by the Liberal Democrats. I was overjoyed to see that they had taken our draft clauses for each of the two proposed amendments almost without change, and Nick Herbert quoted selectively from my brief in his speech.

I was in good spirits on that day because there were only ten Labour MPs on the Committee of 18 members, so if we could persuade just two of them to vote with us, or one to vote and one to abstain, we could carry the amendment. And two of those Labour members, Celia Barlow, the MP for Hove, and Stephen Pound, the MP for Ealing, had both told constituents in letters that they supported law change. This might just be a great day.

I should have known better, I suppose, and when I saw who was going to bat for the Home Office, my heart sank. Hazel Blears must rank as one of the most annoying politicians ever to have been elected to Parliament. Although only about four feet tall, she has the astonishing ability to seem always to be talking down her nose at you. A frequent panelist on Question Time, she would always have me throwing things at the telly whenever she spoke.

Even when she was exposed by the *Daily Telegraph* in 2009 as having claimed large amounts of expenses on a house that she designated as her 'second home' for Parliamentary purposes, while telling the Inland Revenue that it was her 'primary residence' to avoid paying tax on the profits when she sold it, she managed through her manner to imply that she was a study in virtue, waving a cheque for £13,000 which she had magnanimously decided to pay to the Inland Revenue in lieu of the tax she had avoided.

On this day, in front of the Committee, she was bobbing up and down grinning like a Cheshire cat, making ridiculous remarks, indulging in petty point-scoring, rather than behaving with the gravitas of a Minister of State that the taxpayer had the misfortune to be funding.

On the first 'forum' proposal, that if a case could be tried in more than one country, the default presumption should be that it would be tried in the UK, Blears' line was that the amendments were both anti-American and unworkable, even though they would have applied to every single country, were manifestly easy to administer, and simply mirrored the practice in most other countries.

She gave the same short shrift to our other proposal, which was that until such time as the Americans had actually ratified the new Treaty, they should be unable to take advantage of its evidential provisions. Again, few people would regard this as being overly contentious, but for Hazel Blears such proposals were apparently utterly preposterous, and the Tories should be ashamed of themselves for having the temerity to raise them.

You get the Government you deserve, I guess. When it came time to vote, Stephen Pound found himself urgently called away to other business, and Celia Barlow dutifully voted with her Minister. A triumph for Parliamentary democracy and the principles of our elected representatives.

In the big scheme of things, defeat that day was just another bump in the road, I thought. Despite Blair's best efforts at "reform", the upper chamber of Parliament did not have a Labour majority, and so could not be whipped in the way that the supplicant MPs in the Commons could be. So when the Police & Justice Bill reached the Lords in July, the amendments would be put back in, and there was still a real possibility of law change before our appeal reached the Law Lords.

But as a statement of intent by the Government, things couldn't have been clearer. We don't care how sensible these measures are. We're not going to implement them, because that might be an admission that we got it wrong in the first place, and we don't do those.

It must be great to be a Government Minister. You get paid a nice six figure salary, and a boatload of taxpayer-funded expenses. And you get to mess with people's lives, and go on television trying to sound as if you care.

The reality is that they didn't care. They cared about themselves. They cared about their chauffeur driven cars and their expenses for second homes. They cared about the possibility of elevation to the upper house, and the title that went with it. And all of these things depended to a large extent on doing what Tony or Gordon wanted, not on doing what was right for the country or for their constituents.

So, come April 2006, I was relying on the House of Lords to keep us out of Texas, either through the upper House standing firm on law change or through the Law Lords ruling in our favour on our extradition appeal. We figured it would take about a year before they would hear the case, so the Spring of 2007 would likely see the dramatic climax.

Or at least that was the plan.

NOT A LEG TO STAND ON
21st June 2006

If I was stunned when Mark told me about the High Court judgment in February 2006, it was as nothing compared to my shock when Mark rang me on 21st June to tell me that the Law Lords had refused to hear our appeal. No reason given. Just the terse fact that they would not be hearing the case.

This was not on the radar. Not for any of us. Of course the Law Lords would hear the appeal. We were the test case for a controversial new piece of legislation. There were a host of other cases lined up behind us, waiting on the resolution of our case to establish the law. The High Court judges had certified three separate points of law as being of public importance in our case. We might not win, but they would at least hear it.

But they wouldn't.

And that was pretty much that. We immediately filed an emergency application with the European Court of Human Rights, asking for them to order a stay of execution on our extradition while they considered our case. We had no real hopes that they would say yes, and they did not surprise us, replying within a week that while they would look at our case, they would not intervene to stop the extradition.

Game over.

The next three weeks were pretty surreal. We lurched from hope to despair more times than I care to remember. The media worked themselves up into a complete frenzy. It was no longer necessary for Melanie to call anybody or make any prompts. The papers by now would call me direct, and the TV and radio stations likewise.

Melanie was called by Karl Watkin, a self-made businessman who wanted to organise a demonstration of other businessmen. Melanie advised that making it part of the *Telegraph* campaign would be a good idea, and so it was that on 29th June, over a hundred city figures walked slowly from the Institute of Directors on Pall Mall to the Home Office building on Marsham Street, accompanied by press and camera crews, to deliver a petition of several thousand signatures which would doubtless go straight into the Home Office shredder.

Watkin had wanted a noisy affair, but the route took it through the Government's new exclusion zone that prohibited demonstrations near Parliament, and as he observed to a newspaper, we might all have been arrested under terrorism legislation. Which would have been a rather delicious irony.

Jeff Randall from the *Telegraph* rang me. He was perplexed because he had been asking some very senior contacts of his at RBS why they weren't either helping us or at least taking a position on us, and no-one was giving him any answers.

So I told him.

"RBS are over a barrel, Jeff. Read the Batson Report into a deal they did called Enron Teesside Operations Limited. Then read the reports of the Nigerian Barges trial in Houston. Then read the Thompson Memorandum. Then look at the outstanding Class Actions in the US courts in which RBS is a defendant. Then join the dots. If they do anything other than what the DoJ has told them to do, they're going to get fucked. People will go to jail, very senior people, and it will cost the bank billions. It's a thousand times bigger than our case for them".

He rang me back a day later. One of his best business reporters, Katherine Griffiths, had been looking into the story and thought it was potentially devastating. Could I help her understand it all?

Of course I could. But did Jeff realise how high the stakes were, I asked, if they were genuinely thinking about publishing on the subject?

He said he would go away and think about that, while I helped Katherine through the quagmire that was Batson's report.

On 3rd July, Jeff rang me and told me they were going to run the story the following day. He figured that the obligation to put the truth into the public domain overrode any potential negative consequences for RBS and its directors.

The next day, the article appeared. It talked about the Batson report and drew the connections with the US civil cases, and the potential financial consequences for RBS. It didn't however mention the Nigerian Barges case and the potential criminal liability. I was mildly disappointed that they had pulled their punches.

I need not have been, however, because the following day Jeff Randall himself went the whole hog in an opinion piece, hinting at criminal culpability by some of RBS's most senior executives.

He rang me that very morning. "Bingo", he said. "I've just had a call from somebody very senior over there, who I can't name obviously, begging me to call off the dogs".

"Sad, isn't it?"

The reality is that you couldn't really blame RBS for throwing us under the bus, as a purely business decision. Our lives and liberties were as nothing compared to the other issues at stake for them.

Much as I may have reason to hate Fred Goodwin, it would have taken a very principled man to have done the honourable thing ahead of the interests of the RBS shareholders. RBS might have lost its banking licence in the US, and there was every chance that some of his board colleagues would themselves have been indicted, which would have had the almost certain consequence of billions of dollars of judgments against them in the civil cases for being up to their eyeballs in Enron's 'wrongdoing'.

Alternatively, he could let us swing in the breeze, per his instructions from the Department of Justice, and hope that everything could be quietly hushed up

What would you have done in his shoes?

A FOOT ON THE GROUND
July 2006

What do you do when you know you're going away in a week and you don't know when you're coming home again? I would be lying if I said the thought of doing a runner didn't occur to me. It occurred to me often during the early days of July 2006, not least because I can't count the number of people who said, in all seriousness, 'go; go now'. I even got the odd call from total strangers offering me the means to do it, for a small consideration, of course.

Our timing couldn't have been much worse in many senses. Just a few weeks previously, the jury had duly found Ken Lay and Jeff Skilling guilty on multiple counts. Even though Skilling, in particular, had been acquitted on the majority of counts, the guilty verdicts on the rest were still going to result in a huge sentence. He would eventually receive over 24 years.

Ken Lay, the Chairman of the once great company, who had come across as arrogant and defensive on the witness stand, would die of heart failure shortly before his sentencing, but after announcing his intention to appeal, and under US law his conviction would therefore be expunged. It wouldn't stop the US Government pursuing his wife for all their assets, however.

The mood around Houston was ugly.

Ultimately, though, running away was never on the cards. What, after all, would it achieve? I would become what the Department of Justice wanted everyone to believe I already was. A fugitive from justice; and as Roman Polanski would find out to his cost in the autumn of 2009, the Department of Justice isn't in the habit of forgetting about you, no matter how long you've been away.

There were practical considerations too. If you run, do you take the family? Almost impossible to hide a family. And then what about our parents? Do you deprive your children of all contact with their grandparents?

Above all, however, I've always believed that running away is never an option in life. Whatever the odds, you have to look the devil in the eye.

So although I often joked about it with friends, running away wasn't on the agenda. Getting a new lawyer, though, most certainly was.

If I was going to turn up in Houston in a few days' time to face charges carrying a maximum penalty of thirty-five years in prison, I figured I needed a local attorney. There were a host of reasons for this, not least of which was the cost of having a firm in Washington when the client is a couple of thousand miles and a time zone away.

What had convinced me, though, was the Nigerian Barges trial, which I had followed assiduously from afar back in September 2004. In that trial, there were six defendants, four from Merrill Lynch, and two from Enron's in house accounting department. The bankers were represented largely by New York attorneys, the Enron defendants by local guys.

The trial ended in five convictions, including all four of the bankers. There was just one acquittal, of a lady called Sheila Kahanek. She had a local attorney, Dan Cogdell, and his closing statement to the jury on her behalf almost had me in tears just reading it from the transcript. There was little doubting its impact when the verdicts were handed down. In that poisonous environment, I reckoned he had worked a miracle.

So I figured that Dan Cogdell should be top on my wish list of attorneys to hire. The question was, would he be available, and could I afford him?

First I ran through the idea with an attorney called Tom Kirkendall, who authored a blog site called Houston's Clear Thinkers, and with whom I had had periodic e-mail correspondence in the past couple of years. Tom was very much a minority voice in the Houston community, suggesting from the word go that the prosecutors were over-reaching, creating scapegoats for their own career advancement. It was a brave stance to take at that time, given the prevailing mood in the city.

I reached Tom on his cellphone as he was stood by the deathbed of an old friend, which was acutely embarrassing, but he insisted on taking the call. He told me how sorry he was about the situation, and how embarrassed he felt about the conduct of his own country. I reassured him that in my view any blame lay squarely with our own spineless Government. His countrymen were just taking advantage of the gifts they had been given.

We talked about possible choices for attorneys, and Tom concurred that Dan was indeed a great option if available. He gave me the names of a few others in case it didn't work out with Dan.

I had to rehearse my opening address to Dan several times, as I guessed that it was unlikely he would ever have heard of me, and ours would not be the most straightforward of tales to tell. You only get one chance to make a first impression, and I figured I needed Dan significantly more than he needed me.

His assistant Rosi put me straight through to him.

"Hey David. We've been expecting your call. When are you due here?"

This was not the opening I had anticipated. Dan called in his associate, Jimmy, who told me he had been following our case closely over the past six months, and that they were really interested in taking it on. No explanation necessary, then. Marvellous. Dan had a caveat, though.

"I need you to understand something if we're going to do this, David. I try cases. That's all the fuck I do. I'm not the smartest guy in the room. A lot of the time I'm just the leper with the most fingers. If you want to get all technical and lawyerly on this shit, I'm not your man. My motions practice sucks. If you want to plead this case out, I'm not your man. But if you want to take this mother to trial, then you've come to the right place".

I could have wept with joy. Dan Lamar Cogdell and James Madison Ardoin III were duly instructed, and I rang Mark MacDougall in Washington to break it to him that we would have to part company. He couldn't have been nicer about it.

Then I rang Gary and Giles to let them know that we had a foot on the ground in the Houston legal community. And some foot it was, too.

FINAL DAYS OF FREEDOM
6th to 13th July 2006

The final week in England was a blur, really. One day just folded into the next.

I seemed to spend an unreasonable amount of time talking to the media. I suppose that the better course of action would just have been to retreat into our shells, but there was something in me that refused to say die.

For as long as we were still in England, there was always the hope that we would stay there. It was difficult to see where redemption might come from, but never give up. We all figured that the only possible path to redemption now would be public pressure on Tony Blair. It was clear that the "bad law" arguments were falling on totally deaf ears in Government, so the only alternative route would be to appeal to the more basic human instincts. So we decided quite late in the day that our wives and children would no longer be out of bounds to the press. We were fully aware of the likely repercussions, but we just didn't see any option, and the girls themselves were really keen to do it.

A little part of me regrets that decision, because in some sense it was a failure of principle. I have always hated politicians and celebrities who parade their wives and children when caught doing something dreadful, hoping in some sad way to demonstrate that they are really just "ordinary" people.

For us, the point was subtly different. Extradition affects families; it means separating them, potentially for years. The "victims" of our extradition were not just the NatWest Three. They were the wives who would be deprived of husbands, and the children who would be deprived of fathers.

On the other side of the coin, that's what happens to soldiers every day. But then that's why we see soldiers' wives and children on the television so often. Because people understand that it's just as hard for them, home alone, wondering if and when daddy is ever coming home.

So it was with us.

We would be accused of cynically exploiting our photogenic families, of course. Such is life. At that particular point in time, we were all agreed that no matter how distasteful it might feel, we would never forgive ourselves if we left a stone unturned, and Melanie was telling us that this was a really big unturned stone.

If I had my concerns about Emma going in front of a camera or a radio mike, I needn't have bothered. She was a natural. Where I am extremely factual, and often overcomplicate issues, Emma would just nail them in terms which everyone could understand.

"You know, no other country on earth will extradite its own citizens without evidence. I mean, why would they?"

In many ways it was a humbling time. We had so much support from so many different sources. The congregation at church were all praying for us. The teachers and parents at school. Our own parents. All their friends. Work colleagues. And we would get letters and cards daily from people who we didn't know, saying how they were right behind us, and we should keep fighting.

I am eternally grateful to all of those people, not just because they made me feel better, but because they gave strength to Emma and the children, and those closest to us. And that would make it easier for me when the day came to leave. I knew that my family would be looked after.

The knowledge that you are not alone is hugely comforting. I know it has always given succour to my Mother, who to this day keeps doing what she does best, writing to MPs and Ministers, constantly reminding them of the cancer that is the Extradition Act. As it is my mission, so it is hers.

By early July, our case was being brought up every single day in the Downing Street briefing to journalists. Tony Blair had boxed himself into a bit of a corner over bail. We had made much of the fact that we would be hurled into prison as soon as we got to America, and held there until we agreed to plead guilty. Because it was the truth. Don't take my word for it. Go and have a look at the United States Attorneys' Manual. It's there. They are required to oppose bail for all extradition cases. Period. And I am not aware of a single case which preceded ours in which someone who had contested extradition to the US was granted bail by a US court.

This was an uncomfortable issue for Blair, because his Government's official line was that we would be entitled to a bail hearing like everybody else—undeniably true, but utterly irrelevant, since the outcome was pre-determined. So in the way that Tony Blair has of trying to put a band-aid over a severed limb and hope no-one will notice the bleeding, he instructed the Attorney General's office to find a solution, and it was a cracker.

Tony Blair announced at Prime Minister's Questions on 12th July that the Department of Justice had confirmed that they would not oppose bail as long as the court put in place the appropriate conditions, and we agreed them. I still laugh at the concept of Blair and Lord Goldsmith trying to negotiate my bail. How ridiculous do you think they looked in America? The leader of what was once the greatest nation on earth, pleading like some small child for a favour to get him out of a public relations catastrophe entirely of his own making.

Still, it all made for good theatre. After all, how many people get their bail conditions discussed at Prime Minister's Questions?

On the 11th July the House of Lords debated the amendments to the Extradition Act that Hazel Blears had so delighted in getting voted down in the Committee stage of the Police & Justice Bill.

It is a sad fact that if you want any sensible debate in Parliament these days, you have to go to the Lords. Because people with decades of experience, and a sense of real duty to their country, take their legislative responsibilities seriously.

Many of the Peers in the upper house are Cross Benchers, unaffiliated to any political party, and much to Tony Blair's disgust his vast majority in the Commons was not replicated in the Lords, meaning that he couldn't just shovel through whatever odious laws he wanted.

His solution was to wreak constitutional vandalism on the Lords, and attempt to fill it with his own grubby little placemen and partisan apparatchiks. He has only partly succeeded.

For the Government on 11th July Baroness Scotland was at her disingenuous best, and for good measure threw a significant amount of mud at us, in particular describing us continually as the 'Enron Three'. It may have backfired on her, as the amendments were approved by the Lords with a significant majority. They would be presented to the Commons in the autumn, but it would be too late for us.

On 12th of July, the day before our extradition, there was a 3 hour emergency debate in the Commons on the extradition laws, which in practice became more of a debate on the case of the NatWest Three. In securing this 'adjournment debate', Nick Clegg, the Home Affairs spokesperson for the Liberal Democrats, had succeeded where the Tories had previously failed. The debate resulted in the Commons voting in our favour by 246 to 4, but none of it mattered much as it was just a symbolic gesture.

We were going to Texas.

I did not get to watch the emergency debate live, because I was in the garden with Mark Eddo of ITV, doing an interview for the evening news. It was while we were filming that the news broke of the death of an ex colleague of ours, who was said to have been involved in the whole LJM affair. There was initially no name, so it was not until later on that we discovered that it was Neil Coulbeck, who had been found dead in woods close to where he lived in Essex.

I don't suppose we will ever know what caused Neil to take his own life. The wires were full of rumours, supposedly from family and friends, that he had been bullied by the FBI. It wouldn't surprise me. When we got to Houston, the tales of intimidation by the FBI were legion. I met some of the people who had been on the wrong end of it. The prosecutors were so adamant that Skilling and Lay should be convicted, that they drew up a list of over one hundred 'unindicted co-conspirators', who might have testified for the two men. They were told that they were themselves possible targets for indictment. They could make up their own minds whether they wished to take the stand.

The FBI took the somewhat unusual step of issuing a press release which denied that Neil Coulbeck was a suspect–not that anyone had ever suggested it–and stated that he had been interviewed in London on 12th June 2002, which incidentally was further confirmation of the trip about which the Serious Fraud Office had denied all knowledge.

Amidst all this activity on the last day, my daughter Jemima had a swimming gala at school, and so Emma and I made our excuses to the various journalists who were still at the house, and headed out.

Emma's parents came to collect the children, because I would be leaving at four thirty the following morning, and we didn't want them being woken. So they would stay with their grandparents that night.

There were a lot of tears as they drove away, and then a quiet supper before I steeled myself to the task of completing our tax returns. An early morning trip to Croydon police station and a Continental Airlines flight to Houston in the company of the US marshals awaited.

PART THREE: TEXAS

WELCOME TO TEXAS–HAVE A NICE DAY
13th July 2006

The flight touched down at about 1.40pm local time at George Bush International Airport in Houston. The plane taxied to a halt and the pilot came onto the intercom.

"Ladies and gentlemen, this is your captain speaking. I'd like to thank you all for flying Continental Airlines today, and hope you had a good flight. Er, we have some special passengers today who are being met by some local dignitaries, so I'd ask you all to remain in your seats while these folks exit the plane. It should only take a minute or so. Thank you for your co-operation, and have a nice day".

The Marshals indicated that we should get up, and took our bags, and we filed off the plane. We had to walk through almost the entire aircraft with people staring. A lot of familiar faces gave us the thumbs up. Some called out their support and best wishes. Many passengers presumably wondered who the hell we were. It was acutely embarrassing, all told.

As we stepped off the plane, two things hit us simultaneously. The first was a wall of heat and humidity. July in Houston is brutal. The second was a wall of large men in uniforms, with guns and faces that said "don't even think about it".

The first person to reach me was an officer from the Houston police department. He was huge, probably 275 pounds, and not much fat. I would guess he had probably been a lineman in his football playing days. He placed his left hand under my right arm pit and started to walk briskly. Since he was about six feet five, and I am five feet nine in shoes, my feet were literally not touching the floor at times. I could have been a suitcase. Gary told me later that it looked hilarious with my little legs going backwards and forwards, although none of us could quite see the humour in it at the time.

We were all three taken in separate buggies on a journey through the long glass corridors of the terminal building. Each buggy had one fugitive and at least 6 uniforms, and blue lights flashing.

We finally arrived at the customs and immigration facility, where we were marched inside and ordered to sit down in plastic chairs along one wall and say nothing. More men in uniform sat at desks in front of us.

I tried to identify all the various uniforms and badges. Some were easy because they wore jackets with big letters on the back, which I had previously thought they only did in the movies.

There were US Marshals, Houston Police, guys from the Customs and Border Patrol ("CBP"), the Immigration and Nationality Service ("INS"), and Immigration and Customs Enforcement ("ICE"). Everyone had guns. Gary told me that he had counted 23 uniformed officers involved in our transportation from the plane to the immigration facility. As we used to say about the American Army when training with them in Southern Germany in the late 1980s, quantity has a quality all of its own.

We hadn't been there long when four new Marshals arrived. They were obviously the relief crew. And this lot looked pumped. All youngish, and all built like brick shithouses. They were scruffily dressed, with shirts or T-shirts outside slacks or jeans, but a couple were wearing the jackets that said 'US Marshal' so that no-one was in any doubt.

Looking around the room my eye was caught by a card on one of the desks, on which was printed the Texas flag, along with the words "Don't Mess with Texas". I would later discover that this had been the slogan of a remarkably successful anti-littering campaign in Houston, but at that particular moment in time, sitting sheepishly in a room full of testosterone and guns, I interpreted it somewhat differently.

Gary was told to stand up, and was led away by the guy who appeared to be the team leader, Deputy US Marshal David Juers. He wore a short-sleeved open neck shirt, which hung down from his vast chest. He looked like he had no neck and his biceps were about the size of my thighs.

Gary was told that he was going to be searched, and we all had a fair idea what that meant. We all went through the same process, but Gary's was the more amusing, so I'll relate what happened to him.

He was led into a room with no windows, and told to face the wall, and place his hands on the wall and spread his legs. From this moment onwards, all instructions were barked rather than spoken. Deputy Juers pulled on a pair of latex gloves. The conversation went something like this:

"Right, you understand that you are now in the custody of the US Federal Marshals service"

"Yes sir".

"I need to inform you that any attempt to escape constitutes a Federal offense punishable by five years' imprisonment, on top of what you are already here for. It will also necessitate me using whatever force I deem necessary, including lethal force, to impede your escape. Do you understand?"

"Yes sir". There was little doubt that this was no idle threat.

"Now I am going to give you a series of instructions. I want you to do exactly what I say. If I say take off your shirt, I mean take off your shirt and only your shirt. Nothing else. Do you understand?"

"Yes sir".

"Failure to do exactly what I say, or any odd movement, may be construed as an attempt to escape. Do you understand?"

"Yes sir".

"Okay, now I am going to search you from top to bottom. I am giving you the opportunity to tell me right now what you have in your pockets or about your person. If I find anything else, that may constitute an offense. Do you understand?"

"Yes sir".

"Right. What do you have in your pants' pockets?"

"Nothing."

"Nothing? You have nothing in your pockets?"

"No sir". We had been advised by Mark Spragg that whatever we carried in our pockets would probably get 'lost', so we had placed any valuables in our travel bags.

"I am now going to put my hands into your pants' pockets. Any movement at all I will interpret as an attempt to escape. Do you understand?"

"Yes sir"

Trouser pockets were duly searched.

"Alright, now take off your shirt".

And so it went on until Gary was standing in his underpants, still leaning with his hands on the wall.

"Do you have anything concealed in your shorts?"

"No sir." Deputy Juers proceeded to check.

"Okay, turn around and face me. Now put your shirt back on."

Gary smiled.

"What you smiling for?"

"Nothing".

"You just smiled at me. Why did you smile? You think this is funny?"

"No sir".

"Then what are you smiling at?"

"Well, I thought you were going to stick your finger up my arse".

"You want me to stick my finger up your ass?"

"No sir. Absolutely not sir".

Gary must have been in the room with Deputy Juers for about ten minutes. When he was led out, I was told to get up and follow. I wondered at the time whether I should volunteer that I had been having some problem with piles, but I figured he'd find out soon enough, and by all accounts he might just cure them for me.

As part of my search, Deputy Juers attempted to take the laces out of my shoes. I had come in an old pair of moccasins, and of course the laces are an integral part of the shoe. Deputy Juers gave up after a while but insisted that they remain undone when I put the shoes back on. I didn't see the logic, but it didn't seem an appropriate time for debate.

After the search, suitably intimidated, we were shackled and told to sit down again. The shackles consisted of a pair of handcuffs attached to a chain belt that went around your waist, so that your hands were together and in front of you, and you could not lift them away from you. And then the paperwork began. Each of us in turn, in manacles, being fingerprinted and iris scanned, and filling out countless forms with members of the immigration department. Well, they did the filling out, as we were shackled, and so it took forever as you had to spell everything out, letter by letter. The accents didn't help much, either. Gary got the obligatory "so where y'all from then?" to which he replied "Scotland".

"What, Scotland, England?"

"No, Scotland. It's a country".

"Is it? Gee, I didn't know that. But it's near England, right?"

"Yes, it's close".

We had all assumed that Americans would have trouble with Gary's Glaswegian accent, but in fact it was Giles with whom they had the most difficulty. That West Country lilt just threw them completely.

When eventually the form filling was finished, an argument broke out. The immigration guys wanted our passports. The Marshals weren't handing them over.

"What you want their passports for?" asked Deputy Juers.

"Cos these guys are illegals. We're gonna detain 'em and then we're gonna deport 'em".

"You can't do that. These guys are due at the Federal courthouse tomorrow. They're gonna get bond".

"Well if the judge grants 'em bond, we're gonna detain 'em, and then we're gonna deport 'em. They're illegals".

"You can't deport 'em". We've just spent the last two years trying to get 'em here".

"They're illegals. We're gonna deport 'em".

The three of us looked at each other in bewilderment as this played out. The argument got more and more heated as it went round in ever decreasing circles. It was exactly as Doug McNabb had predicted in his expert testimony at the magistrates' court some two years previously. It had sounded implausible at the time, as had much of his testimony. And yet here it was, happening in front of our eyes, just as he had described it. For the record, pretty much every single thing that Doug McNabb said about the practice of the legal system in Texas, and the difficulties that foreign defendants would encounter, was absolutely spot on.

With respect to the immigration issue, none of these agencies interacts with one another, even though they all work for the same Federal Government. Each different badge represented a different team with a different set of rules, and their own agendas. ICE and INS couldn't give a shit about how we got there or what we were doing there. Look at this manual here. It says right here that illegals are liable to be detained, and a deportation hearing scheduled. So that's what we're gonna do. And it says right here that we need to take control of their passports.

In the end a compromise was reached, but not before a lot of shouting and finger pointing. I think the compromise had at least something to do with a combination of numbers and physique. The Marshals won on both counts, and of course they had possession of the passports, so if the INS or ICE guys wanted them, they were going to have to come and get them.

The compromise was that the Marshals would keep the passports, but ICE would issue a "detainer", saying that we were liable to be detained and deported. Someone else could sort out the mess if the judge released us on bond the following day.

So then it was time to move. We were told to stand up and face the wall. Marie-Anne's team's work was done. They had safely delivered the package. Deputy Juers was in command from hereon in.

We were asked if we needed the men's room. Gary said yes. It was another somewhat comical incident since the shackles give you very limited reach with your hands, and Gary had significant difficulty getting his button flies undone. The Marshal was not impressed. He apparently wore that look that said "don't even think about asking what I think you're going to ask". Gary didn't.

We were walked out of the office in single file, with Marshals ahead and behind. The drill was that you looked straight ahead, and made no sudden movements. Whenever stopped, you turned and faced the wall to your left. We ended up in a parking garage, and were led to an old white transit van. Before being loaded into the van, they put ankle chains on us, so that our ability to run or even walk was now severely constrained.

The back of the van could seat about 10 people; the prisoners in the back were separated from the two Marshals in the front by a Perspex screen. Each of us was directed to sit in a different row of bench seats. Giles went towards the front. Then Gary, and me towards the back.

Deputy Juers told us that they were sending out decoy vans because there was so much press at the airport. It sounded very melodramatic and a wee bit implausible, but we all nodded, and off we drove.

It had been raining that morning in Houston, and the roads were wet. We had just come off the Interstate into Downtown and were traveling down Capitol when the car in front braked sharply at an amber light. Our driver also stood on the brakes, and we skidded to a halt about a foot from the vehicle in front. There was a pause of about half a second, and then "bang", and the van lurched forward. We had been rear-ended.

This is the point in the movie when masked men jump out of the car in front and the car behind, and hold up the van with automatic weapons, springing the criminal mastermind in the van. In Hollywood films he would be played by an Englishman, because for some reason English villains always seem more sinister.

But no-one got out of any vehicle. Deputy Juers looked in his wing-mirror, then at his driver, and just said "oh shit", shaking his head. Then he turned round and asked us if we were okay. We all said yes. In retrospect, that might have been the time to develop a severe case of whiplash, but it never really crossed our minds, and anyway the Marshals might have had some rather dramatic cure for whiplash which involved re-arrangement of several vertebrae.

"That was one of ours", Deputy Juers explained, motioning backwards with his thumb. We hadn't previously noticed the Ford Sedan which had trailed us all the way from the airport, and which had now become one with us.

As the lights went green, we pulled gingerly away, taking with us the front grill and part of the fender from the Ford, which eventually detached itself and sprung back to its rightful owner, before hanging miserably from the front of the car. They drove on regardless.

Shortly thereafter we arrived at a large, concrete monstrosity of a building. At the time I thought this was the infamous Federal Detention Centre ('FDC')", though it turned out to be the Federal Courthouse. The Ford Sedan pulled up alongside us, and the two Marshals got out and examined the damage to the front. They doubtless had some form filling to do.

We were helped out of the van by the Marshals. This is where I started to get into difficulty. The footchains are probably difficult enough to walk in at the best of times, but when combined with untied laces they produced an effect best suited to the set of a Charlie Chaplin film. Consequently, I kept tripping over myself and had to be helped up the steps and into the building by one of the Marshals.

It was at this exact moment that an enterprising photographer with a very long lens caught the three of us on camera. Giles in profile with his head bowed, Gary half way up the steps, and me at the top being helped by a Marshal. Hand chains, foot chains. Chain belt. All that was missing was a chain connecting the three of us together. Arrogant bankers brought low. The photograph was on all the major internet news-sites within minutes, and was carried on the front of at least one of the UK newspapers the following morning.

Inside, we were taken to the second floor, and then through a security door into what was like an air lock on a spaceship. Once we had been ushered inside, the Marshals closed the door behind us. The door in front of us then opened, and we filed into a small room with some metal benches, and a lot of electronic equipment.

Here we met the clone of the policeman who had met me at the plane. Where the hell did they get all these guys from? It was like *Land of the Giants*. But this guy was very friendly. He was wearing a pair of beige cargo pants, and a light blue T-shirt which was stretched tight over every single part of his torso. On the back it said "Police". He had a baseball hat on backwards, and that also said "Police". I wondered if those ever got stolen. Not his, I imagined.

He was in charge of fingerprinting and photography. A lady behind a computer terminal started with a fresh set of processing–name, age, address. Again, Gary got into difficulty. When she got to "country of origin", Gary said "Scotland".

"I don't have Scotland on my list", she said after a while. "Can I put England?"

"No, you may not put England", said Gary, indignantly.

Eventually it was discovered that her list included "United Kingdom" as a menu option, and Gary reluctantly agreed that this would be okay.

Towards the end of this process, a man in a very smart suit and shiny shoes walked in. I was still being processed, so he introduced himself to Giles and Gary, and enquired as to whether we were being well treated. Difficult to know how to respond to that one. He told them that he was from the office of the Attorney General. We were then moved next door to an odd room which contained some metal furnishings and some cells which looked very grim.

In the meantime, we could hear raised voices next door, where the man in the suit was conversing with the Marshals. He came back after a while and said "everything's going to be fine". The he left and we were alone. We speculated as to whether we were going home, which would have satisfied the definition of "fine" quite admirably.

A few minutes later Deputy Juers came in. He looked a little perplexed.

"Okay guys, I'm flying way outside the envelope here, so I need you to bear with me, okay?"

It was the first time that he had spoken without sounding menacing. It was almost as if he'd been magically transformed. He introduced himself and his guys, so now we knew his first name.

"We're going to take you out of these chains now, alright, and then we're going to go downstairs and get in a couple of cars and go for a drive. You promise me you'll behave, right?"

And so they took us out of the chains and off we went. Before we left the building, the Marshals gave us each an item of clothing and asked us to put our hands together in front of us and then drape the clothing on top, so that if any photographers happened to be outside, there was at least the pretence that we were handcuffed. There were none, so two of us got into one car, and one into another. With 'Agent Dave' and his boys, as Giles decided they were henceforth to be known.

We headed out West on Memorial Avenue and then South for a short hop on the feeder road beside I-610, before pulling in to the front of the Marriott Hotel.

We were taken straight upstairs and shown into a room containing two queen-sized beds, with a door through to an adjoining room.

"I'll share this one with Gary", said Giles immediately. Giles has a great way of organising other people's lives, and often seems affronted when he tells you what you're doing that afternoon, and you have to break it to him that actually you had other plans.

"Fine by me", I said, and walked through the adjoining door to what turned out to be a much nicer room with a single King-size bed. Gary looked crestfallen.

"Okay guys", said Agent Dave, pointing out through the open door and back across the corridor, "we're going to be in these rooms across the corridor here. Now there's no locks on these doors, so we are going to trust you not to leave the room. Can we trust you to do that?"

"Of course".

"Good. Okay, let me and the boys get sorted out in our room, and then we'll get some food organised. Have a look at the room service menu and decide what you want to eat, and we'll get it fixed. Back in a few minutes".

Well this little scenario had not been on any of our radar screens! We all sat around in Gary and Giles' room and went round and round in circles trying to analyse what had happened and what it could mean. Believing that the room may well have been bugged, we spoke very little but instead wrote messages on pieces of paper which we passed backwards and forwards.

We hadn't come up with any answers when Agent Dave and the boys came back in and took our orders for food and drinks. Giles of course asked for a beer. Agent Dave thought about it for a second, and then decided that this wasn't a good idea, so it was soft drinks all round.

And while we waited for the food, and after it arrived, the Marshals sat and chatted with us. And they turned out to be really nice guys. The whole over-aggressive act was a default setting because their day job was catching and bringing back dangerous and violent offenders, many of whom were on the run. Agent Dave gave us his business card which identified his group as being part of the Gulf Coast Violent Offenders Task Force. Imagine if you will Tommy Lee Jones from The Fugitive. They had all been shot at on several occasions, and all loved their jobs.

They told us that the guy from the Attorney General's office had just arrived out of the blue and told them to get us out of chains and the hell out of there, because it was all kicking off. In retrospect, the only explanation we have ever managed to attach to this was the photograph of us in chains being beamed around the world. If it's true, I'd like to express my thanks to the photographer concerned, whoever he or she may be. Great job!

The following morning, Agent Dave was kind enough to offer me his razor because I did not have one. Only Giles had brought a clean shirt, and Gary and I had thought that it might have been taking the piss to ask to use the hotel laundry service overnight. Very prescient of Giles, I thought. I had imagined that we would be in prison-issue clothing on day two, so no need for a spare shirt.

We all had breakfast together down in the hotel restaurant, and then Agent Dave paid the bill and we set off for the courthouse. Before we left, Dave asked that we keep the story of what had happened to ourselves for the foreseeable future, as it was not the kind of thing that they wanted leaking out. The Marriot might be an expensive precedent for the Marshals' service. He also asked that when we arrived at the courthouse, we again cover our hands with an article of clothing, so that people would believe that we were handcuffed.

We arrived at the courthouse before 9am, and pulled up at the front door. This proved to be a neat trick since all the press were waiting around the back, expecting us to arrive in a prison van from the FDC, in our prison green boiler suits. We were taken up to the seventh floor, and put into a jury room adjoining an empty court. The attorneys arrived soon thereafter.

Michael Sommer had come down from New York, Reid Figel from Washington, and Dan Cogdell and Jimmy Ardoin from about five blocks away. It was the first time I had ever met Dan or Jimmy, and also Gary's first meeting with Reid.

Dan looked a little heavier than I had imagined him from his photographs. Fiftyish, I thought, with jet black hair and gleaming white teeth. His handshake was warm, and his greeting seemed heartfelt.

"I'm real sorry you're here, David", he said.

Jimmy was much younger than I had imagined. He looked straight out of college. He wore a blue shirt with a white collar, and his initials in monogram in the material. He beamed at me. "Welcome to Texas, dude." I felt in safe hands.

Reid was taller than Dan and Jimmy, and although I guessed from what Gary had told me that he must be around fifty, he didn't look it. He had mousy hair and wore tortoiseshell framed glasses about twenty years out of date. He looked every inch the intellectual.

Dan and Jimmy had tried to visit me the previous day at the FDC but were told that no one knew where we were, which had rather taken them aback. We told them what had happened. "Well, that's a first. Man, you guys sure are kicking up a bit of a shitstorm aren't you?" said Dan.

Down to business. This was to be an initial hearing at which we would be arraigned, enter a plea, and discuss bond. The hearing would be in front of Magistrate Judge Smith, rather than our trial judge. The Government had confirmed that they would not oppose an application to be released on bond, but that didn't mean it was a given. Not by any means.

Dan pointed out that it was unlikely that the judge would be able to make a decision on bond immediately, and there was a chance that he might remand us in custody pending a full bond hearing sometime next week. Since this was a Friday, that would mean a minimum of a weekend and possibly longer in the FDC. They would argue against that, but we needed to be prepared in case the judge flunked it.

We were visited in the courtroom by the British consul, Judith Slater, and her assistant who gave each of us a standard pack containing a covering letter and some pre-printed information sheets. She wanted to know if we had been well treated, and we said we had. She encouraged us to get in touch with her if there was anything we thought she might be able to help with. "How about getting us home?" I thought.

Our next visitor was less welcome. He was an attorney who came to serve us with subpoenas to give testimony in the Newby Class action. Having been served with one, I thought we would probably be on the wrong end of a few more, as there were still lawsuits flying around all over the place. Luckily, I was wrong. In any event, it was all just a game. We would have to plead the Fifth, and the plaintiffs' attorneys knew it. It suited their purposes but didn't exactly advance the cause of justice much.

Marshal Anne-Marie, my travelling companion on the flight, had by now made a re-appearance, without her sidekick Doralees. Agent Dave and his guys were in no hurry to leave, though. They seemed more than a little intrigued by the whole thing. Presumably they had been told that there was a huge press posse waiting outside, and perhaps they were wondering who are these guys that get extradited here and then put up in a luxury hotel?

After a lunch of Chinese takeaway, we were taken to the court of Judge Smith. There was a very disgruntled posse of press outside who had been barred from the courtroom because it was already full of reporters. There were lots of familiar journalists' faces in the audience when we got in, and we sat down and waited for things to begin.

The routine of a court hearing would become a familiar one. Shortly before the judge enters the court, one of the court officials will say "all rise", and everyone present stands. In comes the judge in his black cape. Then the court official will say something like "the United States District Court, Southern District of Texas, the Honorable Judge Stephen Smith presiding. May God Bless These United States of America". Then everyone sits down.

The next words that are heard are the case name, so for us it was "the United States of America versus David Bermingham, Giles Darby and Gary Mulgrew, case number CR02-597". Gary pointed out to me some time later how intimidating this was. The official has just asked God to bless the United States, and now the United States is against you, so presumably God must be against you as well. That's tough opposition. I mean the US Government has enough going for it already without needing God on its side.

We all three stood before Judge Smith and formally entered pleas of not guilty. He then took representations from the attorneys on bond. This was to be our introduction to the opposition, and as I sat at the defendants' table I tried to get the measure of them.

I was intrigued that Thomas Hanusik was not present. It turned out that he had joined the growing list of Task Force prosecutors who had parlayed their 'successes' in this most high profile of crusades into lucrative jobs in white collar defense work. Hanusik was offered partnership at the Washington firm of Crowell & Moring, joining their white collar and securities litigation practice.

Shame, really. I would have loved to have looked the guy in the eye, if only the once.

In his stead in the Houston courtroom that day, the lead prosecutor announced himself as Leo Wise. He looked about fifteen years old, tallish and a bit gangly, with pale skin and an awkward manner. He wore glasses and an intense expression. I figured he probably wasn't one for beers with the boys in front of the game at weekends. He looked as if he had still been at law school when Hanusik was framing the charges against us. It turned out that he had.

Wise had only joined the Department of Justice in 2004, and the Enron Task Force the following year, as a junior member of the team that prosecuted Lay and Skilling. A graduate from Harvard Law School, he was obviously being fast tracked through the Department, as I didn't see how he could have been given the lead role on a case like ours with his lack of experience unless someone thought pretty highly of him. Or unless they expected us just to roll over and plead guilty on arrival. If they did, they were going to have had a wasted trip from Washington.

Wise's assistant was Jonathan Lopez, or 'JLo' as we would take to referring to him. He also was young, but still older and more relaxed looking than his colleague. As his name suggested, he was obviously of Latino extraction, and much shorter than Wise. He let Leo do the talking, and smiled enigmatically from time to time.

Our attorneys had agreed in advance amongst themselves that it was worth pitching hard for bond to allow us to return to the UK, as we would all be waiving our right to a speedy trial, and the trial could be many months away. Gary in particular was desperate to get back because of the situation with his children, one of whom had effectively now lost both parents. Tony Blair, through his spokesman, had implied to the press before we left that his people would be making quiet representations to the US Government to the effect that the UK Government would be pleased if permission was granted to come back to the UK. We should have known better.

Leo and JLo were having none of it, of course. While the Government would not oppose bond, they said, it nonetheless regarded us as a serious risk of flight, and insisted that we be kept in the jurisdiction. Lord knows, it had been hard enough getting us here, they said. In common with all persons whose extradition the US seeks, we were formally classified there as 'fugitives'.

"Judge, there's no way these men are a flight risk", Dan countered. "They have been on bond in the UK since their arrest in 2004, and have fulfilled every single one of their conditions. When they lost their battle against extradition, they reported voluntarily to a police station in the UK to be brought here. The idea that somehow they would not return here if they were allowed back there now is preposterous. I mean, what possible reason would they have for not coming back, having come here voluntarily this time around?"

"Well, the prospect of thirty years plus behind bars, for one", said the Judge without a single hint of humour. I glanced at the press who were feverishly scribbling away. Nice soundbite, I thought.

Judge Smith was clearly in a quandary. When a Federal Grand Jury in the US hands down an indictment, a failure to report promptly to be arraigned makes you a fugitive. Your behaviour in another country is a matter of no importance. Self-reporting to a UK police station does not constitute coming voluntarily. The US Attorney's manual stipulates that bond shall always be opposed in extradition cases, so the political pressure that had caused them to step back from that position left everyone in uncharted territory.

If the US Government had not opposed our return to the UK, the judge might well have allowed us to go back because that would make his job easy. But they did oppose it, so he was unsure what to do. How could he grant these guys bond when they didn't belong here, and had nowhere to go? If someone is a flight risk, an alien, and has no permanent residence in the US, or indeed even any friends, then it made perfect sense that they should be locked up.

Dan, sensing that any hesitation would work against us, stepped in. "Your honor, if I may suggest, I would be more than happy to take these gentlemen into my personal custody while we find some more permanent accommodation for them locally".

"What, all three of them Mr Cogdell, in your house?"

You could almost hear the collective intakes of breath around the courthouse. Leo and JLo looked at Dan as if he'd just lost his mind.

"Yes, your honor. I know that there is the potential for this to precipitate Cogdell versus Cogdell Four (he told us later that he had had three previous divorces), but in the circumstances I would be happy to do this, yes".

"Alright. I need to go away and read all of these papers. We will reconvene in 45 minutes and I'll give you my ruling then. Thank you all."

"All rise", said the clerk. And off he went.

"Are you mad, Dan?" I asked, once he was gone. "We met you for the first time three hours ago".

"Dude", he said, curling his forefinger to his thumb until they almost touched, "he was that close to putting you into the FDC for a minimum of a weekend and probably longer. And believe me, it ain't a picnic in there. And anyway, you're my client. If I don't like the other two after a couple of days, I can just tell Judge Smith that it ain't working and he can lock 'em up", he smiled.

Forty-five minutes later we all reconvened. The judge said that the decision was too complex for final ruling now, and that we would reschedule for a full bond hearing the following Friday. Leo and JLo would have to make the long trip back to Washington, only to return a week later for another forty-five minute hearing.

In the meantime, Judge Smith was going to release us into the custody of Dan, subject to electronic monitoring, and nightly curfew. Giles and I would also have to post $100,000 cash as security, and Gary $20,000.

We spent about half an hour getting our electronic monitors fitted. They are a two piece kit. A large plastic block about three inches square and an inch deep that is attached to your ankle on a rubber bracelet, and a phone-like device which is about the size of the old walkie-talkies. The bracelet acts as a proximity device, bouncing signals from the phone, which communicates its position via satellite to the home station. If the bracelet goes out of range of the phone (more than about 10 feet), an alert is sent to Pre-Trial Services.

Given that all mobile phones these days have built in GPS capability (even if the manufacturers tell you they don't), and the Apple i-Phone has about a million times the functionality of this electronic tracking kit, it always amused me how big and cumbersome it was. I could only imagine that it was all part of the psychological warfare. It's cumbersome, it's noticeable, and people would constantly ask what it was. Stigma. Fuck 'em. I didn't care.

I tried not to care that the life of a battery about twice the size of a packet of cigarettes was about six hours, when a mobile phone would last the best part of a week. More psyops. I wasn't going to let it get to me.

I did rather care about paying $9 a day for the privilege of carrying this junk around, though. Over the time that we were in Houston, we each paid nearly $6,000 to some company called Behavioral Interventions in Boulder, Colorado. It's a name that would have belonged well in *A Clockwork Orange*, or *Nineteen Eighty Four*, I always thought. I imagined it being run by a relative of some senior official in the Texas State Government with a soldering iron and a box of old radio parts.

Fitted with the latest high tech tracking gizmos, we made our way into the sunlight outside the courthouse. Agent Dave had warned us that it was a pretty hostile crowd, meaning that they were jostling amongst themselves for position. He said that if things got at all ugly, he and the team would take us back into the courthouse pretty sharply.

Dan said a few words on our behalf. He thanked the Marshals, whom he said had treated us extremely well. He didn't mention the luxury hotel. I said a few words, mostly directed at my spineless Government back in England. Then a white Hummer and a dark BMW pulled up and we were off. There was a real scrum amongst the photographers as we tried to get into the vehicles.

"Holy shit", said Dan as we drove away, "those motherfuckers are mean. I have never seen press like that in my life".

Situated a few blocks from the courthouse downtown, Dan's office was nothing like any attorney's office I had ever been into before. Very rustic, with beige walls and rough stone flooring, and a lot of old, heavy dark wood furniture. A baby Grand Piano sat in the clients' waiting room.

The attorneys (the firm was an affiliation rather than a partnership as such) all had individual offices off the hallway. They were trial lawyers, and by the look of the press cuttings that adorned the walls, they had kicked some serious ass in their time.

Dan's office was on its own at the bottom, past Rosi Nunes, his PA, who acted as gatekeeper, and behind huge old barn-like double doors. Inside, to the left was an old pedestal desk with green leather top, two upholstered carver chairs and an old leather sofa. The only concession to modernity was a table set against the wall, with a computer keyboard and two flat screen monitors.

The office was full of knick-knacks—models of motorcycles and trucks, and a very expensive-looking motorcycle racing helmet. There were pictures on the walls, and the backs of the doors were covered in handwritten messages and cards. It had a really cosy feel to it.

On the wall above Rosi was a big blow-up of an article about Dan's defence of Sheila Kahanek, still the only Enron defendant to have secured a verdict of not guilty. There was a picture of Dan looking very lawyerly, and Sheila looking very businesslike. Just outside his office was a table, on top of which sat a T-Shirt with a picture of a pair of hands far apart, and the slogan "it's this big".

There was also a copy of an e-mail to Dan from one of the jurors in the Kahanek trial, telling him what a great job he had done, and how he made all those other out of town attorneys look real stoopid. The e-mail finished with the advice "Don't Mess With Texas". Second time in two days. This was getting a bit scary.

There wasn't much we could do, and so Dan suggested that we use his phone to call home as he had "some snakes to kill"—e-mails and other routine stuff. The three of us waited in turn to phone home and tell our loved ones that we were not in prison.

Emma had been kept updated by several members of the press, including Mark Eddo, but was glad nonetheless to hear from me. She told me about all the sympathetic calls she had received, not just from friends and family but from members of the press. She had even been sent a huge bouquet of flowers by a guy from the local TV news channel. Little things like that make dealing with bad situations a whole lot easier. There is the sense that others share your pain.

Then Dan, having killed his snakes, said he would take us to our new home. From downtown we headed north on Interstate 59. Dan clocked that we were being followed, and so he made a detour onto the Hardy Toll Road, because he had an EZ-Pass that enabled him to drive though the toll booth without stopping. He was confident that our pursuer would have to stop and queue. He was right. We made our escape.

CASA COGDELL
13th July 2006

Prior to leaving the office, Dan had sent a text to his wife, alluding to the War of Independence.

"The British are coming. The British are coming. To our house!!!!"

Robin, his wife, had just texted back. "Awesome!!!"

We would spend over two weeks at Casa Cogdell, as one of the newspapers nicknamed it. There was much amusement in the Houston community that Dan had taken us into his home, but it was just a mark of the man, and our first real experience of the Texas hospitality that would take all of us by surprise.

Dan and Robin lived in a place called Humble, some thirty miles north east of Houston, with Dan's son Hunter and Robin's daughter Jamie, both of whom were away on summer camp when we first arrived, meaning that Gary and Giles could occupy their rooms while I took the guest bedroom.

Robin greeted us as long lost friends, and took no time in opening a bottle of wine that would set the tone for our stay.

The house was new, in a nice development consisting almost exclusively of detached houses on relatively small plots of land. For some reason many Houstonians are not that interested in having big gardens, or 'yards' as they call them, so they build large properties on small sites. It's not that land is at a premium. Quite the opposite. But typically the yard will be big enough for an outdoor kitchen, a swimming pool, a patio or deck area and not much else. I guess it may have something to do with the oppressive summer weather, when being outside just means drowning in sweat and getting eaten alive by mosquitoes.

Robin was Dan's fourth wife, a fact to which he had alluded in court that day. She cannot have been taller than five feet, but she was no shrinking violet, and would occasionally be seen sporting a tight T-shirt emblazoned with the words "Yes they're real—real expensive". Enough said.

Living with Dan cannot be an easy thing, as he comes with a lot of baggage. Robin, presumably like her three predecessors, found herself sharing her man with his two other loves; his work and his toys. Dan was, to put it mildly, a petrol head. He collected cars and motorbikes, and they had to be the top of the range. He had a limited edition Ducati 990S, and a Kawasaki ZXR600 that he had just had specially and expensively altered so that the diminutive Robin could ride it.

And he had a selection of motocross bikes which he used to race at weekends, when at his age he should have known better. The following year he would all but destroy his knee and the surrounding ligaments riding cross-country. He was in plaster for weeks, and hobbling for months.

All around the garage were pictures of Dan in leathers at various bike meets, with friends who happened to include Julia Roberts' one time husband, the musician Lyle Lovett. Lyle had played at Dan's Christmas party the previous year.

Dan was a Texan through and through. Brash, with a mouth like a sewer from time to time, but a wonderful turn of phrase and a heart as big as an elephant. And Robin, for all her lack of height, had him under her thumb. When I went to bed that first night, I already knew that I had landed on my feet.

The following day we were all up relatively early, still on UK time. Gary was downstairs when I got down, and was trying to use the coffee machine to make tea. It was a disaster. Not many Americans drink tea, and kettles are a rarity. We settled eventually for coffee.

An old friend of Gary's called Jim Moonier flew in from Hawaii that day to see if there was anything he could do to help. He drove us downtown to get us sorted out with cell-phones. I had never possessed a mobile phone before so didn't know where to start.

As with all things in America, you start with a social security number. Which of course we didn't have. In the end 'Moon' had to put the phones onto his Cingular account.

When we got "home" late in the afternoon, Robin had been to the video store and got a selection of DVDs. We had stopped by a wine store and bought a case of wine. We had pizza and wine in front of the TV and watched a film called Fun with Dick and Jane which stars Jim Carrey It had been running for all of about 10 minutes before we realised that it was a spoof on the collapse of Enron.

Robin was beside herself with embarrassment. Certainly it is difficult to imagine a less appropriate film, but that just made it all the funnier. When the credits rolled at the end, there were special thanks to Ken Lay, Jeff Skilling, Andy Fastow, Ben Glisan and others. The only real surprise was that our names weren't on the list.

The following Monday, Dan arranged for us to meet with an immigration attorney. The guy looked at all our paperwork, and the I-94 cards which indicated that we had been paroled due to "significant public interest". He hummed and ha'd for a few minutes, and threw in the odd loud exhale of breath for effect, before giving his verdict.

"Well, gentlemen, the best way I can put it is this. You are here lawfully but not legally. Technically, you are still on the plane."

Well, that was clear then. Still, he reassured us that we weren't going to be picked up any day soon, and so we would remain lawfully but not legally at large for nearly two years thereafter, before finally being sent home as convicts with the immigration detainer stamped in our passports.

On 21st July, a week after our initial appearance, we were back in front of Magistrate Judge Smith for the bond hearing proper. By now, Giles too had secured a Houston attorney, in the shape of the local legend Dick DeGuerin, which had caused a bit of a stir with the press.

As we assembled at the courtroom in preparation for the judge's entrance, JLo handed each of our attorneys a small bundle of papers, which would be appendices to the Government's written brief for the hearing.

It seemed that we were indeed the privileged few. Not only did we get to spend our first night in a swanky hotel courtesy of the US Government, but now we were each being handed work permits, a document that so many millions of illegal immigrants would die for. The Government would argue that if we were to be released, we should be required to work. That should be a laugh.

Not so funny was the copy of the letter dated the day before from Paul Close of the United Kingdom's very own Crown Prosecution Service. Mr Close opined that it would be 'imprudent in the extreme' for us to be allowed to return to the UK.

My thoughts at the time were of the numerous morning and afternoon press briefings at 10 Downing Street just before we were extradited. The Prime Minister's official spokesman had got himself tied in all kinds of knots about the representations which were being made to the US Government about our bail, and the possibility of our being allowed to return to the UK. He had clearly implied that yes, they were asking for us to be allowed to return home.

Paul Close's letter revealed a rather different strategy. Under no circumstances should these guys be allowed anywhere near their country.

I hope Mr Close is proud of himself. I still search through the Queen's Birthday and New Year's honours lists, looking for his name, perhaps knighted for his services to the Special Relationship.

It was a pivotal moment for us. If we were required to stay in Houston, then every day spent on bond would be a day out of our lives. We would be thousands of miles away from everything we cherished, strangers in a strange land, trying to earn sufficient money to pay for our own living in Houston, our families back home, and our legal teams. And if convicted, we would get no credit whatsoever against our sentence for the time spent in Houston. The odds would be stacked against us, and the result all but inevitable. All the Department of Justice would have to do to win would be to keep pushing back the trial date.

Judge Smith was duly persuaded of the Government's argument, and we were given our long term bond conditions. We would be confined to an area encompassing Houston and a small distance around it. We would have electronic monitoring and nightly curfew. We would be required to find employment. And we would not be allowed to be in each other's company other than in the presence of one of our attorneys.

Oh yes, and we would each have to post a bond of one million dollars, of which a large chunk would be in cash—half a million for me and Giles, and two hundred thousand for Gary. This, conveniently, represented all our liquid assets as reported to the Pre-Trial Services department, leaving us no ready money to pay attorneys' fees and living costs.

Both Giles and Gary had come armed with a mountain of pledges of security from friends and family. Not cash, but pledges. The judge dismissed them without a second thought. Cash would do fine, thank you. They would have to sell assets.

All in all it was a shitty day. Leo and JLo left satisfied that the case was now in the bag, and we were left wondering how it is that this nation could constantly trumpet the virtues of its criminal justice system. Can't afford to fight your case anymore? Don't worry, just sign this plea deal and it can all go away. There's a good boy.

Well, fuck 'em.

Gary and I retired to Casa Cogdell, bloodied but unbowed. Giles, meanwhile, was off in Dick's DeGuerin's light aircraft to spend the weekend at Dick's ranch in Marfa, West Texas, some six hundred miles away. Dick had requested permission from Judge Smith at the bond hearing, and since neither Leo nor JLo had any idea where Marfa was, they found themselves unable to object.

Giles called from the airstrip before they took off, terrified. He told us that the plane only had one propeller, and it was at the front. I assured him that this was a good place for it, and that he should only be concerned if at any stage during the flight it ceased to be there.

I was jealous as hell. I had obtained a private pilot's licence while in the Army over twenty years previously, and would have loved to have made that trip, flying low over the vast emptiness of Texas. Giles, by contrast, would probably have rather driven a nail through his hand than get into the little Cessna.

Dan and I sat out that night drinking red wine. He smoked a cigar, I had several cigarettes. Over the course of the previous week, we had all got to know him and Robin quite well. There was no doubt that Dan was a special man. He had a way of connecting with people. It's a gift with which few are blessed, and as a trial lawyer it gives you a huge edge.

Dan quickly put me straight on my views on the case. Forget the righteous indignation. Forget the truth. No-one's interested—at least not in a courtroom.

Trials are a game, played for enormously high stakes. The psychological pressure of a criminal trial can crush the strongest of men. But the winner is almost inevitably the side that defines the issues, that gets the jury to focus on the evidence from their point of view. And to do that, you need to be able to connect with each member of the jury on a personal level. If they like you as a person, then their natural inclination will always be to see an ambiguous fact in the light most favourable to you, and often trials turn on the smallest of things.

I already felt part of the Cogdell family. Robin had a huge personality and great warmth. She loved Dan unconditionally, and so any friend or client of Dan's would be welcome in her home. It was a characteristic of the Texans that we would quickly come to love.

Texans are a breed unto themselves. They came late to the Union, having previously been a country in their own right, with their own embassy in London, and to this day they still have the ability to walk away from the Union. A good number, given the option, would do so. Many see themselves as Texans first, Americans second.

There was no doubt, this place was special. But Houston was a City still very much wracked by the death of its largest company, and it left a community hopelessly divided. And Texans being Texans, the opinions at either end of the spectrum were quite extreme. The majority were still for shooting first and asking questions later. And we were on the wrong end of that sentiment for many.

Dan mused about the bond conditions. After all, his future fees were at stake. I had already sent him a sizeable amount of money, but we both knew that it wasn't enough to get us to trial. On the face of it, I could either pay him, or give the money to the court, but not both.

"Can you find another half a million bucks, David?"

"I'm going to have to, aren't I?"

"Well, you can always agree to be remanded into custody."

"Could I defend this case from inside the FDC"?

"Not a chance".

"Then I'm going to have to find it, aren't I?"

"Yup".

SWITCHING HORSES
July 2006

When your backs are against the wall you really find out who your friends are. It took me just one phone call to secure the promise of a loan for my bond money. I would not be remanded in custody. I could have wept. Giles, ever the pragmatist and no fan of debt, elected to sell his house, which was the only substantial asset he had left. Gary had no house, and so had to part with something that he regarded as far more precious; his shareholding in Celtic Football Club.

The philosophy of the Department of Justice is very straightforward–put the defendant in a position where no sane person would do anything other than agree to plead guilty. For most people, merely the cost of going to trial is sufficient to induce a plea, given that even if you win you cannot recover your fees. The "trial penalty", as evidenced by the cases of Jamie Olis and Jeff Skilling, weighs just as heavily. Assert your innocence and lose at trial, you will be crucified on sentence. Put your principles aside and plead guilty, you will serve a fraction of the time.

For us, there was the added psychological pressure of being far away from home and family, where every day was a day out of your life which you could never recover. Time, therefore, was the friend of Leo Wise and Jonathan Lopez, and they would use it judiciously against us. But at that moment, they must have thought that the bond conditions alone would be enough to finish us off.

It is easy to understand why the prosecutors will always ask for someone to be incarcerated. Once inside, your ability to conduct a defence is all but eradicated. Without the direct intervention of Tony Blair, it is certain that we would have found ourselves languishing in the Federal Detention Center, game over.

If you need evidence, take the case of the larger-than-life character Allen Stanford, the founder of a financial services company based in Houston, who was accused of financial impropriety in the immediate wake of the Bernie Madoff scandal in early 2009. He was thrown into the FDC as a flight risk; within a year, his attorney stated:

'Mr. Stanford's pretrial incarceration has reduced him to a wreck of a man: he has suffered potentially life-impairing illnesses; he has been so savagely beaten that he has lost all feeling in the right side of his face and has lost near field vision in his right eye. The major injuries from his assault while in prison required reconstructive surgery under general anesthesia and was performed while he was under restraint.'

Federal Detention Centers are grim places. I've been incarcerated in more than one, although thankfully never for long. Your accommodation consists of a seven by ten foot cell which you share with another inmate, who statistically is likely to be facing drugs charges.

The only positive thing about pre-trial detention is that when you finally agree to plead guilty, you will get credit for time served. But don't imagine for one moment that you can think about defending yourself. You can't, and the prosecutors know it. And the judges know it. Pre-trial detention in a white-collar case is a summary verdict of guilty without the boring necessity to examine any evidence or hear any witnesses. It is extremely expeditious justice.

I had long harboured a concern as to how Gary and Giles would react when we touched down in the land of Enron. Everybody talks a good fight from an armchair several thousand miles away, but you need to be able to look into their eyes in the heat of battle and see what lies behind. If the truth be told, for all my bravado I wasn't sure how I would react when we arrived. The bullets need to be flying before the question is truly answered.

That both of them made the sacrifices that they did to raise their bond money told me something, therefore. They were not about to fold. If we stuck together, we might just give the prosecutors a run for their money, no matter how badly the system was stacked against us. But if any cracks appeared, the prosecutors would divide and conquer. Turn one defendant, and then start using him or her as leverage to get the others to fold. First one in gets the best deal. Last man standing gets screwed.

The team dynamics were interesting. To a degree the attorneys reflected the personae of their clients. Dan was all for trying this Mother, as he would continually say. He particularly fancied the idea of going up in a

Texan court against a couple of young boys from DC. He reckoned the jury would just hate Leo.

Dan's associate, Jimmy Ardoin, was just a couple of years out of law school but clearly a bright and able guy, and not short of self-confidence. He had persuaded Dan to give him work experience whilst still at college, which had turned into a full time position, and within months Dan was letting Jimmy run his own cases. Jimmy was full of youthful enthusiasm, and pronounced himself happy to babysit the NatWest Three when they wanted to go drinking together, in order to comply with the terms of our bond. So Jimmy was definitely a good guy.

Dick DeGuerin for Giles was studiously middle of the road. He saw that the odds were against us, but he too quite liked the idea of taking these guys on. He didn't pretend to understand much about the case at this point, but his partner Matt Hennessy was already getting up to speed, and would in time probably understand the case better than any other attorney. He had the added advantage of being a really nice guy.

Reid Figel for Gary was Mr Doom. Our chances of winning at trial were about twenty percent, he would say. The e-mails were horrible, and we made a boatload of money. Any decent prosecutor would need no more than that, and we should be working towards negotiating a plea, however much we all thought we were innocent. As an ex-chief of the Fraud section of the Department of Justice, you ignored him at your peril.

It was an eclectic group, therefore, but the spread of talents and viewpoints made our early decision-making informed. And all were agreed on the direction that we should be taking. Plan for trial. Attack is the best form of defence. Even if your intention is to plead guilty, your negotiating position in the great game will always be better if the other side thinks you might just be serious about going to trial.

Where Dan was the hard drinking, cussing petrol head, happy in a smoky sports bar with a bourbon, Dick was the gentleman cowboy, at home amongst Houston's social elite, a glass of fine wine in his hand.

He wore a cowboy hat and boots to court every day with his suit, and had impeccable manners. He owned a sizeable ranch to the North West of Houston, and his place in Marfa, to which he would regularly fly himself on Friday afternoons. He was one of a small handful of attorneys who commanded universal respect amongst the Federal judges in Houston.

Dick, like Dan, tried cases. The harder the case, the higher the profile, the more likely it was that Dick would be interested. Even when the cases were gruesome in the extreme.

Dick had recently tried a high profile murder case where his client was a colourful multi-millionaire cross-dressing local celebrity accused of killing and dismembering his neighbour, whose body parts he then wrapped up and threw into Galveston Bay. He did not deny the act, but claimed self-defence. The case turned on the lack of a head, the only body part not to have been recovered, and he walked.

Dan's comparable case involved the torture and alleged murder of a local man by a gang of cowboys. They had apparently used a cattle prod on their victim, who died at the scene, and one of them had recorded the man's screams as the grisly tale unfolded.

Dan represented one of the accused, and in a piece of theatre that you would only find in the courtrooms of Texas, he used the cattle prod on himself in front of the jury to demonstrate that it couldn't really be said with certainty to have killed the boy. He also went out of his way to play the tape of the dying man's screams as often as he could to the jury, to desensitise them to its impact. The cattle prod, along with a newspaper clipping announcing the not guilty verdict for his client, hung in pride of place in a showcase next to the door to Dan's office.

Gary, meanwhile, was undecided about his attorney. We all knew what we needed as a collective legal team—one major firm to do all the motions practice, and the other two to handle the trial. Much of American law is about filing motions. Mountains of filings. Lots of legal argument. Large firms can cope with this kind of heavy lifting. That's where most of their billable hours come from. Small firms can't.

We already had our trial attorneys. Reid's firm could do all the motions practice standing on their heads, but it would come at an enormous cost, and they billed by the hour. A local firm would be much cheaper and easier to work with.

Dan suggested Thomas Hagemann of the law firm Gardere Wynne, who had represented another of the defendants in the Nigerian Barges trial. There were many parallels between that case and ours, and Tom's experience would potentially be invaluable.

We all got together in Dan's conference room, and Tom arrived with Marla Poirot, another partner from the firm. They had done their research on our case, and were keen to take it on.

"This is a slam dunk honest services case", said Tom.

We all looked at each other, nonplussed. What was one of those, then?

"Here, look at the indictment", offered Tom. "It charges theft of property and honest services fraud. They are different things. Look at paragraph 10.

"...devised and executed a scheme to defraud NatWest and GNW and deprive them of money and their right to honest services"."

The long and the short of it was that Leo and JLo didn't even need to prove that we had stolen any money. All the prosecutors had to do was to argue that we owed NatWest a duty to disclose, and we hadn't disclosed, and we were done. You could be found completely innocent of stealing any money, but the penalties for failing to disclose would be the same as if you had walked out of the bank with a mask on and a large bag marked "swag" written all over it.

"But hang on a minute", said Gary. "There's no way that's a crime in the UK. Failure to disclose? That's an employment law thing."

"Not over here it isn't. What do you think the Task Force convicted the Merrill bankers on? Honest services fraud".

Mark MacDougall's words came back to me. Every time there's another crisis, the Government takes the opportunity to develop new areas of criminality. The honest services statute was originally enacted to deal with dishonest politicians and public servants. It was not supposed to impinge upon the duties owed by employees of private corporations, but the US prosecutors were trying to extend its remit. It was a very powerful weapon for them, because the boundaries of what constitutes an 'intangible right of honest services' were totally vague, which gave the Government huge leeway. Especially in highly charged white collar cases where the jury would be itching to convict.

"But anyway, if this isn't a crime in the UK, we have specialty protection. We can't be tried for that".

The laughter rang around the room.

"I don't think that would be a very long conversation with Ewing Werlein", opined Dan.

Judge Ewing Werlein Jr had been appointed to our case from the moment we were indicted and, as is the system in the Federal Courts, he would remain with the case until its conclusion. He had also presided over the Nigerian Barges trial, and he wasn't known for his sympathetic views of defendants. It was agreed amongst the lawyers around the table that he would not give a fig as to whether we had been extradited on a false premise. We were there to stand trial under US law, and he would be presiding over said trial.

From adversity comes opportunity, however. The Government's case in the Barges trial had pushed the interpretation of the honest services provision to a new level, and Tom Hagemann was hopeful that the Fifth Circuit Court of Appeals would overturn the convictions. Judgment on that was due within weeks. If the Barge defendants had a good case on appeal, our arguments were stronger still. How on earth could a US domestic statute be used to criminalise a purported breach of a contractual relationship between a foreign firm and its foreign employees? This was surely a step too far.

The fact that the indictment charged the deprivation of 'money and [the] right to honest services' in the same sentence meant that the two allegations were inextricably linked. So if the honest services allegations could be struck out, then the whole indictment would arguably fall down.

Tom and Marla were itching to get started. They had a large firm behind them and they could do all the motions practice with ease, reusing a lot of the work from the Barges trial. Why reinvent the wheel? They were local, and they knew the Enron story inside out. It was a slam dunk, I thought, as the meeting broke up.

Life, however, is never that simple. A day or so later Dan took a call from a major Washington firm, wanting to offer their services pro bono. Hiring Dan and Dick was a statement that we weren't going to roll over and plead guilty, and these guys wanted in on the action. Great for their profile, I guess.

So now Gary had three choices. He decided he needed to go to Washington to meet with Reid Figel, and the firm who were offering to act for free. Jimmy Ardoin agreed to go with him, and the court duly granted permission.

When Gary came back two days later and announced his decision, it prompted a huge argument and ultimately I stormed out in a huff, having thrown all of my toys out of the pram. Gary was going to stick with Reid. It seemed to me that this was piss-poor decision making. Reid's firm were an unknown quantity, situated a couple of thousand miles away and billing by the hour. He had a choice of another such firm, also an unknown quantity, who would do the same work for free, or a local firm who knew the ropes, lived just down the street, and would cost a fraction of what Reid and co would bill. The answer was simple, surely?

If I'm brutally honest about it, and I said as much to Reid some eighteen months later, I think this decision cost us the opportunity to go to trial. Though many would say, and depending upon which day of the week it is I might agree, that this was a blessing in disguise, and that we might still be in Texas right now had we elected to stick it out.

But from where I stood in July 2006, we were handicapping ourselves early. The costs would be crippling, and our resources were minimal. There would come a time when the psychological pressure of the mounting bills would be too great. The first one to run out of money would become the 'weakest link'. It wasn't a question of 'if', just 'how long?'

I vented my spleen to Jimmy the next day. Jimmy, however, sided with Gary. Having actually sat in Reid's offices and met the guys who would work on the team, Jimmy was in awe. Kellogg, Huber, Hanson, Todd, Evans and Figel LLP was a relatively small firm, but replete with some of the finest legal minds in the country.

"Dude, half of these guys have clerked for the Supreme Court. They're just awesome. It was a privilege just to be sat in the same room as them".

If attorneys were motor cars, I would have bought the old pick-up truck, and Giles the rather shinier, sleeker version. Neither would turn heads in the street, but the mileage was good, there were several litres of muscle under the hood, and when the weather turned and the tarmac road ran out, you wouldn't want to be driving anything else. Gary, meanwhile, had just acquired himself a Lamborghini, on tick.

Tom and Marla at Gardere Wynne were duly given the bad news, and we hunkered down to begin the fight in earnest.

Every day added a little more to our understanding of the practicalities of the US justice system. It was pretty terrifying, but no matter how bad things ever look on any given day, it is always easy to find people much worse off. If we had been brought against our will to Texas, we had at least managed to engineer a situation where we had a shot at a defence, or so we thought. Others would not be so lucky.

HOME FROM HOME
August 2006

Our first priority while waiting to see the case against us was to find new digs. Jimmy took a considerable amount of time out of his schedule to ferry us around, looking for apartments. In common with most residents of Houston, he drove a giant pick-up truck, a black Ford with a series of gaudy orange lights across the top of the cab.

Gary, Giles and I could not live together, as that would have breached our bail conditions, so we would have to find three separate apartments. It was a blessing in disguise, of course, because although it meant significantly greater aggregate costs, it probably assured our sanity over the coming two years.

In the end, all three of us found accommodation just outside downtown on Memorial Drive. Gary and Giles each took apartments in a complex called the Left Bank, just on the edge of the swanky River Oaks area which was home to many of Houston's wealthier residents. I found an apartment a little closer to town, on Jackson Hill. Both complexes were gated, serviced, and with gym and pools. If we were going to be stuck somewhere for a protracted period, we might as well be comfortable, and in UK money they were dirt cheap.

My little apartment had two ensuite bedrooms, meaning that Emma and the children could stay, even if it was cramped. It also had a tiny cubby hole that served as a study, in which I would almost live for many months at a time, hunched over a desk in front of my little computer, surrounded by papers. It was quiet and without distractions. In short, perfect for the conduct of a defence.

Because we were aliens, on bond, with no social security numbers, Dan had to sign up to all of our leases in the name of his firm. I have often wondered what the hell we would have done without him. He even sorted us out with bank accounts, through his personal banker, a lovely guy called Chuck Bolton, who turned up at Dan's office one day to drive me to the bank and sort out the formalities.

Chuck, it transpired, was no fan of the Federal Government, not least because recent changes in the law had caused him to have to dispose of a large part of his arsenal of automatic weapons. On our way to the bank, we discussed the relative merits of the Belgian FN rifle and the British forces' SLR. Chuck even owned a Browning .50 machine gun, which can shoot holes through armoured vehicles, and regaled me with stories of his sixteen year old son getting familiar with the entire range of his weaponry. Only in Texas, surely?

Things began to fall into place. Dan called me one day at the beginning of August, and asked me to come down to the office, where I found him with his feet up on his old desk, smoking a cigar.

"Dude, you're luckier than a dog with two dicks", he said. I countered that I didn't feel particularly lucky, being stuck five thousand miles away from my family and facing thirty years in prison. But it turned out that I had two reasons to be extremely happy. The first was that the Fifth Circuit Court of Appeals had just overturned the convictions of the Merrill Lynch defendants in the Barge trial. The honest services theory was indeed flawed, it seemed.

My second cause for joy was sitting in the parking lot outside the office. A cream Cadillac DeVille. Unbeknownst to me, Dan had persuaded his aged father, whose eyesight was failing, to give up his car, and Dan wanted me to have it for as long as I was in Houston. If it was a million miles away from the car I would have chosen, it was nonetheless a car, and a splendid car at that, and in a city like Houston you cannot get around without wheels.

I looked at it and laughed. It seemed about four hundred feet long, and when we got in to take it for a spin, it felt more like a hovercraft than a car, gliding over the humps and bumps in the road. It had a five litre, eight cylinder engine that would happily have powered a bus, and drank fuel at a prodigious rate, although at just over two dollars a gallon, its effective cost was still a fraction of what it cost to run a car half the size in England. It was without any shadow of a doubt a vehicle for a retired executive or a drugs dealer.

Dan thought it was hilarious. "Pimp my Brit", he said.

My little package was almost complete. A roof over my head.

Communications. And now transport. I managed to secure long distance employment, working by internet for a small business in London, writing reviews of retail financial products, identifying risks and generally giving overviews for potential investors. This job would cover my overheads while in Houston. Gary introduced Giles and me to Skype, the free internet videophone service which enabled me to talk daily with Emma and the children, and to see them, which was a massive boost to morale.

Giles and Gary were the first to organise a social life. Troy Lochlear, one of the other attorneys in Dan's office, was intrigued by the three Brits, and immediately struck up a friendship with Giles, that seemed to revolve mostly around beer. Troy, though, was also a manic 'soccer' fan, and regularly played in a five a side league at a local sports hall called Kicks, which was very close to where we all lived.

Giles and Gary took little persuading to join his team. I turned out for one early game, tweaked my knee and decided that uninsured medical care in the US was something I didn't need to add to my list of worries, so I retired. I would watch the boys from the sidelines, and join in the beers afterwards.

The practicalities of playing football with an electronic ankle bracelet on are not straightforward, however. The bracelet itself is cumbersome and has a tendency to cut into your skin when you run. And the large phone device to which it speaks cannot sensibly be attached to a pair of football shorts.

Consequently, Giles and Gary would have to keep popping back to the sidelines every minute or so to make sure their phone was still saying that it was in range of the ankle bracelet.

Our circle of friends began to grow. For the most part I piggybacked off Giles and Gary, whose Left Bank apartments turned out to have quite a few sympathetic neighbours, including Kyle and Lucy, a young Scottish couple who worked locally for energy companies.

I became a regular at St Theresa's Catholic Church in Memorial Park. On my first ever visit there, only days after moving into my apartment, I was somewhat taken aback to hear an English voice saying the mass. Father Phil Lloyd, the pastor, was born in Shropshire, and moved to Houston in 2001. As if to leave me well and truly flummoxed, the fina hymn that day was "My Country, 'tis of Thee", sung to the tune of "God Save The Queen".

The families all came out shortly after we settled in. Emma came initially only with Jemima, unsure whether the journey would be possible with all three, and keen to see what awaited her on arrival. Satisfied that Houston was not the nightmare that she envisioned, she returned a few weeks later with Freddie and Archie, and thereafter would come every school holiday with all three for a couple of weeks at a time.

My closest friends locally were Bart and Alix Stafford, who had read an article about us in the *Houston Chronicle* shortly after we arrived, and wrote to the journalist offering us their hospitality. Alix is English, and Bart a local. They were sufficiently moved by our plight that they wanted to help in any way they could. In the first instance, that meant dinner for Gary and me, and thereafter introductions to a lot of the English expat community.

When Emma's parents came to stay just before Christmas in 2007, Bart and Alix insisted that they stay at their house rather than book into a hotel, and after our repatriation, in 2009, Bart diverted from a business trip to Europe to come and visit me in Springhill prison, near Bicester. Truly great people

If you're going to get stuck anywhere in the world, you could do an awful lot worse than Houston. Although it is very much an 'oil town', it has an awful lot going for it. With the exception of the brutal summer months, the weather is generally lovely if a little humid. If you are into art and culture generally, Houston is your place. It has several theatres, wonderful museums, art galleries 'to die for', a world class ballet, great sports facilities, lots of green spaces, and a road network that enables you to travel great distances in relatively short timeframes. Oh yes, and world class shopping malls, with everything at half the UK price, as Emma would discover to her delight....

Little wonder, in fact, that many of the expats that I met had arrived in Houston twenty five or thirty years ago on a six month or year-long assignment, and had never gone home.

The issues of size took some getting used to. Everything in Texas is bigger. The people are bigger. Some, like the policeman we had met on arrival, were giants. Others were just morbidly obese. Portions in any restaurant were beyond ridiculous, but as the staff were always happy to put any leftovers in a box to eat the following day, you effectively got two meals for the price of one.

All in all, it could have been a hell of a lot worse. By securing bail, we had given ourselves a chance. Not a great one. But a chance nonetheless, which was more than most people would have got. It would be up to us to make the most of it.

THE CASE FOR THE PROSECUTION
August 2006

Having entered a plea of not guilty, America's Speedy Trial Act allowed us the opportunity, in common with all criminal defendants, to be tried within seventy days, and Judge Smith had entered a nominal trial date for that September. Everyone involved knew that it was never going to happen, because we couldn't even begin to prepare our defense until we had seen the evidence against us, and this was not going to be a straightforward case.

However, as with all things in the American justice system, the charade had to be gone through so we could formally waive our rights to a speedy trial at the status conference set for early September. Prior to that, the US Government would have to send us the evidence.

It would take them over a month.

The Government's case, when it finally arrived, came in the form of three compact discs, under a covering letter from Sean Berkowitz, then head of the Enron Task Force. Two of the discs contained all of the documentary evidence, and the other was said to contain voice recordings of the three of us.

"Well that should be interesting. No one's ever mentioned us being tape recorded before. That's probably illegal in the UK", I mused to Jimmy.

"Don't make no difference now, David. Wire taps are admissible evidence in Texas, no matter how they were obtained, so it's coming in".

I was actually quite excited. You know that rather queasy feeling you get in your stomach when you are just overwhelmed by anticipation. Possibly for the first time it dawned on me that maybe Gary had lied, and was about to be found out. Maybe Kopper's statement really was true after all, and Gary had been recorded concocting some scheme with him or Fastow. That would certainly be a turn up for the books.

But surely not?

No, indeed. It was quickly apparent that, far from being contemporaneous records of a fraud taking place, these recordings were from nearly two years' later, between the 12th and 15th November 2001, when the three of us were working at the Royal Bank of Canada. Obviously RBC had decided to record all our telephone calls immediately after we had gone forward to the compliance department to report our suspicions about the transaction.

I wondered whether Leo or JLo had even listened to them.

Three hours later I was convinced that they had not.

The recordings painted a fascinating and utterly compelling picture. Not of three crooks thinking they were on the verge of being rumbled, but rather of three guys who were desperately struggling to understand what might have happened some eighteen months previously, and worrying about what impact all of this might have on the running of their existing business.

There were one or two quite amusing moments when Gary was giving his verdict on one or more senior members of the bank as people. The very different characters of all three of us came across beautifully. Me at times abrasive, always clipped and factual. Giles see-sawing between cheery and business-like on the one hand, and maudlin and worried on the other. And Gary talking endlessly, as Gary does.

As each segment finished and a new call began, I kept expecting this to be the one that had Gary or Giles saying something utterly incriminating. But after three hours and nearly a hundred calls, there was nothing of the sort. It was an excellent portrayal of a busy office where this issue was just one problem of many that needed to be worked through to a solution.

I was quickly forming the view that Leo and JLo had substantially no understanding of this case. They had been handed the file after Hanusik left, and had probably let it gather dust until we were extradited, presumably expecting us to immediately seek to negotiate a plea. No need, therefore, to do any work on the case itself.

This was good and bad. Good, because knowledge is power. Whatever my thoughts about Hanusik having been lazy or incompetent in putting together his case, he was at least on the spot at the time, and so presumably had a decent working knowledge. These guys by contrast had exactly no experience on this case.

Bad, however, because presumably their understanding of the case had been shaped by the same press coverage and DoJ bullshit that had poisoned all of our court hearings to date. They probably thought we were slam-dunk guilty, and that was never a good place to have the prosecutors, either in preparation for trial, or in negotiating any deal. You want them to realise that in fact their case sucks. I reckoned Hanusik almost certainly knew that. These guys probably didn't.

Still, I was going to have some serious fun with Gary and Giles that evening. I knew there was no way that either of them would have listened to the tapes.

I called the boys and told them that we needed to meet. I tried to sound as serious as I could and intimated that it was best that we didn't discuss the content of the tapes over the phone, which we all assumed would be tapped. By the time I got to the bar where we had agreed to meet, both of my co-defendants were sitting at a table, beer in hand, looking utterly terrified.

"Is it bad, mate?" asked Giles.

I just blew hard, tried to look as serious as I could, and said "well, it depends on your definition of 'bad', Giles", which I knew would hit the spot. I then looked at Gary. "Is there anything you wanted to tell us, Gary?"

But facing his instant expression of shock and horror, I couldn't keep a straight face. I am the world's worst liar, and I can't keep up any sort of pretence for more than a few minutes. Besides which, I was itching to tell them the truth.

The following day I began reading all of the documentary evidence. Dan had sent the discs off to a local printer, who had turned them into thirteen thousand pages of documents at a cost of a couple of thousand dollars. Reid Figel and Dick DeGuerin's offices undertook similar exercises, at similar expense, for Gary and Giles.

One thing was immediately apparent. Over ninety percent of the documents had come from RBS in the UK. The remainder was a hotchpotch of stuff from Enron, CSFB, LJM, and KPMG, auditors to LJM.

Now that we had finally got to see the case against us, it was abundantly clear, as we had always contended, that it belonged firmly in the UK.

I looked in vain for any single document that might have corroborated the prosecutors' assertions that the February meeting was about a fraud. There was none. Not a single one. They just made it up, and all the courts in the UK accepted it as fact. It was total, complete and utter rubbish. Of pivotal importance in the extradition proceedings, but rubbish nonetheless.

Nor was there anything remotely resembling a 'smoking gun' in the pack, on ANY issue. Other than my inflammatory e-mails from February 2000, there was really nothing vaguely incriminating. On the contrary, there was a ton of stuff that was highly exculpatory, in particular relating to the valuation of the SwapSub asset, which had been the subject of such debate in the High Court.

No matter. The American courts don't care a jot how someone has come to be in the jurisdiction. So the prosecutors bullshitted the UK courts to get you here? So what? Stoopid limeys. Serves 'em right.

Also in the pack of documents was my letter of 28th March 2000, from which it was abundantly clear to any person capable of understanding English that we had no idea what Fastow was up to, some several weeks after the alleged time when we had cooked up this wonderful scheme, and at a point in time when, unbeknownst to us, Fastow had already agreed with Enron to unwind the investment.

I was utterly dumbfounded. I had always assumed that they could not have seen this letter, because it so clearly ran against the central narrative of the indictment, showing as it did that we had no idea what Fastow was up to. But there it was.

The Government had divided the documentary evidence into a "core" pack, of about two and a half thousand pages from various sources, which they indicated would be the documents most likely used at trial, and a non-core pack, exclusively from RBS, of a further eleven thousand. My letter was in the 'core' pack.

I concentrated on this set, initially skimming them looking for the really important stuff, then went back and read every page in detail, indexing each document for date, author and content.

Now call me old fashioned, but if you're going to allege a robbery, you would think you would need to identify a victim. But here, amongst the thousands of pages of documents that supposedly formed the case against us, the victim was notable only for its total absence. Much as it had been in the extradition pack.

The allegation in the indictment was as plain as day:

'devised and executed a scheme to defraud NatWest and GNW.......by recommending to GNW that it sell its interest in SwapSub for only $1 million, when the defendants knew GNW's interest was worth far more....'

In normal circumstances, it is for the prosecution to prove its case to a jury. Consequently, you would have expected at least some evidence that $1 million was not a fair price when the asset was sold. Some testimony perhaps. Some documents, maybe. Something. Anything.

Not one thing.

To this day, I have never seen a single document that suggests that NatWest even thinks it was robbed. No document, and no witness statement. I have seen it suggested that banks are notorious for not admitting to frauds against them because they don't want to wash their dirty linen in public. Perhaps, but that argument simply didn't apply in our case. The world and his brother knew that we were supposed to have defrauded them of all this money. It wasn't something they could hush up.

Instead, there was document after document that supported our assertion that a million dollars for the SwapSub asset was a fair or even excessive price. All totally independent, corroborative material. GNW. Campsie. Coutts. RBS. KPMG. Powers. Batson.

Under normal circumstances, you would think we would have been overjoyed, but Reid consistently put paid to that. Facts don't matter. Perception is everything. NatWest got $1 million, CSFB got $10 million, and we got $7 million. Explain that to the jury.

We couldn't, of course. We had no idea why Fastow had paid CSFB $10 million. It made no sense.

And we knew that unless we could solve that little conundrum by the time we came to trial, we would likely be going down with all hands. It doesn't matter that the constitution says that the prosecution must prove its case beyond reasonable doubt. The prosecution gets to go first, and also has the last word before the case goes to the jury. This was Houston, a City still going through the 'anger' phase, and still a long way short of 'acceptance'. The jury had you guilty as you walked into the courtroom, unless you could prove otherwise. In their shoes, I'm sure I'd have felt much the same way.

GILES TURNS UP FOR WORK
August 2006

Having waded through all of the documents, the picture was crystal clear. There was no real evidence here. The prosecution's entire case was built around the e-mails, even though they clearly had nothing whatsoever to do with the investment that we had made and they weren't even vaguely contemporaneous with the decision to sell the SwapSub stake.

As Reid had put it, 'they look horrible, and you made a ton of money'. For most prosecutors, that would be enough. As Dan consistently said, trials are not about the truth, they're about who defines the issues.

On that measure, we would always be up against it. When you're staring at the ceiling of a prison cell, contemplating the years of incarceration ahead, it's scant comfort to know that yours was the moral victory.

Reid had even managed to throw cold water on the tapes of our conversations from RBC, which we had suggested ought to be giving us an instant ticket home.

"Hearsay", he had said.

Bizarre though it may seem, the rules on evidence in a criminal trial in the US are entirely asymmetrical. The prosecutors could take any one of those tapes and introduce it at trial as evidence of our guilt if they thought it supported their case. If we wished to introduce one in our defence, however, they could argue that it should be excluded as 'hearsay' evidence.

Dan was more positive, explaining that there were quite a few exceptions to the hearsay rules, but even he could not be certain that we would be able to use the tapes.

I am a bit of a cynic, but my overriding impression of the rules of evidence in America is that if something helps the prosecution, then it will almost certainly be admissible. If it helps the defense, you may well struggle to get it in.

If it is genuinely exculpatory material, the prosecutors are supposed to have a duty to reveal it to you. Since the penalty for not doing so is rarely that the case gets dismissed, however, some prosecutors take a fairly nuanced view of their disclosure obligations.

The Enron Task Force seemed to have a rule book all of their own as to how they went about their business, which was the securing of convictions by whatever means necessary. To them, it appeared, the end would always justify the means.

Dan told me of his run-in earlier that year with a member of the Task Force. Dan represented another Enron defendant, Ken Rice, who had agreed to plead guilty and would give evidence for the prosecution in the trial of several of the Enron Broadband executives. Dan had been spotted at some stage having a conversation with one of the Skilling defense team, who as a local attorney was well known to Dan. They had just been exchanging pleasantries, but the Task Force member wrote an e-mail to Dan's client suggesting in a fairly threatening manner that he change his counsel. Dan had responded by firing off a letter to this guy suggesting that he shoved it where the sun didn't shine.

There was little love lost, and the stories of prosecutorial abuse were legion. The prosecutors had used the same 'unindicted co-conspirators' tactic in the Barge trial and the trial of Lay and Skilling to ensure that potential witnesses for the defense were unwilling to testify. In the multi-defendant case related to the Enron Broadband business, a witness would take the stand to tell how he had been threatened with indictment if he testified. Brave man indeed, but one of only a handful to resist the threats.

Plan A, therefore, had to be getting the indictment dismissed. Or at a minimum getting the honest services stuff taken out of it, because if the prosecutors could be forced to pursue only the allegation of theft then we were in with a shout. If they could prevail at trial arguing failure to disclose, we were sunk, because we had never made any secret of the fact that we failed to disclose the investment to the NatWest compliance department. In fact, we had testified to exactly that in the extradition hearings.

In the meantime, since the motion to dismiss was largely a series of dry legal arguments into which we could have little meaningful input, we set about planning our defence if it did come to trial. In large part the momentum for this came unexpectedly from Giles.

I hope Giles will forgive me if I say that he had spent most of the four years since our indictment with his head in the sand, hoping it would all go away. He wanted no part of any attempt to fight the UK Government, nor of any media campaign to get the law changed or stop our extradition. His philosophy was that the more we struggled, the worse they would make it for us.

It's not that he was never there. It's just that he always deferred to the lawyers, and never seemed to want to take any affirmative action. For the last year before our extradition, I rarely copied him on any correspondence with Gary. It was a great shame, because of the three of us, Giles has far and away the best organisational brain. His project management skills are truly excellent, and I had always regarded this as being a project. Complex, certainly. Unusual, absolutely. But a project nonetheless.

Finally, though, in August 2006, something somewhere triggered in Giles' brain, and he turned up one day at Dan's office and walked straight to the whiteboard.

"Right", he said. "We need to fight this thing".

He broke down the defence of the case into a number of key topics, and allocated them to each of us to research using all available tools at our disposal.

Giles finally recognised that in a case like this, you cannot rely on the attorneys to find the answers. You have to give them the answers, and then let them find the way of explaining it to the jury.

Shortly after we had arrived, I had asked Dan to set up a meeting with Sheila Kahanek. I was intrigued to meet the only defendant who had looked the devil in the eye and come out ahead. Dan talked effusively of her case management skills, and how she had worked harder than any defendant he had ever represented.

We ended up having dinner together with Dan and Robin in Mortons, one of Houston's best known restaurants. Sheila was adamant. You have to run your own defense. You have to do the donkey work yourselves. There is no substitute for preparation. Poor old Jamie Olis had been sunk because his attorneys had not been able to find the exculpatory needle in the haystack of documents produced by the Government. Chances are they didn't recognise the significance of many of the documents that they were looking at, because it was all complex finance and accounting stuff.

Sheila would have found the needle, I had no doubt.

So when Giles finally decided to get his act together, I was overjoyed. I knew that once he started working on the documents, he would realise that we really could defend this case, and that would fire him up even more. And with Giles on the case, the job would get done.

Amongst my assigned projects were the CSFB conundrum, demonstrating that the meeting of 22nd February could not have been a fraud, and proving that $1 million was a fair price for GNW. All were tasks that played to my strengths because they were document intensive, and highly detailed.

Gary, by contrast, was allocated some of the 'big picture' stuff, which we would need to set the scene for our defence, such as the background to the takeover of NatWest by RBS. This wouldn't directly rebut the evidence against us, but it would create the canvas onto which we would paint our defence, so that the jury would have a far greater understanding of the context in which these events were happening, and in which the e-mails could be read.

The summer and autumn months were therefore busy. The families came out at different times, which was a huge fillip for us all. We quickly settled into routines. Mine involved getting up at around 7am and going for a swim. After breakfast, the day would be spent working on the case, either at Dan's office or in my little cubbyhole in the apartment. Towards tea time I would go for an hour's walk in Memorial Park, which cleared my mind and enabled me to get some fresh air. Sometimes in the evening we would go out for drinks, but more often than not I could be found back at my computer.

Weekends were mostly about sport. All major league sports in the US are organised around the TV schedules, meaning that you can spend pretty much your whole weekend watching some kind of game. Summer is baseball. Winter is American Football. Basketball spans the two of them.

Houston had major league franchise teams in all sports. The Houston Texans were the local football team. They were a young team, with a new state of the art stadium. The Houston Astros were a decent if unspectacular baseball team, but had in their ranks one Roger 'The Rocket' Clemens, the legendary pitcher who despite being nearly forty was still regularly dominating games with his pitching.

The Houston Rockets basketball team completed the major league franchises, but during my two years in the City I never once saw them play. Basketball is a sport that leaves me cold.

Giles, being a fanatic, quickly became a walking encyclopedia on American sport, and would strike up conversations with complete strangers in bars about the stats on the Patriots versus the Dolphins that coming weekend, and who had the most rushing yards in the division. This total addiction earned him the undying affection of Troy Lochlear, who pretty much adopted Giles as a member of his family, and the two of them became almost inseparable.

Beyond the sun rising every day, there was only one constant in life. On a Sunday afternoon, Giles could be found propping up the bar at The Wet Spot, a ramshackle old sports bar on West Gray, just outside downtown. His transformation into the status of local was absolute, except that he eschewed the use of the word 'dude' in favour of his traditional 'mate'.

I contented myself with the agonies of watching Arsenal at the Richmond Arms. It is a sad fact that you can watch more live Premiership football in Houston than you can in England. Even Carling Cup matches are all live on TV over there. Arsenal did me the favour of winning no silverware the entire time I was away, and would veer from the sublime to the utterly pathetic on a game to game basis.

Like all overseas footie bars, the Richmond Arms was full of Mancs, few of whom could identify the City of Manchester on a map, but who felt they were best mates with Wazza and Giggsy nonetheless. Despite that, and the fact that George the barman was a Spurs fan, it was an allround good place to be, serving English breakfast with a pint of Boddingtons in time for the Saturday kick-offs. The NatWest Three quickly became part of the furniture, to such an extent that after a while the barmaids wouldn't even bother to ask what we wanted. It just arrived. Top barmaid and general lovely person was Kristina Kelly, who was never quite sure whether she supported Liverpool or Spurs, but insisted on organising a party for us before we left to go to prison.

Every time I turned up there, I half expected to see Kevin Howard, who in better years had pretty much lived there. Kevin, however, wasn't likely to risk a confrontation with Mulgrew, and stayed well away.

September saw us back in court to set a new trial date. Coordinating the diaries of three sets of trial attorneys, one Federal Judge and two prosecutors pushed this back to September 2007, another year away. As I had been pushing for a date no later than April, this was not a welcome result, and I knew full well how it would be received by Emma back home in England.

Leo Wise had announced to the trial judge, Ewing Werlein, that "your honor, the United States is ready to proceed to trial", which produced a fair amount of snorting from the defense table, and prompted Reid to tell him that he clearly didn't understand the case. It was a somewhat unexpected and aggressive gambit, and Leo bristled visibly at the comment.

Thereafter, we just had to put our heads down and get on with the trial preparations. We would meet periodically in Dan's office to take stock, and occasionally fight like cats and dogs.

On one such occasion, I made the mistake of calling Giles the word that dare not speak its name, to which he has a pathological aversion. I had just finished regaling Giles with a theory that I was developing on the case, at the end of which he had retorted with something like "right, now back in the real world". To which I had taken no little objection.

I got about as far as "listen to me, you supercilious little c___", when the red mist came over him. Giles had bought his lunch in Subway across the street, and on this occasion it consisted of a large meatball sandwich, dripping in hot tomato sauce. It's about as grim as it sounds, and probably guaranteed to shorten your life expectancy by about a decade. But whatever else it might have been, aerodynamic it was not.

In one seamless movement, Giles stood up and launched it at me from across the boardroom table. At this point, everything seemed to go into slow motion. As he pulled back his arm to throw, tomato sauce splashed all over the wall, the windows and the blinds behind him. In the air, the sandwich came to pieces and sprayed itself in an arc over the whole of the wall behind me. Jackson Pollock would have been proud. In fact, the only things in the entire boardroom that were not covered in tomato sauce and meatballs were me, and Gary who walked in just at the moment that the sandwich was thrown.

Had I had any lunch handy, a cheeseburger or even a small caliber tuna sandwich, this would have been the moment at which Giles caught it square in the face and went down like a sack of potatoes. Being foodless, I just sat staring in disbelief at the scene, trying hard not to laugh. Gary had no such qualms. When Giles left the room to get some cleaning materials, Gary said that it had made his whole year, and promptly began texting everyone he knew....

Dan being Dan, his reaction on being told was that he needed to get the boardroom redecorated anyway, and that now at least he could charge it to Giles. He also took to saying "step away from the meatballs" whenever things got at all heated in a meeting.

Giles, for reasons best known only to himself, decided to self-report the incident to his pre-trial services officer, who promptly despatched him on an anger management course. This created more problems than it solved, since the course was run and attended by a motley collection of violent felons and ex-cons, who were trying (in some cases unsuccessfully) to come to terms with their predisposition to shoot some guy 7 times in the head because he put the wrong kind of music on the jukebox. Giles found it illuminating, but it was of course a clear breach of his bail terms which forbade him from associating with felons.

One of the tips from the course was to go through each day and sort the day's events into "wins" and "losses". So for instance a loss would be where you lose your temper, and a win would be where you manage to control it. Sometimes of course the two can become difficult to distinguish. One of the guys told the class that the previous day was a win because he had not killed or beaten to a pulp the guy who had slept with his girlfriend. All agreed that this was indeed a win. But it was also a loss, he said. When asked to explain, he said that he hadn't found the guy yet.

Pre-trial services helpfully suggested that perhaps Giles should not go to any more classes.

KANSAS CITY SHUFFLE
Autumn 2006

Of my allotted tasks, the first was the easiest. I had to assemble a cohesive argument, supported by evidence, as to why $1 million was a fair price for the SwapSub asset in March 2000. I identified a list of RBS personnel and others who could potentially be called to give evidence on the subject. It ran to thirteen people, including the partner at KPMG who had done an analysis for the Campsie audit.

Next topic was CSFB, and this had really become the nub of the whole case. Why the hell did Fastow agree to pay $10 million for something which pretty much everyone thought was worthless?

It made no sense, and unless we could give a plausible answer to this question to a jury, we were probably sunk.

There's always an answer. It's just that the truth is often stranger than fiction.

One of the most interesting documents in the entire Government evidence pack was a CSFB internal memo dated 20 March 2000, addressed to a number of senior CSFB officers, looking for permission to sell their interest in the SwapSub asset for $10 million.

It was intriguing on a number of levels. The first was the date. Everyone was assuming that the NatWest and CSFB deals to sell their stakes in SwapSub were done at the same time, and that consequently the disparity in price was solely due to our 'fraud'. But since this memo obviously preceded their sale, and yet was dated some 10 days after NatWest had already sold its interest in SwapSub, it suggested very strongly that Fastow had approached CSFB to sell their half much later than NatWest—up to 2 weeks later by the look of it. With the wild fluctuation in the values of the underlying stock, that alone could account for the disparity in price.

Could the value have moved from $1 million to $10 million in 2 weeks? Easily. It sounded a lot, but in fact a mere 5% movement in value would do it. It would have been a very simple argument, and simple is good in front of a jury.

Except that it still didn't gel with the evidence, in a rather unexpected way. The memo included a mark to market valuation of the SwapSub stake as at 17 March 2000, of $5.8 million, which would have meant that CSFB's fifty percent stake was worth only $2.9 million, even before factoring in the discount for the stock restriction. Using KPMG's calculation for the stock restriction would give a "fair" value of minus $17.1 million. And yet Fastow was apparently offering $10 million for it. Now Fastow was many things, but stupid wasn't one of them. Something did not add up.

There was another memo dated the following day in which CSFB's analysts projected forward a 'theoretical' valuation of the SwapSub stake assuming that they held it until December 2000, and that the stock price of RhythmsNet rose dramatically in the meantime. On these new assumptions, $10 million would be a reasonable price.

I thought it was akin to selling your house based on an arbitrary assumption that house prices would rise two hundred percent over the following year, and using that potential future value as the asking price today. Utterly nonsensical.

For the very first time, I found myself asking a new question. Was everyone looking the wrong way?

There is a great film called Lucky Number Slevin, in which the audience is introduced to the concept of the Kansas City Shuffle, where 'you go left when everybody else looks right'. For the Kansas City Shuffle according to Bruce Willis in the film, you need a body.

Maybe we were the body.

It was always assumed that NatWest had been screwed because they got $1 million, Enron had been screwed because they paid $30 million, and the fair price was probably the one paid to CSFB–$10 million for each partner or $20 million total.

But we had conclusive evidence that our $1 million price was fair. No one had ever taken that argument to its logical conclusion and asked "well if NatWest got a fair price, then is it possible that the payment to CSFB was unfair?"

I kept scratching away. I was particularly troubled about some e-mails to and from CSFB's equity derivatives group in October 2001, shortly before Enron imploded. They made no sense, because they appeared to link the SwapSub deal to a huge position that CSFB had in some complex derivative products called equity forwards, involving Enron's stock.

One e-mail, dated 10 December 2001, talked about keeping hold of a pile of Enron shares 'until [March] 02 when holding period appropriately meets 2 years'. Which implied that CSFB had acquired these shares in March 2000, the month of the SwapSub unwind.

I sat in my study one night, and quite haphazardly typed keyword searches into Google. "CSFB Enron derivatives"; "CSFB Enron equity derivatives". Lots of irrelevant 'noise'.

I tried again. "CSFB Enron Equity Forwards".

Bingo.

The very first result was a link to an interim ruling in a civil case, in which it seemed that CSFB was being sued by the Enron estate for fraudulent preference, in relation to a series of large derivatives contracts involving Enron stock in November 2001. There wasn't a huge amount of information in the online document, but the case number was all I needed, because that would enable us to see all of the filings through the US court system.

The next result was a link to a website set up by the Federal Energy Regulatory Commission (FERC), which contained tens of thousands of Enron e-mails. The FERC had published these in response to the scandal surrounding Enron's manipulation of energy prices, most notably during the Californian energy crisis in which there had been rolling power blackouts across the state.

This site was not exactly user friendly, but it did throw up some very interesting results. There were apparently a number of banks with whom Enron began derivatives trading in its own stock in early 2000, including CSFB.

The following day I brought home the filings from the CSFB civil suit to pore over.

The action accused CSFB of forcing Enron to purchase millions of its own shares from CSFB for cash at a price way above the market price, just weeks before Enron's bankruptcy

CSFB had, it seemed, purchased these shares pursuant to a number of equity swaps and equity forward contracts, some apparently dating back to early 2000 and had sat on the shares, continually rolling over (or extending) the equity derivatives, until November 2001. At that point things were looking very bad for Enron, and CSFB had refused to extend the contracts any more, as was their right, obliging Enron to buy back the shares for over $70 per share, when Enron's stock at the time was trading below $10. Enron had to fork out over $200 million in cash, at a time when its finances were stretched to breaking point.

I built a spreadsheet that modeled all of the contracts referred to in the lawsuit, with dates and aggregate valuations. Somewhat frustratingly, the contracts only went back as far as June 2001, but the summary had said that the original deals had been transacted in 2000, and had been periodically extended thereafter.

Having finished the modeling, the aggregate value of the contracts was exactly the same as a figure that had been quoted in one of the e-mails from the equity derivatives group in November 2001. There was no doubt these were the same deals. And the lawsuit was alleging that some had been put together in early 2000, which seemed to corroborate the possibility that they were indeed linked to the SwapSub unwind. It was tantalising.

I wrote a three page note entitled "CSFB and the Mysterious Tale of the Equity Forwards", and appended all of the curious e-mails and my spreadsheet. I then circulated it amongst the whole team by e-mail. My basic argument was as follows:

By November 2001, CSFB seemed to have written contracts over several hundred million dollars' worth of Enron stock. What if CSFB were warehousing these huge amounts of stock, and hedging their position by entering into swaps and forwards with Enron, as a means of supporting the Enron share price in the market?

In other words, they might have bought the shares to create a huge demand and artificially push the Enron share price up, whilst making sure that Enron would assume all the risk on the deal through forward contracts and swaps, derivatives that ensured that if the price went down then Enron would make up the difference.

And if the SwapSub Enron stock was part of that huge stockpile, that could certainly explain their payment of $10 million, as a fee for an equity backed financing transaction.

I ran through the whole theory with Jimmy over a beer the next day. His response was succinct.

"Dude, if you're going there you'd better be damned sure of your ground, and I would advise you to tread real careful. It's no defence to a charge of driving under the influence to say 'your honor, everyone in the bar that night was drunk'."

PEELING THE ONION
Autumn 2006

When I get an idea in my head, I am like a dog with a bone. The whole mystery began to consume me during the autumn months of 2006.

To take the case to trial, we needed to answer three questions unequivocally.

First, why was $1 million a fair price? We knew we could do that, but to knock the ball out of the park we would need an expert witness to corroborate the documentary evidence.

Second, why did CSFB get $10 million? I was on the trail of this one, but more I dug, the more confused I became. Dan sent a letter to Leo and JLo asking them to give us copies of all the documents relating to CSFB's equity derivatives trades with Enron.

Third, we needed to know what the hell had happened at Enron. How on earth could they have agreed to pay Fastow $30 million for something that was so obviously worthless? Fastow had testified that he had lied to Rick Causey, Enron's Chief Accounting Officer to procure the payment, but how could no-one in the Enron finance or accounting department have questioned the price being paid? How could the auditors have missed it?

We were not without friends and helpers, and periodically we would get together with some of these guys and try to make progress on unsolved issues. Others offered support but maintained their distance lest they end up on the wrong end of the Government.

Ben Glisan, the first Enron executive to go to prison, and the first to reappear, called Dan out of the blue one day, and offered to help us in whatever way he could. Dan didn't trust him an inch, but as far as we were concerned, Ben had always been one of the good guys during his time at Enron, whatever our thoughts on his testimony in the Barges trial and Lay-Skilling. And we reckoned that Ben, who had himself been an investor in Southampton, knew that the allegations against us were bullshit.

Unfortunately, our dalliance with Ben was short lived. Before we could get him in and ask him all the really serious questions that we needed to be answered, his attorney closed him down and told Dan to back off, and that was that.

Less constrained was Jeff McMahon, the former Treasurer of Enron, and no friend of Andy Fastow. McMahon had been one of the few people willing to give testimony before the Congressional hearings in early 2002 (Skilling also testified, which was later held against him). Fastow and Kopper had both invoked their Fifth Amendment right to silence.

McMahon was a client of Dan's and had seemingly been within an ace of being indicted for several years. When Fastow was fired in November 2001, as Enron was struggling to stay afloat, McMahon was promoted into his job as CFO, and consequently was at the tiller as the ship went down. In the eyes of the Department of Justice, this made him a crook, but they had struggled mightily to build a case against him, not least because he hadn't done anything wrong, other than carry an Enron business card. For some, that was enough.

Jeff was also a client of Tom Kirkendall, the attorney whose advice I had sought before selecting Dan. Tom did not do criminal work, but represented a number of ex-Enron clients in the myriad civil suits that were flying around, and Jeff was on the wrong end of a number of those.

More importantly, though, Jeff knew Giles and Gary very well from the heady days of 1999 and 2000, and liked them both enormously. As far as he was concerned, these were friends in need, and he would do whatever he could to help.

Jeff gave us more help than he could ever have imagined. He came with Tom to Dan's offices and gave us an insider's understanding of what motivated various key players in the whole Enron story, and how the company actually functioned on a day-to-day basis. What were the key drivers to decision making, and what was the process by which decisions were routinely made. In short, a template of what should have happened when Enron agreed to buy the SwapSub stake from Southampton in March 2000, if the procedures had been followed.

It was Jeff who unwittingly solved the puzzle of why Enron was willing to pay $30 million in cash for an asset that seemed to be worthless. We knew from the documents that Fastow had negotiated the price directly with Rick Causey, Enron's Chief Accounting Officer. Causey had never been accused of being party to fraud on the transaction, and seemed to have made no personal profit on the deal, so what could have possessed him? Powers suggested that he was asleep at the switch, but this was too simplistic, since Jeff confirmed that Causey had people who would have been running the numbers for him.

"Why on earth would he have agreed to this, Jeff?" asked Giles.

Jeff thought about it for a moment. "Were there earnings involved?" he asked.

My heart stopped. Giles and Gary looked at me, and there was only one thought going through our minds. 'Holy shit–that's it'.

Enron did many clever things over the years, straining the bounds of complex and arcane accounting rules. Many of these transactions, such as the Raptors, would subsequently become infamous and would be scrutinised by lawyers, accountants and academics. But despite all the opprobrium that the LJM vehicles attracted, and the pivotal role that the unwind of SwapSub played in our alleged fraud, no-one ever took a microscope to the mechanics of that same unwind, which was by some distance the most Alice in Wonderland piece of accounting I have ever seen.

As with so many things in our case, everybody had been looking through the glass the wrong way, ourselves included. If you analysed this stuff using 'normal' market assumptions, you would always come up with the wrong answer. Jeff provided the key. Look at everything through the optic of earnings, not absolute value. It was, said Jeff, the key metric for Rick Causey.

And when put like that, it was all so obvious. Almost all American companies are focused on their stock price, because both employees and senior management take so much of their compensation in stock. Enron, though, was a company almost obsessed with its stock price, to such a degree that even the elevators had a live feed to the stock market. And, as I discussed earlier, stock price is almost always driven by earnings. So if your stock trades on a multiple of (say) twenty times earnings, then one dollar of earnings turns into twenty dollars of market value in the stock.

How we didn't see this earlier has always vexed me. After all, we had operated on exactly that same principle for that short period when

NatWest was the target of the hostile takeover. The edict from the top had been simple; maximise earnings, to increase the value of the company.

Once you understood this, the logic of paying a large amount of cash to achieve a smaller amount of earnings was clear. At the time of the SwapSub sale, Enron's stock traded at nearly seventy times earnings

Consequently, paying $30 million in cash to create, say, $10 million in earnings was equivalent to 'buying' $700 million of stock value for $30 million.

To you and me, they would just have wasted at least twenty million dollars, surely? But to them, it was a trade they would do all day, every day. It was predicated, like so much else that happened during the first decade of the twenty first century, on the assumption that there would always be an unlimited supply of finance.

Now at this point the logical person would say "well, if paying $30 million would have created $10 million of earnings, then presumably paying $1 would have created $40 million of earnings, because Enron would have been better off by $30 million". And indeed that is what one might have imagined.

But that would be to misunderstand the accounting la-la land in which Enron's relationship with SwapSub sat. I had spent literally days staring at internal LJM spreadsheets with scores of calculations, none of which appeared to make any sense. Until Jeff unlocked the box.

By doing what he did, Fastow managed to create a scenario in which the overall transaction created a tidy profit for Enron on what would otherwise have been a significant loss-making trade. It was warped but brilliant.

Enron had a problem, and Andy came up with a solution. That solution would come at a price. $30 million would do nicely, please, but don't worry, it won't actually 'cost' you a penny.

It's all too easy to look back now with the gift of hindsight, as an armchair expert. What's more difficult is to see things within their context at the time. Was Andy Fastow the embodiment of pure evil, as so many people would have you believe? Over the years, I have come to a more nuanced view. He was a human being, with frailties, one of which was that he was very greedy. But then most of us would probably plead guilty to that one, whether it's for money, power, admiration, or honey-glazed donuts. Certainly the decisions that led me to invest in Southampton can be ascribed only to vanity or greed—take your pick.

Andy didn't need the money, so what was his motivation? Maybe to prove that he didn't need to depend on his wife's billion dollar inheritance. Or maybe it was envy of those less able than himself who had amassed huge piles of Enron's stock simply by arriving on the scene early, who were now rich beyond the dreams of avarice as a result of what he saw as his efforts.

I don't think there is any doubt, even in his own mind, that Andy stepped across the line into criminality. He lied to Rick Causey about where the $30 million was going and he and Michael Kopper had seemingly been lining their own pockets at Enron's expense for some years prior to the SwapSub deal.

But once you understand what happened with the SwapSub unwind, you perhaps get a little glimpse into the mind of a somewhat tortured genius.

There is no doubt whatsoever that Andy Fastow moved the pieces around the board. But my best guess is that he didn't think he was robbing Enron at all. He saw that they had a problem, he fixed it, and he thought that $30 million was a reasonable price to pay for the fix.

THE GRAND OLD DUKE OF YORK
Autumn 2006

The autumn of 2006 in London saw the renewal of the attempt to get the Extradition Act changed in the UK Parliament. Prior to our extradition, the House of Lords had reinserted the amendments that Hazel Blears and her merry little band had thrown out in the Commons Committee stage of the Police & Justice Bill earlier in the year.

After the summer recess, the Bill came back to the Commons, and we were prepared. Melanie had been working feverishly over the summer with Liberty, Justice and all of the newspapers to ensure that everyone was singing from the same song sheet.

On 24th October Home Office Minister Joan Ryan took to the despatch box as the latest unfortunate to hold the title of Minister for Extradition, in place of Andy Burnham. She began thus:

"The adoption of these amendments by the other place was a bad day for international co-operation in the fight against crime. Today, we have the opportunity to put that right, and it is the last chance to do so."

Her performance over the next two hours and forty minutes was described the next day by Quentin Letts in the *Daily Mail* as 'probably the worst performance I have seen from a Minister. Ever.'

In fairness to Ms Ryan, she was new to the job, was not a lawyer, and had been handed a completely poisoned chalice by her boss, the Home Secretary John Reid, who probably didn't much fancy the debate himself. Of course it didn't matter a jot that Ryan did such a poor job defending the indefensible. The Government had realised that it might well be defeated on this, and so had made the vote a three line whip.

In all, three hundred and twenty Labour MPs turned out to vote for the Government that night, including many who had signed Boris Johnson's Early Day Motion calling for exactly the amendments that they were now opposing. Sadiq Khan, the friend and MP of Babar Ahmad, abstained, but when given another chance to put things right in July 2009 during a Parliamentary debate on Gary McKinnon, he voted with the Government, of which by then he was a junior whip.

The Police & Justice Bill was duly bounced back to the Lords, with the amendments voted down. Melanie was at once tickled pink at the savaging that the hapless Joan Ryan took in the papers, and furious that the Government could be making this a party political issue.

I watched the entire debate live on my computer in my little cubbyhole. The result would make no difference to us, of course. But having fought for so long to try to get the amendments through before we went, I felt it was important that we did whatever we could to try to finish the job.

A few interesting things came out of the debate that day. Kate Hoey, the Labour MP who had written to Emma expressing her disgust at what her Government had done, extracted from Ms Ryan the admission that the agreement of the US Senate a few weeks earlier to ratify the Treaty had been extracted at the price of a promise by the UK Government not to use it to extradite the on the run IRA terrorists who had for so long frustrated attempts to secure their repatriation. Having served in Northern Ireland, the irony was not lost on me.

Also of interest was the concern expressed by John Denham, the Minister who had led the debate on the Extradition Bill for the Government in December 2002, about the apparent haste of negotiation of the new Treaty:

"It seems inconceivable that civil servants would have provided me with a briefing that made no reference to treaty negotiations unless none were under way, and I can only conclude that the treaty signed on 31 March 2003 had not even started the negotiation process when the Extradition Bill was debated in December 2002".

When John Denham made this statement, I all but exploded. He had been a member of the Home Affairs Select Committee in November 2005 which had received a chronology of events from Andy Burnham showing that negotiations on the Treaty had begun in January 2002, and were well advanced by December that year.

I sent an e-mail to Mr Denham suggesting in the nicest possible terms that he may have been misled if he knew nothing of the Treaty in December 2002, and giving him a link to the chronology on the Select Committee website. He replied a day or so later, thanking me for the information, and saying that he would look into it. It was the last I would hear from him.

Ms Ryan also took the time during the debate to suggest that many MPs had been taken in by the campaign of disinformation mounted by the rich bankers. They had constantly said that they would not get bail, and yet they got bail. Just goes to show how easily you people can be taken in, she suggested. She had refrained from mentioning that it was solely the efforts of Tony Blair and Attorney General Lord Goldsmith that had secured our bail. I wondered if she was volunteering their services again for all future extraditees.

The Bill was debated again in the Lords on 1st November. The Government was suggesting, presumably as a sop, that rather than involving a judge in the extradition proceedings, there should be formal guidelines for prosecutors to discuss the issue themselves before coming to a decision which would not be subject to review by the extradition court.

Baroness Scotland did not disappoint in trotting out all the anticipated lines of argument, with an element of her usual sickly sugar coating, and the Lords once again ignored her and voted the amendments back in. The Bill was sent back to the Commons.

On 6th November, Joan Ryan was nowhere to be seen on the front benches. In her place, John Reid himself took the helm. His was as menacing a performance by a politician as any I have ever witnessed. To insert this amendment, he said, would require the renegotiation of up to 20 international treaties with other countries. This was quite simply bullshit. There were already several other amendments, including the human rights bar, that were already in the act and not in the individual treaties.

One of the problems in these situations is that the majority of MPs have no legal training whatsoever, and so they take what their Ministers say in these matters as being gospel, even when it's rubbish. The Labour Government between 1997 and 2010 introduced over 3,000 new criminal offences in the UK, and yet the only Home Secretary or Home Office Minister with any legal background at all was Jack Straw, who left the office in 2001.

Terrifying, isn't it? During the years that followed, criminal legislation was shoveled through the House of Commons at an unprecedented rate by the likes of Caroline Flint (who began her professional life in local Government), Andy Burnham (Parliamentary researcher), Tony McNulty (local councilor), Fiona McTaggart (schoolteacher), Joan Ryan (schoolteacher), John Reid (Parliamentary researcher), Jacqui Smith (schoolteacher) and Alan Johnson (postman). I'm not denigrating any of these professions, just observing that it would not be unreasonable to expect the people in charge of criminal lawmaking to have some background in law, surely?

Reid, though, has never lacked in self-confidence. If any Labour MP had remotely entertained the idea of being persuaded by the overwhelming arguments, or indeed of honouring their promises to their constituents, Reid's performance pretty much made it clear that they could kiss goodbye to any political ambitions if they voted against their Government. In fact, his line was that a vote against the Government was a vote to let paedophiles go free.

The vote of course was whipped again by the Government, and the supplicant Labour lickspittles duly filed in to do the bidding of their political masters.

Back it went to the Lords for debate on 7th November. This time, however, was likely to be the last. If the Lords defied the Commons again, the Government could invoke the little used provisions of the Parliament Act to ensure that the elected chamber ultimately got its way.

I wrote briefings for Lords Goodhart and Kingsland, the Liberal Democrat and Tory Peers who were leading the debate, urging them to keep up the fight and pointing out the blatant discrepancy in Reid's argument. Lord Goodhart informed me that they were going to press ahead with the amendment, so the stage was set for the final battle of political wills.

But the Tories flunked it. Totally. Utterly. I watched with disbelief as Lord Kingsland got to his feet and said that the Conservatives did not feel that they could once again fly in the face of the will of the elected chamber.

Lord Goodhart summed it up admirably for many people that day:

"My immediate thought, on learning of the position of the Conservative party on this issue, was of a poem that many noble Lords will know:

'The grand old Duke of York, He had ten thousand men, He marched them up to the top of the hill, And he marched them down again'.

If one substitutes the name of the noble Lord, Lord Strathclyde, for that of the Duke of York, and 200 Peers for 10,000 men, that is exactly the position which the Conservative party is in now."

And with that, our proposed changes to the Extradition Act were dead.

There was little doubt that Lord Kingsland took no pleasure in what he had to do that day. He was acting under orders from the High Command in the Conservative Party. So when, the following day, I saw a quote from some party flunky in one of the newspapers to the effect that the incident showed that the Conservatives were now ready to take the tough decisions required of a Government in waiting, I rather lost the plot.

I wrote a lengthy e-mail to David Cameron, copied to Boris Johnson and Lord Kingsland, pointing out that if he was unable to understand the importance of basic concepts like habeas corpus and the presumption of innocence, then neither he nor his party had any claim whatsoever on the levers of power.

I got a reply back a few days later from some administrative assistant who thanked me for my 'input', told me that my views had been 'noted', and then gave me a brief and somewhat inaccurate history of the legislation. Reading it was somewhat akin to listening to the taped recording when you're on hold, telling you that the company concerned values your call when you know for a fact that they couldn't give a toss and they are hoping that if the loop plays for long enough you will get bored or frustrated and hang up, thereby making their lives immeasurably easier.

I'm afraid to say my response to Mr Cameron's assistant was largely unprintable.

DOWN ON THE RANCH
Christmas 2006

Disappointments in Westminster notwithstanding, we slipped towards Christmas in relatively good shape. We filed our motion to dismiss the indictment in early November 2006. Reid, David and Kevin in Washington had done a truly outstanding job on it, and its effects were almost instant. Leo Wise and JLo quickly agreed to strike all references to the honest services charges from the indictment. On 6th December Judge Werlein, granted us leave to file a new motion seeking dismissal of the whole indictment.

At worst, therefore, we were facing the original charges of theft of property. If we could just nail the CSFB stuff, and then get documents and witnesses from RBS, I honestly reckoned we could win this thing.

By this stage, my routine in Houston was well settled, and I was looking forward to Christmas. Bart and Alix had invited me to spend Christmas Day with them, and Emma and the children were going to come out on Boxing Day. Debs was coming out for Christmas with the girls, and Julie was bringing her two children and Gary's son Calum, so all three of us would be among family.

We wrote to RBS, identifying a list of 36 individuals that we wished to speak to, who were either current or ex-employees of the firm. Travers Smith duly wrote back, indicating that the firm was representing all of the people that we wished to speak to, and that only one of the 36 was prepared to talk to us. Under US law, that was just about that. If an individual has legal representation, and the attorneys tell you that he doesn't want to talk to you, you cannot contact him directly.

This was a huge blow. If we couldn't get witnesses, then our chances at trial were hugely diminished because under the laws of 'hearsay' we would be unable to introduce any exculpatory documents without the authors or recipients of those documents in the courtroom.

By this stage, we were aware of the Thompson Memorandum, and there was little doubt in my mind that RBS was acting under orders from the Department of Justice, just as Merrill Lynch had been forced to do back in 2003.

We would need to find a way around this, or we were sunk. The Sixth Amendment (so cleverly quoted by John Hardy at our hearing) giving you the right to confront witnesses and bring your own, was drafted by Americans for Americans. If your witnesses are outside the jurisdiction, you've got a problem, buster. Serves you right for being foreign, basically. We had tried to explain this in our extradition hearing, but like everything else that's of practical relevance, it had been dismissed.

We had a great team going by now, a melding of complementary skills. Dan and Dick looked down from fifty thousand feet, not wishing to get too bogged down in the facts. Gary has never got too bogged down in facts. Giles had rolled up his sleeves and been through the entire document pack with a fine toothcomb, and was talking about transcribing the voice tapes, which clearly the Government couldn't be bothered to do.

Jimmy had a good working knowledge of the key materials. David Schwarz and Kevin Huff were largely preoccupied with the e-mails, and Matt Hennessy was probably the attorney who could give the most rounded analysis of everything, in terms that everyone could understand. Reid was still Dr Doom, but that was fine. His practice handled the technical side of the case masterfully.

Dick's attitude was interesting. Like me, he obsessed about why Fastow would have paid $10 million to CSFB. Much as he liked us, I always got the impression that his acceptance of the validity of our case would rest on knowing the answer to this question.

Dan's philosophy was markedly different. Dan always used to say to me "look David, there's always bad facts. You wouldn't be here if there weren't bad facts. And there's stuff we don't know. That's okay". You could look Dan in the eye and ask him whether he believed in you, and he would sincerely say "yes". But it didn't matter, he would go on, because the truth's not what's important in a trial. Dan understood that. Dick needed to be convinced.

My investigations on CSFB occupied me right up to Christmas Eve, when I realised that I had done no shopping for presents or anything else. Not an unusual situation, except that normally I would have been sitting at home when the realisation dawned on me. I am probably the world's worst shopper, in which sense Emma and I are like Jack Sprat and his wife.

Emma will identify appropriate cards and gifts for people months in advance. She thinks about people, and instinctively knows what they will like. Somehow I've always struggled to find that bit of my brain, and when put on the spot at the last minute, I never have an idea as to what would be appropriate.

It's not that I don't like Christmas. It's just that I've never been a big one for gifts, either giving or receiving. Emma would be bringing gifts for the children, so I was only faced with the task of buying for Emma, and also for Bart and Alix on Christmas Day. Not the most exacting of tasks, perhaps, but I still struggled.

Christmas Day significantly exceeded my expectations. I had imagined I would be thoroughly miserable without the family, but I had a good session with them on Skype when I woke up, and so was in good spirits when I arrived at the Staffords' for what turned out to be a really lovely afternoon. Emma would be arriving the following day with the children, having set off at some ungodly hour in the morning, so all was well with the world.

Or it would have been. Instead I got a call very early in the morning from a distraught Emma, who was in floods of tears at Gatwick airport. It seemed that her booking through an intermediary firm had never been processed by the company with BA, and consequently she had no seats on the flight.

Now Emma is second only to my best man Miles's wife Sabine in terms of her powers of persuasion, but she had met her match in the BA staff at Gatwick. It was Boxing Day, and here was a woman in distress with three very small children and half a hundredweight of luggage, trying to get to see her husband some five thousand miles away. Through no fault of her own, she wasn't booked on the flight.

They could have bumped some other deserving passengers up into vacant business class seats to make room. Everybody wins. Yes? No. They weren't having any of it. She could pay twelve thousand pounds to sit in business class with her three children, or she could go away.

Eventually Emma had to take the children and her bags home with her, and return the following day. The flight left with a host of empty business class seats. A great victory for bureaucracy, and goodwill to all during this happy season.

The 'world's favourite airline' my arse.

When they all arrived the following day, Emma was more than a little frazzled. It's a long flight for an adult, but with three young children in tow it takes on an extra dimension, and the fact that my bond terms did not allow me near an airport to collect them just exacerbated the issue.

It went downhill from there. I hadn't decorated the apartment. My rationale was that we were heading out in a couple of days to spend the New Year away, but this cut little ice. I can see Emma's point of view now, of course. Being cooped up in my little apartment was bad enough, but when there wasn't even a festive atmosphere it was pretty unforgiveable. I need counseling.

The icing on the cake, though, was my choice of gift for Emma. I had made what many men will recognise as the cardinal mistake of taking my wife at her word when she told me not to buy her anything. Emma knew exactly what she wanted, so she would get it in the Christmas sales in the Galleria in Houston.

As most men apparently know, the innocuous phrase 'don't buy me anything' has two translations, other than the obvious plain English variety which one leaves with the empty champagne bottles at the wedding reception.

The Mars translation (for men): "Don't buy me anything big, but make sure you buy a token present"

The Venus translation: "Of course you've got to buy me something beautiful and expensive, you idiot. And by the way I still expect to go shopping for my "real" present".

Anyway, as you will by now have guessed, I opted for the Martian version. I had at least been consistent in this approach over our twelve years of marriage, but apparently that's not an excuse (believe me, I tried it). Personally, I thought the scented candle was nice. It remained unopened in my apartment until the day I left, a symbolic gesture by Emma.

For weeks afterwards I relayed this tale to anyone who would listen, hoping in vain to find a sympathetic response. None was ever forthcoming. Gary best summed it up: "Bermo, you're a prick".

We had just about resumed talking by the day before New Year's Eve, when all three families converged on Dick DeGuerin's ranch some thirty miles west of Houston. We had got permission from our pre-trial services officers for this, subject to the attendance of Troy Lochlear and his family, Troy qualifying as one of our attorneys for the purpose.

The ranch consisted of a series of small log cabins around a central homestead. Dick and his wife turned up for a day, as did some of their children.

It was the perfect hideaway. There were horses for all, and fishing on a small lake which was stocked with catfish.

On New Year's Eve we sat around a campfire and wondered how the hell we had ever got into this unholy mess, and when it would all be over. Soon, we resolved, even though the trial was still nine months away.

We saw in the New Year with the worst fireworks display in the history of mankind, courtesy of Troy. This being Texas, where everything is bigger, we had expected something approaching Armageddon, and were prepared to shield the children from the impending 'shock and awe'.

Having lit the blue touchpaper, Troy retired to the safety of the campfire, and we were treated to a selection of damp squibs, including rockets that managed about ten feet before falling back to earth. Gary asked whether we had missed the bit on the box that had identified it as a display for dwarfs.

The following day, nursing an almighty hangover, I was determined that I would teach the children how to fish on the lake. Fishing was a big part of my childhood, on holidays in the west of Ireland every summer. Passing down all the knowledge and insights gleaned from years of personal experience is of course one of the joys of parenthood.

It was like a scene from "On Golden Pond", with a lovely long wooden pontoon running out into a still lake. The children all had little rods, and an assortment of baits that could only possibly have been made in America (rubber dayglo frogs legs, for instance). All was going well.

And then Jemima got just a little bit overconfident in the act of casting, leaving a little too much line hanging from the end of her rod before swinging it backwards. I was standing a few yards behind her, proudly surveying another great parenting success, and all I remember is a huge pair of frogs legs coming straight at me, with a triple hook attached.

There was no doubt it was going to catch me in the eye, and add my eyeball to the rubber lure. Now this might well have been a more effective bait for catfish (we had up until this point caught absolutely nothing), but frankly that wasn't really on my mind. Luckily, years of military training followed by nearly twenty years in finance had given me catlike instincts and reactions. I stepped back and fell off the pontoon.

There was a blissful moment of weightlessness followed by a less blissful and not very graceful entry into the water, and a sensation of being swallowed up by weeds. Climbing quickly back onto the pontoon, soaked from head to foot, my first concern was that the children were not alarmed.

I needn't have worried. Jemima dropped her rod and sprinted back to the ranch, howling with laughter and screaming "daddy fell in the lake, daddy fell in the lake". This advance warning meant that by the time I had gathered up all the rods and suggested to Freddie that we call it a day, every person in the ranch with a camera was waiting to record my condition for posterity. This was just as well, as Jeff Fowler, my pre-trial services officer, clearly didn't believe the story as to why my electronic tagging phone had to be replaced, until Giles showed him the photographic evidence.

PANDORA'S BOX
January 2007

January 2007 brought us two giant steps closer to putting the final pieces in the jigsaw. Step one came from a video of a presentation that Andy Fastow, Michael Kopper and Anne Yaeger had given in Merrill Lynch's New York offices in October 1999. Merrill were pitching for the business of promoting LJM2 to the market. They would win the mandate, and would ultimately raise nearly $400 million from a who's who of institutional investors and high net worth clients. Over one hundred Merrill Lynch bankers invested personally in the deal.

A snippet of this video had appeared in the film of Bethany McLean and Peter Elkind's 2003 book *The Smartest Guys in the Room*. The full presentation was a real eye-opener. It gave an extraordinary insight into the magnetism of Andy Fastow. Somehow we had to get this video in front of the jury. This was Fastow the all-conquering CFO at the height of his power.

Our defence had to strip away the preconceptions that had built up in the minds of a jury in the intervening years, take them back in time, and show what happened in its proper context. In October 1999, as this video so clearly showed, Fastow was the king, who had the American financial community eating out of his hand.

Dick DeGuerin asked Giles very soon after he met him why Giles had decided to invest with Andy Fastow. Giles, in his normal frank manner, had responded that it had been an honour and a privilege to have been asked. Dick had scoffed at this response, but the Merrill video bore witness to Giles's attitude. Probably every single senior banker in that room had invested personally in LJM2, not because they liked the underlying business proposition, but because they wanted to invest alongside Andy Fastow.

We insisted that we show the video to Dick, in its entirety, with us in the room to make sure he saw it all. Not least because it gave another very strong clue as to why Fastow might have been willing to pay $10 million for the SwapSub unwind the following March. As if we didn't already have enough of those.

At the time of this presentation, LJM1 was only three months old. We had yet to complete the November restructuring that would net NatWest $22 million. The unwinding of SwapSub was nowhere on anybody's horizon. And Fastow was pushing Merrill hard for a much larger investment in LJM2. The central plank of his argument was 'look at my past successes'. He and Michael Kopper walked them through various other structures, including the RADR and ChewCo deals, ending with LJM1. And when it came to LJM1, Fastow was clear. It had already been a major success, and as a consequence he fully expected the limited partners to be participating in LJM2.

Of course. How could he possibly sell LJM2 to new investors if the banks that had put the equity into LJM1 were not going to participate in the new fundraising? How on earth would he explain that? And LJM2 was going to be twenty or thirty times the size of LJM1, with Fastow earning a 2% fee each year on all the cash raised.

Dick did not need to be prompted. He got it straight away.

"Were CSFB in LJM2?" he asked.

"Yes".

"How much?"

"Guess."

"$10 million, by any chance?"

"Spot on".

"Were NatWest?"

"No", said Gary. "We turned him down flat".

Dick sat back in his chair.

"Finally", he said. "Finally this makes sense. This, a jury can understand."

The prosecutors had given us a small number of internal CSFB documents from the end of 1999, when the bank had been mulling over the invitation to participate in LJM2. The documents revealed that in late December that year, permission was given for an initial $5 million investment, plus a further $5 million only if LJM1 had returned them at least $5 million more by the time the investment needed to be made. It linked in nicely with the Merrill Lynch video.

By this stage, I had worked myself up into a little frenzy of anger and frustration at not being able to figure out exactly what had happened with the $10 million payment to CSFB. I like certainty. We had nothing but speculation, and too many possible theories.

We had many friends in the legal and business community locally, who were almost exclusively of the view that our case brought shame on their justice system. In late January, one of these attorneys, at my request, obtained electronic transcripts from the interviews of all the relevant CSFB bankers in the Newby civil action, back in 2004. Thousands of pages of sworn testimony, all of which was in the hands of the Government, we knew, and none of which they would give to us.

I sat down at my computer with a glass of red wine and began to skim through the transcripts. I began with Marybeth Mandanas, in the expectation that hers would be the most detailed account, as she had been the hands-on deal person on the LJM transaction.

Marybeth was interviewed by a number of separate counsel, and I smiled as she skillfully danced around how CSFB had folded in the November 1999 restructuring and allowed Andy Fastow to walk away with $14 million.

As she described it, this was a natural consequence of the partnership agreement, and only NatWest had disagreed. There was quite some discussion about my apoplectic reaction, and why it was that CSFB had decided to side with Fastow, but Marybeth walked away relatively unbruised from the encounter.

I was really looking for any link to the equity derivatives trades, but I would be disappointed on that score. Instead, most of the discussion focused on the November 1999 restructuring, and the disposal of SwapSub in March 2000.

It was late in the evening when I reached page 550 of the transcript. I had to read the passage several times to make sure that I wasn't seeing things. Almost too excited to speak, and probably a little incoherent from the several glasses of wine that I had consumed, I picked up the phone to David Schwarz. I needed someone to share this with, and he was the only person I knew who might still be around. I was not disappointed.

"David Schwarz, you sad bastard. Go home".

"I will, soon. What causes you to be ringing me at this ungodly hour, Mr Bermingham?"

"Well, I assume you're sitting down. What if I told you that there was hard evidence that CSFB valued the SwapSub asset at less than zero?"

"I thought they valued it at $2.9 million?" he said, referring to CSFB's memo of 20th March, with the spurious valuations to justify the $10 million sales price.

"Yes, but that was on March 20th. What if they valued it at less than zero on 9th March, the very day before NatWest agreed to sell for $1 million."

"Well, that would be very good indeed."

"As in 'next plane home' good?"

"Probably not that good, but very good, certainly. So do we have such evidence?"

I read him the passage from Marybeth's testimony. On 9th March 2000, in an internal e-mail exchange which was read into the record by one of the attorneys conducting the deposition, Marybeth had said that

"the Enron share price has been moving around today. With the latest numbers from Carmen's group, the net market asset value of Swap Sub, given the value of the options, is negative $1 million."

She went on to say

"that would indicate that as long as we sell for something positive, given the negative value, we should be okay."

There was a long pause on the line. I was not going to hurry David. His view of life was generally almost as negative as his mentor Reid's, and I wanted his opinion to be unalloyed when he delivered it.

"Where did you get this from, David?" he asked eventually.

"I'd rather not say", I said defensively, protecting my source.

"Well, if this is going to be of any use to us, we have to have obtained it legally. Did we?"

"Of course", I said, having no idea whether we had or not.

It's a nice little irony that the US Government has no such strictures on its own evidence gathering, but as a defendant you've got to jump through hoops. Just because it was evidence that should have been produced to us

by the Government, evidence which quite clearly pointed to our innocence, that didn't mean it would be given to us or admissible in trial.

"Well", said David, "assuming that we haven't obtained this material
unlawfully, I would say that this is very very good news."

As that was about the most enthusiastic I had ever heard David on the
subject of our case, I figured that the Houston attorneys would be ecstatic.

And indeed they were.

Tom Kirkendall opined that if this had been a civil case, we could have
applied for a summary judgment in our favour right then and there, and
that would have been the end of it.

This little e-mail, though, was but the start of it. The more I read of
the transcripts, the more I realised we might just have opened up Pandora's
box.

QUID PRO QUO
Spring 2007

Reading through the transcripts was like excavating an ancient site, scraping away at a small detail and revealing an entire frieze. The picture that was emerging, although still incomplete, was beyond even my very fertile and conspiratorial imagination.

Two things became abundantly clear, however. The first was that the US Government had failed to turn over some extraordinarily exculpatory documents, and the second was that the High Court in London had been completely misled in our extradition proceedings.

Neither would help us much now. A Texas court wouldn't give a stuff whether the US Government had hoodwinked some limey court. And as for the Government not turning over material, well, it was probably innocent mistake, wasn't it? After all, there were a lot of documents.

To this day I cannot put my hand on my heart and say I know why Andy Fastow agreed to pay $10 million to CSFB for its stake in SwapSub. The only person who knows the answer to that is Andy Fastow. The one thing I am pretty sure, though, was that it had nothing whatsoever to do with the stake being worth $10 million.

The Newby transcripts revealed the extent of the relationship between the bank and the company. According to one call report, CSFB made over $50 million of revenues from Enron in 2000, and they were expecting a similar number for 2001. In comparison with CSFB, Natwest had just been picking scraps off the floor.

Rick Ivers and Marybeth Mandanas did not seem to feature in any deals other than LJM and SwapSub, which suggested that they were product specialists brought in specifically to put together and manage that one transaction, and its follow-on business.

Far from a straightforward and identifiable series of transactions between Enron and CSFB, the picture that emerged was of a blurred relationship where one thing was constantly traded off against another, and the lines between Enron and LJM became very indistinct, the common thread being Andy Fastow.

Fastow leaned heavily on CSFB at the end of 1999 to participate in LJM2, to which they committed $10 million of equity, and just as heavily in October 2000 to participate in LJM3, to which they committed $25 million, although this entity never actually formed. In between, he pressured them to be the lead bank in a revolving credit facility to LJM2.

Fastow was unabashed in his negotiating style with CSFB, frequently using references to how much money they had already made as a lever to further business. As early as August 1999, Rick Ivers' notebook evidenced a call in which Fastow had indicated that he hoped to be able to distribute $7.5 to $10 million to CSFB before December from LJM Cayman, and that he wanted it put straight into LJM2.

Most of the really jaw-dropping stuff about Southampton came from Ivers and Mandanas. In total contradiction of the Government's theory in our indictment, they testified that the structure of the SwapSub unwind, including the creation of the vehicle that would become Southampton, was CSFB's idea and they had been pushing it for some time before Fastow agreed.

So much for the prosecutors' theory that we were secretly plotting our little scheme with Fastow and Kopper.

An entry in Michael Kopper's diary suggested that the one day difference in closing date between the CSFB and NatWest sales to Southampton was there to justify the different pricing of the two stakes. Kopper also mulled over the possibility of characterising CSFB's payment as being $1 million for the equity, and $9 million of 'advisory fee'.

I was spitting with rage by this time. It made a total mockery of our indictment. The prosecutors may not have known what did happen, but sure as eggs were eggs it was not what they had accused us of, and that they failed to mention any of this highly exculpatory material during the extradition proceedings was absolutely shocking.

There was more to come.

The transcripts revealed that CSFB had been pitching off-balance sheet finance structures to Enron from as early as January 2000, involving equity forward contracts on Enron's own stock. These pitches had become more focused in mid-February, when apparently Enron was seriously looking for ways in which to repurchase a large block of its own shares without hurting its credit rating. Oh really?

In the first week of April 2000, CSFB began to transact a series of equity swaps. The dates, amounts and prices were all detailed, and it took almost no time to work out that these were the initial trades that would ultimately get rolled into the equity forward contracts that were the subject of the civil lawsuit.

At last, I thought, the connection was made.

The timing of the deals, so close to the SwapSub unwind, was surely beyond coincidence? The deals were originally documented with ECT Investments as the counterparty. ECT Investments was the Enron subsidiary that owned the stake in Rhythms Net. There was so much circumstantial evidence. But no more than that.

The April 2000 deals, however, involving approximately 1.7 million Enron shares, were the first of a series, and Fastow was very much the driver behind them. Over time, CSFB would engage in similar transactions involving a further 4.2 million Enron shares, and Enron would periodically lean on CSFB to get their internal limits increased in order to transact some more.

I had absolutely no doubt, and exactly no concrete proof, that CSFB had agreed to do these trades around the SwapSub repurchase. The e-mails, the dates of the trades, the number of shares involved, the entity involved, and the aggregate value of the deal, all pointed to the same conclusion.

But so what? There seemed to be a mass of evidence here that CSFB and Enron had entered into a series of agreements designed to provide Enron with off balance sheet finance, but it wasn't clear how any of this helped us.

It certainly didn't prove that Fastow had paid $10 million for the programme. He might well have done, but there was no direct link. He might have paid $10 million to ensure that CSFB participated in the equity raise for LJM2. But there was no direct evidence of that either. It was clear beyond doubt that Fastow made a direct link between LJM1 and LJM2, and had told CSFB so in no uncertain terms. Quid pro Quo. But there was no direct evidence of this being the reason for the payment of $10 million. CSFB themselves thought that they were being paid extra by way of a structuring fee, it seemed, for coming up with the idea of Southampton. So did Kopper, evidently. Perhaps that was it? But a $9 million structuring fee?

The very last transcript that I looked at was that of a member of the CSFB equity derivatives group. In it, he was questioned about a memo that was written on 6th July 1999 by the local Houston relationship manager in CSFB.

In the body of the memo, he described the development of a hedging program for CSFB's investment in LJM. This hedging program would ultimately lead to the SAILs transaction in November 1999, when Fastow would help himself to $14 million of the banks' money, but in July 1999 the programme was very much at conceptual stage.

The memo set out what amounted to a balance sheet of the LJM enterprise, including the Enron shares, the debt owed to Enron, and then a line item which simply read:

"After Tax Gift to Fastow–$10 million".

WITNESSES AND EVIDENCE
–A FOREIGNER'S GUIDE
Spring 2007

We had a pretty good idea now what had happened between Fastow and Enron and some very interesting theories about CSFB, and we were about ninety nine percent sure that the prosecutors had made none of these connections, so it seemed to me that we were in the driving seat.

Dan, ever the realist, cautioned me against thinking in straight lines.

"Dude, if I were Leo, I'd get a custodian of records on the stand, show the jury your e-mails, show them the money, and rest. No Fastow, No Kopper, no nothing. A good prosecutor would know that Fastow and Kopper are likely terrible witnesses for them. Kopper really sucked in Barges. A good cross examination of Kopper could win the whole case for us. But if they don't put him up there, we've got no-one to cross."

"But surely we could put him or Andy on the stand?" I asked.

"Yes, in theory we could. But a jury would get real confused if a witness for the defense seems to be against you. And anyway, cases can be won and lost in cross-questioning. If you haven't pretty much demolished the Government's case before you even get up to present your defense, you're likely going to lose. The jury has to be listening to your story already thinking that the Government's case is shaky. They have to have reasonable doubt. So the simpler the Government make their case, and the fewer witnesses they put up, the harder it will be for us. Right now, we've got to hope that young Leo will want to grandstand, and put a whole bunch of witnesses up there. If he does that, I think we're in good shape. But we won't know that till the morning of trial, will we?"

"Jesus Dan, you're supposed to be on my side. You sound like Reid Figel".

"Look David, I am on your side. It's just that you still seem so hung up on this innocence thing. The prisons here are full of 'innocent' people, some of whom really are innocent. Stop obsessing on the truth, and keep focused on what we can argue at trial".

He was right, of course. But at least knowing what had happened would enable us to start constructing the formal framework of our defence. As Dan had always said, the winner at trial is the person who defines the issues. We could now define the issues, I thought.

As a start, at Dan's request I put together a short bullet point framework for Dan's opening arguments. Each side gets fifteen minutes right at the start of the trial to tell the jury what they're going to be arguing, before the prosecution begins its case in chief. Those fifteen minutes could be the most important of our lives. If Dan could use that address to get the jury to see the prosecution case through our eyes, we could win. No doubt in my mind.

Dan took one look at my brief, ran it through his laminating machine, and stuck it to the wall behind his computer.

Our job between then and September would be to put meat on the bones. And meat meant witnesses. We had a mountain of good documents, but they were useless without witnesses. Had those witnesses been in the US, we could have subpoenaed their testimony. Even if they had pled the Fifth, their silent presence in the courtroom would have allowed us to enter all the exculpatory documents into evidence. For someone outside the jurisdiction, however, there are no such automatic subpoena rights.

Giles came up with the idea of writing a personal letter to each RBS witness, and sending all of the letters to Travers Smith, requesting that they be passed on to their clients individually. It took only a couple of weeks for Travers Smith to respond that no-one's view had changed.

In the meantime, Leo and JLo had responded to Dan's pre-Christmas request for CSFB documents. In a letter dated 22nd January, they said that the documents which were the subject of the request had "no bearing or relevance to the instant case and will not be turned over".

Nice. Particularly in light of the Newby testimony which threw a whole new light onto the CSFB situation.

As it stood, therefore, we had a whole bunch of exculpatory evidence with respect to the NatWest side of the deal, but no witnesses. On the CSFB side, we could subpoena witnesses but didn't have the documents.

It still rankles with me that the prosecutors can get away with this. There are clear rules as to what they are supposed to turn over, but break ing the rules carries no penalty worth its name, so they routinely ignore their obligations. More than one appellate brief in the Enron trials noted how the prosecutors had hidden exculpatory materials, but none would ever be punished for it. On the contrary, many would parlay their 'successes' on the Enron Task Force into lucrative jobs in private practice.

By the beginning of February, therefore, I was angry and upset. The possibility that we might just get a fair fight was becoming less and less likely. It was abundantly clear that the prosecutors would put whatever obstacles they could in our way, and RBS would evidently do likewise, presumably with no real choice but to act under orders from Washington.

We might still win, but it would be against huge odds if we did.

Every day spent in Texas, every dollar spent on new motions, every rejection of what should have been a reasonable request, was just another turn of the screw. The sheriff always gets his man.

MOTIONS, MOTIONS
March 2007

On 15th March 2007 we all got together in Judge Werlein's courtroom for a hearing that would prove pivotal to our case. We had filed a number of significant motions prior to a January deadline, and Judge Werlein would now hear oral argument from each side as to whether these motions should be granted, before going away to make his decision.

An interested spectator was my sister Claire, who had come to stay for the week. Her timing was perfect, as she arrived towards the end of the Houston Rodeo and Livestock Show, which is a three week festival that really needs to be seen to be believed.

It is a quite astonishing logistics exercise and an incredible juxtaposition of old meets new, with horse drawn wagons and livestock being driven down the streets of downtown in the shadow of gleaming skyscrapers. But most of all it is the single biggest concentration of testosterone outside of the 101st Airborne Division (the "Screaming Eagles").

The event kicks off in style with the World Championship Bar-B-Que Contest, a three day marathon knock-out event involving the best of the world's rib and beans chefs (as long as they come from Texas). It is really just an excuse for an almighty piss-up, but they sure do it in style.

Thereafter, as well as the ongoing livestock show (which is truly a very educational event, particularly for the children), the main competitions begin, and last for three weeks.

We went one night to see some of the action. And it was raw. There was steer roping, steer wrestling, bronco riding, and of course bull riding.

Broadly, the events can be categorised into "fastest to catch it" and "longest staying on it". The latter are far the more entertaining. In general terms, whatever species you are riding, you have to stay on for a minimum of eight seconds to score points. There are then points added or deducted for style and various technical aspects which were largely beyond me.

Eight seconds. I wondered who came up with it as a measure. If the symbol of machismo in Texas is being able to stay on something for more than eight seconds, it begged the question as to why there was not a population explosion? It might also have explained our New Year's firework display.

The highlight of the whole evening, though, came after the adult events and before the obligatory country and western band took to the arena. This was the calf-wrestling. Twenty eight children (girls and boys) of between 13 and 15 are put into the arena with fourteen calves. Each child has a rope halter. The first fourteen children to catch and haul a belligerent calf into a square in the middle of the arena get to look after the animal for a year before showing it at the following year's livestock show.

Now this event was truly outstanding. Children were being trampled, crushed, kicked and generally beaten up for a good ten minutes before the last calf was eventually caught. It was like Jeux Sans Frontiers on steroids. I tried to imagine the scene if they tried this in England. The elf 'n' safety Nazis would be putting people in prison. And yet. It was fantastic. The audience loved it. The children loved it. It was brutal. As a metaphor for life, it would be difficult to beat. God Bless America.

And back to business.

The two key motions for discussion in front of Judge Werlein that day were our second motion to dismiss the indictment, and our motion to use the Mutual Legal Assistance Treaty between the US and the UK to request that the UK authorities compel RBS to produce a vast number of documents for use in our defence. These would include internal reports from 2002 and 2003 that would show beyond doubt not only that NatWest had not been defrauded, but that it did not even think it had been defrauded, we were sure.

First and foremost, however, the second motion to dismiss.

On behalf of all three defendants, Kevin Huff from Reid Figel's team stood up to address the Judge. Kevin had graduated *summa cum laude* from the University of Utah before going on to Columbia University Law School. He had clerked for both the US Court of Appeals in Washington, and then for Supreme Court Justice Antonin Scalia. CVs didn't get any better than this.

His boyish looks and soft-spoken manner disguised a razor sharp mind and an alarming support for the death penalty, something about which he and I would argue from time to time. The difference was that my side of the argument was purely theoretical. Kevin, by contrast, had seen more last minute requests for reprieve than he could care to remember, and had been required in many instances to frame the response of the court.

Our motion, to my mind, was all but unassailable. Kevin was calm personified under questioning from Judge Werlein. Leo and JLo had turned up with a specialist from the Department of Justice in tow, who put their side of what was a highly technical legal argument.

The nub of it was whether the domestic wire fraud statutes could be used to criminalise behaviour by foreigners in a foreign land, when the victim of the crime was also foreign, and where any underlying duty to the employer, if it existed at all, existed under foreign law.

The further argument in our motion to dismiss was whether the indictment could stand at all after the honest services provisions had been struck from it, our argument being that it would be impossible to tell whether a Grand Jury would have returned the indictment if the 'theft of property' allegations alone had been put to them.

I didn't think Kevin Huff could possibly have done any better, and in my normal 'born optimist' way, I found myself glowing warmly when both sides were done. Lord knows I should have known better after our experiences in the High Court, but several people had looked at our motion in the previous weeks, and the overwhelming consensus was that even Ewing Werlein, who by nature was a pro-Government Judge, would have trouble turning it down.

The arguments on the Mutual Legal Assistance Treaty motion were less straightforward. We did not know when or where any of these internal RBS reports would have been created, so we asked for 'all' such reports. Likewise we asked for all of our e-mails, and all and any documents relating to the transaction and to a series of other transactions which we named.

We wanted to be able to illustrate the context in which the LJM transactions, including SwapSub, took place. That at the same time that we were selling SwapSub, we were selling lots of other assets; that there was an internal imperative to create earnings in order to fight the hostile takeover by increasing the value of GNW. As with the Fastow video from Merrill Lynch's offices, we needed the jurors to be able to imagine the office at

NatWest during that chaotic and remarkable period at the start of the new Millennium.

For us, knowing that internal RBS reports existed wasn't good enough, we knew. But we had to try, so we did. Likewise, asking for all documents relating to the asset sales wasn't good enough, but we had to try. We couldn't identify documents individually which had been written over seven years ago. So we were up against it. We knew that.

Judge Werlein listened intently to all of the arguments, before retiring to consider the papers. We would get a written ruling in a few weeks. In the meantime a timetable was set for some of the pre-trial disclosures, including expert witness reports.

On the eve of the hearing, Leo and JLo had given us a package containing some of the CSFB documents that we had requested. Almost the very first one was the e-mail of 9th March 2000, identifying that their current valuation of SwapSub was negative $1 million. But the following sentence, which read "that would indicate that as long as we sell for something positive, given the negative value, we should be okay", had been redacted.

Dan was incensed. They had only given us these censored documents to pre-empt any complaint to the Judge at the hearing that they were withholding exculpatory materials. But if they thought this would be the end of it, they were wrong.

We faced a difficult decision, however. If we filed a public motion explaining what we wanted and why, it could potentially be explosive, and the papers would certainly pick up on it. That could be good and bad. Good because it might move public opinion behind us, and might even bounce JLo and Leo into realising that their case was actually total rubbish. Bad, because it would give the Government a good steer as to exactly where we were going with our defence, and consequently plenty of time to prepare witnesses and find ways to frustrate us. The entire element of surprise would be lost.

It would take almost three months to decide which way to go on that, and in the meantime we had to try to get a couple of expert witnesses by a deadline which was now only weeks away.

DENY, DENY, DENY
April 2007

It took Judge Werlein three weeks to rule on our various motions. I spent most of that time believing that we could be just days away from a flight home. I spoke to numerous people about our arguments for dismissing the indictment, and all agreed that we had a good case. It's one of those great acts of self-delusion to seek comfort in the opinions of others, without ever asking yourself what you would say to them if the roles were reversed. You would hardly say 'sorry matey, but let's face it, you're screwed', would you?

Dan and Jimmy, to their credit, had always maintained that Werlein was a pro-Government judge, and that it was extremely unlikely that he would find in our favour. But I had discounted their views in favour of the opinions of some of the finest legal minds in our local downtown hostelry, The Char Bar.

The ruling, when it came, surprised even Dan and Jimmy. They had confidently predicted that it would just read 'Motion Denied', without reason. Instead, Judge Werlein produced a 22 page savage destruction of our arguments on pretty much every motion.

In case we had ever harboured the notion that we might get some even-handedness, what we got was Judge Werlein describing our 'naked self-interest' as part of his rationale for denying the motion to dismiss the indictment. He was, in effect, making a finding of fact without ever having seen a single piece of evidence. We had argued that the statute should never have been allowed to apply to our alleged conduct. In response, he was effectively saying that since our conduct was so egregious, of course the statute should apply to us, issues of jurisdiction notwithstanding.

I'm not sure now why I was so shocked. In effect it was no different to everything that had happened to us during the extradition hearings in England. The naked prejudice that came from accepting the allegations as the truth was all-pervasive. It begs the question, though, as to just what exactly is this mythical concept, the presumption of innocence?

Our motion to get discovery of documents from RBS was also summarily denied as being far too wide and vague. No, we couldn't force them to give us any documents. As a sop to us, Judge Werlein asked the prosecutors to see if RBS would be willing to make documents available on a voluntary disclosure basis. Some chance.

Our motion to compel the prosecutors to produce exculpatory materials was also denied. Leo and JLo had told the judge at the March conference that they had complied with their obligations, and even if that was rubbish, as we knew that it was, it was accepted.

Judge Werlein gave us until May 15th to submit any expert reports that we wished to use at trial, and sent us on our way, tails between our legs.

Emma and the children were staying with me for Easter when the ruling was published. We had gone down to Galveston for a week to stay at our favourite little hut on sticks by the Gulf, and Jimmy rang to give me the news. It was difficult to hide my disappointment, but we were well used to this by now. Soldier on.

The following week a delegation of our attorneys flew to London to interview witnesses for the defense. The single available witness represented by Travers Smith had to be interviewed in their presence, at their offices. This presented the risk that their client, RBS, would immediately report back to the Department of Justice, effectively giving the prosecutors a sneak preview of our defence. But in the circumstances we had little option.

The interview went particularly well. The potential witness was shown a number of documents and e-mails of which he had been a recipient or author, and asked questions about them. Several were correspondence between back-office people at the time of the sale of SwapSub by NatWest, and he concurred that the sale had been conducted according to all standard procedures, and that the valuation had been independently discussed.

The guy was not willing to travel to the US to give evidence, however. He had no wish to set foot on US soil, he said. He would be happy to give videotaped testimony from the safety of the UK, which is never as good as the real thing. Frankly, none of us could blame him. We were just really grateful that he was prepared to talk at all.

There were five other people that we had contacted directly, because they no longer worked for RBS. All five met with our lawyers. So when our delegation arrived back on US soil they were content that we had some decent witnesses as to the context of what was going on at NatWest in 1999 and 2000. It was all good background stuff, and the witnesses would all be well received, the attorneys thought.

But we still didn't have any witnesses to the facts. We didn't have Dai Clement. We didn't have Allen Hing. We didn't have any of the people who were 'in the room' on the SwapSub transaction. And we needed them. We needed them to be able to introduce the documents that we had uncovered that showed that it was all nonsense.

Although Dai was at the Royal Bank of Canada, and thus not represented by Travers Smith, he had his own attorneys, presumably paid for by RBC, and they had indicated that he would not speak with us. In some ways I feel a bit sorry for Dai, because his treatment at the hands of the Department of Justice in 2002 had apparently been extremely unpleasant, and we assumed that they had made him one of their 'unindicted co-conspirators' who could make up his own mind whether he wanted to give evidence for his friends and risk indictment himself.

But the three of us shared the opinion that if the boot had been on the other foot, we would at least have been willing to meet with the defense attorneys, if only to listen to what they had to say.

Allen Hing, by contrast, had previously indicated his willingness to talk to us, through a friend. But when Travers Smith told us the opposite, and informed us that they represented him, we were legally unable to talk to him. Allen was one of the senior back office employees, a trained accountant, and directly responsible for the management and accounting of the entire structured finance portfolio. He knew all of the assets inside and out, and had been involved in the sale of SwapSub. He was a key witness, and we were desperate to be able to talk to him. But we weren't going to be allowed to.

Our only recourse would be to try to get a court order compelling the testimony of Allen, Dai and the other key witnesses who we needed, if only to introduce exculpatory documents, and getting that order was going to be no mean feat.

DEAL OR NO DEAL
April 2007

Judge Werlein's ruling concentrated our minds on the trial timetable, and in particular, the looming deadline for expert witnesses. We reckoned that we needed two. The first would testify as to the valuation of SwapSub at the time that NatWest sold its interest. The second would testify that the presentation on 22nd February could not have been part of any scheme to defraud.

In America everything, including justice, comes at a price. With expert witnesses, you gets what you pays for, and we couldn't pay for much. We shopped around for potential candidates, but most wanted something comfortably in six figures just to get out of bed.

After numerous false starts, and several weeks later, Matt Hennessy found us an expert for the February 2000 presentation who would not charge the earth, and Jimmy identified a Dallas-based firm who specialised in doing the donkey work for complex financial expert witness cases, who would prepare all of the analyses for the second expert at a fraction of the cost of the great man doing it himself. They had a panel of potential expert witnesses for different types of case, and would find the right man for the job.

Matt's expert was a jovial local guy, who had long worked in complex energy commodities and risk management. He was given a prodigious quantity of documents to take away and read. When subsequently asked if he thought it was plausible that the three of us could have been the box marked 'NewCo' in the presentation, he roared with laughter.

"Is that the Government's contention?" he asked. When told that it was, he roared again, and said "I would liken that to three kids turning up at a Rolls Royce garage with the money they made from selling ice cream on the sidewalk". He observed that since NewCo was supposed to transact over $200 million of derivatives with a AAA rated bank, there was no way on earth that NewCo could be owned by three guys off the street.

It was stating the obvious. We all knew it. Gary had previously pointed it out. But it was nice that our man could get there so quickly from a standing start. And he agreed that the structure proposed could not possibly have been done without all of Enron, the two banks and Fastow knowing exactly who owned NewCo. We had found the right man, no doubt about it. He had testified as an expert in other complex white collar cases, and had an easy manner which would play well with a local jury, we thought.

The right man for the other job, however, was beyond our budget and unavailable for the September 2007 trial date, which was hugely disappointing. But we liked the Dallas-based guys, so we instructed them to do the financial analysis and begin to prepare the report. We would find someone to testify to it, we were sure.

The finished product, when it came, was truly outstanding. It analysed the SwapSub asset at the time of sale from the perspective of both NatWest and CSFB, using all of the contemporaneous e-mails and valuations from each bank, replicating their models, and commenting on the sufficiency and comparative merits of each. It also included an objective, third party valuation. It examined the price history and volatility of both the Enron and RhythmsNet share prices, and how these impacted upon implied and actual valuations.

It was total vindication for us. There was not one single way in which you could look at the transaction at the time and find that $1 million was an undervalue. In fact, by almost every single measurement, it was if anything a substantial overvalue. Absent any inside knowledge on our part as to what Fastow was about to do, there was no way that NatWest was defrauded. The sale was completely fair.

Even the 'brainiacs' in Washington, as Dan had taken to calling Reid, David and Kevin, were impressed.

All we needed now was to find the mouthpiece for the report. We might well have come up short had it not been for Judge Werlein's unilateral decision to push back the trial date. He called a conference of the attorneys on 30th April, and informed them that he had decided that the time allocated in September for the trial looked insufficient, and that he was therefore going to postpone it until 22nd October, when there was a larger window available.

On the same day that Judge Werlein announced the trial delay, the prosecutors approached Matt Hennessy offering a deal to Giles. It was a text-book manoeuvre. They must have known that the delay would be a huge psychological blow to us, because it meant more dead time spent in Houston, so perhaps they struck opportunistically. It was a fair guess that Giles would be most susceptible on paper to doing a deal. He had a wife and five children back home, and of the three of us he was the one with the least paper evidence against him. He had been party to very few of the damaging e-mails, and Kopper had not directly fingered him in his affidavit.

The prisoner's dilemma is a well-known problem in game theory. Take two prisoners and put them in separate rooms. Offer each a deal if he confesses and turns on the other. The first one to confess gets liberty or at least a massively reduced sentence, and the other will get the maximum. If neither agrees to co-operate, the chances are that each will serve a short sentence or no sentence at all because the prosecution case is so thin. But for each prisoner, even if innocent, the dilemma is to decide whether the other will confess.

In a perfect world, no-one would be seduced by this kind of primitive torture. But the world is not perfect, and the psychological pressures of the criminal justice system will take their toll on the hardiest of individuals. As a foreigner, separated from all that you know and love, and facing the possibility of a long time in a prison thousands of miles from home, the pressures are extreme.

It therefore must have been something of a surprise to Leo and JLo when Giles told them, in the nicest possible terms, where to stick their offer of a deal. It was an epic statement, frankly, and might have been translated as 'Fuck you. That may be what you guys do over here in America, but back home where I come from, things like the truth and loyalty to your friends actually count for something'.

We filed a motion asking for more time to find our expert, arguing that potential candidates who had previously ruled themselves unavailable for the September 2007 trial date might be available for the new October dates.

Leo and JLo's response was a study in petulance. Whether this was due to their annoyance at Giles' refusal to engage with them, we shall never know. We had just done a very rare piece of press, an article which had appeared in the *New York Times* documenting our existence in legal limbo, and Leo appended the article to the Government's response to our motion, saying that if we had time to be doing articles like this, we should have had time to find an expert witness. Judge Werlein promptly granted our motion, which Dan put down entirely to the pettiness of Leo's argument.

Having been so firmly rebuffed by Giles, Leo and JLo promptly moved on to me. Their tactics, though, were pretty silly. They gave Dan a packet of 'hot' documents that they believed formed the nub of the case against me, presumably to persuade Dan that they understood the case really well, and that they were going to have a really easy time prevailing at trial.

Their choice of documents confirmed instead what we had always suspected. These guys had absolutely no idea whatsoever about the case. As Dan had previously observed, that's not necessarily a good thing, because it would likely force them to run a very simple argument at trial, which would mean few witnesses and so not much for him to work with. The chances of Fastow appearing as a witness appeared slim.

But Dan used the opportunity of the prosecutors' approach to wind Gary up, pointing out that it was obvious that the Government saw him as the most culpable of the three, and joking about my ongoing plea negotiations. If it was in bad taste, it was pretty much par for the course amongst us. But there was a serious subtext. We all knew that once I turned down the offer of a deal, the prosecutors would move on to Gary. And it was no secret that Reid and the gang in Washington thought that a plea bargain was the best solution. Dan took the opportunity to call Giles and me in to his office to ask us whether we thought Gary would turn on us.

Giles was incensed. He gave Dan one of those lectures that only Giles is capable of delivering, about honour and friendship, and character.

"Well okay Giles, I hear you", said Dan. "But you need to be alive to the chance of a separation". The fact that Gary's daughter was now missing was not lost on any of us, and what sane person would be unaffected by that, and his inability to do anything about it from five thousand miles away?

Alternatively, we could use the situation to our collective advantage.

Once they had been rebuffed by Giles and me, the prosecutors would know that we were not going to be easily turned over as individuals. So as long as Gary didn't turn against us, we could potentially now negotiate from a position of relative strength. We could authorise Reid on behalf of Gary to engage with the prosecutors on the possibility of a deal for all or none, and see what came of it.

In the meantime, we would continue to prepare for trial. The more holes we could make in the Government's case, the stronger our negotiating position would be, even if we decided to do a deal. And the longer we could spin the Government out focusing on a deal, the less likely they were to be preparing properly for trial.

Information was power, I thought. The Government was blinking, and drawing them out on what they might be prepared to offer us would help indicate how desperate they were to avoid a trial. I was more than happy to play that game.

BEST MODERN PRACTICE
May 2007

Back home in Britain, things were becoming a little tense on the international extradition front. If Baroness Scotland and Tony Blair had thought that America ratifying the Treaty nearly four years after it was signed would finally quieten down the furore, they were to be disappointed.

The Americans continued to request the extradition of scores of British citizens. Two of the defendants who had been behind us in the queue were having slightly more success in resisting their deportation. Ian Norris, the former chief executive of Morgan Crucible, was fighting extradition on allegations of price fixing and obstruction of justice, in relation to the market in carbon products in the late 1990s.

It was a case on which Caroline Flint had made the mistake of commenting in 2004 that there would be no extradition since the allegations pre-dated price fixing being a crime in the UK. She hadn't counted on the ingeniousness of the UK Crown Prosecution Service in doing the bidding of its American masters, and reframing the charges against him as the common law UK offence of conspiracy to defraud, which would permit extradition.

Norris's predicament followed what was becoming a recognisable pattern in the post-Enron era. Morgan Crucible and its US subsidiary entered into an agreement with the Department of Justice in December 2002 which would prevent the companies being indicted in return for a payment of $11 million, but which would exclude four individuals including Norris, who were hung out to dry. The irony was that it was Norris himself who had originally reported the cartel activity to the European Union. No matter. He was indicted almost exclusively on the hearsay evidence of two supposed 'co-conspirators' who had themselves done deals with the Department of Justice.

Gary McKinnon, the Scottish computer geek who had hacked into the Pentagon computers from a PC in his bedroom shortly after 9/11, looking for evidence of UFOs, was arguing quite persuasively that he should be tried in the UK if anywhere, not least because the prosecutors had threatened to see him 'fry' as a cyber-terrorist if he refused to enter into a plea bargain and waive his rights in extradition.

Since our arrangements had been trumpeted by David Blunkett and Caroline Flint in 2003 as 'best modern practice in extradition', it would probably have been helpful to Blair and Scotland if other countries had demonstrated an equal willingness to hand over their citizens. Regrettably, no such help was at hand.

On 22nd May 2007, the British authorities announced that they had overwhelming evidence that a former KGB agent, Alexander Litvinenko, had been murdered in London by Andrei Lugovoi, a Russian citizen. Litvinenko had been granted political asylum and citizenship in Britain in 2000, and was a prominent critic of the Putin regime from his home in London. In a plot line reminiscent of the world of George Smiley, it was alleged that Lugovoi had travelled to London in 2006, met with Litvinenko in a restaurant, and poured a liquid containing the radioactive isotope Polonium 210 into his tea.

After a painstaking investigation lasting many months, the UK police managed to find a trail of Polonium 210 that stretched from Moscow to London, through several hotels and restaurants, and back to Moscow again on a British Airways jet. And the trail coincided perfectly with the movements of Lugovoi, who Litvinenko had met on the day of his poisoning.

Tony Blair immediately called for the extradition of Lugovoi. The Russian Government immediately told him to fuck off. "We don't extradite our citizens", they said. This was a tad unfortunate, because Russia was one of the new countries, including the US, to whom we were now happy to extradite our own citizens without even asking for evidence, supposedly on the basis that the arrangement was reciprocal. Seemingly the Russians had a different understanding of the concept of reciprocity. They wouldn't even extradite their citizens if there were evidence provided.

Attorney General Lord Goldsmith intervened angrily. "This murder was committed on UK soil, the evidence is in the UK, a UK citizen was killed and other people put at risk and it is therefore right a suspect should face justice in a UK court."

The irony of this was not lost on us, since these were exactly the arguments that we had used to push our case for a UK trial, and which had been so roundly rejected by Goldsmith's own lawyers, and the High Court.

The Attorney General added that he had requested "constructive and rapid co-operation" from Russia over Mr Lugovoi's extradition. He got a response which was certainly rapid, if unconstructive. 'Fuck off'.

Some two years later, Foreign Secretary David Miliband used a trip to Moscow to press the argument for extradition. He too was sent away with a flea in his ear. In the intervening period, Lugovoi had been made a member of the Russian Parliament and enjoyed the patronage and protection of his former spymaster, Vladimir Putin. David Cameron would fare no better than Miliband in 2011.

Nor were our European partners any more willing to roll over and deliver up their citizens, the letter of the law notwithstanding. In 2009, the Crown Prosecution service issued a European Arrest Warrant in respect of Dr Daniel Ubani, a German national who was wanted on manslaughter charges after killing David Gray, a British pensioner, with a massive dose of a painkiller whilst working his very first shift as a locum in England in February 2008.

The Germans, however, had other ideas, and promptly prosecuted Dr Ubani locally, giving him a nine month suspended sentence, and not barring him from practising. The CPS were furious, having spent 14 months painstakingly building their case, but their German counterparts merely expressed surprise that the CPS didn't understand the rights of countries to prosecute their own rather than extradite them.

By 2007, indeed, the realisation was beginning to dawn on many other countries that the UK was now a soft touch for extradition. The requests began to pour in, particularly from countries like Poland, where all allegations of crime, no matter how trivial, must be decided in court. In the fiscal year 2007-2008, 37% of all requests under the European Arrest Warrant were from Poland. By the following year, according to Home Office statistics, the total number of Eurowarrant requests had nearly doubled to 3,526.

There were requests for individuals accused of theft of a hairbrush and a mobile phone. The UK authorities had no option but to process each request, and, almost inevitably, put the individuals on a plane. The system rapidly began to be overwhelmed by the sheer volume of trivial applications, and the costs of processing each would of course be borne by the UK taxpayer, diverting funds from other areas of UK justice.

By early 2010, the UK would be sending an average of one plane-load of people just to Poland every week.

In July 2009, a young Briton named Andrew Symeou was extradited to Greece on a European Arrest Warrant to face charges of the murder of another British man in a nightclub. The evidence against him consisted almost entirely of statements beaten out of his friends by the Greek police, which were immediately retracted after their release from custody. It made no difference whatsoever.

After his extradition, he was denied bail, and was moved on his 21st birthday to the High Security Korydallos prison, whose conditions were condemned by the European Court of Human Rights as degrading and inhumane. It was described by Amnesty International as the worst prison in Europe. Symeou would eventually be granted bail but forced to remain in Greece, and was subsequently found not guilty at a trial in June 2011.

In May 2010, just six days after the Labour Government's ejection from power in a general election, a 52 year old firefighter named Gary Mann was extradited to Portugal under a European Arrest Warrant to serve a two year sentence for causing a riot at the 2004 European Championship football tournament. Arrested and tried within 48 hours of the event in 2004 alongside 11 other defendants, Mr Mann had met his lawyer only 5 minutes before the trial, had been unable to call witnesses, and had been unable to understand most of the proceedings due to poor translation. A UK police officer who had been posted to Portugal during the Championships described the trial as a farce. After the trial, the Portuguese deported him, then changed their mind and asked for him back.

In his High Court Appeal against extradition, Lord Justice Moses stated that he thought the case against Mann was highly questionable, but that the Extradition Act left him powerless to act.

The following month, the High Court began to hear the appeal of Edmond Arapi, an Ethnic Albanian legally resident in the UK, against the decision of the magistrates' court that he should be extradited to Italy to face a sentence of 16 years in prison on charges of murder. Arapi had been tried and convicted in his absence on the flimsiest of identification evidence. Documents produced by his legal team in the extradition proved that he was not even in Italy at the time of the alleged offence, let alone anywhere near the scene of the crime. No matter. His obvious innocence was irrelevant.

Mr Arapi was one of the few lucky ones. Faced with a growing press awareness of his case, and compelling evidence that it was a case of mistaken identity, the Italian prosecutors came to the High Court and withdrew their application. Mr Arapi was represented by our old friend John Hardy QC, who commented that "with respect, this case is outrageous—there is no other way to describe it". Outrageous it might well have been, but had the Italian prosecutors not been willing to own up to their mistake, you can be absolutely sure that Mr Arapi would now be languishing in an Italian prison.

Not so lucky were five young British men wanted as suspects in a case of drunken violence in Greece. The five had not even been charged, and denied all involvement in the incident, but the Greek authorities wished to interview them as suspects, and the Eurowarrant procedures would permit this, said the High Court in June 2010.

Best modern practice, indeed.

ANNIVERSARY PRESENTS
June 2007

As the deadline for the expert witness reports drew nearer, we were still struggling to find our second expert. Those that were available we couldn't afford. We had someone lined up but he wasn't the ideal choice.

On 6th June, Emma flew out for a few days. It was the first time she had come alone, and it coincided with our wedding anniversary. Conscious of the horlicks that I had made of Christmas, I had taken counsel from Bart and Alix Stafford as to what I should do by way of celebration, and the consensus was that taking Emma to a local spa hotel for the night would be a good idea.

I booked us a room at the Houstonian Club, which was only a couple of miles away from my apartment, and had all the pampering and treatments that any woman could want.

The day went much to plan, until about 6pm, when my mobile phone rang. It was Jeff, the guy who had prepared the expert report on valuation, and had been looking for the expert to present it. He wanted me to join a conference call with someone who had long been his prime target for the role, but had so far proved out of reach. The guy had said that he might be prepared to do it, but he wanted to know more about the wider background before he would make up his mind.

The deadline for the report was Tuesday. It was now Saturday evening. I was faced with a dilemma. Jeff was adamant that it had to be me who spoke to the potential witness.

I left Emma by the pool, and headed for our room for the call. It would only take ten minutes, I told Emma.

An hour later, we were still on the phone when Emma came back to get ready for dinner. And another half hour later, when Emma stood in front of me in the little black number with her arms folded, tapping her foot on the floor, we had still not finished.

The mystery man was an eminent professor at one of Texas's top business schools. He was an expert on derivative pricing, published in more respected journals than you could shake a stick at, and had served as an expert witness in some very high profile cases. He was as sharp as a needle, and had read Jeff's report from cover to cover.

The report was a no-brainer for him. He could give it standing on his head. He complimented Jeff on a great piece of work, and made some suggestions as to small changes that might be made here and there. But what really interested him was not the dry financial analysis in the report. It was what the hell had happened. As a local man, with a profound interest in business, he had followed all of the Enron press assiduously and so knew all about Andy Fastow and his dealings. But this transaction had always puzzled him, because so much about it didn't make sense.

I was extremely reticent to go into what I thought had happened, because we were then truly stepping into the possibility of a prosecution challenge on the basis of taint. But he kept trying to construct the arguments as to how to get a jury to understand that both $30 million and $1 million were fair prices. Eventually I could no longer stop myself.

"Look, that's not right, okay, and it's not what we are going to be arguing at trial. $30 million was never a fair price for Enron to pay. Fastow just picked a number out of the air. Then they pumped up the stock price on the day of sale to make the numbers work for everyone."

"But that makes no sense", he retorted. "How did no one at the company ever pick that up?"

"Because Andy circumvented all of the normal processes, and the auditors just missed it".

"And you knew nothing about what he was doing?"

"No".

There was a long pause.

"I need to go away and think about this", he said. Then he told me what his going rate would be for an assignment such as this. It was way too much money. I looked up at Emma. I couldn't believe I had just spent an hour and a half of our anniversary on the phone, and that I could have saved about 89 minutes of the time if we had just asked that question at the beginning of the call.

I told him that we couldn't afford that sum, but thanked him profusely for taking the time to have the call with me, and then put the phone down.

"I hope that was worth it", said Emma.

"It wasn't", I said. "Sorry. No more calls, I promise. Let's go to dinner".

The following morning my cellphone rang again. It was Jimmy.

"Where are you, dude? I've been trying to call you at home."

I told him.

"Well, you've got some explaining to do. Can you tell me just exactly what you told that professor on the phone last night?"

"Jimmy, do me a favour. I'm trying to enjoy my anniversary with my wife. I wasted an hour and a half on the phone last night, only to find out that there's no way we could afford the guy anyway. So what I really don't need right now is a lecture from you on what I should or should not have said to someone who is not going to be an expert witness for us anyway, okay?"

"Well, if that's the way you want it, fine. It's just that I have just taken a call from him. He wants to do it. And he's offered to do it *pro bono*."

I'm not often lost for words, but this was such an occasion. It seemed that the professor had got himself so worked up about the whole thing that he felt it was his civic duty to help. If the report itself was a fantastic bit of work, having an expert witness who would be giving his services without payment was about as good as it could possibly get. One criticism of expert witnesses tends to be that they are guns for hire, and that they may say whatever is required of them because they are being paid to do so. Their fees must be disclosed in the report.

I could imagine the look on JLo and Leo's faces when they got to the section entitled Compensation Disclosure, and read "I have agreed to perform this work pro bono. My compensation is not dependent on the outcome of this matter". With apologies to Emma, it was the best anniversary present I have ever had.

NEW BROOMS
June 2007

We submitted the two expert reports to Leo and JLo on 12th June, the deadline. We thought they would be filed as part of the court papers, and so Judge Werlein would be able to read them, but that wasn't how it worked. Those reports would only be seen by him if we went to trial, along with the rebuttal reports from the prosecutors.

We really wanted Werlein to see the reports, mainly because it might just encourage him to believe that there was another side to the story. We asked the attorneys if we could send him a copy directly but were told that this was not permissible.

As it turned out, Werlein would never see either report. No-one would except the prosecutors.

June 2007 saw a changing of the guard in Britain. Tony Blair sold his personal stock at the top of the market, and flounced off into a sunset of lucrative American advisorships and speaking tours, finally handing Gordon Brown the premiership he had so long coveted. As hospital passes go, it was a blinder.

Within minutes of taking office, Gordon Brown was faced with attempted terrorist attacks on Glasgow airport and London. He couldn't have known it, but the economy was also about to pitch off the top of the cliff onto which he personally had driven it. Even the weather was against him, with biblical amounts of rain causing widespread flooding around the country. All that was missing was a plague of locusts.

Around the same time, the Department of Justice announced that it was opening a probe into corruption at British Aerospace, involving allegations of billion dollar bribes being paid to Saudi royalty as part of the lucrative Al Yamamah contract that had been negotiated during Margaret Thatcher's premiership. In one of his last acts as Prime Minister, Blair had overseen the quashing by Lord Goldsmith of the Serious Fraud Office enquiry into the deal, citing national interest.

Baroness Scotland was appointed Attorney General in place of the outgoing Lord Goldsmith. And Digby Jones was a surprise new member of the Government, being given a Peerage and a job as a Trade Minister, although he did not take the Labour Party whip. As a strong supporter of ours, Digby had kept in contact since we had been in Houston, so having someone on the inside could only help us, I thought. He had been assiduous throughout in taking no position on our innocence or guilt, but thought that our extradition denied us an opportunity to fight our case and offended his sense of fair play.

Gordon Brown's first Prime Minister's Questions took place on Independence Day. He was asked by Menzies Campbell whether he was going to renegotiate the extradition treaty with the US. It was a matter for ongoing discussion, he said. Meaning 'no'.

Meanwhile, John Tiner, the outgoing head of the FSA, called for the regulator to be given American-style plea bargaining powers, including the ability to offer immunity to whistleblowers. It was something that Baroness Scotland would quickly start pushing on the prosecuting authorities.

We made some progress on document discovery. To our great surprise, RBS agreed to allow us to have copies of all of our e-mails from June 1999 to April 2000, and duly sent 36,000 pages of documents in electronic form.

It wasn't what we really wanted, of course—we were after the internal reports. But it was better than a kick in the nuts, and would at least help us with the broad picture. So now, about ninety five percent of the documents in the case had come from the UK!

There was a lot of good stuff in there, but the most fascinating revelation was the ratio of business emails to personal ones. In my case, it was about 90/10. Giles's was about 50/50. Gary's was 10/90, the inverse of mine. It was a damning indictment on one of us, but we couldn't agree which one.

After much soul-searching, we decided that we had little to lose by going nuclear with JLo and Leo on the CSFB stuff. They were continuing to refuse to give us the documents that we wanted, because we would not tell them why we wanted them.

So screw them.

We would go public with a motion for discovery; the downside of revealing our hand to the prosecutors was more than outweighed by the potential advantages. It would show the prosecutors as being disingenuous and in breach of their obligations of disclosure. It would also be extremely newsworthy back in the UK, since it would effectively accuse the prosecutors of lying to the High Court about their knowledge of all these documents during our extradition proceedings.

The motion was filed on 9th July. Publicly. It was a humdinger, crafted as ever by the brainiacs in Washington, giving a compelling counter-story, which would effectively be our argument at trial. The asset was worthless. Even CSFB had thought it worthless. It wasn't us who dreamed up the unwind of SwapSub, it was CSFB. And the $10 million that they received was in fact payment for a series of services rendered to Fastow and/or Enron.

The cat was now well and truly out of the bag. As Tom Kirkendall observed, in a civil case that would have been the end of it. We could all have gone home.

The response from both the prosecutors and CSFB was instant. JLo and Leo filed a slightly hysterical motion with the court saying that "the defendants' requests are moot, the materials they are requesting are irrelevant, and their arguments are inaccurate".

They went on to say that "the defendants are attempting to derail the focus of this case and the indictment". Well, they got that last one right. If the real story derailed the Alice in Wonderland tale in the indictment, we were all in favour.

They made a bit of a schoolboy error, however, in arguing that they did not have access to most of the documents that we were seeking because those documents were part of the Newby civil litigation, to which the US Government was not a party. In response, we produced the court order from 2004 granting the US Government's request to become an interested party in the Newby action, and thereby get access to all deposition testimony and documents.

Before Judge Werlein could rule on our motion, JLo and Leo had duly provided us with all the documents that they said they didn't have. And what a little treasure trove it was.

CSFB, meanwhile, had been contacted by several members of the UK press, asking for their response to our motion. Michael Herman at *The Times* was the first to get a quote, and it was a cracker.

"This new filing is a disingenuous attempt to shift blame away from the three individuals. The evidence establishes that Andrew Fastow conspired with them to cheat the limited partners including CSFB. CSFB was a victim of their fraud."

In the circumstances, their reaction was hardly surprising. Several of the major banks, including CSFB, were still defendants in the Newby litigation, and the last thing they needed was to get embroiled, directly or indirectly, in the mess that was Southampton.

The one piece still missing in the jigsaw was the UK witnesses. On 2nd August, we filed a motion requesting that Judge Werlein use the provisions of the Mutual Legal Assistance Treaty to ask the judicial authorities in the UK and the Cayman Islands to order videotaped testimony from 6 individuals. Five of these were hidden behind the shroud of RBS and their gatekeepers, Travers Smith.

Allen Hing was the most critical, as he had written or received a number of very exculpatory documents in our case. As a member of the back office, and a trained accountant intimately involved in most aspects of LJM and Swap Sub, he was potentially pivotal in our defence.

As gambits went, this then was our last and most important throw of the dice. The task wasn't straightforward. Not one single attorney on our team could find any precedent for this kind of request. The Mutual Legal Assistance Treaty was designed as a means whereby Government officials in different countries could ask each other for help. Although the Treaty did not preclude use indirectly by defendants, it did not exactly facilitate it. We had to rely on the co-operation of Judge Werlein, whose views on us as people seemed to have been well flagged in his response to our motion to dismiss the indictment.

Video testimony was highly unsatisfactory. First because a jury is likely to fall asleep watching a video, as opposed to watching a live witness on the stand. Second because, as it took place before the trial, our attorneys would not be able to use relevant material that may have come up during the trial itself when interviewing the witnesses. Thirdly, because Leo and JLo would be able to work out their counter-strategies in advance.

But, as with pretty much everything else in the US justice system, beggars can't be choosers, especially when they're foreign beggars, and something would most certainly be better than nothing.

Shortly after we had arrived in Houston, Leo and JLo had taken a plane to London to collect more documents and witness statements from the, by necessity, ever-so-co-operative RBS. Having argued during our extradition that the witnesses and evidence were all to be found in Texas, the prosecutors no longer had to keep up that pretence once we had been extradited.

All we needed was for Judge Werlein to grant our motion. Not a huge ask, surely? After all, it was no skin off his nose.

WINDS OF CHANGE
August 2007

It had been over a year since our extradition. A year out of our lives. But it felt as if we were on the home stretch, now. The families were all in town for varying periods over the summer holidays, and then it would be heads down for the trial in October, and if there was a God we would be back home by Christmas, vindicated.

Summer in Houston is brutal. From early June through to about October, the daily average temperature is in the high nineties, with humidity near one hundred percent. You get drenched in sweat walking from your air-conditioned car to your air-conditioned apartment.

Of the three of us, Giles was best equipped to cope. He had been born in India, and had no problem with the heat. Like the proverbial mad dog, he would happily lie out in the midday sun, and by the beginning of August was nut brown. I would stay out of the furnace as much as humanly possible, venturing out for my daily walk around Memorial Park much later in the day, when the edge had gone off the heat and the sun was starting to sink below the trees. Even then, the humidity was stifling.

Emma and the children arrived on 26th July and would stay until 20th August. All three defendants and their families headed off down to Galveston, to stay in different holiday homes. Troy Lochlear and his family also came down, so that we would be able to meet up periodically. The first such date was 7th August, the birthdays of Emma and Deborah Darby. Giles had taken a condo in a development at the south end of the Island, with a large communal pool and bar, which was designated as the meeting place.

The day before the big get-together, I received a call from Jimmy. "Bad news dude", he said. "Werlein's just bumped the trial date again". His excuse this time was that he had spoken to the State judge in a capital murder trial that clashed with our October date, and he had decided that the murder trial really should take precedence, even though it was only a State case. Consequently, our new trial date would be January 2008.

"How often can he keep doing this, Jimmy?"

"Often as he wants, dude".

Emma was remarkably sanguine. She immediately saw the opportunity to extend her stay in Houston. But by the time we got to Giles' place the following day, it was clear that her philosophical approach was not shared by Debs or Julie. What should have been a really nice occasion turned into a series of arguments, seemingly with me and Emma on one side and everyone else on the other.

The majority view was that it was the final straw. Gary had always wanted to plead the case out, reflecting the view of his counsel, Reid. I had always wanted to go to trial. Giles had been happily plodding along in the middle, initially leaning strongly towards Gary, but conscious that we needed to prepare for trial to stand any chance of ever getting a good deal. More recently, he had begun to swing behind going to trial, as we slowly built our case and he saw that we just might win against all the odds.

This had knocked him sideways, though. Debs and Julie were adamant. We needed to cut a deal and get home. They saw nothing but conspiracy. Every time we looked like getting close, the judge was finding reasons to put back the trial. He knew we were stuck thousands of miles from home, and he just kept on pushing it back. And we knew from his ruling on our motion to dismiss that he thought we must be guilty.

That just increased the risk of a mistrial. Giles reckoned it was substantial, and it was difficult to argue with him. We might put on the best defence in the world, but if one redneck juror wanted to see three bankers hang, the trial would end deadlocked, and then we would be stuck around for another year, facing another set of fees which we didn't have. And jurors can be heavily swayed by a direction from the judge.

When things are going your way, you naturally accentuate the positive. When they go against you, the focus naturally shifts to the negative, and try as I might I couldn't turn anyone around, so in the end I gave up and we went back to our little shack on stilts. I sat up for hours that night with Emma after the children had gone to bed. We sat out on the deck under a warm, moonlit sky, drank a lot of wine and smoked a ton of cigarettes.

"This could get ugly", I said.

"Do you think you can get Giles back?"

"Unlikely".

"So are you stuck with doing a deal?"

"Not if I don't want to".

"But what happens then?"

"I'm not sure. History says that there will always be a deal for Gary and Giles, with or without me. It happened in Olis. It happened in Lay and Skilling when Causey pled out. The question is whether the Government will give them a decent deal unless they give evidence against me."

"But they wouldn't do that, would they?"

"Not in a million years. And anyway, what is there for them to say?"

This was a new variant of the prisoner's dilemma. I tried to run through all the possible iterations, but whichever way you looked at it, going our separate ways was unlikely ever to end well. I could go to trial and win, in which case the boys would forever regret doing their deal. I could go to trial and lose, or get a mistrial; either way I could face years in the US alone while Gary and Giles went home.

No, either we all went to trial, or we all pleaded guilty. As always, we would be strongest if we stuck together.

And if we were going to do a deal, the time was now, before any possible tensions or fissures between us became evident, and played into the hands of our enemies.

It just felt such a betrayal, though. We were so close. So many people had supported us. Believed in us. And now we might just chuck in the towel after all these years of fighting. And what would it all have been for?

I began writing the headlines. We would get torn to shreds. Greedy bankers finally admit it was all lies. "See?" says Home Secretary, "I told you it was right to extradite them. How could you all be so stupid as to be taken in by their slick PR campaign?"

How could we ever look people in the eye again? How could I ever look the children in the eye again? What would I ever say to Liberty, who supported us? And Melanie? And my parents? Our friends?

Emma had it right though. "Look, nothing's changed. We know the truth. Your friends will always be your friends. Those who walk away weren't friends, were they?"

"What if I decide to fight on?"

"I'll back you. Always."

"And if I lose?"

"If you lose, you lose. You've worked so hard. You've earned your day in court."

THE DUMBEST GUYS IN THE ROOM
August 2007

The beach house at Galveston was the perfect place to be at this time. Having delayed their return flights, Emma and the children would not be leaving until the end of August, and I figured that the latest trial delay meant that I could have a few more days 'off' without impacting our preparations.

Our life was gloriously simple. Early morning runs along the beach before it got too hot. Lazy days playing with the children. The occasional trip into town. Plenty of time in the evenings after the children had gone to bed to ruminate on the future. With the benefit of time, cigarettes, alcohol, and sensible discussion with Emma, I got myself into a position where I could see the way ahead with some clarity.

Until now, I had analysed most things through the narrow prism of self-interest. If I believed something was right, I would argue with Gary or Giles and between us we would come to a decision. The universe of interested parties was three as far as I was concerned.

Now, for the first time, I was confronted by the fact that there were actually eighteen interested parties. The three of us, three partners, and twelve children. And this decision would have a bearing on all of their lives. We owed it to them to act in the interests of all.

Getting to that point in the thought process was not straightforward, however. It took me a ridiculously long time to realise what I should have realised in about five seconds flat. We weren't fighting for the good of humanity. We were fighting for ourselves. Yes, there were issues of principle involved, but it wasn't a life or death thing. It was about pride and reputation. I was no freedom fighter, sacrificing family to a higher cause. I was a banker who had made a whole lot of money doing a deal with a guy who turned out to be a crook. If I pled guilty I wouldn't be letting the world down, however much it might stick in the craw.

Sometimes we adults have a way of overcomplicating things. My daughter Jemima, who will undoubtedly be a lawyer when she grows up, has the gift of clarity of thought. Before our extradition, when we had sat the children down and explained that I might have to go away, Jemima, aged eight, had observed simply:

"Well, that's just really silly. Why can't they have a trial here?"

Now, sitting in Galveston one afternoon, she managed to hit the nail on the head once more:

"Daddy, if you just say you did it, will they let you come home?"

"Well, yes, they probably would".

"Well then why don't you just say you did? No-one cares, do they?"

Once I had finally got myself straight mentally, things fell into place quite quickly. I would still continue to try to persuade Gary and Giles to go to trial, but if I failed, then I would fall in behind them on a joint plea deal. Splitting the three would never be an option.

I knew that I had little or no chance of persuading Gary himself of the merits of trial. His lawyers were now engaged with the prosecutors on the subject of the deal which they had been recommending since we arrived.

Consequently, I would work on Giles. If he were with me, he might just be able to carry Gary. Their friendship ran far deeper than mine did with either of them, and Giles knew well how to play Gary.

Working against me, I knew, was the fact that the family issues for both Gary and Giles were far more acute than for me. Gary, because his former wife had disappeared from the UK, taking his daughter with her, and as long as he was stuck in Texas there was absolutely nothing that he could do. His son, meanwhile, was living with Julie and her two children, all of whom desperately wanted him to come home. Giles, of course, had five daughters and a wife, all equally keen to put an end to this.

My plan, therefore, was to accentuate the positives in our case, and the ideal opportunity came when on 2nd September we had received no rebuttal expert witness reports from the Government. This was their deadline, and once they had missed it, they could no longer produce an expert witness at trial to contradict ours. The best that they could do would be to try to undermine our witnesses in cross-examination, something that I considered extremely unlikely given the pedigree of our guys.

Dan pointed out again that the absence of expert witnesses for the Government suggested the nightmare scenario of them running a slimmed down case with almost no witnesses for him to attack.

Undeterred, I gambled with my approach to Giles, and lost spectacularly. I suggested to him that I could all but ensure his acquittal at trial. Consider, I said, that there was very little documentary evidence against him. All they really had was 'guilt by association'.

I volunteered, therefore, to get up on the stand and take all the heat. I told him that I would testify that with retrospect my behaviour had been reprehensible, that I had withheld information on the Southampton deal from the bank. I would state that I had no recollection of speaking with Giles about the offer before I returned to the UK from the US, by which time NatWest had sold its stake in SwapSub.

These statements were true, and I was happy to put my name to them by way of a mea culpa, and let the jury decide whether that amounted to a crime. Giles would not have to take the stand—his lawyer could say without much fear of contradiction that there was no evidence that Mr Darby had any knowledge with respect to the offer before NatWest had sold its stake. Giles would be in the clear.

I thought it was a brilliant gambit. I couldn't have been more wrong. Far from seeing it as a means to guarantee his own acquittal, Giles just took it as being an admission of my own guilt. He hurriedly called a meeting with Jimmy, and asked me to repeat my offer to him, which I duly did. Jimmy shrugged. "So what dude?"

"See", said Giles. "Bermo's admitted it".

"Admitted what?"

"That he knew about the deal and we didn't".

Jimmy paused and looked at me somewhat quizzically. I motioned for him to respond as he saw fit.

"Well, first of all I don't think he is saying anything about his own state of mind that isn't already demonstrably true by reference to all the documentary evidence, and second of all he's not saying that you didn't know, he's just saying that he doesn't recall telling you, which is not quite the same thing, Giles".

When Giles has something in his head, it is quite difficult to dissuade him using anything as obvious as common sense and logic. After a while, we decided to let it lie.

It would become a running sore, though. It pissed me off more than a little because I actually thought it was a magnanimous gesture, giving a jury the opportunity to vent its anger on me if they needed a lightning rod. Giles didn't see it that way, though. I had 'admitted' that my behavior was 'reprehensible', and that was tantamount to saying that I was the bad guy.

The negotiations with the Government got underway. Dan and Jimmy, sensing my frustration, were at pains to point out that they didn't think the thing would go anywhere. They were convinced that the prosecutors and our side would never agree on what part of our behavior constituted a crime. In the meantime Dan was content to let the whole charade continue, with Reid driving the bus, because for as long as the Government thought we were looking to do a deal, their minds wouldn't be on trial preparation.

Now in a normal world, both sides would have sat down and discussed what we were supposed to have done wrong. If agreement could be reached on that, we could talk about an appropriate sentence. But of course this was not a normal world. This was the parallel universe of the US criminal justice system. The starting point was to agree the sentence and the monetary penalties, if any, and then try to find something by way of a crime that matched the agreed sentence.

Having come to terms with this new paradigm, so began the worst commercial negotiation I have ever been a party to. Let's put it this way; if someone who worked for me had negotiated as badly as we three did over the course of the next month, I would have fired the bastard on the spot.

There are many gambits and strategies in successful negotiation. Giles likes to work out the fairest deal in advance, and put it on the table as a first and final offer, with a detailed explanation as to what everybody gets out of it. It's such an unusual tactic that it quite often disarms the other side, who promptly agree, and it saves a huge amount of dancing around and point-scoring.

Personally, I favour the more traditional approach where two parties start some distance apart, and end up meeting somewhere in the middle. Offer, counter-offer, etc. But again, the object is to have everyone thinking that it's a good deal, as this maximises the opportunities for further business.

We started off with all the right intentions. The three of us agreed to a series of points defining our position. The attorneys wrote these down, and Reid went into battle.

Over the course of the next month, we ended up with a deal that was so far away from our original position as to be absolutely laughable. We had started with a target of a 12 month sentence, and a maximum of 24 months. We ended up with 37 months. We said no to RBS being regarded as a victim of fraud. We ended up with RBS being designated the victim. We said we wanted to go straight back to the UK to begin our sentence. They said no chance.

Of all the things that we wanted, we achieved only two. The first was that the deal would be guaranteed, a so-called '(c)(1)(C) plea'. This meant that Judge Werlein would have no discretion in sentencing. He could either take it or leave it. We had seen enough of Judge Werlein to reckon that relying on his leniency would be an act of extreme folly.

The second was that the prosecutors agreed to write into the deal that they would not only support our repatriation to the UK under the prisoner transfer treaty, but would use best endeavours to expedite it. They could not guarantee it, because responsibility for saying 'yes' to transfers lay with another part of the Department of Justice, who would not be bound in advance, but the prosecutors indicated that it was pretty much a slam-dunk.

This was their ace card. Once we were back in the UK, we would be subject to UK rules, which included automatic release at the half-way point of any remaining time. In the Federal system, there is no parole, and as a foreigner you are not entitled to any time off for things like drug and alcohol rehabilitation programs, which can dramatically reduce sentences for US citizens. Nor will you be allowed to serve your sentence in an open prison, as US citizens can do.

The prosecutors played their hand skillfully. This may have had something to do with the fact that Leo Wise had been replaced by an older and more experienced prosecutor called Wes Porter. The latest rescheduling of the trial to January had produced a clash for Leo on another trial, and so Porter had been drafted in to replace him. Dan saw him as a far more formidable foe.

The prosecutors knew that what we really wanted was to get home, and so they used a carrot and stick approach. They said that if we agreed to plead, they would get us home quickly. No guarantees, of course, but they would do their best. If we didn't plead, and lost at trial, not only would they push for the maximum sentence, but they would refuse to support any transfer request, meaning that we would spend the whole sentence in a US prison.

They figured, correctly as it turned out, that we wouldn't really dig our heels in on sentence because once we were back in the UK every day only became half a day, and anyway the mere fact of being back in the UK, and close to our families, would be pivotal. And so it proved. The three of us folded like a cheap suit.

Once we had notionally agreed the price of our ticket home, it fell to the prosecutors to produce the first draft of the 'allocution', which would form the statement of facts around which we would plead guilty. Now we had to find a crime to fit the punishment.

My irritation at how the negotiation was conducted was perhaps tempered by the expectation that the whole thing was only a charade, and that we would never be able to agree what it was that we had done that was actually criminal.

As expected, Dan, Jimmy and I had a really good laugh when the prosecutors circulated the draft document. Mulgrew was the main man, the corrupt persuader. He it was who had approached Fastow and Kopper with the plan to steal from our employer. Darby was the facilitator, and I was the mechanic.

There was no way that we were going to get from that position to one remotely resembling the truth, I thought. The trial would be proceeding, and the good news was that now we had a really good idea as to the case the prosecutors would be running.

Reid, though, wasn't remotely downbeat. This was all just part of the game, he told us. As games go, there wasn't much enjoyment in this one, I thought.

We put together a red-line amended copy of the document, which deleted pretty much all of the prosecutors' theory of the case, and inserted instead what had actually happened.

When it was finished, there seemed to be something missing.

"How is this a crime, Reid?" we asked.

"Theft of information", he said, matter-of-factly. "By not reporting to NatWest that you had been offered the opportunity to invest, you deprived them of the ability to do so".

If you scratched below the surface, the lunacy of the proposition instantly became clear. We had deprived NatWest of the opportunity to buy the asset which it had just decided to sell. Or, looked at another way, we deprived NatWest of the opportunity to participate in Fastow's fraud on Enron, which to most independent observers might have been a better analysis of the facts.

The best thing to do, therefore was not to scratch at all. It was true that we had not informed NatWest when we were granted the option. We had told the FSA exactly that back in 2001. If that could be construed as being a crime without further interrogation, then job done. According to Reid, it was. It was not a case he as a prosecutor would ever have indicted, he said, but if you held your nose and stretched the definitions of the statutes a bit, you could get there.

The document bounced back and forth a few times between Reid and the prosecutors, without changing anything fundamental. The prosecutors accepted that our presentation of the 22nd February hadn't been some fraud, as Thomas Hanusik had been so keen to tell the extradition court in 2006 when trying to establish jurisdiction. They accepted that we had no knowledge of what Andy Fastow was up to with Enron, contrary to all of their pleadings in the UK.

On 19th November 2007, the document ceased moving and the music stopped. I suppose I had been hoping that the whole thing would fall over, and it hadn't. In the back of my mind, I had perhaps been waiting for Judge Werlein to grant our motion to compel video testimony for the UK witnesses, which might have derailed the plea negotiations. But it had been three and a half months since we had submitted that motion, and he had just sat on it.

Even if he now ruled in our favour, we would have no hope whatsoever of being able to get the testimony prior to the scheduled trial date. The trial would have to be delayed again, and this time it would be for many months because the diaries of our various attorneys were already full after our January trial slot.

It was game over. After all these years, we would go out not with a bang, but with a whimper. We may have fought a good fight, but we had lost. Everywhere.

The greatest irony of all, perhaps, was that six years to the day after we walked into the offices of the Financial Services Authority in London and gave them a detailed account of what we had done, we had now agreed a statement of facts with the prosecutors that was identical in every material respect to the account that we had given to the FSA, except for the bit at the end that said "this is a crime".

We had been extradited on the basis of some total bullshit theory, by a bunch of prosecutors who had withheld vital and exculpatory evidence, and now we were back to square one, six years older, millions of dollars poorer, and five thousand miles away. Our account had never altered. Not one jot. But where the FSA had seen no wrongdoing, the US law would now criminalise our actions.

I didn't feel like a criminal. I just felt deflated. Over the next few days I had to tell Melanie and Mark Spragg, and apologise for letting them down. Melanie was keen to ensure that the press knew why we were pleading. They needed to be fully briefed. I was adamant that they shouldn't be. They would write what they wanted, and any attempts to try to spin the story might well backfire on us. Let the cards fall as they may. There wasn't much point trying to put lipstick on this pig.

Emma and my parents were more pragmatic, since they had been living the whole thing with me day by day, and ultimately I think they were just relieved that it would all be over soon. The prosecutors set a re-arraignment hearing for the following Wednesday, 28th November.

But we hadn't quite finished shooting ourselves in the foot. There was one final act to play out, and we couldn't possibly have handled it worse.

In order to get home under the prisoner transfer treaty, our 'crime' had to be a crime in the UK as well. You need this concept of 'dual criminality' because it would be unlawful for someone to be imprisoned in the UK for something that was not a crime under UK law.

The problem, though, was that it was quite arguable that there was no

UK crime. After all, on the basis of exactly the same statement of facts six years ago, the Financial Services Authority had not found that we had not done anything wrong, let alone criminal.

And if there was no UK crime, then we had a major problem. It was the ultimate irony. We would have been extradited on the totally false premise that there was a crime, and now we wouldn't be allowed home because there wasn't one. So would have to serve our entire sentence in a US prison, even though the only reason we had pleaded guilty in the first place was to return to England.

We needed Mark Spragg, therefore, to put the draft wording of the statement of facts to the Ministry of Justice in the UK and get their agreement that this would indeed qualify as a crime

Mark spoke to the Ministry of Justice in London, who refused to give an advance ruling. They would only look at it as and when the Americans had agreed to a transfer, and we couldn't even apply for a transfer until we had gone into prison. Reid communicated this to Wes Porter and JLo. Their response was curt. Sign up now, or the deal's off.

It would perhaps have been a great time to have stood our ground. But of course we didn't. After a long conversation with Mark Spragg, who said that he could of course guarantee nothing, but that he was sure that the UK authorities could be persuaded under the circumstances, we let it go.

After everything else, we were going to sign up to something which didn't even guarantee us the one thing that we all needed. A ticket home. And by the time we found out that we had screwed up, if we had, there would be no way back. We would already be in prison, and we would be stuck there for three years.

If Kopper and Glisan were the Smartest Guys in the Room, there was no doubt on God's earth. We were the dumbest.

WHATEVER IT TAKES

28th November 2007

It was a day like many others in most respects. The air was cool, and bright sunshine glinted in the windows of the downtown skyscrapers as I headed into town mid-afternoon. But today we would throw in the towel. Today we would walk into a courthouse and say "hey, you know we've spent the last five and a half years telling everyone that we're innocent of these charges? Well we've changed our minds. It was all rubbish. We're all guilty, and we've agreed with the nice members of the Enron Task Force that 37 months in the pokey and a whopping great fine are the right penalty for our malfeasance, if it please the court."

They say that when you drown, the moment before you die is actually very peaceful, almost pleasurable. Having struggled for however long to breathe, the realisation finally that there is no air and that the water has filled your lungs puts the mind at rest, and you drift into unconsciousness and death thinking calm thoughts. Now how the hell anyone knows this is beyond me, but as I drove into town that day I had a similar sense of peace. It was all over. I could stop struggling now.

I arrived at Dan's office shortly before 3pm. Giles and Matt were already there. Gary was nowhere to be seen. He had gone for lunch with Reid, and we had a fair idea that it was going to be an uncomfortable session for Reid. In law, no attorney can allow a client to plead guilty who doesn't think he is. As an attorney, Reid is about the most "by the book" guy I have ever come across. There is no grey, only black and white. So Gary had to agree that yes, he really was guilty. And Gary was not only convinced that he was not guilty, he had no intention of allowing Reid to begin to persuade him that he was. Gary maintained that correspondence through his lawyers whilst negotiating his departure from GNW included what amounted to a disclosure of the transaction, albeit after we had signed the option agreement with Michael Kopper.

We tried to explain the dynamics of this to Dan, who just cast his eyes to heaven. "Mulgrew has wanted to plea bargain since the day you guys fucking got here. This is his party, dudes. We just got sent the invites".

The irony was that of the three of us, I had no issue with it. In America, you can make a crime out of walking on the cracks in the pavement if you want to. I was happy that every single part of the statement of facts was true, and if the attorneys were content to say that this could be construed as a crime, then I was happy to say that I was a criminal. It's just a label. The bit about it being RBS's money was rubbish of course, but that was just window-dressing.

Eventually Reid and Gary arrived. Each looking suitably bruised. Gary was ready to be guilty. We talked for a few minutes about all the possible things that might happen, and then set off for the courthouse. Reid and Gary walked ahead, and the rest of us ambled along behind. When we got to the rear corner of the courthouse, Giles suggested that he and Matt go round the far side, so that we would approach the front entrance from different sides of the building. It seemed vaguely ridiculous, but what the hell?

"Hey Giles", I called, as they walked away. "Look up, and try to smile. Not too much. Just don't glower. They're going to take our pictures. It's up to you how you look in tomorrow's papers. If you want to look like a crook, be my guest."

Dan, Jimmy and I walked around the corner of Smith and Rusk and headed down toward the entrance to the courthouse. There was a whole posse of TV cameramen and newspaper photographers waiting for us. I tried to wear a neutral face as we walked, and said a cheery "afternoon guys" to them as we went inside.

The courtroom was relatively full of press, but there were also a large number of our local friends there. We thanked people for coming, and then sat down and waited.

And then the usher shouted "all rise", and Judge Werlein walked in. After the normal preliminaries, he called all of us to stand before him. Our attorneys stood behind us.

We had one and only one mission. To get the judge to accept the plea agreement. Nothing else mattered. But nothing could possibly have prepared us for the forty minutes that followed. I thought afterwards that it was significantly worse than the 'resistance to interrogation' training that I had done in Denmark when in the Army some 25 years previously. It was pure psychological torture.

The object of this hearing is for the judge to look you in the eye, ascertain that you have decided to plead guilty of your own free will, and remind you of all the lovely things that the US legal system offers defendants that you will be giving up by not going to trial. In the circumstances, it was almost beyond parody.

If he had just asked "are you making this decision of your own free will, and do you believe that you're guilty?" I think we would all have had a relatively easy time saying "yes your honor". But he had to make it difficult, didn't he?

He wanted to know if we were on medication, or had ever been, or were drunk or on drugs, or subject to psychological problems. A whole string of questions which went on for what seemed like an age. And then he began asking us if we realised what we were giving up by pleading guilty. The first thing, apparently, was the right to subpoena documents and evidence that may be favorable to us. As he was reading all this out, I started to think "You're having a laugh, aren't you? That'll be why you have either denied or failed to rule on EVERY SINGLE motion we have ever put before you asking for documents, over the period of the last eighteen months. That's the "right" that we're giving up, is it? You know what, you can keep it. Enjoy."

"Yes, your honor", we all said respectfully.

And, he continued, we were forfeiting our Sixth Amendment right to compulsory process for obtaining witnesses. "Oh yes, I remember, that was the subject of the motion that we filed asking you to grant us access to six key UK witnesses, who we can't subpoena because they're in another country. And now it's four months later and you still haven't ruled on it. That right to compulsory process".

"Yes, your honor".

But the *piece de resistance* was still to come. This was the bit where he had to establish whether we were pleading guilty of our own free will, or whether we were acting under some form of duress. "Now let me think about that for a moment. We've been cooped up in this place for the last eighteen months, five thousand miles from our families and friends. Unable to do any meaningful work to support ourselves or those back home. You've denied or sat on all of our motions to get evidence. You'll delay the trial for the fourth time if we refuse to plead. We've run out of money. And the Government has said that if we go to trial and lose, they will ensure that we serve our full sentences here, without parole. Does that constitute duress? I suppose not".

"No your honor".

Trying to restrict your answers to "yes, your honor" or "no your honor", when what you really wanted to do was jump over the bench and throttle the guy was an interesting exercise in restraint.

Still it went on. Next he asked each of us about our role in the 'crime', and in doing so it seemed to me that he hadn't even bothered to read the statement of facts. But if he thought we were just going to stand like sheep for this one, he misjudged us, or at least he misjudged Giles. The first question he asked concerned a fax that Giles had sent.

"And when you sent this fax, Mr Darby, you were well aware of all the millions of dollars that you were going to make?" It was presumably supposed to be a rhetorical question.

"No your honor, that's completely incorrect. In fact the statement of facts clearly demonstrates that we had no idea at all what we were going to make, or what Mr Fastow was up to. If I could draw your attention to paragraph 29, it reads as follows". And God bless him, Giles began to read it out loud in the courtroom, as if the judge was incapable of reading it for himself.

"On or about March 22, 2000, and unbeknownst to the defendants", he stressed these words for emphasis) "Fastow, acting on behalf of LJM Cayman, secured an agreement from Enron to pay LJM Cayman/Swap Sub $30 million to close out the Rhythms Net hedge and to recover the Enron shares used to fund Swap Sub. To obtain Enron's agreement, Fastow represented to Enron that one of the limited partners would receive $10 million, and falsely represented that the other limited partner would receive $20 million."

"So you see your honor, we had no idea what he was doing either on the 17th March when I sent this fax, or on the 22nd March when he was signing his deal with Enron. In fact, we didn't find out for over two years what he had done".

I glanced to my right where prosecutor Jonathan Lopez was standing, and he was nodding in the direction of the judge at this stage.

I felt like screaming. "Judge, for the love of God read the statement of facts. It surely can't be too much to ask, can it? It's not very long, it's written in English, and it tells you what we did that's supposedly a crime. Here in paragraph 28? I'll give you a hand:

"The defendants' receipt of an option to acquire for their own personal interest a portion of the NatWest interest in Swap Sub that they had been tasked with selling violated NatWest's conflict policies. The defendants concealed from NatWest their acquisition of the option, and their eventual acquisition of NatWest's residual interest in Swap Sub."

See, easy, isn't it? There were no plots in smoke-filled rooms. No dark and secret meetings on how to divvy up the spoils. No attempts to hide value from NatWest. Nothing. Just a failure to inform our employer of the opportunity to make an investment. Just as we told the FSA over six years ago, and they said "so what?" And now we're going to go to prison for three years for that, five thousand miles from our homes. The least you could do is have the courtesy to know how bloody stupid this is".

Eventually it was over. JLo said that he was happy that henceforth we be allowed to associate with one another. The judge reluctantly agreed. By his demeanour that day, I think he would have preferred to have remanded us straight into custody, and was disappointed that the Government was not asking for that. He set sentencing for February 22nd 2008, and we all stood for him to leave.

Once outside the courthouse, Reid made a statement on behalf of all the clients. Very low key. Dan and Matt were in no mood to do pieces for TV. Dan might have told them what he really thought!

So we retired to the Char Bar with the attorneys and had several drinks. We were joined by Tom Kirkendall and Jeff McMahon. Tom had been at the hearing and commented that he had been watching JLo's body language, and could sense his relief when it was all over. "They really did not want to take this one to trial", he observed. If that was supposed to make me feel better, it didn't.

The mood was very sombre. I felt completely deflated. Reid and David Schwarz made their excuses and left with Gary. No sense intruding on pri vate grief, perhaps. Knowing that we had done the right thing didn't make it any easier. All we could do now was hope that we could get into and out of prison as soon as possible. The long journey home had begun.

All over bar the shouting, or so we thought.

KILLING TIME
Christmas 2007

I woke up the next morning with a hangover and mixed feelings. On one hand, a sense of total release. On the other, the inescapable feeling that we had let everybody down. I've never been one for feeling sorry for myself. But there was my belief that we would have caused enormous damage to the campaign for law change. All those many people who had supported us would now be damned by their association with us.

I figured that we would have been crucified by the UK press, but a little piece of me was rather beyond caring. Surprisingly, though, the coverage was at worst neutral. Almost all of the papers had failed to grasp that our plea agreement bore little relation to the indictment on which we had been extradited, but in the circumstances that was hardly surprising.

Even though it annoyed the hell out of Melanie, we couldn't argue this point. It would certainly be one of life's greatest own goals if we spent time briefing the press on what we had actually pleaded guilty to, only then to have that used as the excuse not to allow us back in because it was not a crime in the UK.

Even so, Martin Wolf at the *Financial Times* wrote a piece entitled 'Judicial Torture and the NatWest Three', which rather eloquently set out the case for changing our extradition arrangements with the US. In his first paragraph, discussing our case, he said:

"The fact that these three men pleaded guilty does not prove they were. It demonstrates that the offers made by US prosecutors are of a kind sensible people cannot refuse. The pressures the former can exert make it rational, even for the innocent, to plead guilty. I do not know whether that happened here. But it would not be very surprising."

I immediately suspected Melanie's involvement. She, it turned out, had immediately suspected mine. We were thus both pleasantly surprised to find that neither had talked to him. As Melanie pointed out, the continuing battle for law change relied on people being able to see beyond our case, and our failure to rebut the consensus that we had just been lying al the way along was not helpful. But she could see that we had no realistic option, and that hopefully we would be able to set the record straight once we returned to the UK.

With the weight lifted off our shoulders, we could look forward to our last Christmas as free men for a while, but before that there was the little matter of Jimmy's wedding. While we had been in Houston, Jimmy had met and got engaged to a fellow attorney called Megan with whom he had been at college some years previously, and they had asked all three of us to be ushers at their wedding. It was pretty humbling in the circumstances, as it took place just three days after we had pleaded guilty. The dress was dinner jackets, and Gary opted for the kilted version, thus ensuring full attention from all assembled womenfolk at the reception.

"Gee, are you really from Scotland? That's in England, right?"

Maura, Dan's receptionist, got sufficiently merry at the party to put her mobile phone up Gary's kilt and take a picture, which she gleefully sent around to everyone the following Monday. It wasn't pretty.

Emma and the children came out the week before Christmas, together with Emma's parents, and we all went down to Galveston. At that time of the year the days were still warm, and the nights cool. We had long walks and plenty to talk about. There were a good few tears, but plenty of laughter as well.

We spent Christmas Day with Dan and Robin and their extended family, which was a really kind gesture on their part. Dan's banker Chuck Bolton, the gun fanatic, was also there. Dan had bought presents for all of the children. Even Dan's Mother had bought a present for us. It might not have been the Christmas Day that I would have chosen, given the circumstances, but it will remain one of the most memorable. The Texans are certainly a breed apart, and when it comes to hospitality and kindness there are few who can rival them. We were blessed.

The next formal step along the journey was the sentencing hearing, on 22nd February, which was not nearly as painful as the re-arraignment. In fact, an altogether different Judge Werlein turned up that day. Not only had he seemingly read the papers by now, he had also read the many hundreds of letters that had been sent to him by friends and colleagues of ours. This was something that had been suggested by the attorneys, and it seemed to have worked quite magically.

All three of us stood up and made a public apology for our actions. For my part, I was genuinely sorry. Sorry that I had put so many family and friends through so much hell over the past few years. Sorry that I had put vanity and greed before natural instinct back in 2000.

Too clever by half, perhaps, and a lifetime to regret it.

Judge Werlein, for his part, was charm personified, and wore a slightly avuncular smile throughout. He had been really impressed with the letters on our behalf, he was quite sure he would never see any of us in his courtroom again, he agreed our pleas, and he wished us well in our future endeavours.

He agreed to our request that we self-report to whatever prison the Bureau of Prisons should allocate, and recommended that the BoP send us to Allenwood, as that was the nearest to New York, through which we would have to travel when going home. He also recommended that we be allowed to serve our sentences in a minimum security open prison, something we knew that the BoP would ignore because we were foreigners.

As we got up to leave, Jonathan Lopez came up and addressed me for the first and only time. He extended his hand and wished me well. Something in his eyes said that he didn't feel terribly proud about this outcome. He seemed like a nice guy. Just doing his job.

Outside the courthouse, amongst the throng, there was a BBC camera crew, and I took the opportunity to say that I was looking forward to the two Governments working together again, to get us home this time, per the terms of our agreement.

In Washington, the Department of Justice press machine was releasing a statement long on triumphalist rhetoric and short on any connection with reality:

"Through the tireless work of our prosecutors and investigators, the fraudulent investment scheme devised by these three defendants and their co-conspirators methodically became unraveled piece by piece. This case demonstrates the Department's unwavering vigilance in addressing corporate fraud matters."

All that remained was to kill time before reporting to prison. We had been told that it would probably be a month. It turned out to be nearly three. Dead time, none of which would count against our sentences, just like the nineteen months we had already wasted before we were sentenced. That was just time out of our lives. Lost forever.

During those last few months, though, we all had many visitors from the UK. Since we arrived there had been a steady stream of family and friends making the long trip, but as the time approached for us to go inside, the frequency picked up.

Even Melanie came across for a weekend, and left feeling that Houston was not such a bad place to be stuck for all that time. She had expected me to be very depressed, she confided, but found me in good spirits. I had experienced a moment of epiphany a week or so before she arrived, which had exorcised all of my demons, and I was keen to share it with her, as I knew that she, more than anyone else outside of my family, felt as deeply about all this as I did from the perspective of principle.

It had always rankled with me that once we were extradited, Blair and his cronies had won, whatever the result. If we went to trial and were found innocent, they would be able to say "see, there's nothing wrong with the US justice system". If we went to trial and lost, they would be able to say "see, these guys were guilty". Either way, the result justified the fast track extraditions.

But one evening, sometime in December, I had a 'eureka' moment.

It all became clear. The single best way to persuade people that the extradition laws should be changed would be to demonstrate by example that once extradited, you have no chance. And in doing what we had done, we could now show that. Maybe.

Far from letting down all the people like Melanie and Liberty, we might just have done them a huge favour. After all, what happened to us in practice was pretty much exactly what we had foretold during our extradition proceedings. We wouldn't get access to witnesses or documents. We would run out of money. The trial would be years away. The icing on the cake was the prosecutors' carrot and stick approach to the plea. "Sign up, and you can go home. Go to trial, and we'll make sure you are here for many years".

There had always been a few people who 'got' this. Martin Wolf of the *Financial Times* was clearly one. Digby Jones was another.

Of course, all of this presupposed that anyone would be willing to listen.

I wasn't alone much those last few months. Emma made several more visits, including one during the Houston Rodeo. My parents came out for a few days, and my father came again on his own. My best man, Miles, came up for two weekends from his home in Atlanta. Friends from the village diverted business trips to spend time with me. It was a good feeling. It made me realise that we were going to be okay.

And in Houston itself, the warm blanket of friendship was wrapped around us by our circle of local friends. Bart & Alix, and the English expat crowd. Joan Gol, Bob & Dorothy Norlund. Bob & Teresa Rose, originally friends of Jim Moonier. Kyle and Lucy, the young Scottish couple who lived in the same apartment block as Gary and Giles. Ernie and Mark Spillard, both Arsenal fans. And Tom Valega, a local attorney who I had met some months previously in the Richmond Arms, watching an Arsenal game. Tom is that rare American who 'gets' football, and he and I would spend many an hour drinking beer and talking footie. He would write to me constantly during my incarceration, mostly about football, and we have stayed good friends since.

The NatWest Three experienced little but kindness and sympathy. Not one person walked away. Friends don't do that. In the Richmond Arms several of the locals confided in us that they too had found themselves on the wrong side of the US justice system at various points in time.

I played a lot of golf. I drank a lot of wine. I smoked a lot of cigarettes. I went to the cinema a lot, and became aware for the first time just how many movies have Texas as a backdrop.

I had plenty of time for contemplation, and I thought about the trip home. It would have several stages, and would involve numerous prisons, and it would take quite some time, I knew. But I was going home.

The lease ran out on my Houston apartment at the end of March, while we were still waiting for our movement instructions from the Bureau of Prisons, and Dan and Robin insisted that I move in with them. So I arranged for a local charity to come and pick up all of the contents of my apartment, and walked away with my computer and a small bag of clothing. On her previous few visits, Emma had steadily been taking back clothes and papers, so that I was by now down to a minimal number of personal possessions. If only all house moves were this easy.

Dan and Robin had moved house since our arrival in Houston back in 2006, but there was a nice symmetry to it, I thought, with my stay beginning and ending with them, like bookends to a chapter in my life. I stayed for six weeks in the end, which I suspect was about five weeks more than they had originally figured when they made the invitation!

Robin was a social smoker, like me. We would sit outside in the evenings with a glass of wine and smoke ourselves silly. We talked about everything from childhood to church, from parenthood to prison. Robin's life had not been easy, and she didn't have any illusions about being low maintenance, but she appreciated her life with Dan, and all of its ups and downs.

Dan preferred cigars, and when he and I sat out in the evenings we inevitably ended up discussing whether we had been right to do the deal. But in whatever direction the conversation meandered, we always came to the same conclusion. If we got home quickly, then it would have been the right decision. You only have one life and one family. You can never get back time spent away from them.

CHALK AND CHEESE

The Blair and Brown years were replete with homage to our cousins across the Pond. Blair and his Ministers cast their eyes enviously towards the Land of the Free, seduced by so much, understanding so little. When you live in a world of soundbite and spin, it is natural to look at results rather than methods. Or should we say 'outcomes', because 'results' is so yesterday?

In criminal justice, the US were clearly the world leaders in 'outcomes'. The numbers spoke for themselves. With conviction rates running at north of 95%, they were surely a model for the world. The US has the highest prison population in the World, at 2.3 million. They also lead the world in the rate of incarceration, at over 750 people per 100,000 of population, compared with 150 in the UK, and less than 100 in France and Germany. Only Russia comes close, with a rate of just over 600.

That the US incarcerates more people than India, China or Russia must surely be a worrying statistic, not something to be proud of. But to a Minister in Blair's Home Office, outcomes were all important, and the US outcomes were awesome.

And the secret was, well, not a secret at all. Plea bargaining accounted for nearly 97% of all convictions. Convictions were good, so therefore plea bargaining must be good. It stood to reason.

The conclusion that the UK must move towards plea bargaining was in no small way aided and abetted by a populist press, and the truly abject performance of many of the UK's prosecuting agencies, in particular in the field of white collar crime. The Serious Fraud Office had a lamentable record of prosecutions, and neither the FSA nor the OFT ever seemed to get a case to court.

Something had to be done.

There can be little debate that the concept of someone who is guilty being encouraged to plead guilty and therefore save everyone the time and expense of a trial is a good thing for the administration of justice. It is not a new idea, and it has long been established in the UK that reductions in sentence, of up to one third of the term for a guilty plea are possible, the important principle being that the judge is the sole arbiter in the sentencing decision.

The US system, of course, is radically different, with the prosecutor able to make deals with defendants that will all but guarantee a particular outcome.

In April 2008, the Attorney General, Baroness Scotland, outlined proposals for the first formal plea bargaining system in the UK. Actually, it wasn't 'plea bargaining', as she was keen to point out, it was 'plea negotiation', there being apparently a significant difference between the two.

Under the new system, which would at first be limited to fraud cases, defendants could be offered a range of possible sentencing outcomes in exchange for a guilty plea, but the actual sentence would still be determined by the judge, who would be able to reject the ranges being offered.

Whatever may have been the merits of this proposal, it seemed to me unlikely to work in practice because the incentives to the guilty were neither so large nor so compelling as to produce the 'right' outcome.

My objection to the US-style system of plea bargaining is that its practical implementation rewards the guilty and penalises the innocent. If you have a system where the 'risk-reward ratio' is so skewed in favour of pleading guilty, then few sane people, even if innocent, will opt to go for trial, meaning that prisons will be full of the innocent.

By contrast, as a guilty man, you only have upside in an arrangement that enables you to reduce your possible punishment not only by pleading guilty, but by giving evidence against others. The more people you help to convict, the less time you will personally serve in prison. Such a system encourages people to 'misremember' things in favour of the Government.

Add into the mix that a US prosecutor's curriculum vitae will depend upon conviction statistics, and that many prosecutors aspire either to political office or lucrative private practice as a defense attorney, and you have a toxic combination which will always penalise innocent defendants.

Thankfully, in the UK, we are still a long way from such a situation, and one of the reasons is that we do not have the equivalent of the Federal Sentencing Guidelines, which enable a prosecutor not only to threaten a defendant with literally hundreds of years in prison, but also to secure a likely sentencing outcome in advance merely by choosing which charges to lay. The disproportionality between the two can be absolutely vast. In the UK, the judges still have great discretion in matters of sentence.

Mark Spragg was asked to take part in a radio debate on Lady Scotland's new measures, and outlined his objections based on his personal knowledge of our case, and how the system works in practice in America. Mark's concern, which I share, was that the new rules would be the thin end of the wedge, because although relatively benign, they would inevitably be added to over time until we eventually replicated the US system.

I made my objections by e-mail to Stephen Hockman, QC, designated as the leader of the working group on the new rules. I suggested that if we were heading towards the utopia of US outcomes, we would need to build another 420,000 prison places, to hold approximately five times the current prison population. I wondered if anyone had budgeted for this?

In May 2010, the outcome of two cases starkly demonstrated the problem. The first was a fraud case in London in which a 'co-operating defendant', Robert Dougall, had agreed to plead guilty to helping bribe Greek State doctors in his role as director of marketing at a subsidiary of US healthcare giant Johnson & Johnson. He admitted to involvement in £4.5 million of payments to Greek surgeons to encourage them to use his company's products.

When it came to his sentencing, the prosecutors recommended a suspended sentence, as per their agreement with him. The trial judge had other ideas and sentenced Dougall to 12 months in prison. The sentence was suspended on appeal, but the appeal court judges pointed out to the Serious Fraud Office that fraudsters were still criminals, and that they should not assume that co-operation would mean a lighter sentence.

The second case was not strictly speaking a plea bargaining case, but had a lot of elements in common. It was the first prosecution brought to trial by the Office of Fair Trading under the 2002 Enterprise Act. This legislation encouraged whistleblowers in cartel cases to come forward by offering immunity from prosecution in return for co-operation.

The prosecution was a hugely political affair, because it originated from an investigation that began in June 2006 and involved both the OFT and the US Department of Justice. Virgin Airlines had come forward to report that some of its senior executives had colluded with others from BA in fixing the price of fuel surcharges on their transatlantic routes.

There was immediately speculation that the BA executives would face extradition to the US, but an agreement was apparently struck between the two Governments that the UK would pursue the investigation, which must have been a huge relief to the individuals involved.

A year later, BA agreed to pay fines of £121.5 million to the OFT, and $275 million to the Department of Justice after pleading guilty to charges of price fixing.

Criminal charges were also brought against four BA executives. All four men denied the charges.

The case came to trial at the end of April 2010. The chief witnesses for the prosecution were the Virgin Airlines chief executive Steve Ridgway and two former executives, William Boulter and Paul Moore, who had exchanged admissions of guilt for immunity from prosecution.

Two weeks into what should have been a six month trial, the case collapsed in farce. Some seventy thousand pages of documents that should have been given to the defendants by Virgin had not been, and some of these documents pointed quite strongly to their innocence.

As the counsel for defendant Martin George, Clare Montgomery QC observed, whistleblowing was "the world turned upside down. If you say you are honest in making an agreement, then you may go to prison. If you say you did nothing wrong, then you're at risk of being charged. But if you say you were dishonest, then you and your company will not be punished, and you will keep your job".

She highlighted the incentive for the Virgin witnesses to "remember more and more about what happened", perhaps "to make the case against British Airways stronger".

Julian Joshua, a cartel lawyer, succinctly identified the flaw with the whole approach: "You are relying largely on witnesses who have an agenda. They have to admit they are dishonest and then the prosecution has to bring them as witnesses of the truth".

When you step back and look at how the law works, its lunacy is self-evident. In order to gain immunity from prosecution, you must first admit that you have personally engaged in dishonest conduct, and then agree to give evidence against others. If you are not prepared to admit that you were dishonest, then you will not be granted immunity.

In one of life's little ironies, after the case collapsed the OFT, with egg all over its face, said that it intended to review very carefully the basis and extent of Virgin's 'co-operation', implying that the immunity from prosecution might be removed. This would have been a cruel twist indeed for Steve Ridgway, the Virgin Chief Executive, whose admitted dishonesty was on the record.

In the meantime, the BA executives left court as innocent men, but hypothetically now faced action from the Department of Justice, whose methods of gaining convictions are of course far more certain of success.

At the heart of these two cases lies a fundamental dilemma, and it is this: Given the choice between a guilty man going free, and an innocent man going to prison, which would you take? The US has long been in the latter camp, while the UK has always been in the former. The former emphasises due process, the presumption of innocence and the rule of law, the latter reflects the fact that Congressmen are frequently elected on their attitudes to crime prevention.

Plea bargaining is the bridge that connects the two camps.

Tread warily.

CALIFORNIA HERE I COME
April 2008

Finally, at the end of April, we got word of our allocations from the Bureau of Prisons. As was common practice in the Federal system, we were to be split up. It is rare that co-defendants are placed together, mostly because it is assumed that they will have fallen out before or during any trial.

My pre-trial services officer, Jeff Fowler, broke the news. Giles got the plum posting of Allenwood, meaning he would have very little travelling to do to get to New York. Gary would be going to Big Spring, in West Texas, and I would be going to Lompoc, in California. My face lit up.

"I've never been to California, Jeff!"

An online search revealed that Gary had drawn the short straw. Big Spring was an awful looking place in the middle of nowhere, with very little greenery around, and not much in the way of recreation areas. It would be hotter than hell over the summer months.

Lompoc, by contrast, was a sea of green, nestling a couple of miles in from the Pacific coastline, some 175 miles north of Los Angeles. A big campus, with what looked like plenty of recreational areas. A good climate, negligible rainfall. If you were going to get stuck anywhere for a protracted period, this was probably as good as it got.

The downside of course was that other than Hawaii, there was no Federal Correctional Institution further away from New York than Lompoc, meaning that my journey home, whenever it began, was likely to be long and interesting. A small price to pay, I thought.

I decided not to tell Gary what I had found out about Big Spring. I figured he would find out soon enough, and he didn't need Giles and me looking smug in the meantime. In fact, Gary would have precious little time to contemplate it, because he was due to report there in five days' time, on 30th April, while Giles was not expected at Allenwood until 7th May, and I had until the 9th to get to Lompoc.

Winding Gary up about the timings was easy pickings. It was clear that the prosecutors regarded Gary as the most culpable, and me the least, I pointed out, knowing that it would hit the spot every time. That's why he would be going in first. I refrained from saying that the choice of Big Spring carried equal significance, because that just wasn't funny.

Finally we could start to unwind our lives in Houston. Gary somewhat frantically, Giles and me in rather more leisurely fashion. The staff at the Richmond Arms insisted on holding a leaving party in our honour, and publicised it on their roadside bill board with a message about not dropping the soap. I rather shamefully declined to attend, as I had my father in town that weekend. By all accounts though it was quite a wild night.

I did go in a few days later, however, to say my farewells to all the bar staff, which was quite emotional. Gary was also there that day, and was flying out with Reid the following morning to report to Big Spring. He told me about his final visit to his pre-trial services officer that morning, which had rather caught him off guard. The guy had asked Gary why we had taken so long to plead.

"You seem like a nice guy, Mr Mulgrew", he had said. "I could have told you two years ago to just plead it out. Saved yourself a lot of time and money. You can never beat these people. No-one ever does".

We said our goodbyes and wished each other well. "Last one home's a cissy", I said as Gary walked away.

I spoke to Reid when he returned from dropping off his charge, and he expressed his shock at what he had found at Big Spring. Gary's time was not going to be pleasant.

A week after Gary departed, Matt Hennessy and Giles set off for New York, where they would overnight before driving the three hours west to Allenwood.

And then there was one.

My last night involved an unreasonable amount of alcohol. Drinks with Dan and Robin at the Char Bar, where the owner Mike and his son Jeremy kept pouring huge gin and tonics for the token Brit who was on his way to the Pen. A tearful goodbye, and then dinner with Bart Stafford at our favourite Mexican restaurant on Washington Street. I was in a bit of state by the time we arrived, and significantly worse by the time Jimmy turned up to take me off Bart's hands and back to stay with him and Megan for the night before our departure the following morning.

Houston to Los Angeles is about a three hour flight. I spent most of it wishing I were dead. Megan came with us, and the plan was that they would rent a car at LA airport, drive me to prison, and then continue up the coastline to San Francisco for a long weekend. So at least someone was going to have a good time of it.

We stopped for lunch in Lompoc town itself, which turned out to be very pretty but lacking a decent restaurant for my final meal as a free man. We ended up having a chicken burger in some fast food joint. We stopped briefly by the side of the road thereafter so that Megan could take a picture of Jimmy and me grinning idiotically under a large sign pointing to the US Penitentiary, before making the last few hundred yards of the journey to my place of incarceration.

As we pulled into the car park, the first thing we could see on the other side of the wire were the sports facilities, including a full size 'soccer' pitch and a baseball diamond. The grounds were immaculate, and a series of sprinklers were watering countless flowerbeds full of exotic plants and shrubs.

There was an air of order and calm about the place, and under a warm Californian sun, cool breeze, and blue skies, it did not exactly exude menace.

"Dude", said Jimmy, "I've been to a lot of closed prisons, and believe me, this is a serious result".

I made a last call to Emma from the mobile phone. We had already discussed that it might be a week or two before she heard from me again, as it is common for new inmates to be placed into the 'hole' for a week or so, for no particular reason other than to make them realise they are in prison. I tried to sound chipper about the whole thing, and we said our final farewell. I switched the phone off, gave it to Jimmy, and asked him to dispose of it.

The reception area, manned by a petite lady behind a desk in a Department of Corrections T-Shirt and cargo pants, had a similar air of welcome about it. She was polite and pleasant, but could find no record of me on the system. It being Friday afternoon, she explained, most of the reception staff had gone home. Jimmy showed her a copy of the court order that required me to report here at two o'clock, and she agreed that we seemed to be in the right place at the right time.

She managed to persuade the guy who ran the post room to come and admit me. There was a short delay while she tried to find something that would enable Jimmy to cut my ankle bracelet off, so that he could take all the electronic tagging equipment back to Jeff Fowler. It being a prison, sharp objects are not in regular use, but eventually the problem was solved with a pair of children's plastic coated scissors which just about did the trick.

Megan then burst into tears, I told her not to be so silly, and she and Jimmy left me to my new owners and headed off to 'Frisco.

The postman smiled at me.

"Come a long way?" he asked.

"You could say that".

POSTSCRIPT

A lot of people have asked me why I didn't write about my time in prison, or to be accurate the ten prisons in which I spent time on both sides of the Atlantic. Doubtless it would have made for a far easier read than *A Price to Pay*. Certainly those were extraordinary times, and I shared them with some of the best and the worst of humanity. But that would be a different story, and wasn't an itch that I needed to scratch. Prison was either my penance for my actions, or the price of the ticket home from America, depending upon your point of view. Or both.

The fact is that the period from 2002 to 2010, when I was finally released from my custodial sentence, was one that I'm not sure I would wish on anyone, but I'm glad now to have been through it because it taught me so much about myself and about others, that I could never possibly otherwise have learned, and I feel a better person for it.

History is constantly being rewritten. It is my fervent hope that the story of Enron will be retold at some stage in a slightly more nuanced light. Some people, like the bloggers Tom Kirkendall and Cara Ellison, have been unwavering in their criticisms of the Enron Task Force over many years. Now, however, as the statute of limitations on criminal actions in America runs out, people who have previously been terrified to speak are finally beginning to come forward to tell their stories. Theirs is a hard task, though. The accepted wisdom that Enron was one giant accounting fraud from top to bottom is a lazy narrative, and one that suits most people in Government and the mainstream media. It will be difficult to displace.

I would highly recommend that anyone with an interest in the 'alternative' truth visits Beth Stier's outstanding site ungagged.net. On it are videos from many people who were caught in the whirlwind of prosecutorial zeal in the period from 2002 to 2006. Their stories are enormously powerful. Gary and I are on there too. We recorded our interviews with Beth, separately and entirely unscripted, before reporting to prison in 2008, and our emotions are raw.

I was a spectator from prison in California when the world financial markets stared into the abyss in the autumn of 2008, and was repatriated to the UK prison system just in time to be shown a five page article in *Esquire* suggesting that the NatWest Three were at least in part responsible for the meltdown, even though we had had exactly no involvement in banking since 2001. As far as polite society goes, I will be forever tarred.

Meanwhile, the iniquities of the Extradition Act continue to be visited upon the citizens of the UK at an alarming rate. Since leaving prison, I have given evidence before a sometimes hostile Joint Committee on Human Rights, whose subsequent report in June 2011 was gratifyingly strong on the need for immediate law change.

I have made my lengthy and relatively intolerant contribution to the Home Office's judge-led consultation on our extradition arrangements, the report on which was published in October 2011 to almost universal opprobrium, concluding as it did that our extradition arrangements were by and large fair and proportionate.

In response, I have given further evidence before the Commons Home Affairs Select Committee in January of this year, in the fond hope that the last word in the argument will prevail.

I continue to give whatever counseling I can to numerous people who are going through the same process that we did all those years ago, and who are usually terrified and confused as to why this is happening to them.

But my efforts pale into insignificance next to those of Melanie Riley, Janis Sharp, Liberty, Fair Trials International, and the many many other people who have campaigned for years to get this unholy state of affairs changed.

I want it to be over. But it isn't. Not yet. Being a profound cynic now in all matters political, I will believe that the Government intends to change the extradition legislation, as both the Conservatives and the Liberal Democrats vowed to do when in opposition, only when the amendments become law.

Until then, the fight goes on.